BODY LANGUAGE IN LITERATURE

Barbara Korte

The tilt of a head, the quirk of an eyebrow, or a shift in position can eloquently portray a wide range of emotions without a single word being spoken. Body language is a critical component of everyday communication, yet the importance of body language, or non-verbal communication, in such a verbal medium as literature has not been fully studied.

In *Body Language in Literature,* Barbara Korte has produced an important interdisciplinary study, by establishing a general theory that accounts for the varieties of body language encountered in literary narrative, based on a general history of the phenomenon in the English language. By focusing on major works of literature, including stories by D.H. Lawrence, Margaret Atwood, and J.D. Salinger, Korte shows body language to be a vital yet unexplored method of communication in literature.

BARBARA KORTE is a professor of English literature at the University of Tübingen in Germany.

THEORY / CULTURE

BARBARA KORTE

Body Language in Literature

UNIVERSITY OF TORONTO PRESS
Toronto Buffalo London

Originally published as *Körpersprache in der Literatur: Theorie und Geschichte am Beispiel englischer Erzählprosa*, © 1993 A. Francke Verlag, Tübingen und Basel, Dischingerweg 5, D-72070 Tübingen

Toronto Buffalo London
Printed in Canada

ISBN 0-8020-0706-6 (cloth)
ISBN 0-8020-7656-4 (paper)

Printed on acid-free paper

Canadian Cataloguing in Publication Data

Korte, Barbara, 1957–
Body language in literature

(Theory/culture)
Originally published as: Korpersprache in der Literatur : theorie und geschichte am Beispiel englischer Erzahlprosa.

ISBN 0-8020-0706-6 (bound) ISBN 0-8020-7656-4 (pbk.)

1. Nonverbal communication in literature. 2. English fiction – History and criticism. I. Title. II. Series.

PR830.N65K6713 1997 823'.009'353 C97-931531-X

University of Toronto Press acknowledges the financial assistance to its publishing program of the Canada Council for the Arts and the Ontario Arts Council.

Contents

Preliminary Note

This is the slightly revised translation of my book *Körpersprache in der Literatur*, originally published in Germany in 1993. I should like to thank Francke publishers for their permission to have the book translated, and also Erica Ens for doing the translation.

Permission to reproduce illustrations was kindly granted by Georg Olms publishers (for Figure 6.1, from Charles Le Brun, *Méthode pour apprendre à dessiner les passions proposée dans une conférence sur l'expression générale et particulière* [Hildesheim, Zurich, and New York: Olms 1982]), The British Museum (for Figure 6.2, Garrick as Richard III), and The Victoria and Albert Museum (for Figure 6.3, *East Lynne*).

In the quotations, emphases marked in bold print are mine.

PART I

INTRODUCTION

1

Rationale and Purpose

Thou shalt not sigh, nor hold thy stumps to heaven,
Nor wink, nor nod, nor kneel, nor make a sign,
But I, of these, will wrest an alphabet,
And by still practice learn to know thy meaning.

Shakespeare, *Titus Andronicus*, 3.2.42–5

Auntie Muriel settles herself on the sofa but doesn't take off her stole or gloves ... Elizabeth remains standing. *Dominate her through height*. Not a hope. (Atwood, *Life before Man*, 215)

She had observed ... his easy familiarity, his sense of being at home in his own body, his comfortable communications with the bodies of others. He radiated presence, immediacy. He touched people easily ... (Drabble, *The Radiant Way*, 169)

Pamela listened dumbly, her posture informing him that she wouldn't be offering any counter-arguments, that whatever he wanted was okay: making amends with body language. (Rushdie, *The Satanic Verses*, 403)

These quotations taken from novels of the late 1970s and 1980s reflect a contemporary trend: a heightened sensitivity to body language or, to use a less popular term, non-verbal communication (NVC).[1] Provisionally, we can define body language as non-verbal behaviour (movements and postures, facial expression, glances and eye contact, automatic reactions, spatial and touching behaviour) which is 'meaningful' in both natural and fictional communication.[2]

The terminology used in the above quotations characterizes them as products of recent decades in which numerous scholarly and scientific publications have devoted themselves to body language. Journalism and popular handbooks have made the results of this research available to the wider public.[3] Apart from literature, the current attention given to NVC has also left its traces in the other arts. In the area of theatre, Scott Burton created *Behavior Tableaux* in which the actors' bodies and their use of space form the sole means of expression. A Frankfurt art exhibition entitled 'Körpersprache' (body language) presented statues with such telling names as 'Hitler's Handshake' or 'Hitler's Party Conference Pose with Hands Covering Genital Parts' (see Rittner 1976, 54). In 1992, the 'Eloquence of the Body' was the subject of another exhibition in the Albertina in Vienna. In a wider context, this interest in body *language* is one aspect of the renaissance of the body to be observed in many areas of life and academic disciplines since the sixties.

The fact that body language is a topical subject does not by itself justify a study of its manifestation in literature. Rather, this study rests on the assumption that body language must be recognized as an important signifying system in the literary text and that skill in using this system constitutes an essential aspect of a writer's art. In what follows, then, we shall concentrate on those aspects of the body in literature which can be subsumed under the broader concept of body *semiotics*, and a semiotic and communicative perspective will form the basis of our approach.

In literary communication, the text serves as the foundation for the reader's construction of meaning and effect.[4] The body language of the literary characters constitutes one subsystem of the text's entire sign repertoire. Permanent features of the face and the physique of a character may also be highly significant; as is well documented, the discipline of physiognomy has left many traces in literature from antiquity up to the nineteenth century.[5] The present study, however, focuses on the semiotics of the body *in motion*: it studies the ways in which the presentation of non-verbal *behaviour* contributes to the text's potential significance and effect.

For one, the body language of a fictional character can be 'read' as a sign (symbol, index, or icon) in the understanding of classical semiotics. Of equal importance, however, are the cases in which the characters' non-verbal behaviour contributes to the effect of a text in addition to or independently of such symbolic meaning. It may, for example, lend liveliness and authenticity to the action portrayed. Contrary to its occurrence in real life, non-verbal behaviour in literature is always 'significant': it is integral to the text's artistic design even when it cannot be read as a sign with a clearly defined meaning.

In chapter 42 of Charles Dickens's *Oliver Twist* (1837–8), a substantial part of the text's meaning is conveyed through body language. Noah Claypole has robbed his employer, an undertaker, with the help of his lover, Charlotte. He goes to London, where Fagin notices him in an inn and tries to recruit him for his band of thieves. In front of the adoring Charlotte, Noah plays the sophisticated man who hopes to become a thief in grand style and expresses his self-image with a grand gesture: '"So I mean to be a gentleman," said Mr. Claypole, kicking out his legs' (267). When Fagin joins the couple, Noah's behaviour changes. To Fagin's seeming confidentiality, Noah first reacts with an 'echo' of the former's body language which is meant to indicate conspiracy but also suggests that Noah is an easily manipulated character:

> 'Yer a sharp feller,' said Noah. 'Ha! ha! only hear that, Charlotte!'
>
> 'Why, one need be sharp in this town, my dear,' replied the Jew, sinking his voice to a confidential whisper; 'and that's the truth.'
>
> Fagin followed up this remark by striking the side of his nose with his right forefinger, – a gesture which Noah attempted to imitate, though not with complete success, in consequence of his own nose not being large enough for the purpose. However, Mr. Fagin seemed to interpret the endeavour as expressing a perfect coincidence with his opinion, and put about the liquor which Barney re-appeared with, in a very friendly manner. (268–9)

Noah's self-confidence is abruptly deflated, however, when Fagin drops his mask of confidentiality and lets Noah know that he has overheard him bragging earlier about his robbery. Noah's shock is evident in his facial expression and eye behaviour:

> Mr. Claypole no sooner heard this extract from his own remarks than he fell back in his chair, and looked from the Jew to Charlotte with a countenance of ashy paleness and excessive terror. (269)

His outstretched legs are now pulled in and hidden. This posture reveals the pretentious Noah to be a coward, who now blames Charlotte for the robbery.

'I didn't take it,' stammered Noah, no longer stretching out his legs like an independent gentleman, but coiling them up as well as he could under his chair: 'it was all her doing: yer've got it now, Charlotte, yer know yer have.' (ibid.)

Only when he is certain that Fagin will not betray him does Noah regain his confidence. The space he occupies increases again with his newly inflated ego:

'Yer speak as if yer were in earnest,' replied Noah.

'What advantage would it be to me to be anything else?' inquired Fagin, shrugging his shoulders. 'Here! Let me have a word with you outside.'

'There's no occasion to trouble ourselves to move,' said Noah, getting his legs by gradual degrees abroad again. 'She'll take the luggage up stairs the while. Charlotte, see to them bundles!' (269–70)

The change in Noah's 'leg language' not only makes for a compact character study, but also contributes to the comedy of the scene.

As even this short example demonstrates, body language appears in the literary text in a variety of forms and serves various artistic functions. Posture and spatial behaviour, facial expressions, gestures, and eye behaviour, both conscious and unconscious, provide the reader with clues to the personal traits, mental states, and interpersonal relations of the fictional characters. Dickens is careful to present the body language of his characters clearly; the narrator's somewhat obvious comments ensure the reader's correct interpretation. In spite of this explanatory effort, another characteristic of Dickens's use of NVC remains effective: it lends vividness and drama to the episode.

That a study of literary body language is relevant is also substantiated by the research conducted to date, which is reviewed in chapter 2. Much of this research, however, is limited to certain writers or periods and frequently lacks a satisfactory conceptual framework. It has not yet produced a comprehensive critical framework which can be used as a heuristic procedure in the analysis of (narrative) texts or which allows for a systematic approach to the study of body language in a broad range of literary texts.

For this reason, one of the main aims of the present study is to develop a critical framework that will make it possible to distinguish and describe the possible forms and functions of literary body language in a way which is not bound by author, period, or individual text. This framework is indebted to the results of modern research in NVC, which, contrary to earlier scientific approaches such as expression psychology, comprises a wide spectrum of non-verbal behaviour. Applied to body language as a *literary* phenomenon, however, concepts of NVC research must be subordinated to the demands of literary analysis and used within a framework of literary theory. This is necessary not least because literature always presents only a selection from the range of NVC that can be observed in real life.

In everyday life, non-verbal behaviour plays a most important role in almost all forms of human interaction. As highly developed social beings, humans are dependent upon 'reading' the reactions of their fellow creatures in as many ways as possible. Body language accompanies all speech, and even when people do not speak, their non-verbal behaviour continually provides information which can be meaningful to others: information regarding feelings, thoughts, attitudes, or interpersonal relationships, which can be only partially coded in words. As Paul Watzlawick has succinctly formulated, 'one cannot *not* communicate' (1968, 49).

Whereas NVC is omnipresent in real life, it appears in varying degrees in the arts. In pantomime, the body is the only carrier of meaning. In theatre and film, body language is automatically present as soon as a character appears on stage or on the screen; here, too, NVC can become the dominant form of expression, as in some forms of modern theatre or in silent film.

Literary texts are much more selective in their presentation of the fictional world than is the case in the performing arts. 'Areas of indeterminacy' (Ingarden 1931) are a characteristic feature of the literary, above all the narrative, text. As John Fowles writes, '[t]he delight of writing novels is what you can leave out on each page, in each sentence' (Stanzel 1984, 116). We shall see that the degree to which NVC is represented in a novel varies considerably depending on period and subgenre. The emphasis given to body language can also vary from one writer to another, within one writer's work, or even within one text itself. In German literature, the novellas of Heinrich von Kleist are notorious for their excessive use of body language. Charles Dickens, Henry James, and Franz Kafka are other writers in whose works the reader encounters body language on almost every page. However, even when body language is rendered only sporadically, it can be highly relevant to the meaning of a text. Even the fact that NVC plays no role at all in some

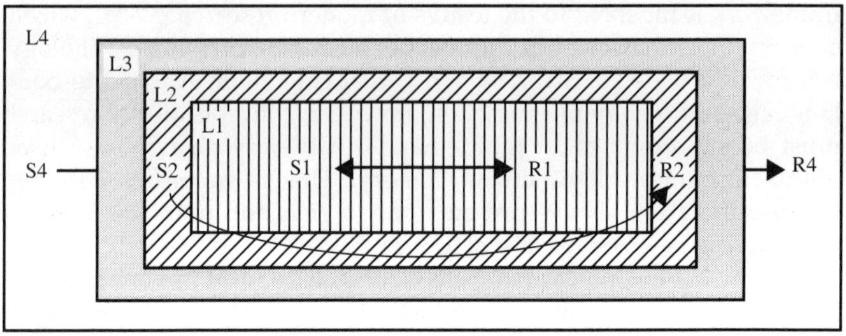

Figure 1.1 The Narrative Communicative Situation

texts does not diminish its fundamental relevance, because the very absence of a phenomenon may point to specific principles of selection and historical inventories of forms and functions, as Gerhard Hoffmann (1978, 3) concludes when he speaks about the treatment of fictional space in the novel.

Basically, body language is used in all literary genres, but there are considerable differences among them. Broadly speaking, poetry offers relatively sparse material for a study of NVC.[6] The role non-verbal behaviour plays in the theatre is obvious, but dramatic texts, which provide the basis for the theatrical performance, vary considerably in the degree to which NVC is specified. In general, the playwright's ability to determine his characters' body language is more limited than that of the writer of a narrative text. The characters' speech forms the core of the dramatic text. Normally, body language is only selectively specified in the stage directions, and only when the author deems it essential to do so. Furthermore, the playwright who anticipates the play's production on stage must also deal with a certain hierarchy of the modes of body language, a hierarchy which does not affect the narrative text. In the theatre, only 'large' body gestures are generally visible to all spectators, and in stage directions regarding NVC, gestures, postures, and spatial relations between characters tend to be given greater attention than expressions of the face. The latter are primarily implied through descriptions or comments made in the characters' speech.

A consideration of all genres would have been beyond the scope of this study. Narrative literature, particularly the novel, offers the most fruitful area for an investigation of literary NVC. It is least restricted regarding the presentation of body language and thus displays the broadest range of its forms and functions. The categories established and the questions posed in a study of narrative literature can, however, be adapted for the analysis of other genres.

Since the present study has chosen a semiotic and communicative approach, a brief look at the narrative communicative situation seems appropriate.[7] In the diagram in Figure 1.1, L4 represents a level of communication outside the text with the real author (S[ender]4) and reader (R[ecipient]4). The levels indicated by L1 to L2 refer to communication levels within the narrative text: L1 is the level of communication between the characters of the fictional world (S1 and R1); the utterances of the narrator (S2), whose direct recipient in the text is a narratee (R2), are located on level L2. L3 represents an abstract level of literary communication which cannot be ascribed to any concrete agent within the text but concerns the communicative potential of the text as a whole.

The primary conveyors of body language in the narrative text are the characters in L1. Within this communicative level itself, there may not be another fictional character who will receive this body language as a message; however, the body language described will always serve as a signifier for the reader.

Narrators and narratees only rarely function as direct senders or receivers of body language, at least as far as *written* texts are concerned.[8] However, occasional examples can typically be found in works of a metafictional nature, which draw the reader's attention to the act of narration itself. Laurence Sterne's *Tristram Shandy* (1759–67), for example, a forerunner of (post)modern metafiction, uses body language in order to create a 'physical' impression of its overt narrative voice:

> Here, – but why here, – rather than in any other part of my story, – I am not able to tell; – but here it is, – my heart stops me to pay to thee, my dear uncle [*sic*] *Toby*, once for all, the tribute I owe thy goodness. – Here let me thrust my chair aside, and kneel down upon the ground, whilst I am pouring forth the warmest sentiments of love for thee ... (Bk 3, ch. 34: 265)

Kurt Vonnegut's *Breakfast of Champions* (1973) is a perfect example of postmodern narrative in which even the boundary between real author and narrator is crossed. The author penetrates his fictional world as a first-person narrator; within the realm of fiction, he meets characters of his earlier novels. The body language of this author/narrator is frequently depicted. The following example, which may be considered a fictionalization of the 'exit-author' principle of modernism, exposes the very convention by which a first-person narrator can report about his own facial expression: a gaze into the mirror. When the 'author' takes leave of his characters, this prompts a tear. The illustration which appears in the text instead of a verbal description of this tear emphasizes the visual nature of the body language:

> I somersaulted lazily and pleasantly through the void, which is my hiding place when I dematerialize. Trout's cries to me faded as the distance between us increased ...
>
> A small hand mirror floated by. It was a *leak* with a mother-of-pearl handle and frame. I captured it easily, held it up to my own right eye, which looked like this: [picture of eye with tear]. (294)

The narrator as a direct sender of body language represents an exception. The communicative level L2 is, however, of central importance for the narrative transmission of body language and distinguishes the presentation of NVC in narrative literature from its presentation in the dramatic text. A narrator in this level may (or may not) choose to describe body language in great detail, comment on it, or filter it through varying perspectives.

The literary functions and effects of NVC cannot all be allocated to individual communicative levels. One of the most important functions of literary body language consists, of course, of communicating information about characters in L1 and their relationships within the fictional world. Body language can play an important role in creating different narrative perspectives (L1 and L2), but it also contributes to the meaning and effect of the text as a whole, such as its coherence or the development of its theme.

This study focuses on the way in which body language manifests itself on the textual levels L1 to L3. As far as level L4 is concerned, factors come into play that have not yet been sufficiently researched, and the questions which would have to be considered in a production and reception-oriented look at body language can be sketched only briefly. It is important to note, however, that the use of body language by an author and its interpretation by a reader occur under assumptions which are never congruent and which may, in fact, be very different.

On the author's side, we must consider, for example, the varying degrees to which he or she is disposed to relate non-verbal aspects of the fictional world. As Gerhard Hoffmann (1978, 27) has shown for the portrayal of fictional space, novelists can be distinguished, in Thomas Wolfe's terms, as 'putter-inners' and 'leaver-outers.' This distinction is also a fitting one to make with reference to NVC. The general role NVC plays in the work of a writer can be considered as a characteristic of this writer's style; within this work, however, the quantity and quality of the body language will also be determined by the theme, structure, and narrative technique of each individual text.[9]

NVC research has proven that the sensitivity to NVC in a person – that is, the person's ability to encode and decode non-verbal information – varies according to his or her culture, gender, and personality.[10] There is also a difference in sensitivity regarding the channels through which non-verbal signals are transmitted: 'Some of us are "seers," some "hearers," some "touchers," etc. We each have our own idiosyncratic pattern and hierarchy of channel-use that derives from an interplay between our relative physical sensitivity in each of those sending and receiving channels, and our cultural training and conditioning' (Katz and Katz, eds 1983, 205). It may be surmised that the degree to which body language or specific modes of body language are used by an author depends on such individual dispositions. In a *Paris Review* interview, Frank O'Connor, for example, gave the following reason for the 'spareness of physical description of people and places' said to be characteristic of his short stories:

> if you're the sort of person that meets a girl in the street and instantly notices the colour of her eyes and of her hair and the sort of dress she's wearing, then you're not in the least like me ... I have terribly sensitive hearing and I'm terribly aware of voices. (Cowley, ed. 1958)

Obviously, O'Connor can be categorized as a 'hearer' rather than a 'seer.' Samuel Richardson, on the other hand, belongs to the 'seers.' As Janet Aikins (1989, 46–7) claims, Richardson was governed by 'a powerful visual aesthetics' and 'fancied himself as a painter in words.' D.H. Lawrence, an amateur painter, may also be assumed to be a particularly 'visual' writer whose novels abound with descriptions of body language. In the case of other authors, a high degree of NVC in their work can be connected to their own bodily eloquence:

> Justin McCarthy put on record that, as a public speaker, Dickens gave 'addi-

tional force and meaning to what he said' by the use of 'his wonderfully expressive hands'; and there is evidence too that he made unusually frequent use of gesture in private conversation. (Page 1988, 155)

Kafka ... according to his friend Gustav Janouch, was known to 'love gestures' and enjoyed incorporating various forms of mimicry into his conversations. (Smith 1976, 10)

In most cases it is difficult, if not impossible, to establish a writer's individual predisposition towards body language. Some general assumptions, however, can be made in comparative studies or on the basis of statistical evaluation. One aspect in particular could become a promising subject for further study: NVC research suggests that, on average, women show a greater sensitivity to NVC than men. One might ask whether this special sensitivity also reveals itself in literature written by women. This question could, however, only be answered by means of a comprehensive sample of texts assembled especially for such a purpose. The texts used as a basis for the present study do not support a reliable conclusion in this matter, although in regard to spatial and touching behaviour, the texts written by women do contain a remarkable number of particularly strong examples.[11] This finding appears to correlate with the observation made in NVC research that women show a special sensitivity for these two modes of NVC.

The degree to which the NVC of a text is decoded by the reader may also vary from one person to another. Individual readers differ, for example, in their ability to transform words into images or kinaesthetic impressions.[12] Empirical studies in this area have not yet been published; however, there are indications that there are also 'seers,' 'hearers,' and 'touchers' among readers. In his *Practical Criticism* (1929), for example, I.A. Richards observed considerable differences in the visualization of poems in a group of readers. Commenting on the reception of narrative texts, Robert Scholes (1982) concludes that 'the visual quality of film reminds us forcibly of how much of fictional narrativity involves the supplying of physical details or the translating of verbal signs into images. Readers who are feeble at such visualizing often fail to realize important aspects of fictional texts' (61).

In particular, a reception study of body language in literature would have to deal with its emotional effect on the reader. The aesthetics of various genres and periods have postulated that the feelings of fictional characters can be transmitted to the reader and evoke his or her emotional reaction. Body language frequently appears to be used in order to elicit this kind of empathy. However, although it has been proven that the area of affect is a domain of *natural* body language, the affective quality of body language in literature has been questioned: 'In real life, the nonverbal seems to have the potential to by-pass thought routes. In literature (with the exception of performed drama), this would not seem to be possible since the written words have to be absorbed by the eyes and consumed by the mind' (Portch 1985, 4). The extent to which body language in the literary text retains its affective potential for the reader despite the particulars of its transmission remains to be determined.

More reliable observations are available as to the historical and cultural conditions which influence the use and interpretation of body language in literature. Literary communication takes place within cultural systems whose models of reality influence both the production and the reception of a text: 'There is abundant evidence from psycho-linguistic research that comprehension does not proceed from straightforward analysis of linguistic structure, but from a complicated process whereby knowledge of language interacts with knowledge of the world: with what is called "pragmatic" or "encyclopaedic" knowledge' (Fowler 1986, 169). Body language in literature is not used and understood autonomously, but within the framework of the writer's or reader's ordinary non-verbal competence, that is, the knowledge of the modes and functions of body language evident in real life. This competence can vary considerably between author and reader if the two do not share the same cultural background. Although in some areas non-verbal behaviour appears to be innate and is thus universally comprehensible, a large amount of NVC is determined by culture-specific codes. Klineberg (1938), for example, observes the following about the expression of emotion in a Chinese novel:

> When we read 'They stretched out their tongues' ... most of us would not recognize this description as meaning surprise, except for the context ... The sentence 'Her eyes grew round and opened wide,' would probably suggest to most of us surprise or fear; to the Chinese it usually means anger ... 'He scratched his ears and cheeks' would probably suggest embarrassment to us, but in the *Dream of the Red Chamber* it means happiness. (518–19)

Even simple body techniques may differ from one culture to another and are subject to historical change, if only because of different fashions of clothing and hairstyle: two hundred years ago a British writer describing a woman as standing, walking, or sitting might have had a very different idea of what these actions implied than would a reader of today.[13] In some cases, the meaning ascribed to an instance of body language at the time of the text's inception can only be reconstructed if one consults etiquette books of the period concerned. Even for literature of the more recent past it can be essential to be familiar with the social norms governing non-verbal behaviour. A famous example is an episode in Henry James's *The Portrait of a Lady* (1881) in which her husband's real relationship to Madame Merle is revealed to Isabel Archer through a breach of non-verbal etiquette:

> Madame Merle was standing on the rug, a little way from the fire; Osmond was in a deep chair, leaning back and looking at her ... There was nothing to shock in this; they were old friends in fact. But the thing made an image, lasting only a moment, like a sudden flicker of light. Their relative positions, their absorbed mutual gaze, struck her as something detected. But it was all over by the time she had fairly seen it. (2:144)

Knowledge of a rule of propriety which has become much more lax, if not obsolete, in our time is essential for an understanding of this episode: the rule which stipulates that a man may sit down in the presence of a standing lady only if he is in an intimate relationship with her. A reader who lacks this knowledge will fail to understand why the behaviour the protagonist has just witnessed will become a culminating point in her development.

A form of NVC particularly subject to changes in meaning is the one in which gesture replaces speech. When the connection between the body language and its verbal meaning relies purely on convention, the gesture can easily become incomprehensible to a reader of another time and culture. An extreme example of this is the mute 'scholarly' debate between Panurge and Thaumaste in Rabelais's *Pantagruel* (1532–3). The gestures of the disputing characters are described in minute detail:

> Adoncques, tout le monde assistant et escoutant en bonne silence, l'Angloys leva hault en l'air les deux mains séparément, clouant toutes les extrémitéz des doigtz en forme qu'on nomme en Chinonnoys cul de poulle, et frappa de l'une l'aultre par les ongles quatre foys; puys les ouvrit, et ainsi à plat de l'une frappa l'aultre en son strident. Une foys de rechief les joignant comme dessus, frappa deux foys, et quatre foys de rechief les ouvrant; puys les remist joinctes et extendues l'une jouxte l'aultre, comme semblant dévotement Dieu prier. (254)

Despite the detailed description, these gestures say nothing at all to the reader of today, whereas they were highly significant to Rabelais's contemporaries, who would have identified them as traditional gestures of mockery and ridicule (see Röhrich 1967, 17).

Body language in literature is not used and interpreted on the basis of ordinary non-verbal competence alone, however. Following the notion of a linguistic competence, literary theory has coined the term 'literary' or 'poetic competence' to identify the knowledge that an author and reader have of the constituents, conventions, and norms of literary texts.[14] In the case of body language, this competence includes the knowledge of conventions governing its representation and of its main literary functions, as well as the awareness that literary body language is significant for the very fact that it has been included in the text. Just as ordinary non-verbal competence is culture-specific, so the competence concerning the forms and functions of body language in literature grows out of the literary traditions of a specific culture and is subject to historical change. It must therefore be emphasized that the present study has been conducted on the basis of European literature and literatures heavily influenced by European culture. European standards will therefore apply for both ordinary and literary non-verbal competence.

The structure of part II of this study follows the premises developed above. Body language in the literary text is interpreted on the basis of two sets of knowledge: first, the reader's ordinary non-verbal competence; second, his or her literary competence. A system of categories for the analysis of body language in literature must, therefore, also include two components. First, we need categories that reflect the reader's knowledge about the general forms and functions of NVC. These categories are provided by modern NVC research (discussed in chapter 3). Second, we need categories to enable the study of the specifically literary aspects of NVC. Such a framework, limited to narrative literature and taking the form of an open catalogue, is developed in chapter 4.

A critical framework made up of these components can aid in opening up, describing, and interpreting a semiotic area of the literary text which might easily be overlooked without such an instrument. Familiar texts may even appear in a new light if their use of body language can be seen more clearly with the help of this analytical tool. The categories are developed in close connection with text analysis, so that their relevance and applicability can be directly tested.

Most examples discussed in part II are taken from novels written in English and a few short stories of various periods; they are complemented by a number of examples from other European literatures. These examples were selected primarily for the clarity with which they demonstrate the various phenomena and concepts discussed. To facilitate understanding and contextualization, many examples were also taken from 'canonical' texts with which most academic readers of the present study will be familiar.

Part III completes the framework of categories with a historical overview. NVC is a central form of human behaviour whose importance has been documented since ancient times. Proverbs and maxims in all cultures prove that people have always been aware of the significance of non-verbal behaviour.[15] Since antiquity various disciplines have also dealt with body language in a more academic fashion – for example, rhetoric[16] and acting theory, as well as the different precursors to modern psychology. In 1603, John Florio wrote in his translation of Montaigne's *Apologie de Raimond Sebond* that 'there is no motion nor jesture that doth not speake, and speakes in a language very easie, and without any teaching to be understood' (1904–6, 2:161). In *The Advancement of Learning* (1604), Francis Bacon declared that 'the motions of the countenance and parts do ... disclose the present humour and state of the mind and will' (1861, 161). It is not surprising, then, that examples of body language can be encountered in the literature of all ages, even though such instances may vary in frequency and form.

Of course, the history of body language in literature cannot possibly be covered within the parameters of this study. Instead, this part of the present study will merely indicate a number of significant changes which body language has undergone in the novel of the British Isles from the sixteenth century to the present. Chapter 5 attempts to show how body language is increasingly gaining ground in the aesthetic of the novel. Chapter 6 illustrates how the depiction of body language in the English novel has been affected by historical developments in non-verbal behaviour itself, by theoretical writings on NVC, as well as by the representation of NVC in other forms of art.

Admittedly, the text sample on which these chapters are based is highly selective in view of the abundance of novels available since the eighteenth century: it consists of only eighty novels (a list of which is given in the appendix). The observations in part II on historical developments and on the frequency of certain modes and functions of NVC are also based on this sample, and thus cannot make any claim at statistical reliability. Throughout the present study, then, statements on tendencies and rates of occurrence will be uncomfortably, but unavoidably, vague. On the other hand, the texts chosen for the sample form a fairly representative cross-section of important varieties of the novel, ranging from canonical 'classics' to popular bestsellers. Furthermore, to avoid tautological results, the texts were selected for this representativeness and not for the quantity or quality of NVC to be found in them. Even if the results gained from the text sample cannot satisfy the statistician, then, they may at least claim to indicate reliable trends.

To facilitate further work in literary body language, this study has two extensive bibliographies of secondary materials. Of these, the bibliography of literary criticism strives to present a fairly comprehensive collection of the scholarly work on NVC in Western literature.

2

Body Language in Literature and the Arts: Past and Present Research

In the fields of literature and the arts, a scholarly interest in body language can be traced back to the last century. Most studies are interconnected with the contemporary precursors of NVC research.[1]

As far as narrative literature is concerned, the earliest philological studies of gesture (most of which originated in Germany) show a strong interest in cultural history. They complemented contemporary writings in folklore, folk psychology, and comparative linguistics that attempted to take inventory of the gestures of various cultures, in particular those of the Greeks and Romans (Sittl 1890) and of the European Middle Ages. Body language in medieval literature and art is important not only because it conveys the emotions of the characters; it also correlates with the high significance of etiquette and ceremony in medieval society.[2] In the 1930s, some German studies of culture-specific body language were clearly marked by racist ideology. A thesis on 'Gesture in the Icelandic Sagas,' for example, was declared to be a contribution to the investigation of a 'Germanic' nature (Graf 1938).

Another line of research before the Second World War examined literary body language as the expression of mental states and thus reflected the interest which expression psychology had shown in NVC since the mid-nineteenth century. Charles Darwin was one of the pioneers in modern expression psychology in Britain; in Germany, Theodor Piderit and Wilhelm Wundt were important early representatives. In the German-speaking countries, expression psychology developed into a flourishing branch of psychology in the 1920s and 1930s and initiated a number of studies in literary body language.[3] In the English-speaking countries, expression psychology hardly affected research in literary

NVC; a rare exception is Klineberg's study 'Emotional Expression in Chinese Literature' (1938).

After 1945, interest in literary body language decreased noticeably; in the German-speaking countries, this was certainly an after-effect of racist writings published during the period of National Socialism. Some folklorists continued to compile inventories of gesture,[4] but most post-war studies are characterized by the awareness that body language in literature also requires a specifically literary approach. In his comprehensive study of gesture in English literature of the Middle Ages, Werner Habicht (1959) emphasizes that, as the literature of that period is not 'true to life,' gestures cannot simply be interpreted as documents of psychology, sociology, and cultural history. Rather, one must investigate the presentation of gesture in medieval literature as conditioned by the poet's way of seeing, his imaginative world, and matters of style.

With the boom in NVC research in the 1970s, the discussion of body language in literature also gained new momentum. However, although this new NVC research in sociology, social psychology, and other disciplines developed a precise and elaborated terminology, literary criticism largely continued to work with traditional and rather broad concepts such as 'gesture' and 'posture.' Besides work on the Middle Ages, such as R.G. Benson's study of Chaucer (1980), an increasing number of studies is dedicated to body language in eighteenth- and nineteenth-century literature.[5] Several studies are also devoted to individual writers of the modern period: Linda Pelzer (1984) investigates the 'Rhetoric of Gesture' in the works of Henry James; David E. Smith (1976) compares the use of body language in the prose fiction of Kafka and Kleist, including essential differences in the narrative presentation of this body language.

In the course of the 1980s, the terminology of NVC research starts to find its way into literary criticism,[6] although it is not always adapted for the special purposes of literary analysis. In some cases, the new terminology is used only to investigate traditional questions concerning literary body language, such as the role it plays in creating character or presenting mental states. However, thanks to the special interest which NVC research takes in human interaction, body language in literature is also explored in a number of new directions – for example, the relation between speech and body language in the communication between fictional characters.

Apart from the work of David E. Smith, questions regarding narrative technique and style in the presentation of non-verbal behaviour have been neglected until now. Fernando Poyatos (1983) names a few basic problems inherent in the presentation of NVC in a verbal medium, but it is obvious that Poyatos is primarily an anthropologist: central concepts of narratology, for example, are ignored, which leads to some deviant interpretations.

The unique manifestations of body language in narrative literature come into sharper focus if compared to the use of body language in the dramatic text. Of course, the presentation of body language in the dialogue and stage directions of a play is limited in comparison to its depiction in a narrative text. Its presentation in the stage directions, given the pragmatic nature of such a text, is also of lesser artistic interest than its portrayal in narrative prose. This might explain why NVC in drama has traditionally received much less attention than body language in narrative literature.

The study of body language in drama begins with a marked emphasis on expression psychology.[7] Studies of a broader scope are much more recent. In the field of English literature, Paul Goetsch (1977), for example, provides a compact overview of the manifestations of gesture in modern drama, and David Bevington's *Action Is Eloquence* (1984) stands out among a series of studies on Shakespeare.

On the whole, literary critics in the English-speaking countries have discussed body language to a lesser degree than critics in Germany, where scholarship of this kind has been embedded in related research performed in philology and expression psychology. In Britain and North America, an increased interest in literary body language can be observed only after the advent of modern NVC research, which has its roots in the United States and Britain.

As a visible phenomenon, body language is a central carrier of meaning in painting and sculpture as well as the performing arts. A comparison between literature and these art forms is especially relevant in view of historical developments, but it also draws attention to the peculiarities in the verbal presentation of body language.

Reflections on bodily expression in painting and sculpture can be traced back to the classical period. There is, for example, Socrates' discussion with a painter and a sculptor in Xenophon's *Memorabilia* (3.10. 4–8). In twentieth-century art history, Aby Warburg worked on an 'atlas' of body language until his death in 1929. This *mnemosyne* atlas was intended to document the way in which Western art 'remembers' and preserves the expressions and gestures of antiquity. Although this project was never completed,[8] Warburg's 'cultural' approach has been a major influence on the discussion of body language in art history. Most of these studies document the history of individual gestures or analyse the body language specific to a period or culture. More general observations on body language in Western art can mainly be attributed to Ernst Gombrich.[9]

In the field of the performing arts, theatre semiotics has made a significant contribution to the development of a classification system for forms and functions of non-verbal behaviour. A seminal German study, to which the present investigation is indebted, is Erika Fischer-Lichte's *The Semiotics of Theatre* (1992).[10] In its portrayal of body language, film can be distinguished from theatre above all in one area: the language of the face. Whereas in theatre the face plays a subordinate role, it may gain a particular significance on the screen. A close-up shot can portray nuances of mime and glance in the most intimate proximity – a closeness, in fact, which may never be experienced in real life. A comparison between body language in film and in narrative literature will therefore accentuate contrasts and parallels that are different from those between narrative and theatrical body language. To date, however, film studies have not yet provided findings that could form the basis for such an investigation.[11]

One last preliminary remark should be addressed to the question of terminology. Before the terms devised by NVC research found acceptance in literary criticism, 'gesture' was the most commonly used term for body language in literature. However, 'gesture' is often defined vaguely and with wide discrepancies in reference, not only in literary criticism. Some dictionary definitions, for example, include every type of body movement; others are restricted to 'expressive' movement. The *Oxford English Dictionary* (1989) defines 'gesture,' in today's usage, as 'a movement expressive of thought or feeling.' *Webster's Third New International Dictionary* (1961) lists two instances of current usage, in which the gesture as an expression of feeling is mentioned only in passing: 'the use of motions of the limbs or body as a means of intentional expression,' and 'a movement usu. of the body or limbs that symbolizes or emphasizes an idea, sentiment, or attitude.' Definitions of 'gesture' also vary as to the parts of the body that are included. In some cases, facial expression is subsumed under 'gesture'; in other cases, the term refers to movements of the body, excluding the face. The vague general usage of 'gesture' has caused each discipline concerned with it to develop its own definition. In literary criticism, 'gesture' is also given figurative meanings that go far beyond the phenomenon of body language. Bertolt Brecht's use of the term 'Gestus' (Brecht 1967 [1938], 482), for example, implies a general disposition of characters to one another and to their environment – that is, the general attitude or stance of a play; it thus resembles Jan Mukařovský's concept of 'semantic gesture' (see Jankovič 1972). For R.P. Blackmur (1942), 'gesture' eventually becomes a synonym for expressiveness: 'Gesture, in language, is the outward and dramatic play of inward and imaged meaning' (6). Even aside from such metaphorical definitions, the meanings of 'gesture' vary widely in literary criticism. David E. Smith (1976, 12) uses 'gesture' in a fairly comprehensive sense: 'Gesture ... includes all movements of the body, facial expressions, reflex reactions and postures which, in some way, reveal the feelings or intentions of a person vis à vis a given set of circumstances.' The most comprehensive definitions of gesture are synonymous with the more recent concept of body language. Since the introduction of the new terminology developed in NVC research, however, the meaning of 'gesture' has frequently been limited once again, and generally only includes forms of body movement, but not facial expression or posture.

Modern NVC research has produced a number of terms with fairly binding definitions. Above all, its terminology is more refined than the established notions of gesture and posture and thus may give rise to questions which have not yet been asked of body language in the literary text. Whereas many earlier studies focused on body language as an expression of feeling, for example, NVC research also draws attention to the phenomenon of non-verbal interaction between fictional characters. Also, various modes of NVC that were usually overlooked under the term 'gesture' now move into the literary critic's line of vision. The areas of haptics and proxemics, for example, have received hardly any attention at all in older literary criticism – although they have been present in literature for centuries.

PART II

A CRITICAL FRAMEWORK FOR THE ANALYSIS OF BODY LANGUAGE IN (NARRATIVE) LITERATURE

3

Categories of Body Language

There's language in her eye, her cheek, her lip,
Nay, her foot speaks; her wanton spirits look out
At every joint and motive of her body.

Shakespeare, *Troilus and Cressida*, 4.5.55–7

This chapter establishes categories which allow the analysis of literary body language on the basis of ordinary non-verbal competence. NVC research has proposed various classification systems for non-verbal behaviour, none of which is entirely satisfactory (see K.R. Scherer, 1984, 161–2). Several of these systems have proved to be useful in the analysis of natural body language, though, and may serve as a basis for an analysis of body language in literature. They have to be modified, however, for the purposes of literary interpretation and criticism. Literary texts never present their characters' NVC in the great variety and complexity to be observed in real life. Many of the differentiations established in anthropological, sociological, psychological, or semiotic research thus are either not relevant in the analysis of literary texts, or only marginally so. This chapter will contain only categories relevant to literary analysis. It is first necessary, however, to define the terms 'non-verbal communication' and 'body language' as basic concepts in the discussion.

3.1 'Body Language' and 'Non-verbal Communication': A Definition of Terms

The term 'non-verbal communication,' established by the psychologists

Ruesch and Kees (1956), has persevered in research literature, although it has been criticized as being vague and divergent in content.[1] In its widest sense the term includes 'the emissions of signs by all the nonlexical somatic, artifactual and environmental sensible signs contained in a culture' (Poyatos 1983, xvi). In most monographs, however, the term has a more limited meaning and refers to communicative non-verbal *behaviour*, that is, to actions or reactions of an organism. According to Laver and Hutcheson (1972, 12), non-verbal behaviour can be separated into non-vocal and vocal behaviour. The latter is usually called 'paralanguage' and includes non-verbal phenomena such as quality of voice, interjection, laughter, sobbing, coughing, and silence. The following discussion is restricted to *non*-vocal aspects of NVC. An examination of paralinguistic phenomena demands parameters specifically relevant to that area and would lead well beyond the boundaries of the present study.[2]

In light of this limitation, this study also uses the term 'body language.' This term is rejected by some researchers – not just because of its association with the popular press. Since NVC primarily serves different communication purposes than speech, the assumption that the body speaks a 'language' is considered to be a misleading metaphor (see Sebeok 1979, 47). However, this metaphor has a long-standing tradition[3] and also appears in serious research, so that it seems justified to adopt the term.

Non-verbal behaviour plays a most important role in social life. In every form of human interaction a large portion of the signals people send or receive, either consciously or unconsciously, are non-verbal – even when the communication appears to be a primarily verbal exchange: 'The vast majority of the message content in virtually all messages we send and receive is encoded and decoded in nonverbal channels. We have seen estimates ranging from a low 65% nonverbal and 35% verbal content in an average message ... to a high of more than 90% nonverbal content ... '(Katz and Katz 1983, xv). Accordingly, the impossibility of communicating non-verbally is perceived as a limitation. In Doris Lessing's novel *The Golden Notebook* (1962), for example, two friends talking on the telephone perceive their inability to communicate through body language as a loss: 'The two women stood by their respective telephones, silent; if they had been in the same room they would have exchanged wry glances or smiles' (259).

Sociological and social-psychological contributions to NVC research have demonstrated how many different roles non-verbal behaviour plays in human interaction. Body language can also be observed in many of these roles in literature: non-verbal behaviour makes it possible for the reader to draw conclusions about the feelings, thoughts, personal characteristics, and attitudes of the fictional interactors; it informs us of their social status and the social roles they play and allows us to assess the power relations between them. Non-verbal behaviour transmits even the finest nuances of interpersonal attraction or repulsion. In the context of speech, it also plays an important role in regulating the conversation; it communicates the listener's reactions to the speaker and can either complement, replace, or contradict a spoken message. In specialized forms of communication such as rhetoric and propaganda, non-verbal action is consciously used as a tool to influence the listener. According to the functional categories of communication established by Roman Jakobson (1960, 353–7), NVC can be said to dominate in the expressive function (focused upon the sender of a message), the conative function (aimed at the receiver), and the phatic function (focused upon the contact between the interactors).

Although there is no question as to the interactive significance of non-verbal behaviour, it can be categorized as 'communicative' only on the basis of a specific definition of communication. A clarification of the potential for communication in non-verbal behaviour leads to the discovery of a set of features that will here be referred to as 'situational frame conditions' of NVC. In relation to literature, these frame conditions are those under which body language is used and understood (or not understood) within the fictional situation (that is, level L1 of the narrative communication model). As we shall see, the effect of body language in literature may depend essentially on the frame conditions under which it occurs. One must also bear in mind that the non-verbal behaviour of the characters may have a meaning for the reader that deviates from its significance within the fictional situation.

Semiotics makes a distinction between signals that are 'communicative' – that is, consciously transmitted – and signals that are 'expressive' – that is, spontaneous, unintentionally transmitted, and revealing an inner state or disposition (see Eco 1977). This criterion for communication is met in the following passage in E.M. Forster's *A Room with a View* (1908). During the characters' first joint meal in their Florence guest-house, Mr Emerson's well-meant but indiscreet offer to switch rooms with Lucy and her chaperone, Miss Bartlett, prompts an exchange of meaningful glances:

Miss Bartlett, though skilled in the delicacies of conversation, was powerless in the presence of brutality ... She looked around as much as to say, 'Are you all like this?' And two little old ladies, who were sitting further up the table ... looked back, clearly indicating, 'We are not; we are genteel.' (25)

As the narrator's paraphrases indicate, the characters' glances replace speech in a situation in which the sense of gentility forbids a verbal exchange of opinions. Here the encoding and decoding of the non-verbal messages takes place consciously and intentionally, just as it would in a verbal exchange.[4]

However, a great amount of non-verbal behaviour takes place unintentionally, and the sender may not be aware of its significance. Often it is precisely the unconsciously transmitted body language that is most significant, in both real-life and literary situations. In their dystopian novels *Nineteen Eighty-Four* (1949) and *The Handmaid's Tale* (1985), George Orwell and Margaret Atwood specifically refer to the unconsciousness of non-verbal behaviour to emphasize the threat under which the individual must live in a totalitarian state.[5] In the worlds described in both novels, people live under the unnatural compulsion to be in control of their bodies at all times; unconscious body language betrays nonconformist attitudes and forbidden feelings. Winston Smith in *Nineteen Eighty-Four* is aware of this danger: 'as he well knew, even a back can be revealing' (6). Atwood's Offred, who is forced to be a birthing slave in a modern theocracy, is afraid that her 'owner' may unconsciously betray his forbidden feelings for her: 'But the Commander could give me away so easily, by a look, by a gesture, some tiny slip that would reveal to anyone watching that there was something between us now' (171). The unconscious non-verbal expression of one's inner state is an elemental trait of human behaviour; however, in the dictatorships described in these two novels, it poses a danger and must be repressed.

The narrow definition of communication as consciously transmitted signals would exclude many dimensions of significant non-verbal behaviour in literature. Our definition of NVC or body language must therefore be based on a broader concept of communication. Paul Watzlawick (Watzlawick, Beavin, and Jackson 1968) defines communication as all behaviour in an interactional situation that has a message value (48–9). One cannot say 'that "communication" only takes place when it is intentional, conscious, or successful, that is, when mutual understanding occurs' (49). According to this definition, NVC or body language is all non-verbal behaviour that can be decoded – that is potentially significant to a receiver – whether it is conscious or unconscious, intentional or unintentional.

However, the intentionality and/or consciousness of non-verbal behaviour may be essential for the meaning it transmits. In Thomas Hardy's *Tess of the d'Urbervilles: A Pure Woman* (1891), the protagonist's purity finds expression, for example, in her attempt to undo her seducer's kiss:

> No sooner had he done so than she flushed with shame, took out her handkerchief, and wiped the spot on her cheek that had been touched by his lips. His ardour was nettled at the sight, for the act on her part had been unconsciously done.
>
> 'You are mighty sensitive for a cottage girl!' said the young man.
>
> Tess made no reply to this remark, of which, indeed, she did not quite comprehend the drift, unheeding the snub she had administered by her instinctive rub upon her cheek. (85–6)

The narrator's emphasis on the unconscious and instinctive nature of Tess's behaviour brings out the natural pureness of her moral character.

Flannery O'Connor's short story 'Good Country People' (1955) is a tragicomic story about deception and delusion. The unattractive Hulga, a doctor of philosophy, who has been looking forward to a long-awaited amorous adventure, is robbed of her artificial leg by Pointer, who is pretending to be a Bible salesman. Hulga's mother lives under the illusion that the 'country people' of the American South represent the epitome of virtue – a notion which her tenant Mrs Freeman knows how to exploit. Mrs Freeman is an expert in manipulating her facial expression: 'Besides the neutral expression that she wore when she was alone, Mrs. Freeman had two others, forward and reverse, that she used for all her human dealings' (169). Just as her naïve mother is deceived by her tenant, so Hulga, in spite of her education, is duped by Pointer, who poses as an innocent country man. Pointer's first appearance makes it clear that he, too, consciously uses body language to suit his purposes and is able to change it from one minute to the next:

> 'Oh!' he said, pretending to look puzzled but with his eyes sparkling, 'I saw it said "The Cedars," on the mailbox so I thought you was Mrs. Cedars!' and he burst out in a pleasant laugh ... 'Mrs. Hopewell!' he said and grabbed her hand. 'I hope you are well!' and he laughed again and then all at once his face sobered

completely. He paused and gave her a straight earnest look and said, 'Lady, I've come to speak of serious things.' (177–8)

In the story's seduction episode, when he literally pulls Hulga's leg, Pointer reveals that it is only his obsession with artificial limbs that has driven him into Hulga's longing arms, and he gives up his deceptive body language: 'When all of him had passed but his head, he turned and regarded her with a look that no longer had any admiration in it. "I've gotten a lot of interesting things," he said. "One time I got a woman's glass eye this way. And you needn't to think you'll catch me because Pointer ain't really my name"' (195). Intentional as opposed to spontaneous body language, then, contributes significantly to the theme of delusion central to this story.[6]

A broad definition of NVC is especially appropriate in the analysis of literature: for a reader who uses a character's body language in the process of constructing meaning from the text, this behaviour is communicative regardless of whether or not it is conscious or intentional, or whether it is decoded or not decoded within the fictional situation itself.

'Zero decoding' (Poyatos 1983, 34–5) can be assumed when behaviour is not decoded by a receiver for whom it could be significant. In his novel *The American* (1876–7), Henry James frequently portrays instances of zero decoding by his protagonist which are closely connected to the novel's central theme. While he is in Paris, Newman, the American, falls in love with the widowed daughter of a French aristocratic family. The Bellegardes, who value tradition and status, are opposed to this relationship and force Madame de Cintré to break off her engagement to the American. Time and again the norms and behaviour codes which Newman imports from the New World collide with the rigid codes of the aristocracy; the customs of the Old World remain incomprehensible to him – including subtleties of non-verbal behaviour. In the following example Newman does receive body language and is aware of its communicative potential, but he is incapable of understanding exactly what it means:

But Madame de Cintré, as she gave him her hand, gave him also a look by which she appeared to mean that he should understand something. Was it a warning or a request? Did she wish to enjoin speech or silence? He was puzzled, and young Madame de Bellegarde's pretty grin gave him no information. (246)

In another passage, Newman does not even perceive meaningful non-verbal behaviour, although the narrator explains its significance to the reader:

> I have said that Newman was observant, but it must be admitted that on this occasion he failed to notice a certain delicate glance which passed between Madame de Bellegarde and the marquis, and which we may presume to have been a commentary upon the innocence displayed in that latter clause of his speech. (253)

The glance which Newman fails to see could give him a clue as to what the Bellegardes, his opponents, think about him. His inability to interpret signifiers and the fact that he misses some of them entirely strengthen the reader's impression of Newman's American 'innocence' and his disorientation in a society foreign to him. In this novel, then, the frame condition of a zero decoding forms an important aspect of the text's significance.

Difficulties in decoding non-verbal behaviour are also thematically relevant in Jane Austen's *Pride and Prejudice* (1813). Pride and prejudice prevent the protagonists from expressing their thoughts on important matters and they must instead rely on vague non-verbal signals. This causes many of the misunderstandings which strain the relationship between the elder Bennet sisters and their lovers. One of the greatest misunderstandings in the novel is Elizabeth's assessment of the frivolous officer Wickham and the mutual aversion that exists between Wickham and Darcy. When Elizabeth sees the two men together for the first time, she becomes aware of the non-verbal signals that express this aversion:

> Mr. Darcy corroborated it with a bow, and was beginning to determine not to fix his eyes on Elizabeth, when they were suddenly arrested by the sight of the stranger, and Elizabeth happening to see the countenance of both as they looked at each other, was all astonishment at the effect of the meeting. Both changed colour, one looked white, the other red. Mr. Wickham, after a few moments, touched his hat – a salutation which Mr. Darcy just deigned to return. What could be the meaning of it? – It was impossible to imagine; it was impossible not to long to know. (72–3)

The question in Elizabeth's narrated monologue ('What could be the meaning of it?') underscores the fact that she cannot precisely decode the body language she has just witnessed, and this will prevent her from giving up her preconceptions in time. Only much later, verbal communication in the form of a long letter from Darcy will explain the meaning of the body language she has observed.

In a fictional situation, meaningful behaviour will also not be decoded when that situation is non-interactive, that is, when there is no other character present to observe the behaviour.[7] Literary texts frequently present characters in non-interactive situations. In *The American*, Newman is often described when he is alone – for example, just after his engagement to Madame de Cintré has been broken off: 'Again and again Newman could only think of one thing; his thoughts always came back to it, and as they did so, with an emotional rush which seemed physically to express itself in a sudden upward choking, he leaned forward – the waiter having left the room – and, resting his arms on the table, buried his troubled face' (440). Here Newman's body language complements the narrator's psychonarration[8] to give the reader a view of the character's inner life; in particular, Newman's non-verbal behaviour conveys the intensity of his despair. The fact that Newman is not seen by any other character contributes to the credibility of his display of feelings – at least to a modern reader of Western culture. Only *because* he is alone ('the waiter having left the room'), can he express his feelings freely, since in modern Western cultures social norms restrict the expression of feelings in an interactive situation.

In natural face-to-face interaction, non-verbal behaviour often occurs in association with acts of speech. Many messages between interactors are, however, primarily or exclusively exchanged non-verbally, as has been stated earlier. In literary texts, too, instances of interaction can be found which consist exclusively of a non-verbal exchange. In Ian McEwan's *The Comfort of Strangers* (1981), a young couple's disturbed relationship is depicted through a detailed study of body language:

> Colin had brought the joint indoors for Mary, and she had refused it – a quick murmur of 'No thanks' – without turning in her seat. He lingered behind her, staring into the mirror with her, trying to catch her eye. But she looked straight ahead at herself and continued to brush her hair. He traced the line of her shoulder with his finger. Sooner or later, the silence would have to break. Colin turned to leave, and changed his mind. He cleared his throat, and rested his hand firmly on her shoulder ... His indecision was wholly drug-induced and was of the tail-chasing kind that argued that if he moved away now, having touched her, she might, conceivably at least, be offended ... but then, she was continuing to brush her hair, long after it was necessary, and it seemed she was

> waiting for Colin to leave ... and why? ... Miserably, he ran his finger along the line of Mary's spine. She now held the handle of the brush in one hand and rested the bristles in the open palm of the other, and continued to stare ahead. Colin leaned forward and kissed her nape, and when she still did not acknowledge him, he crossed the room with a noisy sigh and returned to the balcony. (15–16)

Not only is the verbal communication between the two characters interrupted, but the difficulties in the relationship are also revealed in Colin's tentative attempts at making contact through touch, to which his partner does not react.

The description of interactive body language *accompanying* speech may be problematic in the medium of a printed text, as we shall see later in greater detail. It is therefore not surprising that in many narrative and dramatic texts, conversations between the characters consist primarily or exclusively of verbal discourse, even though a historical trend to incorporate more and more body language accompanying speech is apparent.

In an interaction between characters with verbal *and* non-verbal means, the statement made by NVC is important in its relation to the concomitant speech. This relation spans a wide spectrum, from the mere accentuation of the verbal utterance to the contradiction between verbal and non-verbal statement, of which the ending of Samuel Beckett's *Waiting for Godot* (1956) is a classic and frequently cited example:

> VLADIMIR: Well? Shall we go?
> ESTRAGON: Yes, let's go.
> *They do not move.*

The discordance between speech act and non-verbal action here exemplifies the tragicomic and paradoxical nature of the characters' situation. It also emphasizes that language has deteriorated to such an extent that it has entirely lost its connection to human action.

Since the relationship between the speech and body language of the characters can be essential for the meaning and effect of a text, we need categories to describe this relationship. For natural interaction, Ehlich and Rehbein (1982, 7–8) distinguish between 'comitative' and 'independent' NVC in a verbal context. While the comitative forms are closely linked to acts of speech, the independent forms of NVC achieve a particular quality of their own within the communicative spectrum. Body language can be considered independent, for example, when it gives clues to a character's inner state or to the interpersonal relationship between characters, without these being the subject of the verbal discourse that is taking place at the same time. A passage from Flannery O'Connor's 'Good Country People,' cited earlier, illustrates the difference between independent and comitative body language:

> 'Oh!' he said, **pretending to look puzzled** but with his eyes sparkling, 'I saw it said "The Cedars," on the mailbox so I thought you was Mrs. Cedars!' and he burst out in a pleasant laugh ... 'Mrs. Hopewell!' he said and **grabbed her hand**. 'I hope you are well!' and he **laughed again and then all at once his face sobered completely**. He paused and **gave her a straight earnest look** and said, 'Lady, I've come to speak of serious things.' (177–8)

The body language Pointer uses quite consciously (indicated in bold print) is comitative; it is meant to emphasize his verbal utterance. The sparkle in his eyes, however, has an independent quality: it implies Pointer's characteristics and aims, which he hides behind his verbal and non-verbal masks.

Ehlich and Rehbein also differentiate between a further pair of opposites: 'concordant' and 'discordant' NVC. The former illustrates, strengthens, weakens, or complements a verbal utterance; the latter contradicts it. Ehlich and Rehbein only maintain this distinction with reference to comitative non-verbal behaviour. However, it is often precisely the body language which is *not* directly related to a verbal utterance that is discordant, as is illustrated in the passage from 'Good Country People.' Pointer's sparkling eyes obviously contradict his other verbal and non-verbal behaviour. Thus, it should be possible to combine the two features '± concordant' and '± comitative' freely, not least since the distinction between comitative and independent NVC is not strictly delineated anyway. In the following example from Joseph Heller's antiwar satire *Catch-22* (1961), the degree to which the character Aarfy's body language can be considered independent varies. What is central to the effect of this passage, however, is the discordant quality of this body language. Yossarian berates his friend Aarfy for having killed a prostitute. At first Aarfy does not want to admit to his guilt. In the course of their conversation, however, he becomes increasingly less sure of himself. This is reflected not in his verbal utterances, but in his increasingly discordant *non*-verbal behaviour.

'Aarfy, are you insane?' Yossarian was almost speechless. 'You *killed* a girl. They're going to put you in jail!'

'Oh, no,' Aarfy answered with a forced smile. 'Not me. They aren't going to put good old Aarfy in jail. Not for killing *her.*' ...

'Oh, I hardly think they'll do that,' Aarfy replied with a jovial chuckle, although his symptoms of nervousness increased. He spilled tobacco crumbs unconsciously as his short fingers fumbled with the bowl of his pipe. 'No, sirree. Not to good old Aarfy.' He chortled again ...

'Listen!' Yossarian cried, almost in joy. He pricked up his ears and watched the blood drain from Aarfy's face as sirens mourned far away, police sirens ...

'Oh, no,' Aarfy insisted with a lame laugh and a weak smile. 'They're not coming to arrest me. Not good old Aarfy.'

All at once he looked sick. He sank down on a chair in a trembling stupor, his stumpy, lax hands quaking in his lap ... Aarfy was green. He kept shaking his head mechanically with a queer, numb smile ... (408–9)

Aarfy's non-verbal behaviour climactically reveals an inner state which is disguised by the words he speaks. Ekman and Friesen use the term 'non-verbal leakage'[9] for non-verbal behaviour revealing the true feelings or thoughts of a person, in contrast to what that person asserts verbally. Aarfy's body language leaks out his increasing sense of guilt and his growing fear of punishment. From his discordant body language the reader concludes, as does Yossarian, that Aarfy has feelings of guilt, and expects him to be arrested by the approaching military police. But, along with Yossarian, the reader then experiences the absurdity of the catch-22 situation. It is one of the bitter ironies of this novel that, after the non-verbal climax of the cited passage, Aarfy's increasingly unconvincing words finally triumph. Although he is indeed morally guilty, he is not guilty according to the absurd tenets of military law. It is not the murderer who ends up in jail, but Yossarian, who is guilty of only a minor transgression.

Summary

For the purpose of literary analysis, the terms 'non-verbal communication' and 'body language' refer to the forms of non-verbal behaviour exhibited by characters within the fictional situation. This behaviour can be either conscious or unconscious on the part of the fictional character; the character can use it with an intention to convey a message, or it can be unintentional; it can take place within or outside of an interaction; it can be accompanied by speech or independent of speech. From the perspective of a fictional receiver, it can be decoded correctly, incorrectly, or not at all. The examples above have shown that these 'frame conditions' of NVC can be of great interest in the interpretation of a text. The following set of features shall therefore be incorporated in our system of categories:

I / The non-verbal behaviour of a fictional character is manifested in the presence/absence of another character on the level of fictional action: ± *interactive*.
II / The non-verbal behaviour occurs within/outside the context of the characters' speech: ± *speech*. Body language accompanying speech is either comitative or independent: ± *comitative* (body language which is not accompanied by speech naturally has an independent quality of expression); its relationship to the characters' speech is either concordant or discordant: ± *concordant*.
III / The sender is either *conscious* or *unconscious* of the body language exhibited. Conscious behaviour is either *intentional* or *unintentional*.
IV / The non-verbal behaviour of a character is *decoded/not decoded* by an interactor within the fictional situation (this feature thus presupposes the condition '+ interactive'); the decoding by the receiver can either be *correct* or *incorrect*.

Now that the terms basic to our concept of non-verbal communication have been explained, we can establish a classification framework for modes and functions of NVC. Body language always manifests itself in a particular form (mode) of behaviour. It also plays a particular role within the situation in which it occurs and can thus be assigned to a particular functional class.

3.2 The Modal and Functional Classification of Nonverbal Communication[10]

3.2.1 Modal Classes of Non-verbal Communication

All non-verbal behaviour can be significant in the sense that, apart from its direct practical purpose, a further level of meaning can be attributed to it. This is especially true of behaviour described in literature: because it appears in the context of a work of art, a reader will automatically consider it to have greater significance than similar behaviour occurring in real life. However, even in real life, the boundary between 'significant' and 'non-significant' non-verbal behaviour is blurred and thus the subject of a controversial discussion in semiotics: 'According to the pansemiotic view, all nonverbal behavior is communication ... Those who reject this very broad concept of communication will have to admit that nonverbal behavior is a permanent source of potential messages' (Nöth 1990, 390). According to Mauss (1935), for example, everyday practical actions (such as walking, standing, sitting, or eating) form 'techniques of the body' that are learned and therefore culture-specific. How strongly, for example, the gender-specific clothing of a culture conditions specific behaviour was already observed by Mark Twain, a writer widely noted for his great sensitivity to body language (see Eschholz 1973). In Twain's *Adventures of Huckleberry Finn* (1884), Huck, who has disguised himself as a girl, gives himself away by using incorrect body technique. In an age in which women wore long, wide skirts, they could catch an object with their skirts while sitting down, by moving their legs apart. But Huck, who is used to wearing trousers, catches an object holding his legs together. This practical behaviour provides a woman with a clue to his real gender:

> 'You do a girl tolerable poor, but you might fool men, maybe ... And, mind you, when a girl tries to catch anything in her lap she throws her knees apart; she don't clap them together, the way you did when you catched the lump of lead.' (85)

In E.M. Forster's *A Passage to India* (1924), a sitting posture indicates the cultural and personal relationship between Aziz, a Muslim Indian, and the Englishman Fielding. While intercultural relationships in colonial India are commonly characterized by distance and misunderstandings, Aziz and Fielding become friends right from the start. In Fielding's presence Aziz is thus not at all afraid to sit in the comfortable posture habitual in his culture: 'He sat down gaily on the bed; then, forgetting himself entirely, drew up his legs and folded them under him' (82).

In light of the fact that all non-verbal behaviour has the potential to be significant, we need categories that are able to accommodate all modes of non-verbal behaviour:

I Kinesics

Ever since Ray L. Birdwhistell established kinesics as a discipline in NVC research,[11] the term 'kinesics' has been used with a variety of definitions. Of these, the following is the most widely used: 'the conscious or unconscious psychomuscularly-based body movements and intervening or resulting still positions ... that ... possess intended or unintended communicative value' (Poyatos 1983, 191). Under the general term 'kinesics,' the following submodes of body language can be distinguished:

- body movements
- body postures
- facial expression
- eye behaviour
- automatic physiological and physio-chemical reactions (trembling, change in skin colour, perspiration, etc.)

The area of body movements is further divided into

- gestures
- practical actions

'Gesture' refers to movements of individual body parts that are clearly delineated, for example, nodding, raising a hand, waving an arm, and so on. Such movements have a conventional meaning more frequently than other movements have, and they are often carried out specifically in order to communicate something.[12] The term 'action' includes all other body movements, including body techniques and other practical kinds of behaviour.

II Haptics

The term 'haptics' refers to touching behaviour, which ranges from kissing, embracing, caressing, and holding hands to pinching and hitting.[13] Touching behaviour results from body movement and implies that there is very little distance between the interactants.

III Proxemics

According to E.T. Hall, the anthropologist who established proxemics as an independent discipline, proxemics is to be understood as a general semiotics of space.[14] Hall's research is devoted to the sum total of people's utilization, perception, and conception of space, as well as spatial behaviour. From this vast area, only spatial behaviour will be considered in the present study, since it is kinesically based and thus directly linked to body language. Two particular categories of proxemics to be considered are interpersonal distance/proximity and spatial orientation, that is, the way in which persons arrange themselves in relation to each other.

3.2.2 *Functional Classes of Non-verbal Communication and Their Potential for Expression*

Among the competing models for a functional classification of NVC, the categories established by Ekman and Friesen have found the widest circulation.[15] Their system will also be used as the basis for the present study, along with slight modifications of several categories proposed by Fernando Poyatos (1983). We shall disregard, however, the category of 'adaptors,' as it is defined in modal rather than functional terms and cannot be separated clearly enough from other functional classes. Adaptors are forms of NVC in which a person manipulates his or her own body, the body of another person, or an object. In the passage from Joseph Heller's *Catch-22* cited above, for example, the character fumbles with a pipe and tobacco crumbs, thus giving away his increasing anxiousness. As in this case, the function of many adaptors is the expression of an inner state, and they can therefore be subsumed under the functional categories 'emotional displays' or 'externalizers.' For the purpose of the present study, therefore, adaptors will not be considered as a class of their own.

Frequently, occurrences of body language can be placed in several of the following classes. Gestures which regulate an interaction, for example, can simultaneously imply an emotional state or serve as indicators of a person's temperament. Body language which conveys feelings and interpersonal relationships is especially difficult to separate out clearly. In literature, too, body language will often be found to be multifunctional. However, for the purpose of illustration, mainly unambiguous examples have been selected here.

Emotional Displays and Externalizers

There is widespread consensus in the field of psychology that nonverbal expression is essential for giving an individual access to the feelings of another person. In most cases, however, there is not a simple one-to-one ratio between certain feelings and certain forms of bodily expression: a feeling can be manifested in a variety of forms of nonverbal behaviour, and the same form of body language may imply a variety of feelings – there are tears of joy as well as tears of sadness.

The spontaneous physical expression of several elemental feelings (surprise, fear, revulsion, anger, happiness, sadness) is innate and universal to human behaviour, although there are culture-specific rules that determine the monitoring of this expression in certain environments and social roles (Ekman and Friesen 1981 [1969], 83). Reflection on the body language of feelings, formerly called 'pathognomy,' has a long tradition, beginning in the classical period[16] and continuing from the psychological writings of the Renaissance to those of expression psychology in the late nineteenth and early twentieth centuries. It also forms a main branch of modern NVC research, which has designated a functional category specifically for it: 'emotional display'[17] is the term used for the body language that indicates *momentary* psychological states such as affects and moods.

NVC is superior to speech as far as the communication of emotional states is concerned.[18] The reason for this superiority is found in its primary manner of coding, that is, the manner in which signifier (the nonverbal act) and signified are related to one another. Speech is primarily coded digitally[19] and extrinsically: a discrete meaning is assigned to the signifier (digital), in a binding and fixed manner (extrinsic); the relation between signifier and signified is usually arbitrary. Although NVC can also be coded in this way (see 'emblems' below), its usual manner of coding is analogic and intrinsic. Analogic means that a physical relation or a relation of similarity exists between signifier and signified, so that continual gradations in expression are possible in relation to the degree of meaning that is being transmitted. A facial expression, for example, can reveal nuances of anger much more precisely than a verbal expression can. Intrinsic means that the relation between signifier and signified is noncommittal: NVC does not normally have a 'binding' significance; its meaning can be inferred with only a degree of probability (K.R. Scherer 1977, 278). As a result, a person tends to be less in control of his or her body language than of verbal utterances, a fact which makes body language a fairly reliable source of information regarding emotional states. When verbal and non-verbal cues of emotion are incongruent, the latter are regarded as more trustworthy than the former.[20]

Because of this strong connection between feeling and non-verbal expression, body language has been a favoured mode for representing emotion in narrative literature since antiquity – in spite of the fact that the medium makes it perfectly possible for characters and narrators to express these emotions verbally. Although body language in literature is necessarily conveyed with the use of words, it may still imply the 'unspeakable' elements of many emotions.

The information about a person conveyed by body language goes beyond the person's feelings. This is why Poyatos (1983) amplifies Ekman and Friesen's classification system and adds the class of 'externalizers': 'Externalizers are reactions to other people's past, present, anticipated or imagined reality, to what has been said, is being said or will be said, silenced, done or not done by us or someone else, to past, present, anticipated or imagined events, to our own somatic phenomena, to animal and environmental agents, to aesthetic experiences, and to spiritual experiences' (128). This definition is rather vague and does not clearly differentiate externalizers from emotional displays. Strictly speaking, emotional displays form a subcategory of externalizers. However, they constitute such a distinctive group of non-verbal behaviour that an independent category seems appropriate. It is precisely in the field of literary criticism that the distinction between externalizers and emotional displays is useful, because one can observe historical differences in the use of these two kinds of expression: there are numerous examples of emotional displays in very early texts; externalizers, on the other hand, only gradually gain importance in the history of narrative literature (see chapter 5).

For the purpose of this study, externalizers, as distinct from emotional displays, are those forms of NVC which convey information about a character apart from his or her temporary emotions: relatively stable mental conditions (such as psychopathological states, attitudes, opinions, values, personality traits), but also mental and intellectual activities and conditions. In the following example taken from Thomas Hardy's *Desperate Remedies* (1871), the character's intense reflection, which results in an important decision, is conveyed through externalizers:

> She sat in the attitude which denotes unflagging, intense, concentrated thought – as if she were cast in bronze. Her feet were together, her body bent a little forward, and quite unsupported by the back of the chair; her hands on her knees, her eyes fixed intently on the corner of a footstool.
>
> At last she moved and tapped her fingers upon the table at her side. Her pent-up ideas had finally found some channel to advance in. Motions became more and more frequent as she laboured to carry further and further the problem which occupied her brain. She sat back and drew a long breath: she sat sideways and leant her forehead upon her hand. Later still she arose, walked up and

down the room – at first abstractedly, with her features as firmly set as ever; but by degrees her brow relaxed, her footsteps became lighter and more leisurely; her head rode gracefully and was no longer bowed. She preened herself like a swan after exertion. (111)

Besides such subject-related externalizers, expressions of interpersonal relations (ranging from sympathy and antipathy[21] to power and domination)[22] are also considered to be externalizers. In the area of interaction, NVC, thanks to its analogic coding, also allows for gradations of expression which can hardly be reproduced verbally.

Conveying emotional states, thoughts, attitudes, and interpersonal relationships is one of the main functions of NVC in real life. It is not surprising that in literature, too, emotional displays and externalizers are the most frequently represented functional classes. As early as 1792, the German philosopher Johann Georg Sulzer defined artistic gesture in his *Allgemeine Theorie der Schönen Künste* in terms of these two functions: 'Die verschiedenen Bewegungen und Stellungen des Körpers und einzeler [*sic*] Gliedmaßen desselben, in so fern sie etwas Charakteristisches haben, oder Aeußerungen dessen sind, was in der Seele vorgeht' (314) [The various movements and postures of the body and of individual limbs, insofar as they are characteristic, or are expressions of that which is taking place in the soul] (my translation).

One subcategory of subject-related externalizers remains to be considered: NVC which conveys external characteristics such as age, culture, gender, social roles, or social status. An area of NVC which has received particular attention in the last few years is that of differences in body language between the sexes.[23] An increased interest in externalizers of gender and their social implications is also evident in contemporary literature by women. The feminist writer Marge Piercy, in her novel *Small Changes* (1972), treats gender-specific body language as a subject of extensive and detailed observation. The female protagonists in this novel are particularly sensitive to the social roles women are expected to play, and to gender differences. While she is in the process of coming to terms with her gendered existence, one of the women joins an actors' group. This context provides a frame for a lengthy exposition of male and female body techniques, in which the traditional gender roles are reflected:

Wanda made them aware how they moved, how they rested, how they occupied space. She demonstrated how men sat and how women sat on the subway, on benches. Men expanded into available space. They sprawled, or they sat with spread legs. They put their arms on the arms of chairs. They crossed their legs by putting a foot on the other knee. They dominated space expansively.

Women condensed. Women crossed their legs by putting one leg over the other and alongside. Women kept their elbows to their sides, taking up as little space as possible. They behaved as if it were their duty not to rub against, not to touch, not to bump a man. If contact occurred, the woman shrank back. If a woman bumped a man, he might choose to interpret it as a come-on. Women sat protectively, using elbows not to dominate space, not to mark territory, but to protect their soft tissues.

... A woman walked with a sense of being looked at: either she behaved as if being evaluated by men were a test and she tried to pass it; or she walked with chin lowered, eyes lowered. She pretended that, if she did not look at the men, the men could not see her. She walked very fast, pretending to be invisible, deaf, dumb, and blind. (350)

In Piercy's feminist utopian novel, *Woman on the Edge of Time* (1976), gender-specific externalizers figure among the semiotic systems with which an image of a model future is developed. In the action taking place in the present, the protagonist, Connie, becomes the victim of social 'care.' When she hits her niece's pimp over the head with a bottle because he wants to force her niece to have an abortion, Connie is admitted to a psychiatric institution because of her violent behaviour. Here she is selected to be the subject of an experiment in brain surgery. With the help of a time-traveller, Luciente, she can escape from this present state for hours at a time into a future in which, besides various other deficiencies of the present, the discriminating differences between genders no longer exist. The personal pronoun has been neutralized and replaced by the new form 'per'; men as well as women can become 'mothers'; and men and women no longer exhibit gender-specific body techniques. At first Connie assumes that Luciente is a man because the latter's body language is so 'masculine,' that is, free and confident: 'Luciente spoke, she moved with that air of brisk unselfconscious authority Connie associated with men. Luciente sat down, taking up more space than women ever did. She squatted, she sprawled, she strolled, never thinking about how her body was displayed' (67).

In *The Handmaid's Tale*, Margaret Atwood uses gender-specific body language in order to show the changes American society has undergone after a Puritan fundamentalist coup. The handmaids, recruited for the service of birth-giving, are expected to sit and walk chastely, with bowed heads and folded hands, shrouded in long gowns.[24] In contrast, the reader is reminded of body postures which modern Western women were allowed to assume before the coup: 'Moira, sitting on the edge of my bed, legs crossed, ankle on knee, in her purple overalls' (47). The models whose pictures Offred sees in an old fashion magazine also pose in a way no longer permitted for women in Gilead: 'There they were again, the images of my childhood: bold, striding, confident, their arms flung out as if to claim space, their legs apart, feet planted squarely on the earth. There was something Renaissance about the pose, but it was princes I thought of, not coiffed and ringleted maidens' (165). The non-verbal behaviour required of the women in Gilead indicates how the Puritan dictatorship has undone the achievements of the women's liberation movement. A sitting posture which deviates from the official body technique can thus become a subversive act and also signify an illicit interpersonal relationship. In the following passage, the reference to Offred's relaxed position indicates that her relationship with her 'commander' is no longer only an official one:

> I no longer sit stiff-necked, straight-backed, feet regimented side by side on the floor, eyes at the salute. Instead my body's lax, cosy even. My red shoes are off, my legs tucked up underneath me on the chair, surrounded by a buttress of red skirt, true, but tucked nonetheless, as at a campfire, of earlier and more picnic days. (193)

The first sentence draws attention to the contrast between Offred's forced and her private posture. For Offred, even so trivial a reminder of her earlier existence as a relaxed way of sitting means precious freedom. The significance given to a body technique that is normally taken for granted emphasizes the degree to which life for many people in Gilead has changed.

Illustrators and Regulators

Emotional displays and externalizers can be found in both interactive and non-interactive situations and usually serve an independent purpose of expression, even when they are accompanied by speech. Illustrators and regulators, on the other hand, are forms of NVC which are almost exclusively comitative. Glances and gestures are constant companions to natural speech. Although gesticulation accompanying speech may vary from one individual and, to some extent, from one culture to another,[25] 'the fundamental process of gesticulation is everywhere an integral part of the utterance process' (Kendon 1984, 104), and the listener will normally make corresponding movements.[26]

In narrative literature, the body language concomitant with speech – apart from externalizers and emotional displays – plays, on average, a much smaller part than it does in real life. Regulators in particular are only rarely found in all periods. Quite obviously, the selection process of the literary text makes for a hierarchy of functional classes of body language that is different from that of natural communication. One reason is that body language accompanying speech poses a problem of representation in the narrative text (see chapter 4, pages 95–9).

Illustrators are forms of NVC which emphasize and structure, complete, and support a verbal utterance; occasionally they signal, in a metacommunicative function, how a speech act is to be interpreted, as is the case in this passage from John Braine's *Room at the Top* (1957):

> Mrs Thompson cut in. 'No more of that *Design for Living* humour, Bob Storr.' The smile which accompanied it took the sting from the reproof ... (32)

Following Poyatos (1983, 104–25), one can differentiate between a number of subgroups of illustrators:

- *Language markers*: conscious or unconscious body language which punctuates and emphasizes parts of verbal utterance, underscores its rhythm, or segments it. When body language segments a verbal utterance, different modes tend to correspond with various textual and grammatical elements: head and hand movements correspond with elements within the sentence, whereas a change in body posture generally marks a change of topic.[27]
- *Deictics*: head or hand movements that point at persons, objects, or places.
- *Space markers* and *time markers*: usually hand or body movements that indicate size, distance, place, point of time or duration.
- *Pictographs, kinetographs, ideographs, event tracers,* and *identifiers*: generally hand movements which draw the picture of an object, trace a thought process, depict an object, or clarify abstract concepts (such as 'impossible,' 'absurd'), moral and physical traits of a person, or the quality of objects.

When illustrators find their way into a narrative text, they lend the characters' speech a graphic, vivid, or authentic dimension. This can be seen in the following quotation from Thomas Hardy's *Tess of the d'Urbervilles*. In her report, Tess's mother, a simple woman, uses the pictogram with which the doctor has explained her husband's cardiac illness to him:

'There, it is like this.' Joan Durbeyfield, as she spoke, curved a sodden thumb and forefinger to the shape of the letter C, and used the other forefinger as a pointer. '"At the present moment," he says to your father, "your heart is enclosed all round there, and all round there; this space is still open," 'a says. "As soon as it do meet, so,"' – Mrs Durbeyfield closed her fingers into a circle complete – '"off you will go like a shadder, Mr Durbeyfield," 'a says. "You mid last ten years; you mid go off in ten months, or ten days."' (49)

In *The American*, Henry James demonstrates a marked tendency to complement the speech of his characters with illustrators. A touch or a glance,[28] for example, can give emphasis to an utterance: 'She laid her two hands on his arm. "Will you grant me a last request?" and as she looked at him, urging this, her eyes filled with tears. "Let me go alone – let me go in peace"' (314). Gestures function as deictics, ideograms, or signals of emphasis:

'And you mean to carry my little picture away over there?' and she explained her phrase with a gesture. (39)

'You are very good, sir; I am overcome!' said M. Nioche, throwing out his hands. 'But you have cheerfulness and happiness for two!'

'Oh no,' said Newman more seriously. 'You must be bright and lively; that's part of the bargain.'

M. Nioche bowed, with his hand on his heart. 'Very well, sir; you have already made me lively.' (44)

Newman administered a vigorous slap to his knee. 'I would marry a Japanese, if she pleased me,' he affirmed. (73)

Some kinds of illustrators – for example, deictics, pictographs, or ideographs – can also take the place of speech, in which case they play an independent communicative role. Apart from deictics, which are embedded in the characters' speech, illustrators replace speech when verbal communication is impossible. A vivid example in literature is found in the gestures with which beautiful May directs her young lover in the presence of her blind husband in Chaucer's 'Merchant's Tale':

And with hir fynger signes made she
That Damyan sholde clymbe upon a tree (ll 2209–10)

Regulators, in contrast to illustrators, are quite neutral to the message of the speech they are associated with. They are mainly carried out and received unconsciously and 'maintain and regulate the back-and-forth nature of speaking and listening between two or more interactants' (Ekman and Friesen 1981 [1969], 90). However, the use of many regulators is also determined by culture; the following remarks refer to the norms of Western cultures.

The roles of speaker and listener in a conversation are coordinated by a complex speaking-turn system in which hand and head movements or glances indicate the end of a segment of speech or the taking of the speaking-turn. The listener emits back-channel behaviour which indicates his or her reception and understanding of what has been said.[29] A speaker can gain the listener's attention through touch; the beginning or ending of an interaction phase can be signalled by speaker and listener moving farther away from or closer to each other, or by sitting down or standing up.

Interaction is also regulated when the exchange is non-verbal; in that case, regulators are non-comitative and have a greater potential for conveying a message of their own. Glances and smiles, for example, serve to initiate contact at the beginning of an interaction, as in the following situation in J.D. Salinger's short story 'For Esmé – with Love and Squalor' (1950): 'About the time their tea was brought, the choir member caught me staring over at her party. She stared back at me ... then, abruptly, gave me a small, qualified smile ... I smiled back ...' (92). In such cases, however, the boundary between a regulator and an externalizer of relationship is overstepped: the smiles exchanged between the narrator and Esmé in Salinger's story also point towards the spontaneous friendship which develops in the course of their first meeting. For the purpose of the present study, the category of regulators is reserved for forms of NVC which primarily or exclusively function to regulate an interaction. They are only rarely found in narrative texts, as is also remarked by Anne Marmot Raim (1986) in her study of Maupassant: 'Un écrivain songe rarement à donner au lecteur un compte-rendu précis des details visuels et gestuels qui contrôlent le rhythme du dialogue et il se borne le plus souvent à présenter simplement les paroles des personnages' (94). However, regulators may essentially contribute to the effect of the passages in which they do occur.

In Wilkie Collins's detective novel *The Moonstone* (1868), for example, the prime suspect's fiancée confesses to him, in a long speech, that she has seen him take the missing diamond out of the safe. In her state of anxiety, she does not allow the man, who is also the first-person narrator, to voice his protestations of innocence, and her monologue is repeatedly interrupted by the description of the regulators with which she insists on her speaking role: 'I attempted to speak. She lifted her hand impatiently, and stopped me' (390). Such regulators not only make a long monologue more vivid, but also explain why the suspect cannot defend himself, and the couple's reconciliation is delayed for another few chapters.

An exceptional number of regulators in Salinger's 'For Esmé – with Love and Squalor' serve a different purpose. The conversation between the narrator – a young American soldier waiting to be called up to fight in the Second World War – and Esmé, a precocious English girl, mainly consists of small talk. However, both characters are very concerned with maintaining communication. Their interest in making the conversation last is emphasized by a high occurrence of regulative gestures, especially nodding, with which they signal their attention and their willingness to continue their conversation:

> 'Are you married?'
>
> I said I was.
>
> **She nodded**. 'Are you very deeply in love with your wife? Or am I being too personal?' (95)

> 'Charles misses him exceedingly,' Esmé said, after a moment. 'He was an exceedingly lovable man. He was extremely handsome, too ... He had terribly penetrating eyes, for a man who was intransically [*sic*] kind.'
>
> **I nodded**. I said I imagined her father had had quite an extraordinary vocabulary. (98)

> I said I hadn't been employed at all, that I'd only been out of college a year but that I like to think of myself as a professional short-story writer.
>
> **She nodded politely**. 'Published?' she asked. (99)

The content of their talk is not nearly as important to the characters as the fact that some form of communication is taking place at all. This is implied in the beginning of the story, where the narrator deplores the lack of contact and communication he suffers in the army: 'We were all essentially letter-writing types, and when we spoke to each other out of the line of duty, it was usually to ask somebody if he had any ink he wasn't using. When we weren't writing letters or attending classes, each of us went pretty much his own way' (88). The conversation with Esmé is thus primarily valuable to the narrator because of its phatic, contact-making dimension, and it is precisely this dimension which is stressed by the regulators. The unusually high occurrence of this functional class of non-verbal behaviour, then, corresponds with the story's main theme. This theme is also emphasized by the many farewell gestures which the soldier and the girl exchange, signalling the various steps that lead to the conclusion of their interaction: the two say goodbye four times, they shake hands twice, wave, and finally Esmé sends the narrator a kiss through her little brother. This body language, too, performs the function of regulating an interaction; however, since it is conventional, it rather belongs to the category of emblems.

Emblems

'Emblem' is the term used in NVC research for 'nonverbal acts which have a direct verbal translation, or dictionary definition, usually consisting of a word or two, or perhaps a phrase. This verbal definition or translation of the emblem is well known by all members of a group, class or culture' (Ekman and Friesen 1981 [1969], 71). This kind of body language, usually in the form of gestures, can be used, in the same way words are used, with the intention to communicate.[30] Emblems differ from illustrators replacing speech in their precise lexical verbal translation and their conventional relation between signifier and signified. Well-known examples of emblems are the 'OK' sign, the 'Victory' sign or, in most Western cultures, the act of nodding or shaking one's head to indicate 'yes' or 'no.' Since the meaning of an emblem is established through convention and is therefore culture-specific, emblems may be more problematic to understand than, for example, the universal body language of emotion. On average, emblems of the type defined above are relatively rarely encountered in literary texts (even though they seem to appear more frequently than regulators, which are so important in real-life interaction). Just like regulators, however, emblems can be an essential carrier of significance where they do appear.

In Washington Irving's story 'Rip van Winkle' (1819), for example, emblems help to depict the reaction of a community to the account of a man who returns to his village after a deep sleep which has lasted twenty years. The gestures highlighted in the following passage indicate that the villagers do not believe Rip's story at all and, indeed, consider him to be insane:

The by-standers began now to look at each other, nod, **wink significantly**, and **tap their fingers against their foreheads** ...

Rip's story was soon told, for the whole twenty years had been to him but as one night. The neighbours stared when they heard it; some were seen to **wink at each other**, and **put their tongues in their cheeks**: and the self-important man in the cocked hat, who, when the alarm was over, had returned to the field, **screwed down the corners of his mouth**, and **shook his head** – upon which there was **a general shaking of the head** throughout the assemblage. (66–8)

Irving here makes use of the fact that emblems are always associated with a specific linguistic *community*. The fact that the villagers understand each others' emblems emphasizes their status as members of a group to which Rip van Winkle no longer belongs.

Another form of body language with a conventional meaning is encountered more frequently in literature than emblems that replace speech. For the purpose of this study, the definition of the emblem will therefore be stretched to accommodate such forms of body language that have a conventional *social* meaning, that is, a secular-ceremonial or religious-ritual significance. Like emblems with a lexical meaning, ceremonial and ritual body language can be used and interpreted correctly only when the rules of etiquette or the rites of a culture are known. Thus, Buck Mulligan's behaviour at the beginning of Joyce's *Ulysses* (1922) can be recognized as a parody only if one recognizes his gestures as a part of the ritual of transubstantiation in the Roman Catholic church: 'Solemnly he came forward and mounted the round gunrest. He faced about and blessed gravely thrice the tower, the surrounding land and the awaking mountains. Then, catching sight of Stephen Dedalus, he bent towards him and made rapid crosses in the air, gurgling in his throat and shaking his head' (1:3).

The value placed on social emblems in narrative literature changes according to the world represented in the text. Social emblems are frequently encountered in texts up to the eighteenth century that portray courtly life. Courtly life placed a high value on established standards of behaviour, and the world portrayed in medieval epics and romances, especially, is a 'civilisation du geste' (Ménard 1984, 85), a public world in which the social performance of a person is given a great deal of attention.[31] In their description of social emblems, the following lines of medieval verse narrative are representative not only of the period in which they were written, but also of the courtly literature of later centuries:

Then comaunded the kyng the knyȝt for to ryse;
And he ful radly vpros, and ruchched hym fayre,
Kneled doun bifore the kyng, and cachez that weppen;
And he luflyly hit hym laft, and lyfte vp his honde,
And gef hym Goddez blessyng ... (*Sir Gawain and the Green Knight*, ll 366–70)

Fil Pandarus on knees, and up his eyen
To heven threw, and held his hondes highe,
'Immortal god,' quod he, 'that mayst nought deyen,
Cupid I mene ...' (*Troilus and Criseyde*, Bk 3, ll 183–6)

The high value placed on social emblems is reduced in narrative literature as the portrayal of a public and representative world recedes into the background and is replaced by a new type of bourgeois novel. This novel increasingly portrays everyday events and reflects the private values of a society that has freed itself of courtly ideals and maxims of behaviour (see Vosskamp 1973, 142).

This does not mean, of course, that social emblems disappear entirely from the novel. Joyce's *A Portrait of the Artist as a Young Man* (1916), for example, features a high number of emblems of prayer, which are essentially linked with the novel's theme: Stephen's preoccupation with the question of God and whether or not he feels a calling to become a priest. The modern novel also describes conventional forms of greeting, which at times are enhanced with an additional interpersonal significance and thus simultaneously function as externalizers:

He went without speaking to where the dying man sat and took his outstretched hand. It was retained. There was a moment's silence, a shared emotion, an immediate and mutual recognition of what had been so lacking with the woman outside. (Fowles, *Daniel Martin*, 192)

Jack laughed and put out a ham-like hand. He tried to out-grip me but he couldn't manage it. (Braine, *Room at the Top*, 41)

Bowing and curtsying as emblems of greeting were gradually replaced by the handshake in the nineteenth century.[32] In many cultures, the handshake has a much older social meaning as an expression of friendship and reconciliation that is found in novels as different as John Lyly's *Euphues* (1578) and E.M. Forster's *A Passage to India*:

'I for my part,' said Euphues, 'to confirm this league give thee my hand and my heart.' And so likewise did Philautus, and so shaking hands, they bid each other farewell. (*Euphues*, 150)

'I must go back now, good night,' said Aziz, and held out his hand, completely forgetting that they were not friends ... His hand was taken, and then he remembered how detestable he had been, and said gently, 'Don't you think me unkind any more?'

'No.'

'How can you tell, you strange fellow?'

'Not difficult, the one thing I always know.'

'Can you always tell whether a stranger is your friend?'

'Yes.'

'Then you are an Oriental.' He unclasped as he spoke, with a little shudder. Those words – he had said them to Mrs Moore in the mosque at the beginning of the cycle, from which, after so much suffering, he had got free. Never be friends with the English! (*A Passage to India*, 305–6)

The following excursus deals with an aspect of literary body language which can be called 'emblematic' in a wider sense. In the examples to be discussed, an essential effect of the entire text depends on the fact that a meaningful tension is established between body language and its verbal paraphrase.

Excursus: 'Emblematic' Narrative

In folk literature, the 'narrative of gesture' has a long-standing tradition.[33] One group of these stories centres on a character's misinterpretation of emblematic gestures. In chapter 1 of the present study, a variant of this tradition has already been considered: the contest of gestures between Panurge and Thaumaste in Rabelais's *Pantagruel*. In this debate, each participant misinterprets the emblems of his opponent. What the two 'scholars' take to be gestures with a most learned verbal paraphrase, is, in fact, a body language of rude abuse. The two texts to be discussed in this section do not belong directly in this tradition, but they, too, illustrate how an entire text can hinge on a tension existing between body language and the word.

Italo Calvino's *Il castello dei destini incrociati* (1973) is a classic of postmodern narrative. The first-person narrator's discourse consists of a verbal translation of the stories which the mute characters in the castle tell each other non-verbally, using tarot cards and various forms of body language:

> The handsome youth made a gesture, as if to demand our full attention, and then began his silent tale, arranging three cards in a row on the table: the *King of Coins*, the *Ten of Coins*, and the *Nine of Clubs*. The mournful expression with which he set down the first of these cards, and the joyous look with which he showed the next one, seemed to want to tell us that, his father having died ... he had come into possession of a considerable fortune and had immediately set forth on his travels. This last notion we deduced from his arm's movement in throwing down the *Nine of Clubs*, which ... reminded us of the forest through which we had recently passed. (7–8)

In two ways, this novel represents a postmodern break with the art of the realistic narrative: its structure is dictated by a (card) game, and the relation between its signifiers and its signifieds is highly ambiguous. As the mute narrators use gestures that do *not* have a binding, conventional meaning, the first-person narrator's 'translation' of their gestures is not reliable. The reader does not have the assurance that the verbal story actually is the story which the original, mute narrator wanted to communicate. The non-verbal signifier and the signified provided by the verbal narrator are only loosely linked, and the reader is invited to loosen this link entirely and join in the game of signification. The reader is free to retell the story of the mute characters in his or her own words – with the help of the tarot cards and the body language depicted in the text.

It is not surprising to find a discrepancy between body language and verbal transcription exploited in a postmodern text. But such a discrepancy may also be at the core of a more traditional narrative, such as Charles Dickens's story 'The Signalman' (1866). Here the challenge to give gestures a precise verbal interpretation – that is, to read them as emblems – makes for a central effect of the story.

The first-person narrator meets a signal-box operator who is posted at a railroad tunnel and to whom ghosts have appeared three times. Each of the ghosts has made a specific gesture. After two of these apparitions, accidents have happened, so that after the third apparition, the 'signalman' expects another accident. The first-person narrator, however, is a much more competent reader of 'signals'; he is able to understand and paraphrase the ghosts' gestures, which the signalman can only describe:

> 'I never saw the face. The left arm is across the face, and the right arm is waved, – violently waved. This way.'
>
> I followed his action with my eyes, and it was the action of an arm gesticulating, with the utmost passion and vehemence, 'For God's sake, clear the way!' (17)

The signalman, on the other hand, has interpreted the gesture merely as a signal of alarm, not as a concrete indication of an impending crash ('clear the way'). The second apparition predicts a death, which occurs in a passing train. Once again, only the first-person narrator is able to paraphrase the gesture verbally; the signalman relates only the signifier, but not the signified:

> 'It leaned against the shaft of the light, with both hands before the face. Like this.'
>
> Once more I followed his action with my eyes. It was an action of mourning. I have seen such an attitude in stone figures on tombs. (18)

The third apparition, which has not yet been followed by an accident when the signalman and the narrator first meet, repeats the first gesture. Again the narrator gives its meaning: 'He repeated ... that former gesticulation of "For God's sake, clear the way!"' (19). The signalman still does not understand the exact significance of the body language he has witnessed: '"What is its warning against?" ... "What is the danger? Where is the danger?"' (20–1).

The tragic ending of the story confirms the narrator's correct interpretation of the body language. When the third accident finally happens, the train engineer wants to warn the signalman with gestures *and* words, but cannot prevent him from being run over:

> 'I said, "Below there! Look out! Look out! For God's sake, clear the way!"'
>
> I started.
>
> 'Ah! it was a dreadful time, sir. I never left off calling to him. I put this arm before my eyes not to see, and I waved this arm to the last; but it was no use.' (24)

Only when the ghosts' gestures are read as emblems with a verbal 'translation,' can their message be fully understood. The signalman does not recognize the gestures as emblems and thereby misses their essential significance.

If one considers 'The Signalman' as a story of imperfect semiosis, of a missed understanding, the first-person narrator achieves an additional, essentially moral dimension, and an interesting blank becomes apparent in the text. The communication of the meaning of the emblems occurs exclusively on the story's communication level L2 (see page 9), that is, through the 'I' as narrator. It does not appear to take place on communication level L1, that is, between the 'I' as character and the signalman. There is no indication in the text that the 'I' as character expresses his interpretation of the gestures to the signalman, even though he is expressly asked for an interpretation. Thus the moral question arises of whether or not the narrator is responsible for the signalman's death. Is the act of telling the story an implicit admission of guilt? Such an interpretation might be supported by the fact that the exclamations and body posture of the 'I' as character at the story's beginning can be linked with those of the man who finally causes the signalman's death:

> 'Halloa! Below there!'
>
> ... so steeped in the glow of an angry sunset, that I had shaded my eyes with my hand before I saw him at all. (11)

An analysis of the body language in 'The Signalman,' then, reveals a dimension of the story that goes beyond its common interpretation as a ghost story. The relation between gesture and language emerges as a central issue, which opens up a new way of appreciating the story.

Summary

So far, we have seen that body language in fictional situations can be analysed with the same functional categories that are used in the analysis of natural NVC. In literature, however, these functional classes appear in different proportions to their appearance in natural communication: on average, in narrative literature, emotional displays and externalizers dominate; of the classes of body language that accompanies speech, illustrators figure more strongly than regulators, while the latter are very important in real-life communication.

The discussion above has shown that the effect of literary body language may depend primarily on the functional class it belongs to. The following observations will show that in other cases, the expressivity of body language can be mainly traced to its specific mode.

3.2.3 The Expressivity of Non-verbal Modes

Kinesics

Mobile parts of the body differ in their quality of expression according to their neuro-anatomic conditions and their visibility. The face has the highest capacity for non-verbal signalling because of the great number of stimuli that can be perceived in it and because it is almost constantly visible (Ekman and Friesen 1969, 90). It is not surprising, then, that facial expression is placed very high in the hierarchy of non-verbal modes represented in narrative literature.

Facial Expression The face is the most prominent part of the body. Since most of the senses are concentrated in the face, it can be described as the area of the body with which people encounter the world and in relation to which they usually locate their sense of self (Allport 1961, 472). Above all, it is the part of the body which makes it possible for human beings to 'know' each other, as Georg Simmel has formulated in his *Soziologie* (1908, 485). The immobile features of the face are read for indications of age, gender, nationality, attractiveness, and, despite the scholarly discreditation of physiognomy, personality traits. Because of the flexibility of its muscles, however, the face also serves as a most subtle externalizer and, above all, emotional display: 'Emotions are shown primarily in the face ... There is no specific body movement pattern that always signals anger or fear, but there are facial patterns specific to each emotion' (Ekman and Friesen 1975, 7). Thus, facial expression is the area of body language which has enjoyed the longest tradition of examination in scholarly research – in physiognomy and in expression psychology in the late nineteenth and early twentieth centuries, as well as in modern NVC research.[34]

The 'aesthetic significance of the face' (Simmel 1901) has also been acknowledged quite extensively. Painting and literature have developed the genre of the portrait. The description of the face plays an important role in narrative prose as well as in poetry.[35] Although the theatre is limited in its ability to make use of facial expression, the dramatic text not infrequently indicates facial expression through comments or descriptions in the characters' speech.

Facial expressions, especially as emotional displays, are represented in the narrative literature of all periods. Since many examples for this have already been given and more will be encountered in other contexts, it is not necessary here to give further illustration. However, the face is not always a reliable indicator of emotional states. Because of its high visibility and social significance, it is also the part of the body that is most liable to be monitored and thus has the greatest potential to deceive (Ekman and Friesen 1974, 288). The frame conditions of consciousness and intentionality are therefore most relevant with regard to facial expression, in real life as well as in literature.

The contrast between spontaneous and controlled facial expression is emphasized, for example, in George Orwell's *Nineteen Eighty-Four.* Facial expressiveness poses a constant danger to the inhabitants of the totalitarian state; every departure from the ideologically decreed expression is considered a punishable 'facecrime' (53), and people are constantly forced to play expression games:[36] 'To dissemble your feelings, to control your face ... was an instinctive reaction' (17). This unnatural degree of facial control underlines the restrictiveness of the political system described. A tragic irony in the novel lies in the fact that, in spite of his own facial control, Winston does not suspect that O'Brien's trusting mien might also be a non-verbal lie:

> Then suddenly the grim face broke down into what might have been the beginnings of a smile. With his characteristic gesture O'Brien resettled his spectacles on his nose.
>
> 'Shall I say it, or will you?' he said.
>
> 'I will say it,' said Winston promptly. (138)

Winston's belief that he has found an ally causes him to act carelessly and leads him to interpret O'Brien's face according to the normal principle, which holds that a person's spontaneous body language indicates his or her true intentions and emotions.

Gaze and Eye Behaviour 'Sed in ipso vultu plurimum valent oculi, per quos maxime animus eminet' – 'But of the various elements that go to form the expression, the eyes are the most important,' Quintilian writes in his *Institutio Oratoria* (12.3.75). Like facial expression, eye behaviour has a high capacity for expression and belongs to the modes of body language frequently represented in literature.[37] In the narrative text, eye behaviour figures as an important externalizer of interpersonal relationships, but also as emotional display and, occasionally, as illustrator.

The expressive quality of eye behaviour is certainly influenced by the eye's general significance. The world is mainly perceived through the visual sense, and the eye is also a strong stimulus both in human and animal behaviour. Various animal species, for example, have developed so-called eye-spots that function as signals of danger and threat. In all human cultures, too, eyes and their symbolic representation have a rich significance: 'The symbolic and metaphoric properties of eyes and eye-spots are rooted deep in human history, from the potency of the "evil eye" to the all-seeing "eye of God"' (Hindmarch 1973, 303).

Although the reflex reaction of pupil dilation can also be significant,[38] gaze behaviour, whose expressive quality is mainly determined by the direction and duration of the gaze, is the most important factor of eye language.[39]

Eye behaviour is extremely relevant in face-to-face-interaction. Human beings receive a great deal of information about their fellow creatures through observation. People make and maintain contact through looking at each other. Eye behaviour regulates conversations; it conveys information about the interactants and the nature of their interpersonal relationship. In the discussion of interactive eye behaviour, distinctions are normally made between gaze (one person looking at another person), mutual gaze or eye contact (two persons looking into one another's eyes), and avoiding gaze.

To Offred in Margaret Atwood's *The Handmaid's Tale*, who is deprived of most forms of human contact, the unexpected eye contact with a fellow-sufferer is an almost shocking social experience:

> We can see into each other's eyes. This is the first time I've ever seen Ofglen's eyes, directly, steadily, not aslant ... She holds my stare in the glass, level, unwavering. Now it's hard to look away. There's a shock in this seeing, it's like seeing somebody naked, for the first time. (176)

In this central passage, a turning point of the novel, the meaning is carried primarily by the characters' eye behaviour. After Offred has made eye contact with Ofglen, she joins an underground movement; she is now able to look beyond her personal fate and to develop a sense of solidarity with others.

Intense mutual gaze is, above all, an important signal for sympathy, romantic love, and erotic attraction (see Goldstein, Kilroy, and Van de Voort 1976). The role it plays in courting behaviour is portrayed in countless documents since antiquity. In the Renaissance, for example,

Castiglione's *Book of the Courtier* (1561) advised the lover 'to make the eyes the trustye messangers ... bicause they oftentimes declare with a more force what passion there is inwardlye, then can the tunge' (278). The look of love also belongs to the conventions of Renaissance literature, as is evident in the following passage from a prose romance, Thomas Lodge's *Rosalind* (1590):

On the contrary part, Rosader while he breathed was not idle, but still cast his eye upon Rosalind, who, to encourage him with a favor, lent him such an amorous look as might have made the most coward desperate; which glance of Rosalind so fired the passionate desires of Rosader that, turning to the Norman, he ran upon him and braved him with a strong encounter. (300–1)[40]

The chapter 'The Gloves' in Laurence Sterne's *A Sentimental Journey* (1768), which is dedicated to the body language of flirtation, appropriately accentuates the role of the eyes:

There are certain combined looks of simple subtlety – where whim, and sense, and seriousness, and nonsense, are so blended, that all the languages of Babel set loose together could not express them – they are communicated and caught so instantaneously, that you can scarce say which party is the infecter. (101)[41]

Graham Swift's *Waterland* (1983), finally, contains an instance of eye behaviour that is particularly interesting in the way it is narrated. In a central passage of the novel, the sudden awareness of sexual attraction, love, and rivalry in a group of young adolescents is conveyed by their looks:

Your teacher notes, in true historically-observant fashion, the look that Dick directs ... at Mary. A long and searching look you wouldn't expect from a potatohead. A stern, baffled and questioning look which makes Mary stop all of a sudden her giggling, as if at some command, and look back, just as intently, at Dick. He notes how Dick looks at Mary and then how Mary looks at Dick; and he notes how Freddie Parr catches both these looks which Dick and Mary give each other.

And in all this looking at others' looks he too has a look of his own ... most probably a forlorn, a rebuffed look, bearing on top of it only the thinnest veneer of bravery. Because your history teacher (though he's never told her) is in love, it's a fact, with Mary Metcalf. (179)

Dick, who is mentally retarded, is sexually attracted to Mary, a girl with whom his brother, the narrator, has fallen in love. The fact that the latter's rival, Freddie, interprets the looks between Dick and Mary as evidence of a sexual relationship leads to the tragic development of the plot: Freddie's imminent death and, decades later, Mary's and the narrator's unhappy lives. Only the looks exchanged reveal the characters' sudden awareness of their loss of innocence and of a new way of relating with each other. This experience is an unsettling one, which the adolescents do not want to and cannot yet verbalize. The narrator manages to convey this experience through his description of the glances, while maintaining the adolescents' sense of secrecy.

Gaze is a powerful signal of social dominance in both human and animal behaviour. In this context, the asymmetry of the gaze is especially important. The more powerful person in a group sends longer looks and holds stares for a longer time than subordinate members. Avoiding gaze indicates subordination and recognition of the opponent's power. In Graham Greene's *The Power and the Glory* (1940), for example, a communist policeman who is pursuing a fleeing priest enters the Mexican village in which the priest is hiding. The villagers cast their eyes on the ground as an expression of their subordination to the regime: 'The men and women had the air already of people condemned by authority – authority was never wrong ... They stared at the ground and waited' (73).

In contrast, an intense, one-sided stare has the effect of intimidation and threat and can be used as a conscious expression of power. In Orwell's *Nineteen Eighty-Four*, Big Brother's gaze is especially threatening, as 'the eyes follow you about when you move' (5).

Gaze can also be disconcerting because it breaks a rule in northern European and North American cultures which Erving Goffman (1963, 83–4) has referred to as 'civil inattention.' This rule of social conduct protects the individual's privacy from invasive looks. In Orwell's novel this privacy is constantly violated by the omnipresent eyes of the state. Goffman cites a special form of the violation of civil inattention: the so-called 'hate stare' which white Americans in the southern States used to direct at African Americans. In Tom Wolfe's satiric novel about New York society, *The Bonfire of the Vanities* (1987), another form of the 'hate stare' is one of the signs that show how stockbroker Sherman McCoy has fallen in social status:

Everything about the place ... proclaimed tastelessness, shiftlessness, vulgarity, and, at bottom, sheer ignorance. The two men were talking in what Sherman took to be Spanish ... He let his eyes creep up as far as their midsections ... He took the big chance: their faces. Immediately he cast his eyes down again. They were staring right at him! Such cruel looks! (502–3)

With his decreasing status and power, McCoy descends into circles of New York society in which the standards of behaviour he has learned in his own social circles are no longer valid. When the Hispanic Americans present with him in a prison cell do not play by the rules of 'polite' eye behaviour, Sherman, who still sees himself as a privileged WASP, is deeply insulted and feels painfully degraded.[42]

The lack or avoidance of eye contact also makes a powerful statement about interpersonal relationships. In Bret Easton Ellis's cult novel of the yuppie era, *Less than Zero* (1985), the capability for people to establish relationships has deteriorated in a world in which outer appearances are all that matter. 'People are afraid to merge' is a leitmotif of the novel, encountered three times alone in its first paragraph. Throughout the novel, the inability to 'merge' is also apparent in the characters' eye behaviour. In one of the opening paragraphs, the first-person narrator describes the face of a singer on a poster that hangs in his room. What is striking in this description is that the narrator is not able to look into the singer's eyes: 'The eyes don't look at me, though. They only look at whoever's standing by the window, but I'm too tired to get up and stand by the window' (11). In a fairly uncommunicative meeting with his mother, the narrator avoids looking at her; the mother hides her eyes behind dark glasses:

My mother and I are sitting in a restaurant on Melrose, and she's drinking white wine and still has her sunglasses on and she keeps touching her hair and I keep looking at my hands, pretty sure that they're shaking. She tries to smile when she asks me what I want for Christmas. I'm surprised at how much effort it takes to raise my head up and look at her. (18)

Apart from its social significance, eye behaviour also indicates emotions and personality traits. In Henry James's *The American*, for example, eye behaviour helps to build the emotional impact in the episode in which Newman finds out that his engagement to Madame de Cintré has been dissolved. The glances exchanged indicate his fiancée's desperation as well as the iron will and self-confidence of her mother, who has forced the break-up to occur:

Madame de Cintré stood silent, with her eyes resting upon Newman's. She had often looked at him with all her soul, as it seemed to him; but in this present gaze there was a sort of bottomless depth. She was in distress; it was the most touching thing he had ever seen. (312–13)

'Why should your daughter be afraid of you?' added Newman, after looking a moment at the old lady. 'There is some foul play.'

The marquise met his gaze without flinching, and as if she did not hear or heed what he said. 'I did my best,' she said quietly. 'I could endure it no longer.' (318)

Frequent and open glances are characteristic of dominating and extroverted personalities, but such glances are also seen to indicate honesty. On the other hand, the avoidance of eye contact is commonly interpreted as an indication of fear, insecurity, or embarrassment. For example, the protagonist in Margaret Laurence's *The Stone Angel* (1964) is embarrassed after she has married a man who is socially unacceptable. Hagar is ashamed of her husband and cannot look into people's eyes when she feels mortified by his behaviour: 'I'd done my utmost to persuade Bram not to come with me, but he couldn't see what I was making such a fuss about. Mrs. McVitie was there, and we bowed and nodded to one another. Bram fingered female undergarments, and I, mortified, looked away' (59). But people are also embarrassed when they meet Hagar: 'The manager greeted me courteously enough, listened and nodded, cleared his throat and didn't look at me' (113). The fact that people do not look her in the eye underlines Hagar's position as an outsider after she has acted against the ethos of her home community.

Body Movements and Postures In literature, as we have seen in the examples discussed above, gestures are encountered as externalizers and, especially in older texts, as emotional displays. They mainly appear, however, as illustrators and emblems.

Practical actions, on the other hand, usually indicate emotions and character traits. In *Oscar and Lucinda* (1988), a novel by the Australian writer Peter Carey, the male protagonist is a Victorian clergyman who feels he has been called to be a missionary in Australia. Oscar's uncoordinated body movements underscore his nervousness, naïvety, and awkwardness, which make him a lonely outsider in England as well as in Australia. Oscar suffers from extreme hydrophobia, which brings him to a state of panic on the eve of his departure from England; contrary to his verbal assertions, this panic is revealed by the nervous movements of his limbs:

> 'What a splendid place,' he said.
>
> But Wardley-Fish could feel the Odd Bod's agitated feet tapping beneath the table. It was not just feet. It was also fingers, drumming on the chair. The surface of the table assumed a nervous skin of energy. You could experience anxiety merely by touching it. (185)

Body postures[43] are among the non-verbal modes frequently found in literature. In earlier texts they appear as social emblems (bows, curtsies, prayer poses), but they function primarily as emotional displays or externalizers. For example, a stooping carriage of the body may signal mourning, and a limp posture often indicates depression, as is the case with Greene's priest in *The Power and the Glory*, when he is waiting for his execution: 'His head drooped between his knees; he looked as if he had abandoned everything and been abandoned' (205). A character's attitudes and personality traits may also be mirrored in body posture. In Henry James's *The American*, Newman is introduced at the beginning of the novel in a posture which is repeated as a leitmotif, and always emphasizes the 'otherness' of the American in the aristocratic circles of the Old World:

> On a brilliant day in May, in the year 1868, a gentleman was reclining at his ease on the great circular divan which at that period occupied the centre of the Salon Carré, in the Museum of the Louvre ... and, with his head thrown back and his legs outstretched, was staring at Murillo's beautiful moon-borne Madonna in profound enjoyment of his posture. (33)

Newman's casual posture is characteristic of his New World behaviour, and immediately draws attention to the conflict which is bound to develop between him and the members of the French aristocracy who are so rigid in their concern with proper behaviour and social pose. Furthermore, Newman's body posture is accessible, in that his legs and arms are stretched away from his body; it thus signals friendliness and sociability,[44] characteristics which also stand in sharp contrast to the aristocratic code of reserved conduct.

Newman's posture exhibits personality traits of which the character himself is not aware. However, postures can also be effective externalizers of social roles and are sometimes adopted quite deliberately to signal membership in a certain social group, as for instance in Tom Wolfe's *The Bonfire of the Vanities*. Here the self-confidence which McCoy bases on his wealth and status is caricatured in the description of his exaggerated theatrical poses: 'He squared his shoulders and carried his long nose and wonderful chin up high' (49).

Furthermore, posture is effective in communicating the quality of an interpersonal relationship. If one communicator orients himself or herself towards another – for example, in a forward bodily lean or by pointing his or her shoulders or legs towards the other – the addressee is more likely to feel sympathy, intimacy, and trust than if the opposite postures were assumed. The congruence of movements and postures between two people generally indicates a positive relationship between them (see Kendon 1977, 55). In *Oscar and Lucinda*, Peter Carey uses these principles to portray the interpersonal dilemma of his pair of lovers by describing their contradictory poses. Oscar and Lucinda are surprised to discover their affection for each other at first, and are reluctant to reveal it:

> He held out his arms as if he might embrace her and then brought them back across his chest and hugged himself and hunched his back a little ...
>
> Lucinda duplicated his stance without meaning to; that is, she hugged herself, kept her arms locked firmly around her own body while she felt the space between them as if it were a living thing. (377)

Because he feels affection for Lucinda, Oscar impulsively reaches his arms out towards her, but in his bashfulness he embraces himself instead. Through this posture, he seems to be protecting himself, and it therefore does not encourage Lucinda to reveal her feelings towards him. However, she expresses her sympathy quite unconsciously, by imitating Oscar's stance. Ironically, Oscar interprets her posture as a rejection. By describing this body language, the author gives the reader a glimpse into the characters' thoughts and feelings without having to explain in words what the characters themselves cannot verbalize.

Body posture also effectively communicates relations of power: social dominance or subordination. The effect of power on the individual is a central theme, for example, in Joseph Conrad's *The Secret Agent* (1907). This theme is introduced in the beginning of the novel, not least through the description of body language. In the first chapter, Mr Verloc is summoned to the embassy of the country for which he is working as a secret agent; under pressure, he is given the task of arranging a bomb attack.

Verloc's position of helplessness in the face of the embassy is particularly evident in the characters' postures. The character addressing him in the following passage is a secretary to the embassy who is very conscious of his power:

But there was no trace of merriment or perplexity in the way he looked at Mr. Verloc. Lying far back in the deep arm-chair, with squarely spread elbows, and throwing one leg over a thick knee, he had with his smooth and rosy countenance the air of a preternaturally thriving baby that will not stand nonsense from anybody.

'You understand French, I suppose?' he said.

Mr. Verloc stated huskily that he did. His whole vast bulk had a forward inclination. He stood on the carpet in the middle of the room, clutching his hat and stick in one hand; the other hung lifelessly by his side. (19)

The secretary's sense of power is revealed in his relaxed and comfortable posture, whereas Verloc, who must obey the orders of the embassy, takes on the tense and stooped posture of a subordinate.

Automatic Reactions Of all modes of NVC, automatic reactions have the most limited expressive potential: they serve exclusively to indicate emotional states. They are very reliable indicators, however, since they are generally not consciously controlled and can therefore be considered as trustworthy. Automatic reactions are generously represented in all periods of narrative literature. For example, turning pale or blushing, trembling, and fainting are elements of a conventional literary love code which lasted into the nineteenth century and which will be discussed in greater detail later on.[45]

In J.D. Salinger's 'For Esmé – with Love and Squalor,' young Esmé's occasional blush indicates a childlike shyness that makes her endearing despite her snobbish precociousness: '"Would you like me to write to you?" she asked, with a certain amount of color in her face. "I write extremely articulate letters for a person my [age]"' (101). In the second part of the story, automatic reactions (a constant tremble and a nervous tic) figure as a symptom for the psychological disturbance which the first-person narrator, who now appears as 'Sergeant X,' has suffered in the war.

Haptics

Haptics or touch behaviour is a mode of NVC often used in the narrative literature of all periods. Haptic behaviour is encountered as a social emblem, such as, for example, the handshake. Accompanying speech, touch may also function as an illustrator – for example, of emphasis. However, haptic behaviour manifests itself most frequently as an externalizer, both in real life and in literature.

Physical contact is the first form of perception and communication which human beings experience. 'The very first impressions we receive as living beings must be sensations of intimate body contact, as we float snugly inside the protective wall of the maternal uterus' (Morris 1971, 14). Tactile stimulation is a basic human need, and its lack can have disastrous effects. The significance given to touch in all cultures is evident not least in the magical role it plays in many rituals and ceremonies.

In Margaret Atwood's *The Handmaid's Tale*, a prohibition of physical contact emphasizes the inhumane stance which the theocracy Gilead adopts towards the individual. Offred perceives this lack of touch as a most painful deprivation in her isolated life: 'I hunger to touch something, other than cloth or wood. I hunger to commit the act of touch' (21). Longingly, she recalls the physical contact she experienced in her former life as a wife and mother: 'We would lie in those afternoon beds, afterwards, hands on each other' (61); 'What I remember is Luke, with me in the hospital, standing beside my head, holding my hand' (136).

In another utopian novel, Marge Piercy's *Woman on the Edge of Time*, contrasting norms regarding physical contact are also used to differentiate the worlds portrayed. As in Atwood's novel, touch is associated with the better of the two worlds, which, in this case, is situated in the future. In the protagonist's desolate present setting, the psychiatric ward, physical contact is strictly forbidden: '"No PC!" – physical contact – the slogan of the ward' (350). The experience of touch has become so rare in Connie's life that, when she recalls her first meeting with time-travelling Luciente, she remembers particularly the body contact between them: 'she remembered then the touch of that warm, gentle, calloused hand on her bare arm' (36). In the future setting, on the other hand, touch is a frequent and natural expression for harmonious social existence:

> They were literally patted into their seats and she found herself cramped with nervousness. Touching and caressing, hugging and fingering, they handled each other constantly. In a way it reminded her again of her childhood, when every emotion seemed to find a physical outlet, when both love and punishment had been expressed directly on her skin. (76)

Although the need for human touch is universal, the disposition towards physical contact varies among individuals, so that haptic behaviour may become an externalizer of personality traits: touch avoiders usually seek less contact with other people than people who like to be touched and frequently touch others (see Andersen and Sull 1985, 62). The 'stony' protagonist and first-person narrator of Margaret Laurence's *The Stone Angel* has this kind of personality: Hagar Shipley's exaggerated pride prevents her from establishing close relationships with other people, even those within her own family. Repeated references to a lack of bodily contact in her life indicate this trait in Hagar's personality without the need for the first-person narrator to characterize or criticize herself explicitly:

> In that moment when we might have touched our hands together, Bram and I, and wished each other well, the thought uppermost in my mind was – *the nerve of him.* (84–5)

> I walked to the wrought-iron gate of Mr. Oatley's house with him, he wanting to be off, brushing away my words and hands, and I wanting only to touch his brown impatient face but not daring to. (142)

> She put a well-meaning arm around me. 'Cry. Let yourself. It's the best thing.'
>
> But I shoved her arm away. I straightened my spine, and that was the hardest thing I've ever had to do in my entire life, to stand straight then. I wouldn't cry in front of strangers, whatever it cost me. (207)

Only shortly before her death does Hagar realize that the lack of contact in her long life was a mistake, and she overcomes her attitude of *noli me tangere.* Thus the haptic mode gains increasing importance towards the end of the novel. Hagar now touches people more and more often: a tramp whom she meets while she is fleeing from her imminent move to a nursing home, the nurses, and other patients in this home:

> I'm feeling better now. I'm resting easy. My hand remains on his wrist. (211)

> Impulsively, hardly knowing what I'm doing, I reach out and touch his wrist. (216)

> I poke my hand out from the sheet and put it on her skinny hand. (233)

At the culmination point of Hagar's human development, she even allows her son Marvin to touch her – the son she has never forgiven for outliving his older, more favoured brother:

> 'If I've been crabby with you, sometimes, these past years,' he says in a low voice, 'I didn't mean it.'
>
> I stare at him. Then, quite unexpectedly, he reaches for my hand and holds it tightly. (260)

Haptic behaviour is subject to culture-specific norms; every society has rules regarding which areas of the body are allowed to be touched, how frequently and intensively they are allowed to be touched, and who is allowed to touch them. Touch behaviour can thus indicate membership in a cultural group. Northern European and North American cultures are generally considered to be non-contact cultures. As Ashley Montagu (1971) has suggested in his seminal study, tactile restraint is especially characteristic for Anglo-Saxon societies that have been influenced by Puritanism.

In E.M. Forster's *A Passage to India*, the clash between the English and the Indian culture can, among other things, be recognized in the conflict between haptic norms. Mrs Moore is quite open towards the culture of India; however, during her disastrous excursion to the Marabar Caves, she eventually realizes her failure to understand the other culture. The echo in the caves gives Mrs Moore an almost mystical insight into the central problem of cultural understanding: the echo dissolves all differences in words and language, but at the same time, the possibility of verbal communication is also entirely lost. Mrs Moore is prepared for this insight by a non-verbal experience that throws her into a state of panic even before she has heard the echo:

> It was natural enough: she had always suffered from faintness, and the cave had become too full, because all their retinue followed them. Crammed with villagers and servants, the circular chamber began to smell. She lost Aziz and Adela in the dark, didn't know who touched her, couldn't breathe, and some vile naked thing struck her face and settled on her mouth like a pad. (158)

Despite her goodwill towards India, this insult to her British haptic norms in the contact culture of India is intolerable to Mrs Moore. Even before her devastation by the echo, she has thus experienced the disparity of the two cultures in a particularly intense, because physical, way.

Most importantly, however, touching behaviour makes interpersonal relations apparent. In a handshake, the relation is expressed in a formal, ritualized way, but touch is also an important signifier in the less formal kinds of human interaction. Most frequently it is associated with positive feelings. Touch, like eye contact, plays a central role in the romantic love relationship; narratives with a love plot, like Chaucer's *Troilus and Criseyde*, are accordingly full of examples such as the following:

Hire armes smale, hir streghte bak and softe,
Hire sydes longe, flesshly, smothe, and white
He gan to stroke, and good thrift bad ful ofte
Hire snowisshe throte, hir brestes rounde and lite:
Thus in this hevene he gan hym to delite,
And therwithal a thousand tyme hire kiste,
That what to don, for joie unnethe he wiste. (Bk 3, ll 1247–53)

When, on the other hand, a person feels antipathy towards another, physical contact is felt to be uncomfortable, and is avoided if possible. In Thomas Hardy's *Tess of the d'Urbervilles*, for instance, the protagonist's different relationships to the men who determine her life is revealed in her reactions to their haptic behaviour. The way in which d'Urberville touches her, which Tess attempts to resist, takes on the character of penetration right from the start, and thus anticipates the seduction which will take place later: 'He touched her with his fingers, which sank into her as into down' (106). In contrast, Tess always likes to be touched by Angel Clare and responds by touching him, too.

Touch is not only sometimes perceived as being negative, but can also express negative feelings. Tactile hostility manifests itself as openly violent behaviour, such as hitting, but it may also appear in more covert forms. In Samuel Butler's *The Way of All Flesh* (1903), for example, a mother's way of touching her son reveals the hypocrisy of a Puritan home:

'My dearest boy,' began his mother, taking hold of his hand and placing it within her own, 'promise me never to be afraid either of your dear papa or of me; promise me this, my dear, as you love me, promise it to me,' and she kissed him again and again and stroked his hair. But with her other hand she still kept hold of his; she had got him and she meant to keep him. (198)

Under the guise of motherly care, the mother here misuses close body contact in order to force her son to make a confession; her seemingly gentle clasp is actually a torture device.

The ambiguity of touch behaviour is of thematic relevance in Ian McEwan's *The Comfort of Strangers*. In Venice, a young English couple, Colin and Mary, find themselves in the trap of a mysterious older couple, Robert and Caroline. These two can only satisfy their sexual needs by perpetrating violence against others, and they ultimately kill Colin. Right from the start, Robert's touching behaviour indicates that he is taking possession of the English couple:

> 'Look,' Colin said, trying to detach his wrist without appearing violent, 'we know there is a place down here.' The grip was loose but unremitting, a mere finger and thumb looped round Colin's wrist ...
>
> Mary spoke as though to a child. 'Robert, let go of my hand.' He released her immediately and made a little bow.
>
> Colin said, 'And you'd better let go of me too.' ...
>
> Mary smiled over her shoulder. They had arrived once more at the great residence at the fork in the road. Colin pulled Robert to a halt and jerked his hand free. 'I'm sorry,' Robert said. (27)

Although Colin and Mary, as members of a non-contact culture, find Robert's behaviour uncomfortable, they attribute their discomfort to the fact that they are foreigners in a southern country, that is, a contact culture: 'It was customary here for men to walk in public hand in hand, or arm in arm; Robert held Colin's hand tightly, the fingers interlocking and exerting a constant pressure such that to have withdrawn would have required a wilful movement, possibly insulting, certainly eccentric' (100). An unfamiliar culture and their disorientation as tourists prevent the young couple from recognizing Robert's touches as hostile. They thus do not resist his behaviour forcefully enough, just as they are generally incapable of withdrawing from the older couple. Only after it has become impossible to flee does it become evident that Robert's and Caroline's physical contact is openly threatening:

> She began to pull his T-shirt free of his jeans. Robert leaned his outstretched arm against the wall at the level of Colin's head, boxing him in. Caroline was caressing his belly, gently pinching the skin between her fingers ... Robert's free hand was exploring Colin's face, probing his lips apart with his fingers, tracing the lines of his nose and jaw. (119)

In particular, physical contact between men and women can send negative messages. Empirical studies in psychology have shown that touching behaviour differs significantly according to gender. While in northern Western cultures, women touch other women much more frequently than men touch other men in same-sex interaction, men touch women more frequently than women touch men.[46] This asymmetrical relation correlates with observations that have been made regarding the interaction between two partners who have unequal power (regardless of their gender). Generally speaking, the more powerful person will touch the weaker person more frequently than vice versa. One might conclude that some differences in touch behaviour between men and women are also linked to their respective positions of power. A man's apparently gentle touch can thus come to be an expression of his belief to have the right to possess the woman's body.

This power aspect inherent in physical contact is an important element of meaning in Margaret Atwood's novel *The Edible Woman* (1969). The central character of this novel, Marian MacAlpine, experiences an existential crisis when she can no longer identify with conventional patterns of female role behaviour. Marian's problem is most evident in her relationship to her fiancé, Peter. She gradually becomes aware of his dominating role – first through his touch behaviour, which she increasingly finds to be domineering:

> He took me by the upper arm as though he was arresting me for jaywalking, and turned to Len ... I wrenched my arm away from Peter's hand. (76)

> He put one of his hands over mine. (86)

However, Atwood's novel does not side only with the woman; although the man appears to be dominant from Marian's point of view, women are also shown to exercise power. The seemingly subordinate poses which Marian assumes after Peter's marriage proposal, for example, are revealed as a proprietary claim: 'I could feel the stirrings of the proprietary instinct. So this object, then, belonged to *me*. I leaned my head against his shoulder' (87).

Studies in NVC research show that women have, on average, a greater sensitivity to touching behaviour than men have. Girls generally experience more body contact in their childhood than boys do; women therefore tend to react more intensely and positively to touch (see Fisher,

Rytting, and Heslin 1976) and consider touch to be more significant than men do. In particular, they react more sensitively to touch which they consider to be inappropriate or exaggerated.

In literature, haptic behaviour is frequently encountered in texts by male writers, as the examples above indicate. However, it is striking that in novels written by women, the haptic mode is often employed to make particularly important statements. This is the case not only for modern writers such as Margaret Laurence, Margaret Atwood, or Marge Piercy,[47] but also for female novelists of the nineteenth century.

As an unwanted poor relative, the orphaned Jane in Charlotte Brontë's *Jane Eyre* (1847) does not enjoy any affection from her aunt. She suffers from a lack of touch, except for the beatings she is given. Even many years later, her dying aunt allows Jane to touch her only for practical purposes, not as a means to express human warmth:

> I approached my cheek to her lips: she would not touch it. She said I oppressed her by leaning over the bed; and again demanded water. As I laid her down – for I raised and supported her on my arm while she drank – I covered her ice-cold and clammy hand with mine: the feeble fingers shrank from my touch – the glazing eyes shunned my gaze. (1:404)

As a child, Jane enjoys the friendly physical contact she occasionally experiences with her aunt's maids and later with a beloved teacher. Most important of all, however, the relationship between Rochester and Jane is characterized by touch right from the start. In their very first encounter in chapter 12, physical contact occurs when Jane helps Rochester up and supports him after he has fallen from his horse. This passage anticipates their reunion in the second-last chapter, in which Jane once again serves as Rochester's support: 'Then he stretched his hand out to be led. I took that dear hand, held it a moment to my lips, then let it pass round my shoulder: being so much lower of stature than he, I served both for his prop and guide' (2:364). In between these two passages it is Rochester who touches Jane again and again because he needs her. Physical contact in this novel not only reflects the development of a love relationship, then, but also specifies the particular role each partner plays in this relationship.

In George Eliot's *Middlemarch* (1871–2), haptic behaviour helps to communicate the increasing alienation between Dorothea and her elderly husband, Casaubon, as in the following passage, in which Casaubon openly rejects his wife's touch:

Then she went towards him, and might have represented a heavensent angel coming with a promise that the short hours remaining should yet be filled with that faithful love which clings the closer to a comprehended grief. His glance in reply to hers was so chill that she felt her timidity increased; yet she turned and passed her hand through his arm.

Mr. Casaubon kept his hands behind him and allowed her pliant arm to cling with difficulty against his rigid arm ...

Dorothea did not withdraw her arm, but she could not venture to speak. Mr. Casaubon did not say, 'I wish to be alone,' but he directed his steps in silence towards the house, and as they entered by the glass door on this eastern side, Dorothea withdrew her arm and lingered on the matting, that she might leave her husband quite free. (2: 215–16)

By contrast with this episode, Dorothea's final decision for Will Ladislaw manifests itself in a long-awaited clasp of their hands:

While he was speaking there came a vivid flash of lightning which lit each of them up for the other – and the light seemed to be the terror of a hopeless love. Dorothea darted instantaneously from the window; Will followed her, seizing her hand with a spasmodic movement; and so they stood, with their hands clasped, like two children, looking out on the storm, while the thunder gave a tremendous crack and roll above them, and the rain began to pour down. Then they turned their faces towards each other, with the memory of his last words in them, and they did not loose each other's hands. (3:387)

The important role played by haptic behaviour in central passages in women's novels could support the supposition that female writers have a special sensitivity to this mode of NVC. However, further studies, based on a larger text sample, would be needed in order to make a reliable statement about this question.

Proxemics

Compared to haptics, proxemics appears, on average, less frequently in the sample of novels investigated for this study. It is also a mode of NVC which manifests itself, above all, in the more recent novel: between the sixteenth and the eighteenth centuries, descriptions of proxemic behaviour are relatively rare.[48] Proxemic behaviour in the novel thus seems to be linked with an increased awareness of fictional space, which does not generally become apparent in the novel before the mid-eighteenth century (see Hoffmann 1978, 17–19).

Sporadically, proxemic behaviour appears as an emotional display; in Charles Dickens's *Oliver Twist*, for example, negative characters like Monks and Sikes provoke the other characters to shrink away in shock and disgust:

'Do not mind shrinking openly from me, lady ... The poorest women fall back, as I make my way along the crowded pavement.'

'What dreadful things are these!' said Rose, involuntarily falling from her strange companion. (252)

'Don't come nearer me,' answered the boy, still retreating, and looking, with horror in his eyes, upon the murderer's face. 'You monster!' (322)

However, distancing behaviour fulfils its main expressive function as an externalizer of personality traits and interpersonal relationships. Since spatial behaviour is strongly influenced by cultural and social norms, proxemics can also function as an indicator of cultural and social belonging.

Proximity between people represents a strong stimulus, especially when the 'personal space' of the individual is invaded. This space is a zone of privacy which surrounds an individual like a bubble and which only few people are permitted to enter. Violations of this space are perceived as uncomfortable or even threatening; they can produce stress and aggression. The violation of personal space can also represent an intentional threat or provocation, as in the following examples from novels of the eighteenth century:

'Dam'-me, Sir,' said the officer, 'do you call me young?' striking up the front of his hat, and stretching forward on his seat, till his face almost touched Harley's. (Mackenzie, *The Man of Feeling*, 78–9)

'Damme if you don't say every thing that you can to provoke me; and curse me if I'll bear it,' said Fillygrove, advancing with an air of menace. (Bage, *Hermsprong*, 61)

The size of personal space varies according to the personality[49] and acculturation of an individual. E.T. Hall differentiates among four levels of interpersonal distance (intimate, personal, social, and public), which are measured differently according to culture. The proximity, for example, which southern Europeans or Arabs seek when talking to others is perceived as too personal or even intimate by northern Europeans and North Americans. In Alison Lurie's novel *The War between the Tates* (1974), an Anglo-Saxon character is uncomfortable with the distance norms of southern Europeans:

But the bulk of the party is composed of [Danielle's] colleagues in Romance Languages and their spouses ... Erica passes amongst them, smiling and nodding; pausing sometimes for a few words, but always keeping her predetermined interval of two and a half feet. It is not as easy as she had hoped, because of the Romance Language habit of standing rather too close – close enough to breathe, and in some cases spit, on one's companions. But Erica manages it. Over the last months she has learned to keep her distance with everyone – a distance not only physical, but psychological. (218)

As is apparent in the last sentence, the character's exaggerated proxemic sensitivity is not only an externalizer of her cultural background; it also indicates a psychological trait: her difficulty in making contact with other people.

Furthermore, spatial behaviour can indicate a person's social status. High-ranking individuals often cultivate an aura of being unapproachable and are allowed a respectful distance. They also tend to demand the most prominent position within a 'territory,' as is generally the case with dominating personalities. In David Lodge's *Nice Work* (1988), for example, the hierarchical seating order of a group of managers contributes to the social realism of this modern industrial novel:

Vic Wilcox asks Brian Everthorpe to stay for a meeting he has arranged with his technical and production managers. They file into the office and sit round the long oak table, slightly in awe of Vic, serious men in chain-store suits, with pens and pencils sticking out of their breast pockets. Brian Everthorpe takes a chair at the far end of the table, slightly withdrawn as if to mark his difference from the engineers. Vic sits at the head of the table ... (74)

In particular, proxemic behaviour is a reliable externalizer of interpersonal relationships: proximity can serve as a subtle gauge for sympathy or antipathy, friendship or enmity, love or hate, and other types of relationships. In Laurence Sterne's *Tristram Shandy*, for example, interpersonal distance becomes the seismograph of a marital relationship when Tristram's parents discuss the appropriate clothing for their growing son in bed (chapter 18 of book 6). In order to convince his wife that the boy should finally be allowed to wear trousers, Mr Shandy first moves towards her. But when they come to speak about Mr Shandy's own body size, a comment by his wife (which also raises the question of his paternity) makes him withdraw again:

> We should begin, said my father, turning himself half round in bed, and shifting his pillow a little towards my mother's, as he opened the debate – We should begin to think, Mrs. *Shandy*, of putting this boy into breeches ...
>
> – He is very tall for his age, indeed, – said my mother. –
>
> – I can not (making two syllables of it) imagine, quoth my father, who the duce he takes after. –
>
> I cannot conceive, for my life, – said my mother. –
>
> Humph! – said my father.
>
> (The dialogue ceased for a moment.)
>
> – I am very short myself, – continued my father, gravely.
>
> You are very short, Mr. *Shandy*, – said my mother.
>
> Humph! quoth my father to himself, a second time: in muttering which, he plucked his pillow a little further from my mother's, – and turning about again, there was an end of the debate for three minutes and a half. (526–7)

In Fay Weldon's *The Cloning of Joanna May* (1989), the clones, who are the results of a genetic experiment, show their antipathy towards one another in the distance they keep from each other when they meet for the first time. Their need to differentiate themselves from their unwanted, identical sisters becomes evident in the way they take up space: 'They sat as far from one another as they could. Just because they were sisters or half-sisters, they did not see why they should like one another, let alone resemble one another: in fact, the more they thought about it, the less they felt they did either' (294).

As with haptics, NVC research has shown that women have a special sensitivity with regard to their personal space and proxemic behaviour.[50] The examples given above and the text sample analysed for this study are not extensive enough to permit the conclusion that women writers describe proxemic behaviour more frequently than do their male colleagues. But it may be fair to suggest that, as with touching behaviour, female novelists have a particular awareness of the nuances of spatial behaviour. In *Middlemarch*, for example, George Eliot repeatedly implies the nuances of the relationship between Will Ladislaw and Dorothea by giving exact measurements of the distances between them:

He was standing **two yards from her** with his mind full of contradictory desires and resolves, – desiring some unmistakable proof that she loved him, and yet dreading the position into which such a proof might bring him. (3:16)

She did not move, and he came towards her with more doubt and timidity in his face than she had ever seen before ... Seeing that she did not put out her hand as usual, Will **paused a yard from her** and said with embarrassment, 'I am so grateful to you for seeing me.' (3:383–4)

A similar sensitivity for degrees of proximity and distance is found in A.S. Byatt's novel *Possession* (1990):

The room was largely uninhabited: a group of women in jeans were laughing in the opposite corner, and two girls were in earnest conversation by the window, pink spiky heads leaning together. Maud Bailey's excessive elegance was even odder in this context. She was a most untouchable woman; Roland, who had desperately decided to gamble on showing her the xeroxes of the letters, who wanted secrecy and privacy, was forced to lean forward in a kind of pseudo-intimacy and speak low. (48–9)

Within this short passage, the proximity between people talking to each other is mentioned twice. The forced pseudo-intimacy of Maud and Roland is contrasted with the true intimacy of the two girls who are deeply involved in conversation. However, the gender-specific representation of proxemics is also an area that requires more in-depth study.

3.2.4 *The Modal-Functional Classification System*

The aim of this chapter was to define the field of NVC or body language more precisely and to introduce categories for its most important modal and functional classes. Since the interpretation of body language in the literary text occurs on the basis of a reader's ordinary non-verbal competence, its analysis requires categories as they are available for the analysis of NVC in real life. In addition to categories for modes and functions of body language, features are needed to describe the situational frame in which an instance of body language occurs.

The diagram in Table 3.1 summarizes the categories established in this chapter. The top half of the grid lists the modal-functional classification of non-verbal behaviour; the bottom half lists the frame conditions

Modal classification		Functional classification: emotional display	externalizer	illustrator	emblem	regulator
I. Kinesics	gesture					
	practical action					
	facial expression					
	eye behaviour					
	automatic reaction			X	X	X
	posture					
II. Haptics						
III. Proxemics						
Situational Frame Conditions	± interactive			(+)	(+)	+
	± speech			(+)		(+)
	± comitative [1]	(–)	(–)	(+)		+
	± concordant			(+)		+
	± conscious				+	(–)
	± intentional				+	(–)
	± decoded [2]					

[1] only relevant in combination with + speech; [2] only relevant with + interactive

Table 3.1 The Modal-Functional Classification System

of NVC. The boxes crossed out in the upper half mark combinations of modal and functional class which do not occur.

In the frame conditions, a + means that the particular functional category *always* presupposes the condition marked by the positive feature; (+) and (–) indicate the tendency of a functional class to occur *primarily* under the condition marked by the positive or negative feature. Regulators, for example, can be found only within an interaction and are

'For Esmé – with Love and Squalor'		Functional classification				
Modal classification		emotional display	external-izer	illustrator	emblem	regulator
I. Kinesics	gesture		0 / 1	1 / 1	3 / 0	5 / 0
	practical action		16 / 5			
	facial expression	3 / 0	1 / 0	0 / 1	1 / 0	3 / 0
	eye behaviour		6 / 3	1 / 1		1 / 0
	automatic reaction	2 / 0	0 / 4			
	posture		3 / 2			
II. Haptics			1 / 0		3 / 0	3 / 0
III. Proxemics		0 / 1				

Table 3.2 Non-verbal Profile: J.D. Salinger, 'For Esmé' – with Love and Squalor'

usually accompanied by speech. For the analysis of body language in narrative literature, the frame conditions are understood to have the special definitions explained above (pages 27–36). It is also necessary to add that, for the analysis of narrative literature, the feature '+/– speech' includes the various forms of 'inner speech' encountered in the narrative text, that is, forms of the presentation of consciousness such as interior monologue, narrated monologue, or psychonarration.

This grid can be used for a systematic analysis of body language in literature. It can also be employed to establish non-verbal 'profiles,' for example, of a writer's preference for certain modes and functional classes, of the characteristic use of body language in a literary period, or of the characteristic use of body language in an individual text.

In concluding this chapter, I demonstrate the heuristic value of the classification by a comparison of J.D. Salinger's 'For Esmé – with Love and Squalor' and Charles Dickens's 'The Signalman.' In the profiles for the two stories, the frame conditions are not represented, since they are of minor relevance in the comparison.

For Salinger's story, the profile in Table 3.2 can be established. The numbers indicate the number of occurrences per category. The occurrences of NVC in the two parts of the story are separated from each other with a slash mark. The story's first part describes the first-person narrator's encounter with the girl Esmé; in the story's second part, the narrator appears as 'Sergeant X,' a shell-shocked victim of the war. All in all, the diagram demonstrates a fairly high frequency of NVC in this story. Most importantly, however, the distribution of NVC into various modes and functional classes also reveals a significant domination in several areas which can be linked to the story's basic theme.

Facial expression is a modal class of non-verbal behaviour that is usually highly represented in literature. In 'For Esmé,' however, it is comparatively underrepresented. As was explained earlier, the face is an especially effective indicator for emotional states, and in general, the number of emotional displays in this story is conspicuously small. In keeping with the story's theme of loneliness and lack of contact, the story has a subdued emotional atmosphere; emotion becomes evident between the lines rather than in explicit non-verbal drama.

Eye behaviour, as a mode of NVC especially effective as an externalizer of relationships, is more strongly represented. Eye contact first establishes the relationship between the narrator and Esmé, and in the further development of their encounter, the looks exchanged between the narrator and Esmé as well as her brother, Charles, are mentioned repeatedly. This finding correlates with the rather large number of social emblems and regulators commented on earlier (pages 48–9). Haptic emblems and regulators in particular emphasize the dimension of contact: Esmé's handshake, Charles's kiss, but also the latter's childlike attempts to gain the narrator's attention: 'I was about to press her for more details, but I felt Charles pinching me, hard, on my arm. I turned to him, wincing slightly'; 'Ignoring his sister, and stepping up on one of my feet, Charles repeated the key question' (100). The body language of contact and relationships clearly dominates in the first part of the story.

In the second part, Sergeant X is deprived of communication; his only contact is a comrade who has no empathy for his shell-shocked condition. This lack of communication and human understanding is reflected in both the quantity and quality of body language: the types of NVC in which the relationship between the soldier and the children manifests itself in the story's first part occur much less frequently, if at all. In addition, the eye behaviour represented in the story's second part never takes on the form of eye *contact*; it is limited to instances of one-sided gaze:

'The Signalman'		Functional classification				
Modal classification		emotional display	external-izer	illustrator	emblem	regulator
I. Kinesics	gesture			4	5	
	practical action	1				
	facial expression	3	1			
	eye behaviour	1	1	1		
	automatic reaction	3				
	posture		1			
II. Haptics				3		
III. Proxemics		1	1	1		

Table 3.3 Non-verbal Profile: Charles Dickens, 'The Signalman'

X, regarding him hostilely, stated that he didn't want an Eisenhower jacket. (108)

Clay suddenly looked at X with new – higher – interest than before. (109)

Clay looked at him suspiciously. (110)

The greatest portion of body language represented in this part of the story consists of externalizers (practical actions and automatic reactions) which indicate the soldier's desolate emotional state.

The non-verbal profile for Dickens's 'The Signalman' in Table 3.3 demonstrates a completely different use of body language, again determined by the story's theme and its intended effect. In general, body language occurs much more rarely in this story than in 'For Esmé'; there are also marked differences in the types of body language used. The number of externalizers, for example, is comparatively small, as interpersonal relationships and personality traits play a minor role in this story. At the centre of the story are the supernatural apparitions, their 'emblematic' prophecies, and the effect they have on the signalman. Thus the signalman's emotional displays are of major importance: 'I detected in his eyes some latent fear of me' (13); 'while he was speaking to me he twice broke off with a fallen colour' (15). The illustrators in the story also serve almost exclusively to emphasize the signalman's report of his extraordinary experience:

> I asked his pardon, and he slowly added these words, touching my arm: ...
>
> 'This,' he said, again laying his hand upon my arm, and glancing over his shoulder with hollow eyes, 'was just a year ago ...' He stopped, with a fixed look at me ...
>
> He touched me on the arm with his forefinger twice or thrice, giving a ghastly nod each time: ... (18–19)

We have seen in this chapter that the modal and functional categories of ordinary non-verbal competence are of considerable value in the understanding and analysis of body language in literature. To a certain extent, they even permit insight into what is special about literary body language: it is subject to selection processes which lead to a different hierarchy of modes and functions from that in real life. We have also seen that the meaning and effect of body language in the literary text may depend on a special mode, function, or frame condition of the behaviour described. However, the modal-functional classification can be only the first component of a conceptual framework for the analysis of literary NVC. Its second component will have to focus on the literariness of body language in literature.

4

Body Language in the Narrative Text: A Literary-Critical Perspective

> Action is eloquence, and the eyes of th' ignorant
> More learned than the ears ...

Shakespeare, *Coriolanus*, 3.2.76–7

Semiotic systems of everyday reality acquire new or additional functions when they are used in the context of art. Not every single element in real life is felt to be 'meaningful.' In literature, however, every component plays a part, at least potentially, in the reader's construction of meaning and the text's effect. The following observations on theatre made by Keir Elam (1980) generally apply to all forms of art: 'Theatrical messages are non-redundant to the extent that, even where the direct semantic information is low, each signal has (or supposedly has) an "aesthetic" justification, and the reduction of signals will drastically alter the value of the ostended messages and text' (43). The very fact that an element is present in a literary text, then, means that a higher than usual semiotic importance will be attributed to it, and that it may also be interpreted differently from the way it might be understood in a real-life situation.

The higher importance placed on semiotic systems in literature is, in part, a result of the selective portrayal of reality in the fictional text. This selectiveness is especially obvious when it comes to the description of body language. Once a character is embodied on the stage or on the film screen, his or her body cannot be 'silenced.' In narrative literature, however, the characters' body language is easily 'omitted' – as are other aspects of the fictional reality, such as details of space. Just the fact that body language occurs in a narrative text gives it a certain semiotic importance.[1] This importance is further influenced by its status in the text, the special quality of its signified and signifier, and the mode of its presentation.

4.1 Textual Status and Semiotic Quality

4.1.1 Textual Status

Narrative texts differ considerably from one another with respect to the frequency and distribution of the body language they represent. In Henry James's *The American* or Ian McEwan's *The Comfort of Strangers*, body language is a continuous presence in the text; in other works it is used much more sporadically. Bernard Malamud's *The Fixer* (1966), for example, contains, on the whole, relatively little body language. However, this novel ends with an image whose significance depends essentially on bodily eloquence. Yakov Bok, the Jewish protagonist, feels alienated from his religion and the Jewish milieu in Czarist Russia. He tries to lead a life of assimilation in Kiev, but can avoid anti-Semitic persecution for only a short time. When a child is killed, Yakov is accused of having performed a ritual murder. The novel ends with Yakov being driven towards his place of execution:

> The crowds lining both sides of the streets were dense again, packed tight between kerb and housefront. There were faces at every window and people standing on rooftops along the way. Among those in the street were Jews of the Plossky District. Some, as the carriage clattered by and they glimpsed the fixer, **were openly weeping, wringing their hands. One thinly bearded man clawed his face**. One or two waved at Yakov. Some shouted his name. (299–300)

This final image epitomizes the novel's central message. Yakov, who has tried to escape the Jewish tradition, is caught by this tradition in the end – both in a negative and in a positive sense. Traditional prejudice is the cause of his death, but he is also mourned with the traditional gestures of orthodox Jews. In an anti-Semitic society, the only group that sees him as an individual deserving pity is the very group he wanted to flee – an insight that comes too late for Yakov. The gestures of mourning at the end of the novel make a final, implicit comment on the inhumanity of the world it describes.

The general proportion of NVC in a text, then, does not automatically determine the role which body language may play in individual parts of the text. However, this proportion can influence the semiotic importance of individual occurrences of body language in that these may be more conspicuous in a text with a low level of represented NVC than in texts with a consistently high proportion.

4.1.2 *The Body Language Signified*

In real life, many forms of body language – in particular, illustrators and regulators – are 'redundant' if one considers only the information they convey.[2] In the context of art, signs are basically never redundant. However, literary body language differs significantly from that in other art forms with respect to the degree of its semantic content and its semantic clarity.

Many forms of body language have a high degree of semantic content and can figure quite independently as carriers of meaning, especially emotional displays, externalizers, and emblems. This is the case, for instance, in the passage from Graham Swift's *Waterland* referred to above (page 59), in which information about the newly forming relationships between the characters is conveyed almost exclusively through eye contact. But forms of body language that are semantically less 'meaningful' may also play an important role in the effect of a text, as will be shown.

Body language also varies in the clarity of its semantic content. Emblems, with their conventionally binding meaning, and emotional displays that are universally understood distinguish themselves by a particular clarity of their signifieds. However, because of its intrinsic coding, body language is often much more vague than verbal speech. This vagueness is also retained in the narrative text, unless the body language is interpreted by the narrator or a fictional character. Such an act of clarifying the meaning of an instance of body language within the text will be referred to as 'glossing.'[3]

Literature of the nineteenth century, especially, contains a great number of glosses given by the narrator. It seems as though the writers want to exploit the expressive potential of NVC, but do not quite trust its eloquence:

> 'Mrs. Heathcliff is my daughter-in-law,' said Heathcliff, corroborating my surmise. He turned, as he spoke, a peculiar look in her direction: a look of hatred, unless he has a most perverse set of facial muscles that will not, like those of

other people, interpret the language of his soul. (Emily Brontë, *Wuthering Heights*, 17)

It may have been a peculiarity – at any rate it was a fact – that when Bathsheba was swayed by an emotion of an earthly sort her lower lip trembled: when by a refined emotion, her upper or heavenward one. Her nether lip quivered now. (Hardy, *Far from the Madding Crowd*, 155)

One of the favoured forms of glossing in this period is virtual speech.[4] Here, NVC occurs quite clearly as a substitute for speech, but at the same time, the speech act which it is to replace is also spelled out:

Mrs. Proudie looked at her, but said nothing. The meaning of her look might have been thus translated: 'If you ever find yourself within these walls again, I'll give you leave to be as impudent and affected, and as mischievous as you please.' (Trollope, *Barchester Towers*, 1:107)

Farmer Blaize deflected his head twice in silence. 'Bribery,' one motion expressed: 'Corruption,' the other ...

The farmer flung back in his chair. 'Lie number Two,' said his shoulders, soured by the British aversion to being plotted at, and not dealt with openly. (Meredith, *The Ordeal of Richard Feverel*, 65)

A gloss is less reliable when a comparative construction limits its interpretation. In the modern period, this type of glossing still occurs quite frequently. It softens the impression that the narrator is interfering, as in the following quotation from Saul Bellow's novel *A Theft* (1989):

'So she isn't like you?'

'I sure hope not.' Clara made a gesture, **as if** saying, Wipe out these Helmsley Palace surroundings and listen to me. 'Don't forget my two suicide attempts.' (78–9)

In the form of 'as if' clauses, glossing also remains a favourite device in the modern novel because it allows an interpretation of body language from a character's subjective point of view, as Hartmut Binder (1976, 213) has shown for the novels of Kafka. Independent of its reliability, and regardless of whether it is conveyed through a character or a narrator, however, glossing always achieves a highlighting of body language in the narrative text.

As a rule, glossing contributes to a clarification of the body language described. There are some cases, however, in which glossing serves to emphasize semantic ambiguity. Indeed, the effect of NVC in the literary text can essentially build on its inherent vagueness, and in such cases, too, body language may be of considerable semiotic importance.

For example, body language which resists an unambiguous interpretation by the reader may support the impression of a paradoxical and inexplicable world. In Thomas Pynchon's *The Crying of Lot 49* (1966), a gesture at the end of the novel contributes significantly to the purposeful ambiguity which characterizes Pynchon's work. His characters begin a quest but never achieve their goal, or, at least, the text will not reveal the outcome of the search. In *The Crying of Lot 49*, Oedipa Maas believes that she has tracked down a conspiratorial underground communications system. The novel ends with the beginning of an auction sale, in which a collection of stamps linked to this system is to be auctioned off. Oedipa believes she has found the men behind the system; the text, however, refuses to give the reader any information as to whether or not her expectations will be fulfilled. A man who seems to play an important role in the secret organization opens the auction sale with a conspicuous, sweeping gesture:

> Oedipa sat alone, towards the back of the room, looking at the napes of necks, trying to guess which one was her target, her enemy, perhaps her proof. An assistant closed the heavy door on the lobby windows and the sun. She heard a lock snap shut; the sound echoed a moment. Passerine spread his arms in a gesture that seemed to belong to the priesthood of some remote culture; perhaps to a descending angel. The auctioneer cleared his throat. Oedipa settled back, to await the crying of lot 49. (127)

The gesture of the spread-out arms plays an important role in ceremonies and rituals, as the text itself emphasizes ('priesthood of some remote culture'), and thus implies that Oedipa is about to experience a significant moment. The gesture itself is therefore very important; but it is only potentially significant: its precise significance is not revealed to either the character or the reader. Particles of speech implying ambiguity, such as 'seemed' and 'perhaps,' ensure that the gloss of this gesture operates strictly by implication, and emphasize the sense of vagueness: Is Oedipa about to be initiated into the secret organization, or does the reference to the angel descending from heaven imply that she is being threatened by death? Or is this only a harmless gesture used to mark the opening of the auction, because the system of which Oedipa is suspicious does not really exist?

Ambiguous occurrences of body language as in this example are an exception even in literature of the modern period. As a rule, the meaning of the body language portrayed can be derived from its context. However, body language can also contribute to a text's artistic effects in instances in which its 'decodable' semantic meaning or clarity is of lesser importance. In Peter Ackroyd's *The Great Fire of London* (1982), a glossing draws attention precisely to such a lack of inherent meaning: '"How nice to meet you, Mr Coleman." Michael scratched his leg **for no apparent reason**. "How vewy vewy nice"' (128). Here, the character's action is not meaningful in itself; it does not convey any crucial information about the character or his emotional state. Rather, like the character's speech defect, this action makes the episode seem vivid and gives it a dramatic quality, thus contributing essentially to the text's narrative effect.

As we have seen, the degree of the semantic clarity or vagueness of NVC can be an essential constitutive element of a text's meaning and effect. The clarity of body language may also be conditioned by literary convention, at least as long as the convention is in current use.

4.1.3 Literary Convention and the Significance of Body Language

In the examples considered in this section, the significance of literary body language is determined not only by its 'normal' coding, but also, or even exclusively, by a special literary code, that is, by literary convention. Well into the nineteenth century, several areas of literary body language appear as strongly conventionalized; a decline in the use of conventional body language is one of the important developments in the twentieth century.

When body language with a conventional meaning is used in art, it has a high degree of semantic clarity for the receiver who is familiar with the appropriate artistic code. But receivers who are not, or are no longer, familiar with the respective code are confronted with a problem in their attempt to decode this body language. Body language which can only be understood on the basis of a specific iconographic code is often found in painting and sculpture (see Cupchik 1988, 239–42). Some forms of theatre, such as Oriental theatre, also use a conventional body language which can be understood only by the initiated.[5] There are similar examples in certain traditions in Western literature. In the Middle Ages and the Renaissance, folded arms, for example, were a common display of melancholy. In Chaucer's *Troilus and Criseyde,* Pandarus folds his arms as a sign of mourning over the pain of the young lovers (book IV, l 359). In Philip Sidney's *Arcadia* (1590), a woman's melancholy mood is expressed in her 'la[n]guishing cou[n]tena[n]ce with crost armes, and sometimes cast-up eyes' (170).

Another aspect of conventionalization is the use of repertoires or inventories of stereotypical body language. Such repertoires are especially characteristic of folk literature and early literature[6] but can still be found in the nineteenth-century novel. The non-verbal canon of the medieval epic, for example, contains emotional displays such as tears, automatic reactions (turning pale, blushing, fainting, and trembling), and self-destructive acts such as pulling one's hair. The following typical examples are from Chaucer's 'Knight's Tale':

The pure fettres on his shynes grete
Weren of his bittre, salte teeres wete (ll 1279–80)

Whan she hadde swowned with a deedly cheere (l 913)

For ire he quook, no lenger wolde he byde (l 1576)

Allas, the pitee that was ther,
Cracchynge of chekes, rentynge eek of heer. (ll 2833–4)

In addition to such emotional displays, the stereotypical medieval inventory of body language also contained the look of love, and, in particular, many emblems of courtly behaviour.

The same repertoire is found, without substantial modifications, in the romance of later centuries, as in this passage from William Painter's 'The Love of Alerane and Adelasia' (1566):

For Alerane by taking careful heede to the lookes which the Princesse continually did stealingly cast vpon him, saw the often and sod aine chaunces [*sic*] of colour, wherein sometimes appeared ioye, which by and by did ende with infinite nomber of sighes, and with a countenance agreeable to that, which the hart kept secrete and couert, whereby he assured himselfe vnfainedly to be beloued, which caused him to do no lesse ... but to beare vnto her like affection ... The eyes alone did thoffice of the handes and tongue, as trustie secretaries, and faithful messengers of the effects of the minde. (252–3)

In Aphra Behn's *Oroonoko* (1688), even two black lovers change colour in the stereotypical mode. However, the narrator is quick to explain this phenomenon to the sceptical reader: 'And I have observ'd, 'tis a very great error in those who laugh when one says, *A* negro *can change colour:* for I have seen 'em as frequently blush, and look pale, and that as visibly as ever I saw in the most beautiful white' (162). The sentimental and Gothic novels of the eighteenth century continue to use the conventional set of emotional displays, as do many nineteenth-century novels when they strive for a strong melodramatic effect:

'Ah!' said the man: bursting into tears, and sinking on his knees at the feet of the dead woman ... He twined his hands in his hair; and, with a loud scream, rolled grovelling upon the floor ... (Dickens, *Oliver Twist*, 31)

Occasionally, conventional body language is imbued with new or additional meanings and functions, as, for example, in John Bunyan's *The Pilgrim's Progress* (1678). Here, the pilgrim's allegorical journey towards salvation is told using old narrative traditions, especially that of the romance. Accordingly, the novel's body language also derives from a traditional repertoire:

There came also flashes of fire out of the Hill, that made *Christian* afraid that he should be burned: here therefore he swet, and did quake for fear. And now he began to be sorry that he had taken Mr. *Worldly-Wisemans* counsel; and with that he saw *Evangelist* coming to meet him; at the sight also of whom he began to blush for shame. (20)

At first sight, these emotional displays appear to have the same signification as in the romance; however, they do not primarily serve to create an atmosphere of intense emotion. Rather, they are adapted to the purpose of allegory: the pilgrim's fear, desperation, helplessness, or happiness on his journey are portrayed through emotional displays which even the uneducated reader whom Bunyan addresses in his work can easily understand. The glossing of this body language ('quake for fear,' 'blush for shame') further underscores the author's didactic interest.

Summary

In the last two sections, we have concentrated on the signification of body language in literature. However, the semiotic importance of body language is determined not only by the nature of its signified. It may also be determined by the quality of the non-verbal signifier, that is, the way in which body language is executed by a character within the fictional situation. Conventional body language in literature often also has a conspicuous or at least very clear signifier: the intensity of an emotion, for example, corresponds with a large gesture, a violent movement, or an extreme automatic reaction. The signifier is also accentuated when a character's body language is characterized by a distinctive non-verbal style.

4.1.4 *Non-verbal Style*

The distinctiveness of a non-verbal style can be measured against the norms of natural bodily movement that are, to a certain extent, determined by the anatomy of the human body. A harmonious, fluid movement of the limbs is normal for a person healthy in body and mind;[7] this can be used as a standard against which to measure social, cultural, and personal non-verbal styles. The notion of distinctive and/or artificial non-verbal styles has been discussed for the theatre, for film, and for art.[8]

In narrative literature, the assumption of a stylistically remarkable body language rests on its execution through a character, not the way it is verbally described in the text. The following passages from Samuel Beckett's *Murphy* (1938), for example, present a distinctive body language in a fairly 'neutral' verbal style:

When his head moved at last, it was to fall with such abandon on his breast that he caught and lost sight of her simultaneously ...

When Murphy had found what he sought on the sheet he dispatched his head on its upward journey. Clearly the effort was considerable. A little short of halfway, grateful for the breather, he arrested the movement and gazed at Celia ... When she came full circle she found, as she had fully expected, the eyes of Murphy still open and upon her. But almost at once they closed, as for a supreme exertion, the jaws clenched, the chin jutted, the knees sagged, the hypogastrium came forward, the mouth opened, the head tilted slowly back. Murphy was returning to the brightness of the firmament. (12)

He raised his left hand, where Celia's tears had not yet dried, and seated it pronate on the crown of his skull – that was the position. In vain. He raised his right hand and laid the forefinger along his nose. He then returned both hands to their point of departure with Celia's on the counterpane, the glitter came back into his eye and he pronounced: ... (17–18)

> Wylie rose to his feet, hooked the thumb of his left hand in the armhole of his waistcoat, covered his praecordia with his right and said: ... (121)

The mechanical and puppet-like movements described in these examples suggest that the characters are alienated from their own bodies. As we shall see in greater detail below (pages 160–2), this non-verbal style is an integral part of the novel's entire artistic concept.

Non-verbal styles in literature, like language styles, are evident in various domains: they can be characteristic for individual characters, but also for an author, a genre, or a literary period.

Summary

The following catalogue summarizes the aspects discussed in section 4.1. All of them concern the semiotic importance and the semiotic quality of body language in the literary text:

What is the:
- frequency and distribution of body language within the text?
- semantic content } of the non-verbal
- semantic clarity/vagueness } signified?
- distinctiveness of the non-verbal signifier?

As will be shown in the following section, the manner in which body language is presented in the narrative text can have a substantial effect on its semiotic importance, quite independently of its inherent semiotic quality. Furthermore, language and narrative technique determine the extent to which NVC can appear in the narrative text.

4.2 The Presentation of Body Language in the Narrative Text

4.2.1 *Verbalizing the Non-verbal*

All art forms present NVC through a secondary semiotic code. In other words, NVC always undergoes a 'translation' into another semiotic system when it is used in a work of art. Theatre is the only art form in which the signs that relate the characters' body language are 'materially identical with the signs they are meant to signify' (Fischer-Lichte 1992, 130). But even theatre is limited in its ability to represent NVC: subtleties of facial mime or automatic reactions such as blushing are normally 'unstageable' (Poyatos 1983, 331). While theatre and film can portray the body in motion, painting and photography lack the temporal dimension and must therefore select one significant moment of the entire non-verbal act: 'like a photograph, a painting represents a "still" abstracted from the flow of time ... It is apparent that the artist develops a painting as a "peak still," leaving behind the transitional frames that would convey ambiguous information' (Cupchik 1988, 227–8).

Language as the medium of literature is especially limited in its mimetic ability: 'le langage ne peut imiter parfaitement que du langage' (Genette 1969 [1966], 55). While theatrical performance, painting, sculpture, and photography portray body language analogically, literature transcribes the non-verbal into words. Body language that is coded analogically is thus converted into digitally coded signs and loses a measure of its specific potential to communicate degrees of meaning.[9] 'In being a link between us and the nonverbal,' writes Kenneth Burke (1966), 'words are by the same token a screen separating us from the nonverbal' (5). Some writers, therefore, have experienced a sense of limitation or paradox when they have tried to represent NVC in their writing. Margaret Laurence, for example, commented on the irony that 'in all my novels, in some of the scenes that I think are most emotional the characters involved are really saying very little. But, of course, I am describing with words' (Fabre 1983, 201).

Lexical Aspects

The limitations of the verbal medium to represent NVC become immediately apparent when one considers the vocabulary that is available to the writer. In a rare discussion of the process of transforming NVC into language, Harald Burger (1976) differentiates between the various formal-semantic possibilities summarized below and illustrated with examples from Henry James's *The American*:

a. Lexicalized body language, that is, special lexemes and phrases in the dictionary of a language. In all languages, only a fraction of all forms of non-verbal behaviour are lexicalized:

> The artist stared a moment, gave a little pout, shrugged her shoulders, put down her palette and brushes, and stood rubbing her hands. (37)

> Mr. Babcock frowned and winced. (110)

b. Description of non-verbal behaviour:

his smile went through two or three curious phases. It felt, apparently, a momentary impulse to broaden; but this it immediately checked. Then it remained for some instants taking counsel with itself, at the end of which it decreed a retreat. It slowly effaced itself and left a look of seriousness modified by the desire not to be rude. (156)

c. Reference to non-verbal behaviour that is not described but implied through its function or effect. In the following instance, the non-verbal signifier – that is, the manner of the character's expression – can be inferred only on the basis of the glossed signified:

Bellegarde wore a look of mingled perplexity, sympathy, and amusement. (158)

These possibilities vary in the degree to which they offer the reader a concrete image of the body language represented. Some lexicalized expressions, such as, for example, 'to frown,' are connected with quite precise images; others can be used for a wide range of non-verbal behaviour and allow the reader to imagine various kinds of body language. In the following quotation from *The American*, for example, only the general mode of the behaviour is named: '"Your only reason is that you love me!" he murmured, **with an eloquent gesture**' (244). Here, the emphasis is not on the execution of the gesture, but on its expressiveness. Conventionalized body language as discussed above (pages 88–90) is predominantly communicated through lexicalized expressions, because in these cases, too, it is not the quality of the body language that is important, but rather its meaning: a typical emotion or pattern of behaviour whose concrete enactment is of secondary importance.

The most precise portrayal of NVC is possible in case (b). Here it is possible to qualify and concretize body language, both in its signifier and its signified. However, a detailed description of body language does not necessarily mean that its meaning will be communicated with total clarity. The detailed description of a facial expression, for example, can be interpreted in various ways. The meaning of body language can be communicated much more clearly in the cases described in (a) and, especially, (c).

In any case, the detail with which body language is presented will have an influence on its prominence within the text; a long description makes for an effect of 'foregrounding,'[10] as do 'poetic' devices such as the use of imagery. For example, in the following passage from John

Updike's *Roger's Version* (1986), the eye contact between a man and a woman is conveyed through an unusual metaphor:

> She looked up at me, my dear feminist manqué, and there was a glaze: a big-eyed white fish had swum up close to the green aquarium glass and let escape a flash of her furious tedium at going around and around in this tank every day. (37–8)

This metaphor not only emphasizes the woman's body language, it also implies the first-person narrator's particular frame of mind: although the association with the aquarium is motivated by his wife's green eyes, the image of a cold-blooded fish in equally cold water also refers to the increasingly cool relationship between Roger and his wife.

These few examples should suffice to indicate that there is a marked difference between the presentation of body language in the narrative and in the dramatic text. In drama, the characters' body language is frequently given in the stage directions, which primarily have the practical function of directing the characters' behaviour on stage. How body language is described is, thus, generally speaking, of inferior artistic importance in drama than in narrative literature.

Textual and Syntactic Aspects

The limitation of language in the presentation of NVC is also inherent in its linearity. Non-verbal behaviour has a temporal dimension which the printed narrative text can render only imperfectly. Although narrative literature is a temporal art in Gotthold Ephraim Lessing's sense, it is much more limited in its representation of time than other art forms. Theatre and film present non-verbal behaviour just as it occurs in real time; as multichannel media, they are also able to present non-verbal and verbal communication simultaneously. In a narrative text, however, a course of events must necessarily be segmented into discrete units, since they are communicated by discrete linguistic units. The continuity of non-verbal behaviour is thus destroyed, and, in extreme cases, its description in the text can give the impression of a 'peak still' as in painting or photography (also see section 4.2.2, below). In particular, however, simultaneous behaviour is difficult to present in the narrative text. The following diagram shows the relation of body language to speech in a *natural* communicative situation (according to Poyatos 1983, 178). It demonstrates how much body language can be assumed to accompany the exclamation, 'Well, what did *you* think of that!' Only the speaker's body language is represented, but while the statement is being made, a listener will also transmit non-verbal reactions:

SPEECH	BODY LANGUAGE
Well,	raised brows, then facial stillness
what did	lowering brows
you	slightly knit brows + narrow-angle head-nod deictic + gazing at counteractant
think of	same
that!	lateral head-tilt deictic, then stillness with final lingering slight smile

For the narrative text, a linear medium, it is impossible to render the synchronicity of speech and body language implied in this diagram. All simultaneous events in fictional reality must be transformed into sequences and presented successively in the text.[11]

Indeed, the reproduction of speech-synchronic body language in the narrative text can be decidedly cumbersome. In the following excerpt from Samuel Butler's *The Way of All Flesh* (1903), it takes the form of a conspicuous flashback or 'analepsis,' to use a term coined by Gérard Genette.[12]

'Oh, that's the kindest thing of all you have done for me,' he exclaimed, 'I thought all – all middle-aged people liked my father and mother.'

He had been about to call me old, but I was only fifty-seven, and was not going to have this, so I made a face when I saw him hesitating, which drove him into 'middle-aged.' (313)

Representing the listener's non-verbal reaction at the point where it actually occurred (which is indicated by the dash in the speaker's utterance) would have been an awkward interruption of the direct speech. In the following passage from Thomas Hardy's *Tess of the d'Urbervilles*, the report of body language in a flashback seems to be less motivated by textual demands:

He was obliged to explain that he was Tess's husband, and his object in coming there, and he did it awkwardly enough. 'I want to see her at once,' he added. 'You said you would write to me again, but you have not done so.'

'Because she've [*sic*] not come home,' said Joan.

'Do you know if she is well?'

'I don't. But you ought to, sir,' said she.
'I admit it. Where is she staying?'
From the beginning of the interview Joan had disclosed her embarrassment by keeping her hand to the side of her cheek. (424)

However, such extreme delays in the presentation of speech-synchronic body language are usually avoided in the narrative text. Although the linear text can only present synchronic body language either pro- or analeptically, it can at least suggest, through various syntactic means, that a character's speech and body language occur simultaneously. The means most frequently used for this purpose are (a) the interruption of the character's speech by a description of the body language, and (b) the syntactical subordination of the body language to the character's speech.

Both techniques can be observed in an almost excessive measure in the novellas of Heinrich von Kleist. Again and again the characters' speech is interrupted by the description of simultaneous body language; it is usually inserted into the structure of the sentence in a temporal subordinate clause (see Smith 1976, 124). The following sentence from 'Michael Kohlhaas' (1810) is a typical example for this kind of interweaving; my translation into English follows the German syntax as closely as possible:

Inzwischen, sagte der Prinz, nach einer Pause, indem er ans Fenster trat, und mit großen Augen das Volk, das vor dem Hause versammelt war, überschaute: du wirst auf die ersten Tage eine Wache annehmen müssen, die dich, in deinem Hause sowohl, als wenn du ausgehst, schütze! – Kohlhaas sah betroffen vor sich nieder, und schwieg. (47)

In the meantime, said the prince, after a pause, while he walked towards the window, and gazed wide-eyed at the people who were gathered in front of the house: you will have to employ a guard for the first few days, who shall protect you while you are inside your house, as well as when you leave your house! – Kohlhaas looked down in shock, and was silent.

There is a striking syntactical difference in the reproduction of the two non-verbal acts described in this passage. The cumbersome construction of the first sentence serves to subordinate the prince's non-verbal behaviour to his direct speech, and thereby strengthens the impression of the synchronicity of speech and body language. In contrast, the non-verbal reaction of Michael Kohlhaas, which occurs after the prince's speech, is presented in an independent clause.

Other means to signal synchronicity are prepositional phrases and, in the English language, participial constructions, as in these examples from Henry James's *The American*:

'Ah, what an invitation!' murmured Madame de Cintré, with something painful in her smile. (132)

Then, addressing her with the single word which constituted the strength of his French vocabulary, and holding up one finger in a manner which appeared to him to illuminate his meaning, '*Combien?*' he abruptly demanded. (36)

Punctuation, too, can indicate simultaneity. In the following passage from Peter Carey's *Oscar and Lucinda*, the parallel occurrence of a character's speech and the body language of his listeners is marked by ellipses and a set of parentheses. The speaker is Mr d'Abbs, who wants Oscar and Lucinda to approve of his plans for a glass church:

'You are *not* appreciative.' His voice rose and the tremble could not be ignored. Oscar saw how the brown eyes pleaded, even while they closed down with anger. 'I tender no fee, merely the pleasure of doing the job well for you because I care for matters of the spirit ...'

A small vertical frown mark appeared on Lucinda's high forehead.

'... more than most men in this town. As you know, as you know. And I take it,' his voice rose even more as a flock of white cockatoos rose shrieking from the Moreton Bay fig beside the window, 'I take it most uncivilized to be hectored on account of it. Do you see my bill attached?' **(Oscar crossed his leg again.)** 'Do you see an account of my worry? Or my hours? ...' (416–17)

What is remarkable here is that only the simultaneous non-verbal behaviour of the listeners is specially marked by punctuation. The references to the speaker's own paralanguage and body language in the second and third sentence are not marked in any way. This difference seems to point to a convention of (Western) narrative literature: a *speaker's* body language is assumed to be synchronic to his or her speech simply on the basis of syntactic construction (in this case, the interruption of the verbal speech), whereas the simultaneity of a listener's body language requires special marking. Once again it becomes clear how reductively the narrative text goes about its presentation of NVC. In natural face-to-face communication, the listener displays complex behaviour parallel to every act of speech. In narrative literature, the behaviour of the listener finds its way into the text only sporadically, and when it does so, it demands a rather cumbersome description.

In the narrative text, however, the sequencing of body language and speech must also be considered with regard to stylistic decisions: the semiotic importance of body language will be either strengthened or weakened according to its position relative to the character's speech. In the linear text, there are three positions in which body language can be presented in relation to a character's speech: the initial, medial, and final position. The question that follows is whether one of these ways can be seen to be most 'natural' in real-life communication; psycholinguistic research has only begun to deal with this question, but there are some interesting findings.

When the synchrony of speech and body language is not absolute, the initial position of various forms of NVC, in particular illustrating gesture, has been observed to occur most frequently in natural communication: 'One hypothesis that can be offered to account for the fact that gestures precede lexical items (rather than occur simultaneously with them) is that there is a greater repertoire of lexical items than of gestures to choose from' (Beattie 1983, 75).[13]

The study of stage directions in dramatic texts since the nineteenth century also shows such a clear preference for the initial position of NVC that one might regard this positioning as a dramatic convention.[14] The following quotation from Shaw's *Pygmalion* (1914) is quite representative for modern and contemporary drama:[15]

HIGGINS [*in despairing wrath outside*] What the devil have I done with my slippers? [*He appears at the door*].

LIZA [*snatching up the slippers, and hurling them at him one after the other with all her force*] There are your slippers. And there. Take your slippers; and may you never have a day's luck with them!

HIGGINS [*astounded*] What on earth – ! [*He comes to her*]. Whats the matter? Get up. [*He pulls her up*]. Anything wrong? ...

LIZA. Because I wanted to smash your face. I'd like to kill you, you selfish brute. Why didnt you leave me where you picked me out of – in the gutter? You thank God it's all over, and that now you can throw me back again there, do you? [*She crisps her fingers frantically*].

HIGGINS [*looking at her in cool wonder*] The creature is nervous, after all.

LIZA [*gives a suffocated scream of fury, and instinctively darts her nails at his face*]!!

HIGGINS [*catching her wrists*] Ah! would you? Claws in, you cat. How dare you shew your temper to me? Sit down and be quiet. [*He throws her roughly into the easy-chair*].

LIZA [*crushed by superior strength and weight*] Whats to become of me? Whats to become of me? (104)

Consistently, Shaw's stage directions precede the character's speech when the body language is synchronic, or when it actually comes before the speech. The final position seems to be reserved for non-verbal behaviour that follows a verbal utterance.

The dramatic text, then, presents body language that is concomitant with speech in a sequence which can also be observed in real life. This is quite different in narrative literature. Here a tendency to adhere to a 'norm' of sequencing can also be observed, but this norm does not appear to be influenced by a natural pattern. Rather, it is linked with techniques of speech presentation peculiar to the narrative text.

Characteristically, direct speech in narrative literature is associated with a tag, the 'inquit,' which serves to identify the speaker. These inquits are often joined by descriptions of body language, and the description of the speaker's body language can also replace the inquit. When one looks at the position of the inquit relative to the speech to which it is bound, a historical development can be observed: 'In modern prose the inquit tends to come in final position. Second in popularity is the medial position. The initial position was dominant in narratives of the renaissance' (Bonheim 1982, 75). Novels of the Renaissance have relatively few instances of body language in comparison to more recent texts; however, when this body language is associated with speech, it also tends to appear before the speech. A reason for this preference is most likely the fact that the direct speech of the characters often consists of long monologues. In this case, the description of body language in the final position would seem extremely delayed. The following examples of inquit-*cum*-body language from John Lyly's *Euphues* (1578) and Robert Greene's *Pandosto* (1588) are each followed by long monologues; in both cases one can assume that the body language occurs synchronic to the speech:

Having therefore gotten opportunity to communicate with him his mind, **with watery eyes**, as one lamenting his wantonness, **and smiling face**, as one loving his wittiness, encountered him on [*sic*] this manner. ' ... ' (*Euphues*, 91)

Porrus was stricken into a dump at these news, so that, thanking his neighbours for their good will, he hied him home to his wife and, calling her aside, **wringing his hands and shedding forth tears**, he brake the matter to her in these terms. ' ... ' (*Pandosto*, 189)

In novels of the nineteenth and twentieth centuries, the final or medial position is favoured for NVC that accompanies speech. The following dialogue in a passage of Charles Dickens's *Oliver Twist* exemplifies this practice. Mr Grimwig is still suspicious of Oliver, who has just been accepted as a member in Mr Brownlow's household. He convinces Mr Brownlow to test Oliver's honesty by sending him on an errand to his bookseller. The citation is limited to those parts of the discussion in which speech and body language are immediately associated with each other:

'And when are you going to hear a full, true, and particular account of the life and adventures of Oliver Twist?' asked Grimwig of Mr. Brownlow, at the conclusion of the meal: **looking sideways at Oliver**, as he resumed the subject ...

'If he is not,' said Mr. Grimwig, 'I'll – ' **and down went the stick**.

'I'll answer for that boy's truth with my life!' said Mr. Brownlow, **knocking the table**.

'And I for his falsehood with my head!' rejoined Mr. Grimwig, **knocking the table also**.

'We shall see,' said Mr. Brownlow, checking his rising anger.

'We will,' replied Mr. Grimwig, **with a provoking smile**; 'we will.' ...

'Send Oliver with them,' said Mr. Grimwig, **with an ironical smile**; 'he will be sure to deliver them safely, you know.' ...

'You are to say,' said Mr. Brownlow, **glancing steadily at Grimwig**; 'you are to say that you have brought those books back; and that you have come to pay the four pound ten I owe him.' ...

'Oh! you really expect him to come back, do you?' inquired Mr. Grimwig.

'Don't you?' asked Mr. Brownlow, **smiling** ...

'No,' he said, **smiting the table with his fist**, 'I do not.' (84–6)

The final or medial position of body language in relation to speech can be considered the norm of the narrative text since the nineteenth century; the initial position is a departure from this norm and may thus have an effect of foregrounding the body language described.

However, consistent departure from this norm can also characterize the style of an individual author. In the work of Henry James, for example, the initial position of body language accompanying speech is encountered with unusual frequency. The following excerpt from *The American* is taken from the conversation in which Madame de Cintré, in the presence of her family, tells the American that she will not marry him. The body language described can be assumed to occur either before or parallel to the verbal utterance:

Madame de Cintré looked across at the old marquise; her eyes slowly measured her from head to foot. 'I am afraid of my mother,' she said.

Madame de Bellegarde rose with a certain quickness, crying: 'This is a most indecent scene!' ...

The marquise laid her hand on her son's arm, as if to deprecate the attempt to define their position. 'It is quite useless,' she said, 'to try and arrange this matter so as to make it agreeable to you.' ...

'Is *that* all you have got to say?' asked Newman, slowly rising out of his chair. 'That's a poor show for a clever lady like you, marquise. Come, try again.'

'My mother goes to the point, with her usual honesty and intrepidity,' said the marquis, toying with his watchguard. 'But it is perhaps well to say a little more.' ...

Madame de Bellegarde gave a rap with her fan in the palm of her hand. 'If you don't take it you can leave it, sir.' ...

Newman shook his head heavily. 'This sort of thing can't be, you know,' he said. 'A man can't be used in this fashion. You have got no right; you have got no power.' ...

'... Why should your daughter be afraid of you?' added Newman, after looking a moment at the old lady. 'There is some foul play.'

The marquise met his gaze without flinching, and as if she did not hear or heed what he said. 'I did my best,' she said quietly. 'I could endure it no longer.' ...

'In all this matter,' said the marquis, smiling, 'I really see nothing but our humility.' (313–19)

The obvious difference in positioning body language in relation to speech apparent in Dickens and James can hardly be accounted for by the function which the body language has within the fictional situations. Both excerpts contain, for example, illustrators with which the characters emphasize their utterances. Dickens's characters emphasize their sentences by knocking the table; the marquise in James's novel raps her fan. In both cases, body language fulfils an identical function. In view of the fact that the initial position of body language seems to be a 'natural' one in real-life communication, one might speculate whether James's method of positioning the body language of his characters has a more natural effect.[16] But it seems more likely that readers perceive the initial position as a departure from a narrative convention that is part of their *literary* competence, and therefore see it as an instance of foregrounding.

At any rate, the body language of James's characters is more emphatic for syntactical reasons alone: in James's novels the characters are often 'seen' before they are 'heard,' while in Dickens's novels, a greater weight is placed on the verbal part of the characters' behaviour; the non-verbal elements, which come after the speech, have the effect of information that is added as an aside. The body language and paralanguage of James's characters, on the other hand, set the emotional and interpersonal tone of the verbal communication; they are not just 'background music'; rather, their independent quality of expression is emphasized.

The semiotic importance of body language is certainly also influenced by the construction of the sentence in which it is presented. Body language in final or medial position is often rendered in a subordinate clause. This not only suggests the simultaneity of verbal and non-verbal behaviour, but also tends to tone down the importance of the body language it presents: 'Subordination is ... a syntactic form of salience, since the effect of making a clause subordinate is to background it: to demote the phenomenon it describes into a "subservient circumstance" which cannot be understood except in terms of its part in the main clause ... If A is subordinate to B, then A is the circumstantial background against which B is highlighted' (Leech and Short 1981, 221). When body language is reported in a subordinate construction, then, it serves to foreground the speech with which it is associated. In contrast, the body language in an independent clause is not weakened but actually strengthened;[17] most instances of body language in the initial position in James's novel are presented in an independent clause.

Summary

The possibilities for the narrative text of portraying body language are limited from both a lexical and a syntactical perspective. Yet even within these fundamental limitations there are various ways of increasing the prominence of body language through the manner of its presentation in the text. The presentation of NVC in the narrative text is also essentially affected by narrative modes and the structure of narrative transmission.

4.2.2 *Narrative Modes*

Narrative modes are the basic forms of statement with which a narrative text imparts its fictional reality. Helmut Bonheim (1982) differentiates among four elemental narrative modes: the characters' 'speech' (including thoughts and feelings); the 'report' of action; the 'description' of people, objects, and space; and 'comment.' According to their temporal dimension, these modes can be further differentiated as dynamic (speech and report), or static (description and comment).

The prominence of body language can be increased through a narrator's or a character's comment. The other three modes are used in the presentation of body language. However, body language is only rarely presented within a character's speech. In real life, too, the non-verbal behaviour of a speaker or a listener seldom figures as the subject of conversation. For one thing, interactors are often unaware of this body language; for another, it may be considered impolite to mention certain displays of body language. In addition, such mention would often violate the maxims governing conversation as formulated by H. Paul Grice (1975):

> The category of QUANTITY relates to the quantity of information to be provided, and under it fall the following maxims:
> 1. Make your contribution as informative as is required (for the current purposes of the exchange).
> 2. Do not make your contribution more informative than is required ...
> Under the category of RELATION I place a single maxim, namely, 'Be relevant.' (45–6)

These requirements are rarely met for a thematization of body language in conversation. A fictional example in which the above maxims are not violated is found in J.D. Salinger's 'For Esmé – with Love and Squalor.' In the story's second part, Corporal Clay repeatedly draws attention to the symptoms of Sergeant X's nervous condition while the two are talking:

> Undarkened, Clay watched X trying to get a cigarette lit. 'Jesus,' he said, with spectator's enthusiasm, 'you oughta see your goddam hands. Boy, have you got the shakes. Ya know that?' (107)

Since the Corporal does not know to what extent Sergeant X is aware of his condition, his comments are relevant. But although his words do not break conversational maxims, they certainly break the rules of politeness and thus reveal how insensitive a character Clay is.

In the dialogue of plays, references to body language violate Grice's maxims much more frequently than in narrative literature. This is because in the theatre the characters' speech is often the only means to inform the audience about body language that cannot be enacted on stage or that would not be visible to all audience members, such as a facial expression or a change in facial colour. In Shakespeare's *All's Well That Ends Well*, for example, the countess wants to find out Helen's true feelings for her son; Helen's facial expression is an important clue and is thus conveyed in the countess's speech:

> When I said 'a mother,'
> Methought you saw a serpent. What's in 'mother,'
> That you start at it? ...
> What's the matter,
> That this distempered messenger of wet,
> The many-color'd Iris, rounds thine eye? ...
> Yes, Helen, you might be my daughter-in-law.
> God shield you mean it not! 'daughter' and 'mother'
> So strive upon your pulse. What, pale again?
> My fear has catch'd your fondness! Now I see
> The myst'ry of your [loneliness], and find
> Your salt tears' head, now to all sense 'tis gross:
> You love my son ...
> for look, thy cheeks
> Confess it, [t'one] to th'other, and thine eyes
> See it so grossly shown in thy behaviors
> That in their kind they speak it. (1.3.137–79)

In the narrative text, the portrayal of body language is, of course, not limited by visibility as it is in theatre, and a breach of conversational maxims is therefore more weighty than in drama. It is interesting in this context that a dramatist like Oscar Wilde reveals an unusual tendency to report body language within the characters' speech in his narrative prose; dramatic practice seems to affect his writing in another genre:

'You don't understand me, Harry,' answered the artist. 'Of course I am not like him ... You shrug your shoulders? I am telling you the truth.' (*The Picture of Dorian Gray*, 4–5)

'... You have a wonderfully beautiful face, Mr. Gray. Don't frown. You have.' (ibid., 31)

'And now, my dear fellow, I want to speak to you seriously. Don't frown like that. You make it so much more difficult for me.' (ibid., 217)

The main modes used to convey NVC in the narrative text are description and report, between which, however, there is a rather fluid boundary. 'There is often little difference between *report* and *description*: the depiction of a person at rest is ... considered description, the depiction continued when that person begins to move is report' (Bonheim 1982, 22). This is especially apparent in the presentation of NVC. Non-verbal behaviour, of course, has a temporal dimension, but this temporality is more or less weakened through the narrative mode in which it is conveyed. For example, most of the illustrators accompanying speech in the passage from *Oliver Twist* quoted above can be classified as report: 'and down went the stick,' 'knocking the table,' 'smiting the table with his fist.' Here, body language is conveyed with verbs of action and is not embellished any further, so that its dynamic character remains intact in the presentation. A description of body language, however, has an effect of retardation. In general, as a narrative mode, description is 'slow,' or there may be no sense of fictional time passing at all (see Bonheim 1982, 41–2). The more detailed the description of body language, then, the more it loses its 'normal' temporal quality and gains a special emphasis comparable to a slow-motion sequence or a freeze shot in film. In painting, sculpture, and photography, too, body language gains particular importance because it is frozen in its most seminal or 'pregnant' moment, as Lessing put it in chapter 16 of his *Laocöon*. A literary example of 'frozen' non-verbal behaviour can be found in the following passage from Aldous Huxley's novel *Point Counter Point* (1928). At the beginning of a conversation in which important characteristics of the protagonists are revealed, one character is illuminated, both figuratively and literally, in the following description:

Spandrell struck a match. The cigarette between her thin lips, she [Lucy Tantamount] leaned forward to drink the flame. He had seen her leaning like this, with the same swift, graceful and ravenous movement, leaning towards him to drink his kisses. And the face that approached him now was focussed and intent on the flame, as he had seen it focussed and intent upon the inner illumination of approaching pleasure. There are many thoughts and feelings, but only a few gestures; and the mask has only half a dozen grimaces to express a thousand meanings. She drew back; Spandrell threw the match out of the window. The red cigarette end brightened and faded in the darkness. (209–10)

The manner with which Lucy, a member of the British upper class, allows her cigarette to be lit implies her self-centredness and sybaritic nature. The slowing-down of narrative pace in this passage is caused not only by the detailed description. In addition, Lucy's body language is explained and commented on by her observer; her action thus appears extremely drawn out and almost comes to a complete stop by the time the cigarette is lit.

The example from Huxley's novel also draws our attention to the narrative transmission of body language. Lucy's face and her action are described from a particular perspective – that of her observer. Spandrell's consciousness and his past experience with Lucy clearly taint his perception of her body language. The following section will deal more closely with this aspect of narrative mediacy.

4.2.3 *Narrative Transmission*

Narrators and Focalizers

The primary distinguishing feature of narrative literature is the 'mediacy' of its presentation (see Stanzel 1984, 15–38). This mediacy has been the subject of a great deal of research in the area of narratology, which has brought forth a number of descriptive models for the structure of narrative transmission. From these models, the present study has chosen the system originally developed by Gérard Genette (1972) and modified by Mieke Bal (1983) and Shlomith Rimmon-Kenan (1983). Genette makes a basic distinction between 'narration' and 'focalization.' A 'narrator' is the agent of narrative transmission whose 'voice' we hear in the text. A 'focalizer' is the agent through whose 'eyes' the fictional world is perspectivized. A focalizer can be identical with the narrator, but he can also be a character within the fictional world. In the communication model of the narrative text (page 8), the narrator is on level L2, whereas the focalizer can be found either on this level, or on level L1, that is, the level of the fictional action.

A narrator's 'perceptibility' 'ranges from the maximum of covertness (often mistaken for a complete absence of a narrator) to the maximum of overtness' (Rimmon-Kenan 1983, 96). A narrator is 'homodiegetic' when he or she participates in the action told, in other words, where the narrator is also a character of the fictional world. This concept is largely identical with the traditional notion of the first-person narrator. A narrator who does not participate in the action told is called 'heterodiegetic.'

If the focalizer is a character within the fictional situation, the focalization is 'internal.' In an 'external' focalization, the perceiving subject is located outside the fictional situation, and thus is necessarily identical with the narrator. Mieke Bal has completed Genette's system by adding the category of the 'focalized,' that is, the object of the focalization. The focalized can be either 'perceptible' or 'imperceptible' (Bal 1983, 250). Body language is usually a perceptible focalized.

Depending on the narrator and/or focalizer, body language will be transmitted very differently. In particular, the extent to which it will be present at all in the narrative text is essentially affected by the structure of narrative transmission.

An external focalizer in heterodiegetic narration has the greatest potential access to the body language of all characters in the fictional situation. An overt heterodiegetic narrator can comment on and gloss the characters' body language, as is particularly evident in novels of the nineteenth century. Thomas Hardy's narrators, for example, tend to make extensive comments on the characters' non-verbal behaviour. The following is an example from *Tess of the d'Urbervilles*:

> His air remained calm and cold, his small compressed mouth indexing his powers of self-control; his face wearing still that terribly sterile expression which had spread thereon since her disclosure. It was the face of a man who was no longer passion's slave, yet who found no advantage in his enfranchisement. He was simply regarding the harrowing contingencies of human experience, the unexpectedness of things. (277)

As is evident in the final sentence of this quotation, the narrator/focalizer also has access to the character's consciousness. When a narrator refrains from giving such inside views, a character's body language takes on the role it plays in real life: as a perceptible focalized, nonverbal behaviour provides the only clue to the thoughts and feelings of the characters, unless the characters themselves reveal them verbally.

How a strictly external view goes hand in hand with a heightened importance of NVC can be observed in J.D. Salinger's story 'Pretty

Mouth and Green My Eyes' (1951). Here a lack of inside views is essential for the story's overall effect. Through the eyes of an external focalizer, the reader observes a scene in which the male character Lee and a girl are in bed. The scene is interrupted by a telephone call from Lee's friend Arthur. Arthur is waiting for his wife, Joanie, to come home, and Lee calms him down. The name of the woman in Lee's bed is never mentioned in the characters' conversation, but the reader soon guesses that she is, in fact, Joanie. It is especially the NVC that occurs at the beginning of the telephone call that leads the reader to this conclusion:

> A man's voice – stone dead, yet somehow rudely, almost obscenely quickened for the occasion – came through at the other end: 'Lee? I wake you?'
>
> The gray-haired man glanced briefly left, at the girl. 'Who's that?' he asked. 'Arthur?' (116)

Lee's glance can be interpreted as a warning to the woman that her husband is on the telephone. Lee's surprise at the end of the story, when Arthur calls a second time to tell Lee that his wife has just arrived, is also only plausible if the woman in Lee's bed really is Joanie. In any case, the relationship between Lee and the woman has been disturbed by the call; the story significantly ends with the pulling back of a hand:

> Again the girl immediately spoke to him, but he didn't answer her. He picked a burning cigarette – the girl's – out of the ashtray and started to bring it to his mouth, but it slipped out of his fingers. The girl tried to help him retrieve it before anything was burned, but he told her to just *sit still*, for Chrissake, and she pulled back her hand. (129)

In a story which consistently refuses to permit the reader an inside view of the characters, emotional displays and externalizers become important cues for the reader's interpretation.

The limitations of homodiegetic – first-person – narration have been frequently noted. While a heterodiegetic narrator can potentially be 'omniscient,' the first-person narrator is limited in what he or she can credibly know. When reporting body language, the first-person narrator is largely bound to that which he or she can perceive as a character in the fictional situation. An instance of disregard for this limitation is found in a famous nineteenth-century adventure novel, *King Solomon's Mines* (1885), by Henry Rider Haggard. At the climax of the novel, the 'I' and his comrades are lured into a trap by the witch Gagool, out of which she secretly escapes. The text states quite explicitly that neither the 'I' nor his friends notice her departure; nevertheless, the narrator describes the woman's facial expression in order to emphasize her craftiness: 'What we did *not* see, however, was the look of fearful malevolence that old Gagool favoured us with as she crept, crept like a snake, out of the treasure chamber and down the passage towards the massive door of solid rock' (279–80).

Despite the fact that in a first-person narrative there are limitations on the way body language can be perceived, it also has a special significance in this type of narration: for his or her information about the consciousness of other characters, a homodiegetic narrator depends on what he or she is told or can perceive as a participant in the fictional world. In homodiegetic narration, too, non-verbal behaviour thus is an essential and often the only key to the characters' thoughts, feelings, and interpersonal relationships. In Herman Melville's *Moby-Dick* (1851), for example, Captain Ahab is unapproachable and has mysterious motives for fighting the white whale. The first-person narrator, Ishmael, must rely exclusively on Ahab's body language in order to draw conclusions about his character and his intentions:

> I was struck with the singular posture he maintained ... His bone leg steadied in that hole; one arm elevated, and holding by a shroud; Captain Ahab stood erect, looking straight out beyond the ship's ever-pitching prow. There was an infinity of firmest fortitude, a determinate, unsurrenderable wilfulness, in the fixed and fearless, forward dedication of that glance. Not a word he spoke; nor did his officers say aught to him ... (125–6)

In general, the body language of others is a most important clue for all internal focalizers. Frequently, however, the decoding of this body language is difficult and uncertain. This uncertainty is systematically explored in the classic detective novel. Internal focalization is a preferred form of narrative transmission in this genre, because it impedes access to the consciousness of most of the characters involved in the action and thus helps to delay the solution of the crime. The suspense must be maintained until the end; at the same time, however, readers must receive a satisfying number of clues so that they can participate in the game of detection. The body language of the characters can provide such clues without being too explicit. The following quotation is taken from P.D. James's novel *A Mind to Murder* (1963). Here the reader gets the same 'perceptible' information as does the focalizing detective, Dalgliesh. The expressions emphasized in bold print serve to strengthen Dalgleish's uncertain interpretation of the suspects' body language:

She spoke with coy indulgence, the little woman administering a mild rebuke. Dalgliesh looked at Nagle to see how he bore it, but the painter **seemed** not to have heard. He still sat, immobile, on the bed and looked down at them. Clad now in brown linen trousers, thick blue jersey and sandals, he yet **looked** as formal and neat as he had in his porter's uniform, his mild eyes unworried, his long, strong arms relaxed.

Under his gaze the girl moved restlessly about the studio, touching with happy possessiveness the frame of a painting, running her fingers along the window ledge, moving a jug of dahlias from one window to the next. **It was as if** she sought to impose the soft nuances of femininity on this disciplined masculine workshop, to demonstrate that this was her home, her natural place. She was entirely unembarrassed by the pictures of her naked body. **It was possible** that she gained satisfaction from this vicarious exhibitionism. (152)

A focalizing character is also limited in the perception of his or her own body language. As a person is not always conscious of his or her non-verbal behaviour, a psychologically credible account can ensue only when the focalizing character is aware of this body language.[18] This is the case in the following passage from James Joyce's *A Portrait of the Artist as a Young Man*. Stephen Dedalus is punished in school, and experiences his own body language intensely, because he is ashamed of it:

Stephen closed his eyes and held out in the air his trembling hand with the palm upwards ... and at the sound and the pain scalding tears were driven into his eyes. His whole body was shaking with fright, his arm was shaking and his crumpled burning livid hand shook like a loose leaf in the air ... The scalding water burst forth from his eyes and, burning with shame and agony and fear, he drew back his shaking arm in terror and burst out into a whine of pain. His body shook with a palsy of fright and in shame and rage he felt the scalding cry come from his throat and the scalding tears falling out of his eyes and down his flaming cheeks. (50–1)

By contrast, the account of body language of a character-focalizer always stands out when it is not clear that the character is conscious of the body language within the fictional situation. In Defoe's *Robinson Crusoe* (1719), for example, Robinson as first-person narrator gives several accounts of his arrival on his island. Every rendition contains descriptions of his body language, of which he can have hardly been aware in his extreme despair immediately after the shipwreck:

I walk'd about on the Shore, **lifting up my Hands**, and my whole Being, as I may say, wrapt up in the Contemplation of my Deliverance, **making a Thousand Gestures and Motions which I cannot describe**, reflecting upon all my Comrades that were drown'd, and that there should not be one Soul sav'd but my self ... (1:52)

In this first account of his rescue, Robinson mentions gestures indicating despair, specifically the lifting up of his hands. In a later account, he remembers *other* forms of body language:

For Example, I must have said thus. *Sept.* the 30th. After I got to Shore and had escap'd drowning ... I ran about the Shore, **wringing my Hands and beating my Head and Face**, exclaiming at my Misery, and crying out, I was undone, undone ... (1:78)

Quite obviously, the emotional displays described here are not a body language of which Robinson was conscious when he actually performed it. Rather, Robinson as narrator imagines this body language in retrospect, as one appropriate to the situation he narrates and apt to convey the intensity of the deep despair he wishes to portray.

Virginia Woolf's *Mrs Dalloway* (1925) allows us to observe the focalization problem of body language in the context of a modern stream-of-consciousness novel. Peter Walsh is characterized through a non-verbal action that acts as a leitmotif: playing with his pocketknife. This kind of playing is normally an unconscious expression of inner tension or unconscious conflicts and always appears in Woolf's novel when Peter Walsh finds himself in a state of anxiety, as during his first reunion with Clarissa Dalloway. In this reunion episode, the focalization oscillates continuously; it is partly external, partly done by Clarissa, and partly done by Peter:

'And how are you?' said Peter Walsh, positively trembling; taking both her hands; kissing both her hands. She's grown older, he thought, sitting down ... She's looking at me, he thought, a sudden embarrassment coming over him, though he had kissed her hands. **Putting his hand into his pocket, he took out a large pocket-knife and half opened the blade** ...

'How heavenly it is to see you again!' she exclaimed. *He had his knife out.* That's so like him, she thought ... Oh yes, he had no doubt about that; he was a failure, compared with all this ... ***and he took out his knife quite openly*** his old horn-handled knife which Clarissa could swear he had had these thirty years – and clenched his fist upon it.

What an extraordinary habit that was, Clarissa thought; *always playing with a knife ...*

'But what are you going to do?' she asked him. Oh, the lawyers and solicitors, Messrs Hooper and Grateley of Lincoln's Inn, they were going to do it, he said. *And he actually pared his nails with his pocket-knife.*

For Heaven's sake, leave your knife alone! she cried to herself in irrepressible irritation; it was his silly unconventionality, his weakness; his lack of the ghost of a notion what anyone else was feeling that annoyed her, had always annoyed her; and now at his age, how silly!

I know all that, Peter thought; I know what I'm up against, he thought, **running his finger along the blade of his knife**, Clarissa and Dalloway and all the rest of them ... (45–52)

The italicized passages can be attributed to Clarissa as focalizer; in this context, the report of Peter's emotional display is not unusual. In contrast, the passages in bold indicate the same emotional display in contexts which can quite clearly be interpreted as Peter's consciousness. Here the question arises as to whether Peter is aware of his body language, which would contradict normal manifestations of this kind of behaviour, or whether a momentary shift into external focalization is taking place. In the passage highlighted in bold *and* italics, Peter's action seems to function specifically as the point at which a shift in focalization occurs: the body language is the very hinge on which the focus of perception switches from Peter to Clarissa.

In other parts of the novel, too, Peter's body language emerges as a focalization problem. On his way to Clarissa's party, Peter reflects on English society and on his own life. This reflection is interrupted by the following sentence: 'His light overcoat blew open, he stepped with indescribable idiosyncrasy, leant a little forward, tripped, with his hands behind his back and his eyes still a little hawk-like; he tripped through London, towards Westminster, observing' (181). The question as to the subject of focalization in this passage is of essential importance for the reader's image of Peter Walsh. His body language, his idiosyncratic non-verbal style, reflects his place in society. He is an outsider in a society which he can only stumble through, but which he can also observe critically due to his position as outsider ('his eyes still a little hawk-like'). The sudden external view of Peter in the passage quoted above does not represent a break with the internal focalization only if it can be attributed to Peter's imagination – in other words, if it is not a perceptible, but rather an *im*perceptible focalized: Peter's imagined and ironic view of his own non-verbal behaviour, which he recognizes as being symbolic of his place in society.

The extent to which the description of NVC is determined by the mode of narrative transmission can also be seen in texts in which this mode undergoes a change, for example, from homodiegetic into heterodiegetic narration or vice versa, which is linked with a change in focalization. An example is John Fowles's *Daniel Martin* (1977), a novel in which the narrator, in a metafictional mood, at one point regrets the change from heterodiegetic into homodiegetic narration because it restricts the presentation of body language: 'For once a camera would have done better; the queries in eyes, the avoided looks, the hidden reservations on both sides, the self-consciousness' (176).

In Margaret Atwood's *The Edible Woman*, a shift from homodiegetic into heterodiegetic narration can be interpreted as an expression of the protagonist Marian's identity crisis. Here, too, the shift has consequences for the presentation of the protagonist's non-verbal behaviour. In the homodiegetic parts of the novel, Marian's body language is normally understood to be conscious and often also deliberate:

> he brought his other hand over and placed it on top of mine. I was going to bring my other hand up and place it on top of his, but I thought if I did then mine would be on top and he'd have to take his arm out from underneath so he'd have another hand to put on top of the heap, like those games at recess. I squeezed his arm affectionately instead. (63)

In the second part of the novel, which has a heterodiegetic narrator, the frame condition of 'consciousness' is no longer a prerequisite for the report of Marian's body language. There is no indication in either of the two following passages that Marian's body language is perceived out of her own focalization:

> 'Hi Len,' Ainsley said lightly. 'You hung up on me before I had a chance to explain.'
>
> Len wouldn't look at her. 'Marian has already explained, thanks.'
>
> Ainsley pouted reproachfully. She had evidently wanted to do it herself.

'Well, it was somebody's duty to,' Marian said, compressing her lips in a slightly presbyterian manner. 'He was suffering.' (149)

Marian fidgeted with the leather fingers of one of her gloves. 'But I'm not trying to rescue you,' she said. She realized he had tricked her into contradicting herself. (232)

If, in this part of the novel, focalization is delegated by the narrator to Marian, her body language must, again, be understood to be conscious in order to appear psychologically credible. In this way, for example, the following proxemic behaviour can be interpreted as a deliberate measure of caution – Marian feels threatened by her fiancé and moves farther away from him:

Suddenly she felt totally without her usual skill at calculating his reactions in advance. He had become an unknown quantity; just after she had spoken, blind rage and blind ecstasy on his part seemed equally possible. She took a step away from him and gripped the railing with her free hand: there was no telling what he might do. (212)

The focalizer's way of seeing is not only determined by his or her location external or internal to the action. It also essentially depends on the particular make-up of his or her mind. As Rimmon-Kenan (1983, 79–82) emphasizes, each focalizer has a specific cognitive, emotional, and ideological make-up, that is, a mental perspective.

Mental Perspectivization

The perception and communication of the fictional world, and thus also of the characters' NVC, is always biased according to the mental perspective from which it is seen; in some instances, however, the focalizer's subjective perspective can be particularly conspicuous. For example, the portrayal of body language can be strongly influenced by a focalizer's values. In the following passage from James Fenimore Cooper's *The Last of the Mohicans* (1826), the body language of an 'evil' savage clearly implies the ideological and moral convictions held by the narrator-focalizer:[19]

His eye, alone, which glistened like a fiery star amid lowering clouds, was to be seen in its state of native wildness. For a single instant, his searching and yet wary glance met the wondering look of the other, and then changing its direction, partly in cunning, and partly in disdain, it remained fixed, as if penetrating the distant air. (10)

The glistening in Magua's eyes indicates from the start that he is not a 'noble' savage, sympathetic to the white man. His avoidance of eye contact with the white man who is observing him also makes him seem suspect. The narrator's comments such as 'wary,' 'in cunning,' 'in disdain' further help to emphasize the 'negative' meaning of this body language.

When body language is perceived by a character-focalizer, his or her special way of perceiving allows the reader to make conclusions about the make-up of the character's consciousness. Penelope Lively's novel *Moon Tiger* (1987) is a model example of multiperspective narration, where the same instance of body language is often perceived differently by various characters. The multiple perspectives in *Moon Tiger* result from the perspectivist world-view of the narrator and protagonist, Claudia. On her deathbed, she is telling herself the story of her own life. A writer of historical works, she is aware that there is no single view of history, and that the story of her own life also cannot be told from one single perspective: 'The voice of history, of course, is composite. Many voices; all the voices that have managed to get themselves heard. Some louder than others, naturally. My story is tangled with the stories of others ... their voices must be heard also ...' (5–6). As Claudia relates different versions of the events of her life, body language is also remembered from different viewpoints – for example, in an episode from her childhood in which her older brother, Gordon, explains the facts of life to her. The episode is first told from Gordon's perspective:

'Anyway,' he says, 'I know how babies are made.'

'So do I,' Claudia says. But there has been an infinitesimal, a fatally betraying pause ...

She hesitates, trapped. He watches her. Which way will she jump? **She shrugs**, at last, wonderfully casual. 'It's obvious. The man puts his – thing – into the lady's tummy button and the baby goes inside her tummy until it's big enough.'

Gordon collapses in glee. He **rolls about on the sofa, howling.** ' ... '

She stands over him, **scarlet not with embarrassment but with chagrin and rage**. 'He does! I know he does!'

Gordon stops laughing. He sits up. 'Don't be such a cretin. You don't know *anything*. He puts his thing – and it's called a penis, you didn't know that either, did you? – *there* ...' **And he stabs with a finger at Claudia's crotch, pushing the**

stuff of her dress between her thighs. Her eyes widen – in surprise? In outrage? They stare at each other. (26–7)

It is then repeated and interpreted from Claudia's point of view:

'I'm not going to tell you,' she says.

'Because you don't know.'

She could gladly hit him, lolling there complacent on the sofa. And anyway she does know – she's almost sure she does. She says defiantly, 'I do know. He puts his thing in the lady's tummy button.' She does not add that the inadequacy of her own navel for such a performance bothers her ...

He hurls himself around in laughter. He is speechless. **Then he leans forward.** 'I knew you didn't know,' he says. 'Listen. He puts his penis – it's called a penis incidentally – *there* ...' **And he stabs with his finger against her dress, between her legs.**

And her anger, strangely, evaporates; eclipsed by something different, equally forceful, baffling. Something mysterious is present, something she cannot nail or name. **She stares in wonder at her grey-flannelled brother.** (27)

In the first version Gordon, eager for Claudia's reaction, notices that his sister shrugs her shoulders before she answers him – a detail that Claudia does not relate from her own point of view. Gordon also observes her blush, while Claudia's version does not mention this automatic reaction but rather articulates the thought that causes her to blush – a thought which, incidentally, differs considerably from her brother's interpretation. Whereas Gordon's version only reports his act of sitting up, Claudia notices that the space between her and her brother is diminished in anticipation of his intimate touch. Claudia experiences this touch much more intensely than her brother does, as is also reflected in the syntax of her version: whereas in Gordon's version the stuff of Claudia's dress is between his finger and her body ('And he stabs with a finger at Claudia's crotch, pushing the stuff of her dress between her thighs'), in Claudia's version the act is split into two equal prepositional phrases ('And he stabs with his finger against her dress, between her legs') – in her subjective perception, Gordon's finger does not seem to touch her *through* the cloth, but directly. The brother is also less aware of the sexual significance of his touch than Claudia is. The surprised look on her face in Claudia's version indicates that she suddenly has unexpected feelings for her brother. For Gordon, on the other hand, this look might also indicate outrage.

On the one hand, then, the special make-up of a character's consciousness will determine the extent to which NVC is perceived. On the other hand, the extent and the manner of perception also provide clues as to the particular nature of this consciousness. This can also be observed in two novels that have already been discussed in other contexts, Margaret Laurence's *The Stone Angel* and Margaret Atwood's *The Handmaid's Tale.* The narrator-protagonists of both novels stand out in their unusual alertness to NVC, especially with regard to their own body language.

In Atwood's novel, this hypersensitivity is determined by the circumstances of Offred's life. Since she is practically forbidden to talk with other people, non-verbal behaviour provides an essential mode of access to the minds of her fellow human beings. But Offred is also extremely aware of her own body language:

I can sit in the chair, or on the window seat, hands folded, and watch this. (17)

I put my hand out, unfolded, into the sunlight. (18)

I stood in front of her, hands folded. (24)

I know better than to look the interpreter in the face. (38)

My own hands are clenched, I note, tight around the handle of my basket. I won't give anything away. (43)

My hands stay where they are, folded in my lap. Thighs together, heels tucked underneath me, pressing up against my body. Head lowered. (90–1)

As a ward of the state, Offred is strictly regulated in her non-verbal behaviour: folded hands belong to the official body language of a handmaid. It is a matter of life and death for Offred to obey these rules of behaviour, which partly explains why she *must* pay so much attention to her own body language. On the other hand, every moment in which she can use her body freely is precious and consciously experienced, such as a chance to stretch out her hands. Offred's unusual consciousness of her own non-verbal behaviour is a result of the abnormal conditions under which she must live; it implies how the totalitarian state has changed her structures of perception and consciousness.

Like Offred, ninety-year-old Hagar Shipley in Margaret Laurence's novel also finds herself in a critical situation. She is afraid that her son and daughter-in-law will put her into a nursing home and tries to infer their intentions from their body language:

Well, so much is clear. He is referring to Doris. She sighs, one of her deep sighs straight from the belly, and gives him a glance. She lifts an eyebrow. He shakes his head. What are they trying to signal to one another? They spoke before as though I weren't here, as though it were a full gunnysack they dragged from the floor. But now, all at once, they are intensely aware of my open ears. (26)

Hagar also carefully observes herself for indications of her progressive senility:

On the way home, the bus is packed. A teenage girl ... gives me her seat. How very kindly of her. I can scarcely nod my thanks, fearing she'll see my unseemly tears. And once again it seems an oddity, that I should have remained unweeping over my dead men and now possess two deep salt springs in my face over such a triviality as this. There's no explaining it. (77)

The woman who has been in control all her life finds it painful and undignified to have to be dependent on others in her old age. She is afraid of doing anything that may be considered a reason to put her in the home. As in the case of Atwood's narrator-character, then, Hagar's unusual consciousness of her own NVC is also a result of her existential situation.[20]

How powerfully the perception of NVC can contribute to the constitution of a perspective and indicate the special state of a consciousness is particularly obvious in the case of an 'unreliable' report of the fictional action.

Unreliable Narrators and Focalizers

To what extent the unreliability of a narrator's or character's perspective can be distinguished from its 'normal' subjectivity remains a fundamental question in light of the fact that every world-view is essentially subjective. However, when the view of a narrator or character is marked as questionable through features of the text itself, a situation of unreliability can be assumed. Next to direct speech, the body language of characters can play an important role as the corrective tool of an unreliable view. Both direct speech and body language are available to the reader as signifiers independent of their perception through a narrator or character, and an unreliable perception can thus be bypassed.

In his first three novels, the Japanese-British author Kazuo Ishiguro shows his fondness for unreliable narrators. His first-person narrators typically withhold crucial information about themselves because they are repressing events of their lives or do not want to admit to certain truths about themselves. An old painter is at the centre of Ishiguro's novel *An Artist of the Floating World* (1986), set in Japan. Several years after the Second World War, Ono is confronted with the problem of giving his youngest daughter in marriage according to traditional custom. This custom includes long and intricate negotiations between the families, during which investigations into the future in-law family are allowed. An earlier marriage arrangement for the youngest daughter had failed abruptly after promising negotiations – for reasons that are only gradually revealed to the reader: before the war, the artist had joined the ultranationalists who drove Japan into the war. During the war years, he produced paintings that could be used for propaganda purposes, instead of continuing to create pictures of a 'floating world,' that is, art for art's sake. As a member of the state art committee, he was responsible for his former pupil Kuroda's arrest.

Ono's fall into a state of disrepute after the war is only indirectly implied at the beginning of the novel. He claims not to paint anymore because he is too old, but he does not even hang his paintings in his own house. The artist also does not want to see that there is a connection between his past and the problems his daughter is having in finding a husband: 'My own guess is that there was nothing so remarkable about the matter. True, their withdrawal at the last moment was most unexpected, but why should one suppose from this that there was anything peculiar in it? My feeling is that it was simply a matter of family status' (18). In keeping with traditional politeness, his two daughters also never openly articulate this connection to their father; however, their thoughts can be read from their body language, which Ono as narrator reports. Even though Ono himself does not want to accept the significance of this body language, it gives the reader important clues. For example, the elder daughter's nervousness implies that the new negotiations for her sister's marriage will be problematic:

> As Noriko said this, her elder sister – whose gaze until then had been demurely turned away – gave me a swift, enquiring look. Her eyes left me again immediately, for she was obliged to return Noriko's smile. But a new, more profound uneasiness had entered Setsuko's manner and she seemed grateful when her little boy, speeding past us down the veranda, gave her an opportunity to change the subject. (14)

When it becomes known that a member of the groom's family is in contact with the pupil Ono denounced, the daughters' body language is a fairly definite indicator of their anxiety:

> 'An odd thing. It turns out Dr Saito met a former pupil of mine. Kuroda, in fact. It seems Kuroda's taking up a post at the new college.'
>
> I looked up from my bowl and saw my daughters had again stopped eating. It was clear they had just exchanged glances, and it was one of those instances last month when I got a distinct impression they had at some point been discussing certain things about me. (83)

Neither as a character in the action nor as a narrator does the father admit that he is worried about the reappearance of his former pupil. But his actions and his body language give the reader a hint that he can no longer deny the effect which his past behaviour has on his daughter's marriage plans. Under the pretext that he is just making a polite visit, he looks up an old comrade to find out whether the groom's family has made any attempts to investigate his past. In the course of this conversation, an emotional display observed by the former comrade allows the reader to infer the artist's mental strain:

> 'I see. Hopefully their detective will be equally lost as to where to find him. But then sometimes those detectives can be very resourceful.'
>
> 'Indeed.'
>
> 'Ono, you look deathly pale. And you looked so healthy when you first arrived. That's what comes of sharing a room with a sickly man.' (95)

After this conversation, Ono's panic increases steadily. This can be seen mainly in his reaction to the body language of the other characters. In a society in which politeness is maintained even in situations of extreme conflict, Ono does not have to fear being attacked verbally. However, he increasingly perceives this attack in the non-verbal behaviour of others. Ono especially perceives the body language of one of the groom's brothers as a reproach – a brother who was in contact with Kuroda at the college:

> In any case, as we began to eat, I found myself becoming increasingly confirmed in these suspicions. Although at this point Mitsuo was behaving with all due decorum, there was something in the way I would catch him looking at me, or about the way he would pass a bowl to me across the table, that made me sense his hostility and accusation. (117)

Ono's growing awareness of guilt makes him interpret the other characters' behaviour as a reproach, whereas formerly he did not want to read his daughters' body language. Finally, his conscience forces him to make an open verbal confession of his guilt – towards himself and the others.

In this novel, body language first is an important key to information which the narrator withholds. When this information becomes clearer and clearer in the course of the action, the function of the body language shifts. It is no longer important as a corrective for the narrator's statements, but rather becomes an indicator for the artist's sense of guilt: after he has finally stopped repressing his past, Ono no longer reads the other characters' body language as a reproach.

The protagonist Marian in Atwood's *The Edible Woman* is also an unreliable medium, since she is going through a difficult personal crisis: 'Marian's world, and all the people in it, are ... projections of her own disturbed and immature psyche' (Hill Rigney 1987, 29). The impression she has of being oppressed by her fiancé, Peter, grows into a persecution complex. This delusion first culminates at the end of the first part of the novel. During a visit with friends at which the men speak about a rabbit hunt, Marian feels so threatened that she identifies with a rabbit and crawls under a couch in search of protection. When she is freed from this position, Peter's body language – his eye and touch behaviour – appears threatening to her: 'The hot needle of anger in my voice must have penetrated the cuticle of Peter's euphoria. He stepped back a pace; his eyes seemed to measure me coldly. He took me by the upper arm as though he was arresting me for jaywalking, and turned to Len' (76). Then Marian attempts to flee, but is 'caught' by Peter, who wants to bring her home. He still seems dangerous to Marian:

> He glanced quickly over at me, his eyes narrowed as though he was taking aim. Then he gritted his teeth together and stepped murderously hard on the accelerator. (78)

> During a long flickering moment of light I turned and saw him watching me, his face strangely shadowed, his eyes gleaming like an animal's in the beam from a car headlight. His stare was intent, faintly ominous. (79–80)

Interpretations of *The Edible Woman* hinge on the question of whether or not Marian's fears are to be taken seriously. Is her existence, or at least her identity, really threatened by Peter, or is her behaviour paranoid?

Particles of uncertainty ('seem,' 'as though') frequently draw attention to the subjectivity of Marian's interpretation of non-verbal behaviour. If one 'frees' the body language in the citations above of its perspectivization through Marian, it could also be interpreted in a way that is more advantageous to Peter: he feels disgraced by his tipsy girlfriend and treats her first with amusement and condescension, later with increasing anger. The direct speech of the characters, which is not influenced by Marian's perspective, provides enough justification for this interpretation:

> 'Oh come along Marian, don't be childish,' he said brusquely, and took my arm ...
>
> He got in and slammed his own door and started the motor. 'Now perhaps you'll tell me what all that nonsense was about,' he said angrily ...
>
> 'Why the hell you had to ruin a perfectly good evening I'll never know,' he said, ignoring my remark. There was a crack of thunder. (77–8)

Marian's view, then, is relativized. She may very well see herself as a victim of a/the male – as an edible woman – but the text indicates at the same time that this is not the only possible way of seeing. Towards the end of the novel, too, Peter's body language serves to present Marian in an ambiguous light. In order to test Peter's true attitude towards her, she bakes him an 'edible woman,' the central symbol of the novel:

> 'You've been trying to destroy me, haven't you,' she said. 'You've been trying to assimilate me. But I've made you a substitute, something you'll like much better. This is what you really wanted all along, isn't it? I'll get you a fork,' she added somewhat prosaically.
>
> Peter stared from the cake to her face and back again. She wasn't smiling.
>
> His eyes widened in alarm. Apparently he didn't find her silly. (254)

Marian's interpretation of Peter's eye behaviour is positive for her: 'he didn't find her silly.' From her point of view, Peter has understood the significance of the cake (that he simply sees women as objects to be consumed) and is 'alarmed' for this reason. But an interpretation that is less advantageous to Marian is also possible: that Peter does not really find her 'silly,' but completely crazy.

Summary

The last few sections have shown that the structure of narrative transmission determines to what extent NVC finds its way into a narrative text. On the other hand, the way body language is perceived is an important element in the constitution of perspective, and body language may also serve as a means to bypass an unreliable perspective.

In narratology, the term 'perspective' is used in a figurative sense to refer to mental points of view. But a narrative text may also convey the impression of a specifically *visual* way of seeing.[21] A distinctive visual quality can give body language considerable emphasis.

4.2.4 *Visual Perspectivization*

Visual foregrounding, in a very literal sense, can be effected through the suggestion of special proximity to the perceived body language, in the way in which film creates emphasis through a close shot. According to Siegfried Kracauer, film has a special ability to portray what a normal observer is unable to perceive – that which is extremely large or extremely small. Kracauer uses a scene from D.W. Griffith's *Intolerance* to illustrate how strongly an effect of very close perception can create emphasis in a film. In this scene, a close-up of a desperate woman's hands is shown:

> It almost looks as if her huge hands with the convulsively moving fingers were inserted for the sole purpose of illustrating eloquently her anguish at the most crucial moment of the trial; as if, generally speaking, the function of any such detail exhausted itself in intensifying our participation in the total situation. This is how Eisenstein conceives of the close-up. Its main function, says he, is 'not so much to *show* or to *present* as to *signify*, to *give meaning*, to *designate*.' ... Such images blow up our environment in a double sense: they enlarge it literally; and in doing so, they blast the prison of conventional reality, opening up expanses which we have explored at best in dreams before. (Kracauer 1965 [1960], 47–8)

The effect of a close-up of body language in the narrative text is, to a certain degree, inherent in the representation of certain modes of NVC. For example, body postures seem to be perceived at a greater distance than a facial expression or a hand gesture. When the latter are described, they appear to pull the reader closer; their image seems to be magnified.

The ending of Franz Kafka's *The Trial* (1925) shows how the apparent 'proximity' of the body language described can create emphasis. Josef K. is the perceiving subject; he is awaiting his execution. Several references to his vision give the passage a succinctly visual character:

His glance fell on the top storey of the house adjoining the quarry. With a flicker as of a light going up, the casements of a window there suddenly flew open; a human figure, faint and insubstantial at that distance and that height, leaned abruptly far forward and stretched both arms still farther. Who was it? A friend? A good man? Someone who sympathized? Someone who wanted to help? ... Where was the Judge whom he had never seen? Where was the High Court, to which he had never penetrated? He raised his hands and spread out all his fingers.

But the hands of one of the partners were already at K.'s throat, while the other thrust the knife into his heart and turned it there twice. With failing eyes K. could still see the two of them, cheek leaning against cheek, immediately before his face, watching the final act. 'Like a dog!' he said; it was as if he meant the shame of it to outlive him. (127)

K.'s final non-verbal statement, raised hands with spread-out fingers, has been interpreted as a gesture of despair (see Kuepper 1970, 152). It may also be seen as a defensive gesture, or a gesture of shock and fear of death, without any one definition excluding the other. What is most important is that it is a *non-verbal* reaction: K. can only confront the incomprehensible non-verbally, and his gesture, which is his final statement before the execution, has considerable semantic importance. This importance is emphasized by the fact that K.'s gesture must be visualized as a close-up; his fingers can only be perceived from relative proximity. The contrast to the image of the man in the window, perceived to be far away and high up, even increases this closeness of K.'s last gesture.

An extreme close-up of body language can be found in John Updike's *Roger's Version*. In the following quotation, Roger, the first-person narrator-character, is fascinated by his observation of the symptoms of antipathy between his niece, with whom he has a sexual relationship, and his wife:

The chemistry between two women we have fucked fascinates us, perhaps, with the hope that a collusion will be struck to achieve our total, perpetual care. Though Esther in her animated gestures several times reached out to touch Verna as one would Exhibit B, I saw no actual contact occur; rather, Esther's long-nailed fingers froze an inch above the skin of Verna's forearm, whose fine hairs responsively rose up, bristling. (287)

In this situation, Roger poses as a natural scientist who is observing an interesting phenomenon. This is not only evident in his diction ('chemistry,' 'Exhibit B,' 'I saw ... occur'), but also in his report of Verna's reaction to Esther's threatening touch, which would normally not be perceivable at all. The close-up here suggests the magnifying capacity of a microscope through which Roger, the 'scientist,' observes the two women. Thus the body language becomes significant precisely because it is magnified to such an extreme extent: it communicates the women's antipathy towards each other, but in particular, it conveys Roger's distanced and perverse interest in the situation.

The visual perspectivization of body language occurs relatively rarely in the narrative text, but it is a particularly effective means of emphasis. Chapter 6 will address the question of how the visual presentation of body language in the novel is affected by the history of visual media and by the visual arts (pages 235–40).

Summary

The aspects examined for the *presentation of body language in the narrative text* can be summed up in two blocks of questions:

How is an instance of body language 'filtered' through language and narrative transmission?

Is an instance of body language *foregrounded* through
- linguistic means?
- narrative mode?
- the structure of narrative transmission?
- visual perspectivization?

4.3 Literary Functions and Effects of Body Language in the Narrative Text

The discussion so far has indicated a number of ways in which NVC contributes to the potential meaning and effects of a narrative text; in the following sections, these ways will be touched on only briefly in the light of some additional points. Other literary functions of NVC require more detailed attention, however.

Some literary critics separate a body language which serves the function of 'decoration' from forms of body language with other, more 'important' functions. R.G. Benson (1980, 22), for example, comments in connection with Chaucer's *Book of the Duchess* that '[t]he elaborate explanations of her behavior make of the gestures merely decorative additions which supply no information not already in the text.' In contrast, Chaucer used 'organic' gestures in his later, more mature works, 'which ... enhance our understanding of such vital narrative elements as character and plot' (59). Such statements are not only evaluative, they are also by far too general and do not do justice to the broad functional spectrum of body language in the narrative text. This can be demonstrated with a passage from Melville's *Moby-Dick*:

His deep chest heaved as with a ground-swell; his tossed arms seemed the warring elements at work; and the thunders that rolled away from off his swarthy brow, and the light leaping from his eye, made all his simple hearers look on him with a quick fear that was strange to them.

There now came a lull in his look, as he silently turned over the leaves of the Book once more; and, at last, standing motionless, with closed eyes, for the moment, seemed communing with God and himself.

But again he leaned over towards the people, and bowing his head lowly, with an aspect of the deepest yet manliest humility, he spake these words ... (48)

This quotation is taken from Father Mapple's sermon on Jonah in chapter 9. This sermon plays an important role in foreshadowing and directing the interpretation of future plot developments. It would also fulfil this function without the NVC portrayed. Father Mapple's body language can best be described as rhetorical *actio*, which mainly serves to emphasize his words, and thus appears to be 'decorative' at first glance. On the other hand, the preacher's non-verbal rhetoric is not at all 'superfluous': it gives the reader an impression of Father's Mapple's charisma and thus explains the great effect his words make on the fictional listeners. Furthermore, the cited passage follows several pages of direct speech in which Father Mapple tells the story of Jonah. It thus serves to make the sermon more vivid and to give it structure by marking the turning point at which the example moves on to the sermon's moral. After the lengthy exposition on Jonah, the reader is allowed a break, so to speak, which ensures his or her further attention. The body language that seems purely 'decorative' at first sight thus proves to be an organic, multifunctional component of the text. However, it is obvious that the importance of non-verbal behaviour within the narrative action varies from one text to another.

4.3.1 The Place of Non-verbal Behaviour in the Narrative Action

Structuralist narratology has distinguished between the 'existents' (characters, objects, fictional space, and so on) and the 'events' that make up the content of a narrative text. The events of a narrative action can be classified into 'kernels' and 'satellites,' using terms proposed by Seymour Chatman (1978, 53–4). The former are irreplaceable core events; they advance the action by opening an alternative; the latter are events that do not open alternatives but accompany a kernel action.

Body language can function as a kernel event – for example, in pantomime or cartoons where actions are conveyed exclusively non-verbally. In two of the texts discussed earlier, Calvino's *The Castle of Crossed Destinies* and Dickens's 'The Signalman,' body language certainly constitutes a narrative core: both narratives essentially depend on their characters' 'emblematic' body language (see pages 52–5 above). In the modern psychological novel, too, body language may acquire a particular significance within the action. A character's body language perceived by another character may result in reflections or reactions which will greatly influence the subsequent action. In a frequently cited passage from 'The Art of Fiction' (1884), Henry James emphasizes the importance of apparently insignificant events in the psychological novel: 'It is an incident for a woman to stand up with her hand resting on a table and look out at you in a certain way; or if it be not an incident I think it will be hard to say what it is' (35). The passage from *The Portrait of a Lady*, in which the nature of the relationship between Isabel Archer's husband and Mme Merle is revealed to Isabel by means of a breach in etiquette (see page 14 above), perfectly illustrates this statement: this non-verbal event clearly pushes the action forward by advancing Isabel's personal development.

In the majority of examples, body language does not, however, function as a kernel event. As all non-verbal behaviour has a temporal dimension, it is sometimes difficult to decide whether an instance of body language should be classified as a satellite event or, rather, an 'indexical' element[22] which qualifies a character, that is, an existent.[23] Externalizers of character traits or interpersonal relationships are minimal events; first and foremost, however, they clarify states of being which continue to exist beyond their particular moment in the action. With regard to body language, it seems justifiable, then, to assume only one basic distinction: Is body language relevant to the action of the story, or does it fulfil an indexical function? Indexical body language is by no means of secondary importance in the meaning and effect of a text. On the contrary, in most of the functions it performs in literature, body language is to be understood as indexical.

4.3.2 *The Indication of Mental States*

As has become apparent in various contexts, one of the central functions of literary body language is to indicate the characters' mental states and processes. Examples can be found in the literature of all periods, although there are differences in degree. In some genres of narrative literature, body language provides the prime access to the thoughts and feelings of the fictional characters, as in some types of folk literature or in the medieval epic. It is one of the conventions of medieval literature that it communicates mental states primarily through external signs. This preference should not, however, be interpreted as an inability of medieval writers to provide an 'inner' view of their characters: 'The falsity of such a notion must be apparent to anyone even slightly acquainted with the work of the Cistercians or Victorines, whose psychological penetration into the workings of homo interior is most remarkable. The erroneous notion has arisen largely because a literary mode of portrayal has been interpreted as indicative of a lack of native capacity' (L.J. Friedman 1957–8, 109).

In the prose romances of the Renaissance, on the other hand, psychological states are primarily expressed in long monologues. It was noted above (page 100) that body language is usually described prior to such monologues; when it consists of emotional displays, these are almost always concordant with the verbal statement. Body language in the Renaissance romance is therefore, as a rule, only an additional indication of psychological states. It primarily serves to intensify the psychological facts communicated in other ways, in accordance with an aesthetic that laid great emphasis on intense emotional effect.[24] The emotional displays are therefore often derived from a tested and reliable repertoire, and their presentation, too, tends to be emphatic; one strategy for intensification is the cumulation of emotional displays as in the two following quotations:

At this question, Rosader, turning his head askance and bending his brows as if anger there had plowed the furrows of her wrath, with his eyes full of fire he made this reply ... (Lodge, *Rosalind*, 295)

Having given her this bitter reproof, he departed, leaving her weeping the fountain of her Eyes dry, wringing her hands, and like one in a dead Trance overcome with grief, cast upon the earth ... (Forde, *Montelion*, 13)

In both examples, the emotional displays are not the only sources of information for the character's emotional state; not only are they followed by emotionally laden speech, but the narrator's glossing of the body language also leaves no doubt about the character's feelings. This redundancy of portrayal makes for a particularly intense emotional effect.

In the eighteenth-century novel, the relation between language, body language, and feeling is different again. During this period, too, various forms of literature (such as the sentimental and the Gothic novel) developed a poetics in which emotion plays a dominant role. Speech, however, was no longer considered sufficient to express feelings (see chapter 6, pages 215–17); instead, body language became a favoured and often the only means to convey emotional states. In melodramatic moments of the nineteenth-century novel, too, corporeal expression is used to achieve an intense emotional effect.[25] In modern narrative literature with an external focalization, it is also principally body language which allows the reader to gain insight into the characters' inner lives, as we have seen in the discussion of Salinger's story 'Pretty Mouth and Green My Eyes' (see pages 108–9).[26]

In the course of the nineteenth century, the techniques for representing consciousness in fiction were developed and refined, culminating in the modern stream-of-consciousness novel. Obviously, however, even techniques such as the narrated and interior monologue do not entirely replace the body language of mental states. One reason is that from a character's perspective, non-verbal behaviour of other characters is an important clue to their inner lives, and thus is often carefully observed and reflected upon.[27] But also the body language of characters whose thoughts and feelings are directly accessible is often portrayed and gives the reader additional insights into their inner lives. In these cases, NVC accompanies the character's 'inner' speech in a similar way to which it accompanies verbal speech. In the following example from Virginia Woolf's *Mrs Dalloway*, the character's train of thought is interrupted by a brief shift of attention to a gesture which illustrates the content of her thought:

Power was hers, position, income. She had lived in the forefront of her time. She had had good friends; known the ablest men of her day. Murmuring London flowed up to her, **and her hand, lying on the sofa back, curled upon some imaginary baton such as her grandfathers might have held**, holding which she seemed, drowsy and heavy, to be commanding battalions marching to Canada, and those good fellows walking across London, that territory of theirs, that little bit of carpet, Mayfair. (124)

In George Eliot's *Middlemarch*, too, the presentation of consciousness is frequently interwoven with externalizers and emotional displays. In chapter 28, having just returned from her honeymoon with Casaubon, Dorothea feels bored in her new life; she is drearily contemplating her marriage when her eye falls on a portrait of Will Ladislaw's grandmother. The woman's features remind her of Will, who is an important factor in her marital problems. In this moment, body language penetrates into her train of thought, and Dorothea herself becomes aware of the emotional display, a smile, that has been triggered by the thought of Will. The non-verbal behaviour that follows is reported from the narrator's external view:

In the first minutes when Dorothea looked out she felt nothing but the dreary oppression; then came a keen remembrance, and turning away from the window she walked round the room. The ideas and hopes which were living in her mind when she first saw this room nearly three months before were present now only as memories ... Nay, the colours deepened, the lips and chin seemed to get larger, the hair and eyes seemed to be sending out light, the face was masculine and beamed on her with that full gaze which tells her on whom it falls that she is too interesting for the slightest movement of her eyelid to pass unnoticed and uninterpreted. The vivid presentation came like a pleasant glow to Dorothea: **she felt herself smiling, and turning from the miniature sat down and looked up as if she were again talking to a figure in front of her. But the smile disappeared as she went on meditating, and at last she said aloud,** –

'Oh, it was cruel to speak so! How sad, – how dreadful!'

She rose quickly and went out of the room, hurrying along the corridor, with the irresistible impulse to go and see her husband and inquire if she could do anything for him. (2:3–5)

Dorothea's smile indicates that she has feelings for Will, even though she immediately represses this thought. These feelings are still mainly on a preconscious level and, correspondingly, the presentation of consciousness is dropped at this moment. Instead, the display of her emotion is delegated to non-verbal behaviour: Dorothea's smile can suggest something which the character is as yet unable, or only partially able, to verbalize. This body language, then, has a more independent quality of expression than the illustrating gesture in the passage from *Mrs Dalloway* quoted above.

The fact that body language is especially effective in the portrayal of unconscious or preverbal states of mind[28] is also evident in the following example from Ian McEwan's *The Comfort of Strangers*. In the apartment of their new Venetian acquaintances, Mary has seen the photograph of a man. When she observes Colin standing on the balcony of their hotel room, she seems to make a connection, on a preconscious level, between the photo she has seen and Colin. She becomes fully aware of this connection only later, in a nightmare. To the reader, however, it is already suggested through an externalizer of her original thought process. Once again, body language is used in order to avoid verbalizing that which cannot (yet) be verbalized by the character:

> when Colin shifted his position a little, as though stepping around something at his feet, her smile froze, and then faded. She looked down puzzled, and glanced over her shoulder across the water again ... Mary looked towards the balcony, and was able to smile again, but once Colin had gone inside, and in the few seconds she had to herself before he joined her, she stared unseeing at the distant quayside, her head cocked, as though struggling, without success, with her memory. (83)

The increasing tendency for novelists to employ internal viewpoints, then, does not mean that emotional displays and externalizers have become less frequent. However, body language is, to a certain extent, used in new ways. Not only have the techniques for the presentation of consciousness been further developed, but the body language indicating mental states has also been refined and is used to portray powerful emotions as well as subtle states of mind.

4.3.3 The Indication of Interpersonal Relationships

Another main function of body language in the narrative text is to indicate interpersonal relationships between the characters. This function is continually gaining significance in the history of the novel. The exploration of the ways in which people relate to one another, both privately and socially, has become one of the main domains of the modern novel: in many texts considered for the historical part of this study, NVC indicating interpersonal relationships constitutes a large part of the body language described, for example, in the novels of John Braine, Iris Murdoch, Doris Lessing, John Fowles, Ian McEwan, or Anita Brookner. Chapter 5 will show how body language in this function begins to achieve a high status in the eighteenth century, and how an ever-expanding range of interpersonal relationships is expressed with the use of NVC.

4.3.4 *Characterization and Character Identification*

The construction of fictional characters has been considered a creative process taking place in the reader's imagination:

> This means that they are psychic phenomena formed by the reader in analogy to real-life characters, with the difference that their creation is not based on the open context of our experience of life but on the distinct and restricted information derived from the reading of one particular fictional text. This implies that the same categories for subsuming masses of detail (such as type, stereotype, individual, character trait, habit, mood, action, thinking, feeling) are active in the creation of fictional characters as in our perception of real-life characters. (Grabes 1990, 119)[29]

The body language which indicates traits of fictional characters will be interpreted largely on the basis of a reader's ordinary non-verbal competence. Subject-related externalizers can imply the personality structures of fictional characters (dispositions, opinions, attitudes, values) just as they do in real life. For example, when Hagar in Margaret Laurence's *The Stone Angel* shies away from the touch of others, she is characterized as a person who has difficulties forming relationships with others (see pages 67–8). In fiction, as in reality, body language also indicates a person's social and gender role, age, cultural belonging, and social status (see chapter 3, page 42).

In the narrative text, where non-verbal behaviour is mediated through narration, characterizing body language can, however, be strongly coloured by a narrator's perception or complemented with explicit glosses and comments. An example is the characterization of Uriah Heep in Charles Dickens's *David Copperfield* (1849–50). Uriah's externalizers of character traits constantly contradict his verbally asserted 'humility' and indicate his coldness (his fake smile and expressionless eyes) and slyness (his snaky twistings):

> I observed that he had not such a thing as a smile about him, and that he could only widen his mouth and make two hard creases down his cheeks, one on each side, to stand for one ... I observed that his nostrils, which were thin and pointed, with sharp dints in them, had a singular and most uncomfortable way of expanding and contracting themselves; that they seemed to twinkle instead of his eyes, which hardly ever twinkled at all ...
>
> He had a way of writhing when he wanted to express enthusiasm, which was very ugly; and which diverted my attention from the compliment he had paid my relation, to the snaky twistings of his throat and body. (196–7)

Here the body language clearly contributes to the negative characterization provided by the narrator's explicit comments ('most uncomfortable way,' 'very ugly'), and is thus essential in evoking the reader's antipathy.

As a means of characterization, body language appears to occur, on average, less frequently in narrative literature than with the functions already discussed above. This may, perhaps, be explained by the important role which another form of body semiotics plays in characterization. Writers from the Middle Ages until the nineteenth century were influenced by physiognomy,[30] and even in the twentieth-century novel, characterization through permanent physical features is given great significance. When non-verbal *behaviour* is used as a means of characterization, it is also often marked as habitual and thus emphasizes the stability of a character trait:

> Margaret could not help her looks; but the short curled upper lip, the round, massive up-turned chin, the manner of carrying her head, her movements, full of a soft feminine defiance, always gave strangers the impression of haughtiness. (Gaskell, *North and South*, 62)

> It was Alfred's Yule's [*sic*] characteristic that he could do nothing lighthandedly. He seemed always to converse with effort; he took a seat with stiff ungainliness; he walked with a stumbling or sprawling gait. (Gissing, *New Grub Street*, 30)

However, a growing tendency to rely on body language for characterization is apparent even when Johann Kaspar Lavater's *Physiognomische Fragmente* (1775–9) sparked a golden age of physiognomy in the eighteenth century.[31] Since the mid-eighteenth century, a new interest in *individualistic* characterization results in an increased interest in idiosyncratic body language. Sterne's *Tristram Shandy* represents a high point of such individualized body language. Every character in this novel is associated with idiosyncratic facial expressions, practical actions, or postures. Uncle Toby, a philanthropist, is associated with good-natured expressions of the face, Corporal Trim with exaggerated rhetorical poses, and Tristram's choleric father with vehement movements, as in chapter 41 of book 3:

> My father thrust back his chair, – rose up, – put on his hat, – took four long strides to the door, – jerked it open, – thrust his head half way out, – shut the door again, – took no notice of the bad hinge, – returned to the table, – pluck'd my mother's thread-paper out of Slawkenbergius's book, – went hastily to his bureau, – walk'd slowly back, twisting my mother's thread-paper about his thumb, – unbutton'd his waistcoat, – threw my mother's thread-paper into the fire, – bit her sattin [*sic*] pin-cushion in two, fill'd his mouth with bran, – confounded it ... (282–3)

In *Tristram Shandy*, such non-verbal characteristics appear as leitmotifs. Apart from their function of defining a character, they thus also have the function of identifying a character: idiosyncratic body language makes a character easily recognizable by the reader. Identifying a character through features of his or her non-verbal behaviour was especially popular in the nineteenth-century novel; for example, the father in Disraeli's *Sybil* is associated with his benevolent smile, Rochester in *Jane Eyre* with his passionate look, the superficial, beautiful Rosamond in *Middlemarch* with her hair preening,[32] Casaubon in the same novel with the stooped posture of the scholar, the dandies in *The Picture of Dorian Gray* with casual postures in which they rest languidly on armchairs and sofas. Dickens's preference for this device is notorious, especially since his non-verbal leitmotifs are often absurd or grotesque and thus particularly conspicuous. In *Hard Times* (1854), Mr Bounderby is constantly putting his hands into his pockets; Louisa has an expressionless face and looks nobody but her brother in the eye, an expression of her lack of relationships to other people. A secondary character with an odd body language is Bitzer, who can be recognized not only by the way he constantly blinks his eyes, but also by the way he rubs his forehead with his knuckles. The function of a non-verbal leitmotif to identify a character becomes very obvious when Bitzer, in one passage, is introduced by his body language before he is named: 'The light porter placed the tea-tray on it, knuckling his forehead as a form of homage. "Thank you, Bitzer," said Mrs. Sparsit' (87). Especially when a secondary character has not appeared for some time, an idiosyncratic feature of body language is an economical means to remind the reader of his or her essential characteristics. This is important above all in the Victorian novel, in which the length, intricate plot structures, abundance of characters, and the serialized form in which the novels were originally published demand character traits that are easily identifiable and memorable.[33]

However, non-verbal leitmotifs are still to be found in the twentieth-century novel. In Virginia Woolf's *Mrs Dalloway*, Peter plays with his pocketknife; in Somerset Maugham's *The Razor's Edge*, the soft and absent-minded smile of Larry, the mystic and drop-out, is a reminder of his 'otherness': 'He smiled. **I must have remarked twenty times on the beauty of his smile**, it was so cosy, trustful, and sweet, it reflected the candour, the truthfulness of his charming nature; **but I must do so once again**, for now, besides all that, there was in it something rueful and tender' (296). In *The Power and the Glory*, Graham Greene works extensively with non-verbal leitmotifs, in both his secondary and his central characters. The dentist, who appears sporadically, can easily be recognized by his permanently open mouth; the 'half-caste,' the Judas figure of the novel, has the habit of rudely scratching himself, and the persecuted priest, a victim of the regime, is associated with his stooped body posture.

The definition of character through body language is also a highly suitable means to indicate contrasts or correspondences within a group of characters. In Greene's novel, the priest and his communist persecutor are opponents, but they resemble each other in the integrity with which they pursue their respective missions. This correspondence is indicated in parallel body postures, which are presented in an almost identical formulation:

> He [the priest] sat there **like a black question mark**, ready to go, ready to stay, poised on his chair. (15)

> The lieutenant stood there **like a little dark menacing question-mark** [*sic*] in the sun: his attitude seemed to indicate that he wouldn't even accept the benefit of shade from a foreigner. (35)

In Henry James's *The American*, body language is consistently used to draw attention to the contrasts and correspondences among the characters. Newman is characterized as self-confident and naturally relaxed in the way he casually stretches out his legs, or as open and friendly in the way he reaches out his hand as a greeting (see also Pelzer 1984, 25–67). His antagonist, Urbain de Bellegarde, on the contrary, stands out through his stiff non-verbal style and calculated poses; also, he will not give Newman his hand:

'I am delighted to know Mr. Newman,' said the marquis, with a low bow, but without offering his hand. (183)

The marquis was stationed before the fire, with his head erect and his hands behind him, in an attitude of formal expectancy. (204)

The old marquise, who also rejects Newman, demonstrates the same non-verbal rigidity as her son Urbain. In contrast, her second son, Newman's friend Valentin, resembles Newman in his casual and open non-verbal behaviour. He often stands in a relaxed pose, puts his hands in his pockets, has a friendly smile, and willingly greets people with a handshake. Body language links even those characters who seem to have nothing in common at first sight. The first French people Newman gets to know are the Nioches, social climbers and opportunists, who manage to make money even out of their first coincidental meeting with Newman; the daughter wants to sell him one of her paintings, the father offers to give him language lessons. Their flamboyant non-verbal style is essentially different from Newman's natural behaviour. This style is partly an externalizer of their cultural belonging;[34] above all, however, it highlights the Nioches's opportunism; their manner is always calculated to have a desired effect:

The cultivation of the fine arts appeared to necessitate, to her mind, a great deal of by-play, a great standing off with folded arms and head drooping from side to side, stroking of a dimpled chin with a dimpled hand, sighing and frowning and patting of the foot, fumbling in disordered tresses for wandering hair-pins. These performances were accompanied by a restless glance, which lingered longer than elsewhere upon the gentleman we have described. (36)

The old man drooped his head on one side and looked at him with an expression of pain, as if this were an unfeeling jest ...

M. Nioche turned to the confiding foreigner again, and stood rubbing his hands, with an air of seeming to plead guilty which was not intenser only because it was habitually so striking ...

'You are very good, sir; I am overcome!' said M. Nioche, throwing out his hands ...

M. Nioche bowed, with his hand on his heart. 'Very well, sir; you have already made me lively.' (41–4)

With their calculated body language, the Nioches share a characteristic with the aristocratic Urbain, in spite of their different social background and aims. The same is true for the way M. Nioche constantly rubs his hands, something his daughter also does repeatedly; in both characters, this body language indicates the purposefulness of their actions, as well as their anticipated success. Urbain de Bellegarde, too, rubs his hands when he sees a potential way of preventing his sister's liaison with Newman: 'The marquis, who had greeted Newman almost genially, stood apart, slowly rubbing his hands' (238). Thus the negative characters in the novel, despite their social differences, are grouped together through an instance of non-verbal behaviour.

Similarly, body language indicates important correspondences between characters in Margaret Atwood's *The Edible Woman*. The secondary characters in this social 'comedy' are, to some extent, symbolic. They serve as personal correlatives of the identity crisis which the protagonist is experiencing. In particular, Marian's coming to terms with her previous roles, both private and professional, is mirrored in her relationship with the student Duncan. In many interpretations of the novel Duncan is seen as Marian's *doppelgänger*;[35] this interpretation is strongly supported by Duncan's and Marian's body language. In his academic work, Duncan is 'stuck' just as Marian is stuck in her understanding of her female role. An externalizer of this stagnation is a posture typical for Duncan: he sits quietly on his bed, with his back to the wall. This is a position Marian is also found in repeatedly: 'I was leaning back against the wall' (73); 'to sit in this quiet room gazing up at the empty ceiling with my back against the cool wall' (100). She is described in this pose even *before* Duncan appears in the novel: 'In my room, I sat on the bed with my back against the wall, thinking' (43) – new evidence for the thesis that Duncan is Marian's projection rather than a 'real' character. Furthermore, Duncan is a narcissist, whose egocentrism is also emphasized in his poses; he often shrinks into himself and embraces himself:

He stood gazing at me solemnly, shoulders hunched, arms folded across his torso, holding his own elbows. (50)

> He was talking in a monotone, sitting hunched forward, his elbows on his knees, his head drawn down into the neck of his dark sweater like a turtle's into its shell. (91)

His narcissism parallels the extreme egocentrism which Marian has to experience in order to find herself – she takes on a similar, fetal position whenever she is with Duncan: 'She sank back, still with the sheet clutched around her and her knees drawn up' (238).

Apart from its role in characterization, NVC in the narrative text also contributes to the constitution of the fictional reality in other aspects. One of the main functions of NVC, at least in the modern novel, is its role in authenticating the fictional world and bringing it to life.

4.3.5 Authentication

One of the most widely acknowledged functions of literary body language is its contribution to the 'realism' of a narrative text.[36] Unfortunately, the concept of realism in literature lacks a clear definition despite a multitude of critical studies. When the 'realistic' effect of body language is spoken of, however, what is generally meant is an aspect of presentation which has also been referred to with terms such as 'authenticity,' 'reality effect,'[37] 'solidity of specification,'[38] 'formal realism,' and 'circumstantialism,'[39] or 'verisimilitude':

> The sense of being in the presence of actual individual things, events, people, and places, is the common experience we expect to find in literature; and it is this aspect of the illusion of reality that we may call VERISIMILITUDE ... it includes incidental particularities which give us the sense of knowing places, people, times, occasions, etc, as if we were participants or observers ourselves. (Leech and Short 1981, 156–7)

Body language can help to create an impression of authenticity of the fictional world so long as it does not counter the impression of verisimilitude through a bizarre non-verbal style or a heavily distorted perspectivization. An overspecification of details may also counter the reality effect: 'The exhaustive description ... is false to the psychology of perception. We tend not to notice what is not exceptional' (Irwin 1979, 20). Leech and Short (1981) observe the same phenomenon in the context of fictional speech: so-called non-fluency signals (hesitation, pauses, or discontinuous syntax) are typical for spontaneous, natural speech, but they are generally not reported in the characters' conversations in the narrative text. Nevertheless, fictional dialogues do not appear 'unrealistic' for the lack of these signals: 'Since features of non-fluency are normally overlooked by participants in real life conversation, they can be omitted from fictional conversation without impairing the realistic effect' (165). It is therefore not the absence of non-fluency signals that has an unrealistic effect; rather, their presence (as long as they do not occur excessively) makes for a special reality effect. With regard to body language, too, it can be said that its presence can have a particular effect of authentication, but that its absence does not automatically mean a reduced verisimilitude. Body language contributes to the authentication of the fictional world in a number of ways; only a few will be introduced here.

For example, NVC plays an important role in making a conversation in a fictional situation resemble a conversation in real life. As has been shown, complex non-verbal behaviour on the part of both the speaker and the listener is a natural accompaniment to all speech. It can be captured to only a limited extent in the narrative text (see pages 95–9),[40] but the partial inclusion of this non-verbal behaviour makes a fictional conversation seem closer to reality. This effect does not rely only on the fact that behaviour 'normally' concomitant with speech is included in the text. The characters' speech itself achieves a more authentic quality when it is accompanied by NVC. The presence of deictic illustrators, for example, allows the characters' speech to contain exophoric reference (usually in the form of pronouns), which is highly characteristic of natural speech. In addition, the natural fragmentation of speech is imitated more closely when body language complements the characters' speech. Accompanied with body language, the dialogue in the narrative text may approximate natural speech to the same degree as the dialogue in modern drama, which normally anticipates the 'gesturality' at the time of performance: 'In its "incompleteness," its need for physical contextualization, dramatic discourse is invariably marked by a performability, and above all by a potential gesturality, which the language of narrative does not normally possess since its context is described rather than "pragmatically" pointed to' (Elam 1980, 142). The following example comes from the novel *The Tent Peg* (1981) by Aritha van Herk:

'Do you think Mackenzie will keep on doing this?' she asks.

'Coming out in the field? Of course. It's his life.' I stare at her. 'Why?'

'I don't know. A feeling.'

'He seems to be more positive. He was unhappy at the beginning of the summer, but I don't think he'll abandon geology.'

'What makes you guys do it?'

I take my time answering. 'The barrens. Going to places where nobody's been. The possibility of finding a mine.' I gesture at the fire. 'This.' (157)

The final paragraph of the quotation shows how an illustrator permits the conversation to use exophoric reference: 'this' for the fire around which the characters are sitting. In addition, the earlier non-verbal interpolations ('I stare at her' and 'I gesture at the fire') give the illusion of a pause in the conversation[41] and thus contribute to the imitation of a natural speech rhythm:

Without them the dialogue could seem too rapid and glib, too much like verbal ping-pong ... Just as the ten-minute interval in the theatre can somehow make more plausible a lapse of two years in the action of a play, so a number of brief descriptive phrases can dilate a passage of dialogue into something that will pass for equivalence with the time-scales of real life. In short, a set of interpolations with little or no descriptive usefulness can still serve a number of formal purposes. (Irwin 1979, 47–8)

Another area in which body language can contribute to verisimilitude is in the presentation of psychological states, even if older literature often employs a stereotypical and stylized body language for the expression of emotion. The more 'psychological' the novel becomes in its historical development, the more it makes use of a detailed and authentic body language of mental states. In this area, too, Henry James demonstrates a particular gift of observation. In *The American*, even Valentin, who is kindly disposed towards Newman, is uncomfortable when he hears of Newman's marriage plans; he shows his discomfort non-verbally: 'Bellegarde raised his hand to the back of his head and rubbed his hair quickly up and down, thrusting out the tip of his tongue as he did so' (157). After a family meeting, Valentin tells Newman that he will be allowed to marry Madame de Cintré. Not only does Valentin's brother, Urbain, still not accept the marriage, he is also angry about Valentin's lack of good manners; but he can keep his aristocratic composure. His repressed anger is noticeable only in minor details of his behaviour:

M. de Bellegarde looked at his brother with dangerous coldness, and gave a smile as thin as the edge of a knife. Then he removed a spark of cigar-ash from the sleeve of his coat; he fixed his eyes for a while on the cornice of the room, and at last he inserted one of his white hands into the breast of his waistcoat. 'I must apologise to you for the deplorable levity of my brother,' he said ... (209)

As modern popular handbooks of body language tell us, a person who picks off something from his or her clothing is probably reacting to a momentary annoyance, which he or she wants to remove or shake off.

Body language can also contribute to the cultural authenticity of literature. In the novels of Kazuo Ishiguro which are set in Japan, for example, body language helps to establish a cultural setting foreign to the European reader. The bow as a Japanese emblem of politeness and honour is mentioned with striking frequency, as in the following passage from *A Pale View of Hills* (1982):

Mrs Fujiwara saw us and came across the forecourt.

'Why, Ogata-San,' she exclaimed, recognizing him immediately, 'how splendid to see you again. It's been a long time, hasn't it?'

'A long time indeed.' Ogata-San returned the bow Mrs Fujiwara gave him. 'Yes, a long time.'

I was struck by the warmth with which they greeted each other, for as far as I knew Ogata-San and Mrs Fujiwara had never known one another well. They exchanged what seemed an endless succession of bows, before Mrs Fujiwara went to fetch us something to eat.

She returned presently with two steaming bowls, apologizing that she had nothing better for us. Ogata-San bowed appreciatively and began to eat. (149)

Besides numerous bows, in *An Artist of the Floating World* another nonverbal detail is encountered whose authenticating effect has even been emphasized by a reviewer.[42] When she covers her mouth with her hand while laughing, Ono's daughter demonstrates the traditional behaviour of Japanese women:[43] 'My daughter raised a hand to cover her laugh. "He must have been playing cowboys. When he plays cowboys, he tries to speak English"' (35). In this instance, the traditional body language also fulfils another function besides authentication. One of the themes of the novel is the Westernization (especially the Americanization) of Japan after its defeat in the Second World War. Ono's grandson, whose incomprehensible behaviour must be explained to Ono by his laughing daughter, represents this Westernization. His heroes are no longer the samurai which his grandfather drew in his paintings, but rather American cartoon characters like the Lone Ranger and Popeye. The link of traditional Japanese body language and a sentence which indicates the Americanization of the next generation echoes the juxtaposition of the new and the old in Japanese postwar society.

Body language can help to authenticate even fictional worlds that have no direct reference to empirical reality. So-called 'paleofiction' describes a primeval world.[44] In fiction of this kind, body language, as a means of communication inherent in humans and animals, can help to suggest an animal-like and widely preverbal state of primitive humanity. William Golding's *The Inheritors* (1955), for example, describes how a group of peaceful Neanderthals is decimated by a group of *homo sapiens sapiens*. The latter contain the roots of evil in them in a manner typical of the author's view of humankind. In an exemplary analysis of this novel, M.A.K. Halliday (1971) has shown how Golding makes use of various linguistic means to convey the limited cognitive capabilites of the Neanderthals. Golding's Neanderthals do have a language, but it does not always enable them to interpret their environment adequately or to think coherently. Their reactions are still highly dependent on instinct and reflex, and they mainly communicate their thoughts, feelings, and relationships non-verbally:

> Ha said nothing with his mouth but continued to smile. Then as they watched him, he moved both ears round, slowly and solemnly aiming them at Lok so that they said as clearly as if he had spoken: I hear you! Lok opened his mouth and his hair rose. He began to gibber wordlessly at the cynical ears and the half-smile. (38)

> Fa put her hands wide apart, watching Lok all the time. Then she began to bring them together. But though the tilt of her head, the eyebrows moved slightly up and apart asked a question she had no words with which to define it. She tried again. (49)

In these passages, the narrator's glosses emphasize the Neanderthals' limited capacity of verbalization. This makes them different from the superior *homo sapiens sapiens*: 'They did not gesticulate much nor dance out their meanings as Lok and Fa might have done but their thin lips puttered and flapped' (144–5). Apart from indicating different stages of human development, the contrast between body language and verbal language in the last sentence also implies a negative evaluation of language. It has replaced the clear and beautiful, 'dancing' gestures of the Neanderthals. The body of the new human is silenced, reduced to an unattractive flapping of the lips, whose meaning can no longer be easily interpreted, unlike the universally comprehensible body language of the Neanderthals. The language of the new people can be understood only by those who know its code. It thus excludes others from communication and becomes an instrument to spread evil.

A body language typical of age or gender can also function as an element of authentication, as in Anita Brookner's novel *A Friend from England* (1987). Here the first-person narrator becomes aware of her friend's increasing age when she notices her sitting posture, which is typical of older women: 'She sat with her ankles crossed and her knees slightly apart, in that posture that old women adopt' (90).[45] This non-verbal detail is of only subordinate significance for the general content of the passage, but it shows how 'carefully observed' it is. In Salinger's 'For Esmé – with Love and Squalor,' the non-verbal behaviour of Esmé's little brother is rendered with a similar sense of authentic detail:

> Charles gave me the fishy look my question deserved, then wriggled downward and forward in his chair till all of his body was under the table except his head, which he left, wrestler's-bridge style, on the chair seat ... He picked up a corner of the tablecloth and put it over his handsome, deadpan little face. (96–7)

> In response to this compliment, he sank considerably lower in his chair and again masked his face up to the eyes with a corner of the tablecloth. He then looked at me with his exposed eyes, which were full of slowly subsiding mirth and the pride of someone who knows a really good riddle or two. (99)

> I kept looking over at Charles, who had sat down and started to drink his tea, using both hands on the cup. (101)

The childishness of the five-year-old boy, as indicated through these externalizers, provides a foil for the precocious behaviour of his thirteen-year-old sister, who has been forced into the role of an adult through her parents' early death and the war.

Striking differences in gender can especially be seen in spatial and touch behaviour (see chapter 3, pages 71–3, 76–7). Samuel Richardson, who addressed a primarily female readership in his novels, is often considered to have an extraordinary insight into the female psyche. This is supported by the credibility with which he conveys the gender-specific sensitivity for NVC of his female characters, for example, in *Clarissa*

(1747–9). Clarissa reacts extremely sensitively to the spatial proximity of the hated man she is expected to marry:

> Had the wretch kept his seat, it might have been well enough; But the bent and broad-shouldered creature must needs rise, and stalk towards a chair; which was just by that which was set for me.
>
> I removed it to a distance, as if to make way to my own ...
>
> He took the removed chair, and drew it so near mine, squatting in it with his ugly weight, that he pressed upon my hoop. – I was so offended (all I had heard, as I said, in my head) that I removed to another chair ...
>
> I saw that my Father was excessively displeased. When angry, no man's countenance ever shews it so much as my Father's. Clarissa Harlowe! said he with a big voice – and there he stopped. – Sir! said I, trembling and courtesying (for I *had* not then sat down again): And put my chair nearer the wretch, and sat down – My face, as I could feel, all in a glow.
>
> Make Tea, child, said my kind Mamma: Sit by me, Love; and make Tea.
>
> I removed with pleasure to the seat the man had quitted; and being thus indulgently put into employment, soon recovered myself ... (1:100)

Even though Clarissa's reaction seems exaggerated, the description has an authenticity – at least for female readers – which contributes greatly to the novel's intensity of feeling.[46]

Women's greater alertness to touch is supported, for example, by a study of American female college students:

> Women seem to be more concerned about the type of touch than men ... The differences between the two sexes were striking. Males understood the differences among patting, stroking, and squeezing, but were not concerned with the body part being touched. Men felt that warmth, love, sexual desire, and pleasantness all had the same meaning. On the other hand, women were very concerned about the body part involved. They felt that touch on the hands, head, face, arms, and back meant love and friendliness. However, they felt that touch in the genital areas and breasts was a sign of sexual desire. Thus, women distinguished the type of touch and part of body being touched to mean either friendship or sexual desire. Men associated friendship and sexual desire with similar touch. (Richmond, McCroskey, and Payne 1987, 215)

The passage from Penelope Lively's *Moon Tiger* cited earlier in the context of perspectivization (pages 116–17) appears highly authentic with regard to this gender-specific difference – if only, perhaps, to female readers, who can empathize with the girl's sensitive reaction because of their own experience. A haptic contact between the adolescent siblings is first described from the brother's perspective, then from the sister's:

> And he stabs with a finger at Claudia's crotch, pushing the stuff of her dress between her thighs. Her eyes widen – in surprise? In outrage? They stare at each other.

> And he stabs with his finger against her dress, between her legs.
>
> And her anger, strangely, evaporates; eclipsed by something different, equally forceful, baffling. Something mysterious is present, something she cannot nail or name. She stares in wonder at her grey-flannelled brother. (27)

As has been shown, the syntactic structures of the parallel passages alone give an impression of the varying degrees of intensity with which the brother and sister experience this touch. This intensity corresponds with the gender-specific differences that have been established: the brother is puzzled about his sister's strong reaction, shows no sensitivity for the intimacy of his touch; for the girl, however, his touching her intimate parts has a sexual significance, even if she is not fully aware of it.

Observations on gender-specific body language suggest, then, that the impression of authenticity evoked in the reader can vary. What a female reader finds to be an especially accurate description may not cause a reality effect in a male reader at all. An effect of authentication through body language thus depends on the non-verbal competence of the individual reader: his or her everyday knowledge of and degree of sensitivity to body language, as well as familiarity with historical and culture-specific forms of body language.

4.3.6 Dramatization

Another literary function of body language is often mentioned in connection with the authentication effect. Michael Irwin (1979), for example, observes the following about the novels of George Eliot: 'George Eliot's tendency to concentrate too narrowly on the moral and intellectual life of her characters is greatly alleviated by her constant awareness of physical movements and mannerisms' (49). What Irwin describes with the word 'alleviate,' could be more accurately described with the concept of 'dramatization': body language helps to illustrate a fictional event, to make it more scenic, concrete, and vivid.[47] Body language that does not have an authentic effect – for example, a body language distorted for comic or satirical purposes – may well have a dramatic quality.

Every detail of body language makes the fictional reality more concrete. In particular, however, a scenic effect similar to the effect of drama is achieved by the account of body language that accompanies speech: it makes the characters appear as speakers with bodies; their non-verbal behaviour contributes to the emotional and interpersonal tension of an episode, and the episode can be more easily visualized than without the non-verbal 'stage directions.' A very vivid and 'visual' example is an episode from George Meredith's *The Ordeal of Richard Feverel* (1859), in which the young Richard must apologize to a farmer for a fire he has started as revenge for the hiding he has received. Richard finds it difficult to utter his apology, as his nervous blinking indicates behind the façade of his initially arrogant sentences. The farmer enjoys the situation in which the young gentleman must humiliate himself, and makes the situation especially uncomfortable for Richard by calling him a liar and thereby challenging Richard's temperament again:

He commenced blinking hard in preparation for the horrible dose to which delay and the farmer's cordiality added inconceivable bitters ...

'Mr. Blaize! I have come to tell you that I am the person who set fire to your rick the other night.'

An odd contraction formed about the farmer's mouth. He changed his posture, and said, 'Ay? that's what ye're come to tell me, sir?'

'Yes!' said Richard firmly.

'And that be all?'

'Yes!' Richard reiterated.

The farmer again changed his posture. 'Then, my lad, ye've come to tell me a lie!'

Farmer Blaize looked straight at the boy, undismayed by the dark flush of ire he had kindled.

'You dare to call me a liar!' cried Richard, **starting up**.

'I say,' the farmer renewed his first emphasis, and **smacked his thigh thereto,** 'that's a lie!'

Richard held out his clenched fist. 'You have twice insulted me.' ...

'Sit ye down, sit ye down, young master,' said the farmer, **indicating the chair and cooling the outburst with his hand** ...

Richard, disdaining to show signs of being pacified, **angrily reseated himself** ...

'Come,' continued the farmer, not unkindly, 'what else have you to say?'

Here was the same bitter cup he had already once drained brimming at Richard's lips again! ...

The boy blinked and tossed it off.

'I came to say that I regretted the revenge I had taken on you for your striking me.'

Farmer Blaize nodded. (60–3)

What is immediately striking in this episode is its large proportion of NVC, which takes up almost as much space as the characters' speech. Various functional classes of NVC underscore the different facets of the interaction between the characters: there are emotional displays of Richard's nervousness, embarrassment, and anger, as well as externalizers of Farmer Blaize's superior position in the situation and his amusement; in addition, illustrators help to make the scene concrete. Last, but not least, the extensive use of NVC effectively narrows the gap between time of narration and narrated time: the uncomfortable conversation seems just as endless to the reader as it does to Richard. The frequency with which Farmer Blaize's body language precedes his speech also increases this effect, because his delayed answers suggest how Richard is being tortured by the sly farmer.

4.3.7 Excursus: Non-verbal Comedy and Satire

The comic body has a long tradition in narrative literature as well as in the dramatic arts.[48] Because it easily lends itself to distortion and exaggeration, body language can be an especially effective instrument of comedy and caricature, although this is certainly not one of the central functions of body language in literature. On the one hand, a character's non-verbal behaviour itself can be 'deviant' in a manner that is perceived as comical. In the Middle Ages and the Renaissance, there existed a convention, on the theatrical stage as well as in narrative literature, according to which high-ranking (non-comic) characters were presented with a measured body language, while the bodily movements of low-ranking (comic) characters were uncontrolled and exaggerated. A modern example of a comic non-verbal style is found in Peter Carey's *Oscar and Lucinda*. Oscar, the missionary, is an 'odd-bod' whose erratic movements do not fit into the world of 'normal' people. The grotesque effect of his bodily movements is especially blatant when they are parodied by another character in the following episode:[49]

[Mr Borrodaile] clasped his big hands together on his breast. He inclined his upper body backwards from the vertical. He sucked in his ruddy cheeks and raised his eyes like a choirboy in procession. He walked. He was a wooden doll with tangled strings. His legs jerked sideways then up [*sic*]. The upper body swung from side to side like the mainmast of a brig at anchor in a swell. The hands unclasped and clasped and then flew apart to grasp at – at what? A butterfly? A hope? A prayer? (245)

In Aldous Huxley's *Antic Hay* (1923), the satire of social types also relies on striking non-verbal styles. Bojanus, a sophisticated gentlemen's tailor, for example, distinguishes himself through exaggeratedly elegant behaviour, which matches his affected verbal style:

Mr Bojanus looked up archly with a sideways cock of his head that tilted the rigid points of his waxed moustache. The fingers of his right hand were thrust into the bosom of his frock-coat and his toes were turned out in the dancing-master's First Position. 'A light spring great-coat, is it? Or a new suit? I notice,' his eye travelled professionally up and down Gumbril's long, thin form, 'I notice that the garments you are wearing at present, Mr Gumbril, look – how shall I say? – well, a trifle negleejay, as the French would put it, a trifle negleejay.' (31)

In these cases, the characters' body language itself is to be taken as comic; in other cases, a character's body language is perceived in a comically or satirically distorted manner. An example of this type is found in Thomas Nashe's picaresque novel *The Unfortunate Traveller* (1594). The objects of satire in Nashe's *speculum mundi* are individuals as well as representatives of various social and national groups. Time and again, their body language is grotesquely exaggerated by Jack Wilton, the first-person narrator. In one episode, Jack is able to escape a vivisection to be performed by a Jewish doctor in Rome at the last minute. The doctor's anger is manifested in an emotional display which the narrator gives extreme and absurd dimensions:

So swelled Zadok, and was ready to burst out of his skin and shoot his bowels like chainshot full at Zachary's face for bringing him such baleful tidings. His eyes glared and burnt blue like brimstone and aqua vitae set on fire in an egg-shell; his very nose lightened glowworms. His teeth crashed and grated together like the joints of a high building cracking and rocking like a cradle whenas a tempest takes her full butt against his broad side. (294)

Zadok not only appears to be comical through this exaggeration, but he is also satirically dehumanized; comparisons with lifeless objects and animals highlight his dehumanization.

Conventional body language is especially suitable for an ironic or parodic portrayal. In his burlesque of the epic in *Tom Jones* (1749), Henry Fielding uses, amongst other things, the conventional body language of this genre. The burlesque is defined by a ridiculous disparity between subject matter and style. In the following example from *Tom Jones,* a very commonplace event is portrayed in the ceremonious style of the epic. In chapter 8 of book 4, Tom's lover Molly and her rival fight each other tooth and nail in a comic version of the heroic duel. Watching this spectacle, Tom breaks into epic despair: '*Tom* raved like a Madman, beat his Breast, tore his Hair, stamped on the Ground, and vowed the utmost Vengeance on all who had been concerned' (184). In the spirit of the burlesque, these traditional gestures of despair and pain are obviously inappropriate to the banal situation in which they occur.

A further subtype of non-verbal comedy is based on the misunderstanding of NVC. Medieval 'narratives of gesture,' in which body language is decoded incorrectly within the fictional situation (see page 52), are almost always of a comic nature. In the modern novel, the comic potential of such misunderstandings is still occasionally used. In an episode in Iris Murdoch's *Under the Net* (1954), the protagonist finds himself in an embarrassing situation. Squatting on the stairs of a fire escape, he is eavesdropping on some people in an apartment. When he is discovered by the neighbours, he tries to communicate with them through gestures but only makes the situation worse by triggering a series of false decodings:

> Almost in despair I nodded, and added to my smile such gestures indicative of total well-being as it is possible to perform in a sitting position with one's back against a door. I shook hands with myself, held up my thumb and index finger in the form of an O, and smiled even more emphatically.
>
> 'If you ask me, I think he's an escaped loonie,' said the second woman. They retired a little from the window ...
>
> 'Can't you say anything?' called the man on the fire escape.
>
> This was becoming embarrassing. I glared at him, and pointing into my mouth shook my head vigorously. I wasn't sure whether nodding wouldn't have conveyed my meaning more clearly, but the possibilities of misunderstanding were in any case so enormous that it didn't seem to matter much one way or the other.

'He's hungry,' said the woman in the pinafore. (117–18)

As discussed in the last seven sections, body language can contribute in various ways to the constitution of fictional reality in the narrative text. However, body language in literature is also significant outside the immediate role it plays in the fictional situation. For example, it can serve as an image or help to develop the theme(s) of a text.

4.3.8 Body Language Imagery

As a visible element, body language is predestined to be used as an image. In the drama and novel of the Victorian period, for example, melodramatic body language frequently has an additional layer of meaning. In general, melodrama 'demonstrates over and over that the signs of ethical forces can be discovered and can be made legible' (Brooks 1976, 20). Emotional displays in the melodramatic episodes in Dickens's novels are often legible in exactly this sense. Nancy, the gangster bride in *Oliver Twist*, is a fallen woman whose conscience, however, is still intact. A conventional, easily readable body language of affect shows that she is devastated by the knowledge of the crimes committed by Fagin and her lover, Bill Sykes:

The girl said nothing more; but, **tearing her hair and dress in a transport of passion**, made such a rush at the Jew as would probably have left signal marks of her revenge upon him, had not her wrists been seized by Sikes at the right moment; upon which, she made a few ineffectual struggles, and **fainted**. (98)

After completely exhausting herself, she stopped to take breath: and, as if suddenly recollecting herself, and deploring her inability to do something she was bent upon, **wrung her hands, and burst into tears**. (247)

In contrast to Nancy, Rose Maylie is the angel figure of the novel. The gratitude and adoration which Nancy feels for her is conveyed through an emblem of prayer, which leaves no doubt at all as to the novel's moral ideal:

'Oh!' said the earnest girl, **folding her hands** as the tears coursed down her face, 'do not turn a deaf ear to the entreaties of one of your own sex ...'

'Lady,' cried the girl, **sinking on her knees**, 'dear, sweet, angel lady, you *are* the first that ever blessed me with such words as these ...!' (254)[50]

Nancy's ultimate moral conversion as she is dying is also shown with a posture of prayer:

> She staggered and fell: nearly blinded with the blood that rained down from a deep gash in her forehead; but raising herself, with difficulty, **on her knees**, drew from her bosom a white handkerchief – Rose Maylie's own – and **holding it up, in her folded hands, as high towards Heaven as her feeble strength would allow**, breathed one prayer for mercy to her Maker. (302)

The symbolic meaning of this body language is enhanced by another detail: the white, untainted handkerchief, given to her by Rose Maylie, which the dying Nancy is holding up.

Some modern novelists, too, seem to have a particular fondness for symbolic body language. As we have already seen (pages 138–9), the body language in Margaret Atwood's *The Edible Woman* is frequently used with a figurative meaning. In *The Handmaid's Tale*, too, we find a number of strong non-verbal images: for example, in an episode in which Offred reflects on the restrictive circumstances of her life. In these circumstances, even the limited freedom she enjoys in her room becomes a treasured possession: 'But a chair, sunlight, flowers: these are not to be dismissed. I am alive, I live, I breathe, I put my hand out, unfolded, into the sunlight. Where I am is not a prison but a privilege' (18). As an image, the hand reaching towards the life-giving sun points towards Offred's will to survive, a desire that has remained strong in her despite her humiliating role as birthing slave. Atwood's preference for figurative body language emerges especially clearly where she uses body language to develop the theme of a novel.

4.3.9 Thematic Body Language

Examples of body language in a thematic function have already been discussed: in Henry James's *The American*, the characters' postures reflect the opposite world-views represented by the democratic American and the French aristocracy. Newman's frequent inability to decode the body language of his opponents points towards his disorientation in a foreign culture and society, in other words, to one of the main themes of James's entire work. In Jane Austen's *Pride and Prejudice*, similar problems of decoding body language contribute to the development of the central theme already indicated in the title of the novel. In J.D. Salinger's 'For Esmé – with Love and Squalor,' the abundance of NVC that initiates and maintains contact between the main characters indicates the value of interpersonal relationships. In Margaret Atwood's *The Handmaid's Tale* and Marge Piercy's *Woman on the Edge of Time*, body language helps to emphasize the contrast between the 'good' and the 'bad' worlds portrayed in these two utopian novels. Atwood generally has a tendency to use NVC thematically, as shall be shown in a discussion of *Surfacing* (1972) and *Bodily Harm* (1981).

Surfacing presents a quest that combines real, mythical, and psychological dimensions. Both myth and psychology represent areas in which the non-verbal is of particular significance. The nameless protagonist of the novel begins to search for her missing father in the Quebec wilderness; this voyage also leads her into the repressed subconscious of her disturbed self. At the beginning of the novel, she is a stranger to herself, her feelings are numbed, and she has great difficulties in making contact with others – symptoms which are characteristic of schizophrenia.[51] The protagonist's crisis has been triggered by the repressed memory of the abortion of her only child; however, a more fundamental psychological problem is rooted in her childhood. Her parents have confronted the child with contradictory ways of relating to life: 'Her father represents the forces of reason and logic; he is the head. Her mother embodies the intuitional, instinctual realm of gesture and feeling; she is the body' (Grace 1980, 102–3). Instead of a union of the two ways of relating, a split has occurred in the protagonist between head and body, thinking and feeling. The head has gained supremacy: 'At some point my neck must have closed over, pond freezing or a wound, shutting me into my head' (348).

Surfacing is based on the assumption that this domination of the head is harmful. Throughout the novel, the intellect, logical thinking, is associated with *logos*, the word: thought is only possible in categories provided by language. These categories, however, involve fragmentation: language digitalizes reality, separates it into individual words, such as 'head' and 'body': 'The language is wrong, it shouldn't have different words for them ... if the head is detached from the body both of them will die' (323). Thus language, too, is often presented as being negative in *Surfacing*.[52]

In her head-dominated existence, language is the primary means of communication for the protagonist, while she has difficulties in the area of non-verbal communication.[53] She can therefore not express her feelings, because verbal language is only an imperfect means of communication in this particular area:

'Do you love me, that's all,' he said. 'That's the only thing that matters.' ... He must have known what he meant but it was an imprecise word; the Eskimoes [*sic*] had fifty-two names for snow because it was important to them, there ought to be as many for love.

'I want to,' I said. 'I do in a way.' I hunted through my brain for any emotion that would coincide with what I'd said. (349)

It follows that the protagonist's healing has to take place in the area of the non-verbal.[54] What ultimately has to be achieved, however, is a reintegration of the verbal and the non-verbal. This is implied in the protagonist's memory of her mother, whom she has for a long time rejected as a model in favour of her father. Although the mother has chosen to approach life in a natural and instinctive way, it is certainly not a wordless approach. A decisive experience in the protagonist's childhood is her mother's confrontation with a bear she is able to chase away with a combination of language and body language: 'That was the picture I kept, my mother seen from the back, arms upraised as though she was flying, and the bear terrified. When she told the story later she said she'd been scared to death but I couldn't believe that, she had been so positive, assured, **as if she knew a foolproof magic formula: gesture and word**' (326). Before the protagonist discovers this magic formula for herself, she must go through a phase in which the body and the non-verbal finally gain the upper hand after a long period of time. She finds the copies of rock paintings which her father has made as a non-verbal guide towards her destination. When she dives into a lake in search of these paintings, she discovers the corpse of her disappeared father, which triggers the memory of her aborted embryo and initiates a process of self-healing. As another non-verbal clue, the mother has left her daughter a child's drawing, which suggests that a new pregnancy will solve her trauma; she attempts to reunite with her lover, Joe, in order to conceive a new child. This first step in overcoming her lack of relationships is introduced with haptic behaviour: 'I touched him on the arm with my hand. My hand touched his arm. Hand touched arm. Language divides us into fragments, I wanted to be whole' (381). In the final part of the novel, the practice of Indian rites pushes the protagonist's healing process forward.

Rites represent a special area of (emblematic) NVC, in which individual non-verbal acts are joined into one symbolic significance. Although rites can also contain verbal elements, their significance rests primarily on the non-verbal components:

In the first place language is not well adapted to describing subjective emotional experiences and the niceties of social relations, especially for primitive people ... Secondly, verbal expression does not evoke powerful emotional feelings, produce bodily or psychological healing, or effect changes in social relationships ... Thirdly, some personal and interpersonal problems can evidently be handled better if they do not come fully into consciousness, where their contradictions and difficulties would be disturbing or embarrassing. (Argyle 1975, 188)

The more deeply Atwood's protagonist falls into a trance in which she performs her rites, the less significant does language become: 'It must be either English or French but I can't recognize it as any language I've ever heard or known' (412). After the ritual behaviour has ended, however, speech returns, because the mother's model contains 'gesture *and* word'; human beings consist of 'body *and* head.' The relationships the protagonist now wishes to have with her fellow human beings is not possible without any language at all: 'For us it's necessary, the intercession of words' (419).

In Atwood's *Bodily Harm* (1981), touching behaviour is important in the development of and connection between various thematic strands.[55] The question about being touched and not being touched on a figurative level is made concrete in the novel through haptic behaviour. The novel unites a personal with a political theme, as is already evident in the double meaning of the title. The journalist Rennie has survived a cancer operation and the resulting break-up of two relationships, when she is given the assignment to write a travel report on a Carribean island. The mastectomy has left deep scars, both physically and psychologically. On the island, Rennie hopes to be distracted from her anxieties and problems, but instead, she becomes involved in a *coup d'état* against her will.

Like many of Atwood's characters, Rennie is a non-toucher. The trauma of her illness has only exacerbated a problem that has its roots in Rennie's childhood. One of her key experiences was her grandmother's refusal to communicate comfort and safety to her by holding her:

I'm crying, I'm holding my grandmother around both legs ... I want forgiveness, but she's prying my hands away finger by finger ...

As a child I learned three things well: how to be quiet, what not to say, and **how to look at things without touching them.** (53–4)

This strictly visual approach to the world leads to an impoverishment of the individual:[56] Rennie does not make close contacts with others, and she does not participate in the world. Rennie's grandmother, in her old age, is 'punished' for her rejecting behaviour by the delusion of having lost her hands and can only be calmed down when someone holds her hands. Her granddaughter, however, is no longer capable of performing this act of sympathy: 'She puts her own hands behind her and backs away' (297).

Rennie also shies away from touch as an adult. On the Caribbean island she runs away in a state of panic from a beggar who wants to wish her luck by touching her (75). She is repulsed by the hands of Lora, another young woman: 'She wouldn't want to touch this gnawed hand, or have it touch her' (86). On the other hand, Rennie longs to be touched. She falls in love with the surgeon Daniel, who is holding her hand when she regains consciousness after her operation: 'he was dragging her back into it, this life that he had saved. By the hand' (32). She believes that his hands have healing powers: 'the touch of the hand that could transform you, change everything, magic' (195). But Daniel can only heal Rennie physically, not psychologically. The latter happens only on the Caribbean island, where the motif of the magic hands is taken up in several variations: the beggar wants to bring Rennie good luck; an old woman has the gift to heal physically through touch (194). Rennie makes a decisive step towards her psychological healing in her relationship with the adventurer Paul, with whom she has an affair. In spite of her scar, Paul does not shy away from touching Rennie: 'he's touching her, she can still be touched' (204). Paul, then, fulfils Rennie's longing to be touched, but she is still not capable of actively touching someone herself. The final step in Rennie's personal development is linked with the development of her political awareness.

The principle 'to look at things without touching them' has also been formative in Rennie's conception of her career as a journalist. She comes to the island as a professional tourist, and wants to remain so despite the tense political situation: 'There's nothing to worry about, nothing can touch her. She's a tourist' (203). However, she is pulled into the confrontations of the rival parties by everyone she meets on the island, and, significantly, she is touched by all of these people as well.

Rennie ends up in jail as a political prisoner and must share a cell with Lora. Here her process of becoming politically and humanly conscious is completed. Rennie is determined to become a committed journalist should she ever be freed. She also overcomes her fear of touching. Lora, whom she found repulsive earlier, is brutally abused in the prison. Confronted with this form of 'bodily harm,' Rennie remembers her failure to treat her grandmother with sympathy. For Lora, she herself will now practise the magic of touch; she tries to pull the unconscious Lora back to life:

> she has to pull her through ... this is a gift, this is the hardest thing she's ever done.
>
> She holds the hand, perfectly still, with all her strength. Surely, if she can only try hard enough, something will move and live again, something will get born. (299)

Various motifs and plot lines merge in this instance of touch: bodily as well as psychological injury and healing, the past and the future, the political and the personal development of the protagonist. Haptic behaviour is essential in weaving all these threads together.

4.3.10 Technical and Structural Functions of Body Language in the Narrative Text

A number of technical and structural functions have already been mentioned: body language can play a role in the structure of narrative transmission (pages 107–23) or help to establish contrasts and correspondences among the characters (pages 136–8). Used as a leitmotif, it can increase the coherence of the text (pages 135–6). Occasionally, one also finds other ways in which body language serves to establish textual coherence. In the novel of the eighteenth century, for example, the narrators tend to make extensive digressions which interrupt the action of the novel for quite a length of time. The points at which the narrator breaks away from the plot can be marked by a 'freezing' of the characters' body language. When the narrator re-enters the action after his digression, the repetition of the frozen body language serves as a reminder of what had previously been narrated. In chapter 5 of book 5 of Fielding's *Tom Jones*, for example, Tom discovers his teacher, the Philosopher Square, in a compromising pose with his lover Molly:

> as *Molly* pronounced those last Words, which are recorded above, the wicked Rug got loose from its Fastning, and discovered every thing hid behind it; where among other female Utensils appeared ... the Philosopher *Square*, in a Posture (for the Place would not near admit his standing upright) as ridiculous as can possibly be conceived.
>
> The Posture, indeed, in which he stood, was not greatly unlike that of a Sol-

dier who is tyed Neck and Heels; or rather resembling the Attitude in which we often see Fellows in the public Streets of *London*, who are not suffering but deserving punishment by so standing. He had a Night-cap belonging to *Molly* on his Head, and his two large Eyes, the Moment the Rug fell, stared directly at *Jones*; so that when the Idea of Philosophy was added to the Figure now discovered, it would have been very difficult for any Spectator to have refrained from immoderate Laughter. (229–30)

The posture of the unhappy Square certainly contributes to the comedy of this scene; more importantly, however, it serves as the departure for a long excursus about the various episodes that led to Square's exposure. The digression ends with Square being freed from his frozen position:

Square no sooner made his Appearance than *Molly* flung herself back in her Bed, cried out she was undone, and abandoned herself to Despair ...

As to the Gentleman behind the Arras, he was not in much less Consternation. He stood for a while motionless, and seemed equally at a Loss what to say, or whither to direct his Eyes. *Jones*, tho' perhaps the most astonished of the three, first found his Tongue; and, being immediately recovered from those uneasy Sensations, which *Molly* by her Upbraidings had occasioned, he burst into a loud Laughter, and then saluting Mr. *Square*, advanced to take him by the Hand, and to relieve him from his Place of Confinement. (232–3)

In Sterne's *Tristram Shandy*, the gestures and postures of the characters repeatedly function as pins to hold Tristram's intricate narrative threads. In chapter 29 of book 3 the narration of the episode is begun in which Mr Shandy is told that his son's nose was damaged during his birth. In a pose of despair, which is described in minute detail, Mr Shandy collapses on his bed, where the narrator leaves him for the duration of a lengthy digression: 'To explain this, I must leave him upon the bed for half an hour, – and my good uncle *Toby* in his old fringed chair sitting beside him' (256). Only in chapter 2 of book 4 is this posture released with the narrator's return to the course of events. The details ensure that the description of the body language at this point is just as conspicuous as was the first mention of the pose:

My father lay stretched across the bed as still as if the hand of death had pushed him down, for a full hour and a half, before he began to play upon the floor with the toe of that foot which hung over the bed-side; my uncle *Toby*'s heart was a pound lighter for it. – In a few moments, his left-hand, the knuckles of which had all the time reclined upon the handle of the chamber-pot, came to its feeling – he thrust it a little more within the valance – drew up his hand, when he had done, into his bosom – gave a hem! – My good uncle *Toby*, with infinite pleasure, answered it ... (327)

Summary

The functions observed in the last few sections can be summarized in the following catalogue. One should keep in mind, however, that an instance of body language often fulfils multiple functions in the narrative text. Body language that is particularly intended to influence the reader's emotional reaction and sympathy was not specially considered, according to the concerns expressed in chapter 1 (pages 12–13). Since this function is, however, integral to the poetics of some literary genres, it is included in the catalogue.

What role does body language play in the constitution of fictional reality?
- as an element in the action
- as an indication of mental states
- as an indication of interpersonal relationships
- as a means of character definition and identification
- as a means of authentication
- as a means of dramatization

Is body language used:
- as an image?
- in the development of a theme?

Does body language in the narrative text perform a technical and/or structural function?
- in the process of narrative transmission
- in establishing contrasts or correspondences among the characters
- in establishing textual coherence

Is body language intended to achieve a particular effect in the reader?

4.4 Artistic Concepts of Body Language

When unified features can be established throughout a text for the presentation, the semiotic quality, or the functions of non-verbal behaviour, an overall concept for this body language can be assumed. Samuel Beckett's first novel, *Murphy*, shows how such a concept is governed by the general artistic principles of a text.

For Beckett's plays, a particular concept of the body and body language has often been observed. The fragmentation, grotesque distortion, and/or immobility of bodies reflects the existential state of Beckett's characters.[57] This concept of the body can partly be explained by the author's preoccupation with philosophical systems of the seventeenth century, a background which also shapes *Murphy*.

In seventeeth-century philosophy, man is often conceived as a psychophysical mechanism. Beckett's protagonist Murphy is influenced by two of these systems: the monadology of Leibniz and (post-)Cartesian occasionalism. Like the occasionalists, Murphy senses a profound rift between his spiritual and bodily existence.[58] Whereas Descartes believed in a connection between the psyche and the physical located in the pineal gland, the occasionalists denied this connection as existing within the human being. For them, only God can intervene between mind and body. Murphy, however, does not see even God as a mediator between mind and body: an absolute dualism of mind and body determines the action as well as the characters of the novel,[59] and the characters' body language also serves essentially to present the mind-body problem. Passages from *Murphy* were cited above (pages 91–2) as examples for a conspicuous non-verbal style. This wooden, puppet-like style[60] can now be connected with the philosophical background of the text.

The natural sciences and philosophy of the seventeenth century were preoccupied with mechanics, the study of movement. The laws of motion researched in physics were also applied to the psychological and spiritual areas. In the bodily world, the human body was seen as a machine which obeys the principles of mechanics. For Arnold Geulincx, a proponent of occasionalism cited in the novel, the motor of this machine was not human will, but God. Man, in Geulincx's view, can only watch how his body is being set in motion by an extrinsic power, by a puppeteer, so to speak. 'Here we have the entree to that strange detachment with which Beckett's people regard the things their hands and feet do: their tendency to analyze their own motions like a man working out why a bicycle does not topple, and their reluctance to live through the senses without scrupulous interrogation of all that the senses report' (Hugh Kenner 1962, 84). The mind that is separated from its body wants to analyse this body's movements. This analysis, however, means that a movement which is normally perceived as a holistic unit must be fragmented. 'Beckett is, in this sense, an entomologist: he methodically breaks down the language of the body, he dissects it' (Chabert 1982, 27).

Not only is the non-verbal style of the characters in *Murphy* puppet-like, but the perception and presentation of this body language further supports the impression of a mechanical body movement. In the following quotation, an emotional display is presented from Murphy's perspective. His teacher Neary makes a fist in his despair over his unrequited love for Miss Dwyer:

> The knuckles stood out white under the skin in the usual way – that was the position. The hands then opened quite correctly to the utmost limit of their compass – that was the negation. It now seemed to Murphy that there were two equally legitimate ways in which the gesture might be concluded, and the sublation effected. The hands might be clapped to the head in a smart gesture of despair, or let fall limply to the seams of the trousers, supposing that to have been their point of departure. Judge then of his annoyance when Neary clenched them again more violently than before and dashed them against his breast-bone. (7)

Murphy's analysis of the movement is underscored by the way he expresses it in scientific terms. His prime interest is in the pure mechanics of the movement; the message of the body language, Neary's emotional state, entirely slips into the background as it is filtered through Murphy's analysis. Murphy even finds Neary's beating his breast illegitimate according to the laws of movement, while he is reassured when another gesture of despair made by Celia obeys the mechanical law: 'She dispatched her hands on the gesture that Neary had made such a botch of at the thought of Miss Dwyer, and resolved it quite legitimately, as it seemed to Murphy, by dropping them back into their original position' (24). Murphy, whose ideal is a monadic existence, has no appreciation whatsoever for the feeling expressed through this body language. He pays attention only to the body-language signifiers; the signified remains elusive to him. This lack of connection between expression and content corresponds with the lack of connection between body and mind.

The body language of the characters in *Murphy* not only fits into the philosophical concept of the novel; it is also an essential factor of its grotesque humour. As in his plays, Beckett achieves a 'crudely physical humour' (Esslin 1980, 47) in his novels, with clear echoes of silent-film slapstick or music-hall comedy. For example, the exaggerated, melodramatic gestures of some of the characters have a distinctly comic effect:

> Miss Counihan, her statement concluded, turned to go. Neary sank on one knee, on both knees, and begged her to hear him in a voice so hoarse with anguish that she turned back. (33)

> Wylie tore at the handle, calling, 'It is I, it is Needle.' Miss Counihan threw herself on Neary's mercy, not by word of mouth obviously, but with bended knee, panting bosom, clasped hands, passion-dimmed belladonna, etc. (117)

The characters' mechanical non-verbal style also contributes to the text's comic nature, because, according to Bergson (1900), body language has a comic effect exactly when it appears to be mechanical: '*Les attitudes, gestes et mouvements du corps humain sont risibles dans l'exacte mesure où ce corps nous fait penser à une simple mécanique*' (Bergson 1975 [1900], 22–3). Since, in *Murphy*, this mechanical quality stems from the characters' existential problems, the philosophical content and the comedy of the novel are inseparably joined in the semiotics of the body. Of course, this brief discussion could not do justice to the novel's complexity. However, we have seen that the body language in *Murphy* obviously fits into a larger philosophical and artistic concept.

4.5 Specifics of Genre and Author

A few digressions into the area of drama in the present study have shown that there are some differences in the use of body language between dramatic and narrative literature, especially as far as the presentation of non-verbal behaviour is concerned (see pages 99–100, 105). Poetry displays varying capabilities to present body language, depending on its subgenre. Meditative poetry, for example, is less predisposed in this aspect than the dramatic monologue, which always evokes a concrete conversational situation.[61] The fact that many poetic forms are short prevents them from describing a great number of gestures. But in poetry, too, body language can be an important signifier. For example, the theme of Margaret Atwood's 'Against Still Life' from *The Circle Game* (1966) is a couple's troubled relationship.[62] The verbal communication between the man and the woman in this poem has exhausted itself, and on a non-verbal level they also do not have anything to 'say' to each other. The body language which the 'I' in the poem perceives in his or her partner suggests contentment (a smile and folded hands), which is also, however, an indication of stagnation, of the unwanted 'still life' of the relationship. As this poem demonstrates, body language in poetry often tends to have an imagistic character, whereas non-verbal behaviour in the narrative text serves essentially to bring a scene to life or to make the fictional action seem authentic. In poetry, then, there seems to be a different hierarchy of functions of body language than there is for the narrative text or drama.

To date, the connection between 'gesture and genre' in narrative literature has been discussed in some detail only with regard to medieval texts.[63] In general, one might propose that the more attention the text devotes to the elaboration of its existents, the more likely it is that the entire spectrum of body language will be used. Whereas 'realistic' novels occupy one end of the spectrum, folk tales or fairy tales, because of their formulaic nature, generally rely on a limited inventory of gestures.[64]

Stephen Portch (1985) postulates that 'nonverbal moments' have a greater significance in the short story than in the novel (without actually having considered novels in his study): '[the novel] does not depend on them in the same way as the short story does' (37). This statement is true only in certain circumstances. In the short story, body language can be used to indicate character traits or mental states without these having to be described in great detail. The semiotic importance of body language may well be greater in the short story because of the brevity of the text. Body language that constitutes an important element in the action or a thematic core may also occur more frequently in the short story than it does in the novel, as, for example, with the emblems in Charles Dickens's 'The Signalman,' or the touches in Sherwood Anderson's 'Hands,' the first story in *Winesburg, Ohio* (1919), and D.H. Lawrence's 'You Touched Me' from *A Modern Lover* (1922). In Anderson's story, a teacher is accused of homosexuality and scorned by society because of his tendency to touch his pupils. In Lawrence's story, an instance of touch leads to a woman's forced marriage to her much younger and socially inferior adopted brother. As the discussions above have shown, however, non-verbal behaviour in a novel can also have a considerable semiotic importance. The novel and the short story do not differ essentially, but only in degree, as far as their use of body language is concerned.

Author-specific tendencies in the use of body language have been indicated above in the cases of Beckett and Atwood (pages 160 and 152), but this aspect cannot be investigated further within the scope of this study. As a number of studies on the work of individual writers suggest, however, writers appear to differ in their preference for certain modes and literary functions of body language as well as for forms of presenting it. The use of body language also differs according to period, as we shall see in part III of this study.

Summary

The catalogue for the analysis of literary body language can be completed with two final sets of questions:

Is the use of body language determined by a specific concept?

To what extent is the use of body language determined by: - genre? - author? - period?

In concluding part II of this study, I establish the value of the categories for interpretation and demonstrate their interplay within the text in an analysis of the use of body language in two novels. Both are texts in which body language occurs throughout with a high degree of frequency.

4.6 Body Language in George Eliot's *Adam Bede* and Elizabeth Bowen's *The Death of the Heart*

The work of George Eliot belongs to the great 'realistic' tradition of the nineteenth-century novel. In this tradition, the non-verbal behaviour of the characters is generally described with great variety and detail: it plays an important role in making a fictional situation seem authentic and vivid, and in suggesting the characters' mental states and interpersonal relationships. This will be shown in greater detail in chapter 5. Besides such period-specific tendencies, some features of the use of NVC that are evident in *Adam Bede* (1859) are specific to the text and its author.

One of the most prominent functions of body language in *Adam Bede* is its contribution to characterization. At the centre of the novel are the personality traits and developments of its characters, primarily within the triangle comprising Adam, Hetty, and Dinah. In particular, the characters' power to make moral judgments is carefully observed, and glosses and comments on characteristic body language also especially emphasize its moral implications.

Adam Bede is characterized by an honesty that is conveyed, for example, by his upright and naturally dignified posture: 'he looked neither awkward nor embarrassed, but stood in his usual firm upright attitude, with his head thrown a little backward and his hands perfectly still, in that rough dignity which is peculiar to intelligent, honest, well-built workmen, who are never wondering what is their business in the world' (1:372). The two central female figures in the novel, Dinah and Hetty, are contrasting characters whose body language is also diametrically opposite. Dinah, the Methodist, whose human values Adam only gradually discovers, is distinguished by her natural behaviour, the calm expression on her face and a composed posture: 'She had sat in this way perfectly still, with her hands crossed on her lap, and the pale light resting on her calm face, for at least ten minutes' (1:219). The calmness of her body language is an obvious parallel to Adam's, indicating early on that Dinah is a more suitable partner for Adam than Hetty, whom he adores. Another non-verbal attribute of Dinah is her tendency to touch others: for example, when she comforts Adam's mother after the death of her husband, or Hetty after she has been condemned to death for her act of infanticide. This haptic behaviour is a clear externalizer of Dinah's altruistic, active religiosity and her sympathy – qualities that are valued highly in all of George Eliot's novels. In contrast to Dinah, Hetty's non-verbal behaviour shows her self-indulgence and self-love. She repeatedly preens herself in front of the mirror, and even her everyday activities, such as butter churning, are turned into a flirtatious act:[65]

> And they are the prettiest attitudes and movements into which a pretty girl is thrown in making up butter, – tossing movements that give a charming curve to the arm, and a sideward inclination of the round white neck; little patting and rolling movements with the palm of the hand, and nice adaptations and finishings which cannot at all be effected without a great play of the pouting mouth and the dark eyes. (1:114–15)

Frequent comments by the narrator ensure that the messages conveyed by body language are clearly understood by the reader. The characters within the fictional situation, however, have great difficulties in interpreting the body language of their fellow human beings. The theme of (self-)delusion, so often present in George Eliot's work, is a central theme in *Adam Bede*. A number of characters, especially Adam, have to suffer through a process of disillusionment in order to attain maturity. The misunderstanding of body language contributes essentially to the development of this theme of delusion. A famous passage from chapter 15 of the novel denounces the unreliability of physiognomy, especially with regard to Hetty, whose outer attractiveness masks the weaknesses in her personality. Hetty's body language is equally deceiving: it is not read adequately either by Adam, who loves her, or by Arthur, who seduces her. Adam, in particular, is repeatedly noted to misinterpret the language of Hetty's body:

> He thought yesterday, when he put out his hand to her as they came out of church, that there was a touch of melancholy kindness in her face, such as he had not seen before, and he took it as a sign that she had some sympathy with his family trouble. Poor fellow! that touch of melancholy came from quite another source; but how was he to know? (1:288)

> And presently, when Totty was gone, she caught his eye, and her face broke into one of its brightest smiles, as she nodded to him. It was a bit of flirtation, – she knew Mary Burge was looking at them; but the smile was like wine to Adam. (1:364)

> 'God bless her for loving me,' said Adam, as he went on his way to work again, with Gyp at his heels.
>
> But Hetty's tears were not for Adam, – not for the anguish that would come upon him when he found she was gone from him forever. They were for the misery of her own lot ... (2:135)

One of George Eliot's artistic interests was to evoke understanding and sympathy in the reader. As she wrote in a letter to Charles Bray on 5 July 1859: 'I have had heart-cutting experience that opinions are a poor cement between human souls; and the only effect I ardently long to produce by my writings, is that those who read them should be better able to *imagine* and to *feel* the pains and the joys of those who differ from themselves in everything but the broad fact of being struggling erring human creatures.'[66] It is a matter of conjecture to what extent a body language of emotion can affect a reader in this way (see pages 12–13). If manipulation of sympathy can actually be accomplished through NVC, the emotional displays in Eliot's novels, which are nuanced and psychologically authentic, would be especially capable of doing so. Indisputably, though, the body language of feeling evokes sympathy within the fictional situation of *Adam Bede*. Repeatedly, characters discern their fellow characters' inner states through their body language and thus achieve a deeper understanding of each other. For example, Adam's reaction to the news of Hetty's arrest evokes sympathy in Mr Irwine:

Mr. Irwine had sat down again in silence. He was too wise to utter soothing words at present; and indeed the sight of Adam before him, with that look of sudden age which sometimes comes over a young face in moments of terrible emotion, – the hard, bloodless look of the skin, the deep lines about the quivering mouth, the furrows in the brow, – the sight of this strong, firm man shattered by the invisible stroke of sorrow, moved him so deeply that speech was not easy. (2:194–5)

The characters' perception of body language is extremely important in the episode of Adam and Hetty's reunion in prison. Each recognizes how much the other has changed as a result of his or her suffering, and they develop pity for each other as a result:

But he began to see through the dimness, – to see the dark eyes lifted up to him once more, but with no smile in them. O God, how sad they looked! ... The face was marble now; the sweet lips were pallid and half-open and quivering; the dimples were all gone, – all but one, that never went; and the eyes – oh! the worst of all was the likeness they had to Hetty's. They were Hetty's eyes looking at him with that mournful gaze, as if she had come back to him from the dead to tell him of her misery ...

When the sad eyes met, – when Hetty and Adam looked at each other, – she felt the change in *him* too, and it seemed to strike her with fresh fear. It was the first time she had seen any being whose face seemed to reflect the change in herself; Adam was a new image of the dreadful past and the dreadful present. She trembled more as she looked at him. (2:266)

We have seen that the body language in *Adam Bede* makes a central contribution to characterization and the development of the themes of delusion and sympathy. In *The Death of the Heart* (1938), Elizabeth Bowen emphasizes other functions in the body language of her characters. The novel describes a sixteen-year-old girl's failed initiation into the British upper middle class before the Second World War. Body language plays an important role in establishing the social context into which Portia fails to integrate herself. It also effectively conveys the girl's sorrow, which results from this failure.

After the death of her mother, Portia moves in with her older half-brother, Thomas, in London. Her wealthy father had divorced his first wife in order to marry Portia's mother, who came from an unacceptable social class. After the death of her father, Portia and her mother lived freely and independently in the hotels of various European countries. From this environment, she is transplanted into her brother's house. Thomas's marriage to his superficial and pleasure-seeking wife, Anna, has broken down. Thomas is much too involved with his wife's lack of affection and numerous love affairs to be able to befriend Portia; Anna instinctively rejects the girl. The only person with whom Portia can communicate is the housekeeper, Matchett, a woman as lonely as Portia is herself.

The atmosphere of upper-class life is created not only through the description of material attributes, but also through precise studies of language and behaviour. Class-conscious Anna performs the behaviour typical of a society lady; she frequently preens herself, and dainty gestures and postures externalize both her self-love and her enjoyment of luxury:

> Raising her arms, she shook her sleeves back and admired her own wrists. (30)

> Anna swung her feet up on the sofa, a little back from the others, and looked removed and tired – she kept touching her hair back. (47)

> Anna, on the sofa in a Récamier attitude, had acted, among all she had had to act, a hardy imperviousness to this. (49)

> 'All the same,' said Anna, after the kiss, sitting up and moulding back with her fingers the one smooth curl along the nape of her neck ... (242)

This body language achieves a special emphasis when it is parodied by Anna's lover, Eddie, whom Portia eventually also falls in love with: 'Eddie posed himself, leaning sideways on one elbow with Anna's rather heavy nonchalant grace. He drew his fingers idly across his forehead, putting back an imaginary wave of hair' (103). The same mannerisms are encountered in one of Portia's classmates, who promises to become just as fashion- and class-conscious a lady as Anna is: 'Even

Lilian, prone to finger her own plaits or to look at the voluptuous white insides of her arms, sat, during those hours with Miss Paullie, as though Lilian did not exist' (55).

In contrast to Anna and Lilian, Portia lacks social graces and any sense of conventional behaviour; she frequently commits *faux pas*, and her body language is awkward:

Getting up from the stool carefully, Portia returned her cup and plate to the tray. Then, holding herself so erect that she quivered, taking long soft steps on the balls of her feet, and at the same time with an orphaned unostentation, she started making towards the door. She moved crabwise, as though the others were royalty, never quite turning her back on them – and they, waiting for her to be quite gone, watched ... The pointed attention of St Quentin and Anna reached her like a quick tide, or an attack: the ordeal of getting out of the drawing-room tightened her mouth up and made her fingers curl – her wrists were pressed to her thighs. (29)

The tense body language expressed in this quotation is typical for Portia. It is the result of the fear which the girl has developed in her foreign, cold environment. As a tolerated poor relative, she is afraid to make mistakes. An expression of her profound feeling of unprotectedness is the way she embraces herself again and again:

Now, by crossing her arms tightly across her chest, as though to weight herself down with them, she seemed to cling at least to her safe bed. (79)

Portia, by folding her arms over it tightly, locked the eiderdown, her last shelter, to her chest. (297)

The Death of the Heart is a novel about relationships, or rather the failure of relationships that finally causes the 'death' of Portia's heart. Externalizers of interpersonal relationships are therefore one of the main classes of NVC in this novel. Eye contact, in particular, is foregrounded through comments and glosses by the narrator. Thus it becomes very clear that Portia's piercing looks are perceived by many as odd and strange, and that she has therefore learned to reduce her eye contact to a minimum:

Portia had learnt one dare never look for long. She had those eyes that seem to be welcome nowhere, that learn shyness from the alarm they precipitate. Such eyes are always turning away or being humbly lowered – they dare come to rest nowhere but on a point in space; their homeless intentness makes them appear fanatical. They may move, they may affront, but they cannot communicate. You most often meet or, rather, avoid meeting such eyes in a child's face – what becomes of the child later you do not know. (49)

There are only a few people with whom Portia can exchange glances: with fatherly Major Brutt,[67] who is also seen as an outsider in the eyes of the world, and with frivolous Eddie, who cannot give Portia love, but who does feel sympathy for her:

Portia and Eddie, side by side at the table, her diary between them under one of her hands, turned on each other eyes in which two relentless looks held apart for a moment, then became one. To generate that one look, their eyes seemed for the first time to be using their full power. The look held a sort of superb mutual greeting rather than any softness of love. You would have said that two accomplices had for the first time spoken aloud to each other of their part in the same crime, or that two children had just discovered their common royal birth. On the subject of love, there was nothing to say: they seemed to have no projects and no desires. Their talk today had been round an understood pact: at this moment, they saluted its significance. (106)

Portia's eye behaviour, then, suggests how limited her capability is to make contact with other people; on the other hand, it also shows how her relationships to a few people gain a particular intensity, as is evident in the detailed presentation of eye contact in the above quotation.

Touch is rare in Portia's family. The few seemingly tender instances of touch exchanged between Anna and Thomas have hostile undertones: 'Anna wiped complexion milk off her fingers on to a tissue, smartly re-tied the sash of her wrapper, walked across, and gave Thomas's head a light friendly unfriendly cuff ... More lightly, less kindly, she hit at his head again' (239). In this world with its pronounced lack of love, Portia almost desperately seeks haptic contact with the few people who have some affection for her, or who appear to have affection for her: Matchett, Eddie, and Major Brutt:

'But don't, don't keep going off – ' began Portia, desperate. Stopping, she put both arms out, with a rustle of sheet falling away. Matchett, reluctantly softening, inch by inch, unlocked her arms, leaned across the bed again, leaned right down – in the mysterious darkness over the pillow their faces approached, their eyes met but could not see ... But Portia's hand, with its charge of nervous emotion, still crept on the firm broad neck, the strong spine. (83)

Terrified by his voice and face of iron, Portia cried, *'Oh no!'* Annihilating the space of grass between them she flung an arm across him, her weight on his body, and despairingly kissed his cheek, his mouth, his chin. (213)

he felt Portia measuring his coming nearer with the deliberation of a desperate thing – then, like a bird at still another window, she flung herself at him. Her hands pressed, flattened, on the fronts of his coat; he felt her fingers digging into the stuff. She said something inaudible. Grasping her cold elbows he gently, strongly held her a little back. (287)

Portia practically clings to the people whom she trusts. Her eruptive touch behaviour described in these passages has the effect of mute screams of desperation, which are, however, taken seriously only at the end of the novel, when Portia suffers a complete breakdown after her betrayal by Eddie and, partly, by Major Brutt.

As we have seen in these brief analyses, the main uses of modes and functions of body language in *The Death of the Heart* are clearly different than those in *Adam Bede*. In both works, however, NVC constitutes an important dimension of meaning.

4.7 A Catalogue of Questions for the Analysis of Body Language in the Narrative Text

Chapter 4 has shown the great variety of forms and artistic functions in which body language can be encountered in narrative literature. The reader's ordinary non-verbal competence, though it represents an important basis for the understanding of this semiotic area, is not sufficient for an appreciation of its specific uses in literature. The classification grid established in chapter 3 must therefore be completed with the questions discussed in this chapter.

This second set of categories for the analysis of literary body language is not a closed system such as the modal-functional grid, but an open catalogue of questions that can be complemented and modified. It is summarized in the next two pages.

The critical framework with its two components from chapters 3 and 4 can serve as a kind of guide in the analysis and interpretation of a text, and it facilitates a precise presentation of the results of this approach to a text. The categories established in this framework allow for a systematic analysis of the extent to which and the manner in which body language is used in individual texts, by individual authors, in certain genres, and in certain literary periods.

BODY LANGUAGE IN THE NARRATIVE TEXT: AN OPEN CATALOGUE OF QUESTIONS

I Concerning the semiotic importance and semiotic quality of body language in the narrative text:

> What is the:
> - frequency and distribution of body language within the text?
> - semantic content } of the non-verbal signified?
> - semantic clarity/vagueness } of the non-verbal signified?
> - distinctiveness of the non-verbal signifier?

II Concerning the presentation of body language in the narrative text:

> How is an instance of body language 'filtered' through language and narrative transmission?

> Is an instance of body language *foregrounded* through:
> - linguistic means?
> - narrative mode?
> - the structure of narrative transmission?
> - visual perspectivization?

III Concerning the literary functions and effects of body language in the narrative text:

> What role does body language play in the constitution of fictional reality?
> - as an element in the action
> - as an indication of mental states
> - as an indication of interpersonal relationships
> - as a means of character definition and identification
> - as a means of authentication
> - as a means of dramatization

Is body language used:
- as an image?
- in the development of a theme?

Does body language in the narrative text perform a technical and/or structural function?
- in the process of narrative transmission
- in establishing contrasts or correspondences among the characters
- in establishing textual coherence

Is body language intended to achieve a particular effect in the reader?

IV Concerning the artistic concept of body language:

Is the use of body language determined by a specific concept?

V Concerning genre, author, and period:

To what extent is the use of body language determined by:
- genre?
- author?
- period?

PART III

BODY LANGUAGE IN THE ENGLISH NOVEL: TRENDS IN HISTORICAL DEVELOPMENT

5

Body Language and the Aesthetic of the Novel

In most strange postures
We have seen him set himself.

Shakespeare, *Henry VIII*, 3.2.118–19

As stated in the introduction, part III of this study attempts to complement the systematic framework established in part II with a sketch of important historical developments in literary body language, focusing on the novel of the British Isles from the sixteenth century to the present. Based on a small sample of only eighty – albeit fairly representative – texts (see pages 16–17 and the appendix), the observations made in this and the next chapter merely indicate some basic trends. A more reliable study of the history of body language in the English novel would not only have required a vast sample of texts, but would also have to reconstruct the systems of body language codes and the body images specific to each period, based on writings in anthropology, philosophy, theology, medicine, and rhetoric, on etiquette books, and on visual art.[1]

The *period profiles* (see page 79) given in this chapter are therefore deliberately vague: instead of percentage rates, the intensity of the shading given for certain modal and functional classes of NVC must suffice to indicate their relative frequency of occurrence within a certain period. Categories left blank indicate that they are of minor significance in comparison with other modal and functional classes. Since regulators are exceptional in all periods, they are generally not regarded in the period profiles. (It should be noted that the profiles represent only the approximate relations of frequency *within* the individual periods; they do *not* compare the frequency of modes and functions across the various periods.)

This chapter, then, sets out to demonstrate how body language is increasingly gaining ground in the aesthetic of the English novel. In part II we have seen how certain individual tendencies in presenting body language in the narrative text appear to be linked with general developments in narrative literature: social emblems, for example, are especially prevalent in texts which emphasize the public versus the private sphere; extensive narratorial comments and glosses on body language are particularly popular in the nineteenth century; conventionalized body language occurs regularly in literature up to the nineteenth century, but its presence decreases markedly in the twentieth century. Besides such individual trends, however, a general historical tendency can also be observed: the examples cited in part II were mainly taken from novels written since the mid-eighteenth century; earlier texts could be used to illustrate only a few areas. A closer look at the presence of body language in English prose fiction before the mid-eighteenth century – that is, before the novel created by Samuel Richardson and his contemporaries – confirms this comparatively marginal status.

5.1 Body Language in Prose Fiction before Richardson

The profile in Table 5.1 portrays the average distribution of non-verbal modes and functional classes in English prose fiction from the sixteenth to the mid-eighteenth centuries. From the Renaissance until the early eighteenth century, no major development in the literary use of body language could be observed for the texts investigated: emblems and emotional displays emerge as the main functional classes of NVC in the antecedents of the modern novel. Most of the emblems are socially coded, in accordance with the courtly world portrayed in many of the texts. Externalizers of interpersonal relations are mainly those of the love relationship, and thus frequently overlap with emotional displays. This fairly restricted use of the modal-functional spectrum corresponds with the limited literary functions with which body language tends to appear in prose fiction before the mid-eighteenth century: it indicates the characters' emotional states and portrays codes of behaviour.

Furthermore, this body language often derives from a conventional repertoire, and its presentation tends to recur in set phrases. The following examples containing identical formulations are from Thomas

Prose fiction, before 1740		Functional classification			
Modal classification		emotional display	externalizer	illustrator	emblem
I. Kinesics	gesture				■
	practical action				
	facial expression	■			
	eye behaviour		■		
	automatic reaction	■			
	posture				■
II. Haptics			■		■
III. Proxemics					

Table 5.1 Period Profile: Body Language in Prose Fiction before Richardson

Lodge's *Rosalind* (1590), the prose romance which became the source for Shakespeare's *As You Like It*:

Leaning **his head on his hand and his elbow on his knee**, full of sorrow, grief, and disquieted passions, he resolved into these terms ... (329)

At last, fixing his looks on the riches of her face, **his head on his hand and his elbow on his knee**, he sung this mournful ditty ... (362)

John Lyly's portrayal of body language in his *Euphues* (1578) also does not match the verbosity that has given this novel its place in literary history:

Having therefore gotten opportunity to communicate with him his mind, **with watery eyes**, as one lamenting his wantonness ... encountered him on this manner ... (91)

Philautus entered the chamber and ... **with watery eyes** uttered this speech ... (116)

Therefore in all haste, **with watery eyes** and a woeful heart, began on this manner to reason with his daughter ... (147)

In *Euphues*, non-verbal behaviour is described throughout with the same lexicalized expressions; as in many examples of contemporary fiction, the accent is thus clearly on the body language signified; its signifier, that is, the way in which it is carried out by the character, is rarely specified, and its presentation appears to come second in the writer's concern.[2]

At times one can even speak of a marked negligence in the use of body language in early fiction. In one passage of *Rosalind*, for example, Lodge apparently overlooks the fact that an instance of non-verbal behaviour has already been described a few sentences earlier. Saladyne, Rosader's remorseful brother, sits down in pain over his earlier evil-doing before he announces his remorse in a monologue. At the end of this speech he sits down again, even though we have not been told that he had stood up in between:

Saladyne, **sitting down** and fetching a deep sigh, began thus:

Saladyne's Discourse to Rosader (Unknown)

'Although the discourse of my fortunes be the renewing of my sorrows, and the rubbing of the scar will open a fresh wound, yet that I may not prove ingrateful to so courteous a gentleman, I will rather sit down and sigh out my estate than give any offense by smothering my grief with silence ... I set my middle brother to the university to be a scholar, counting it enough if he might pore on a book while I fed upon his revenues; and for the youngest, which was my father's joy, young Rosader –'

And with that naming of Rosader, Saladyne **sat him downe** and wept. (351)

The rather marginal role which NVC plays in the prose romance of the Renaissance is also evident in a comparison with Shakespeare's plays. *The Winter's Tale*, for example, contains a scene in which body language is of central significance. Leontes' fateful jealousy is triggered by an instance of NVC which takes place between his wife, Hermione, and his best friend, Polixenes. In the play, this body language is minutely described by Leontes, who misunderstands it because of his excessive jealousy:

LEONTES Why, that was when
Three crabbed months had sour'd themselves to death,

Ere I could make thee open thy white hand,
[And] clap thyself my love; then didst thou utter,
'I am yours forever.'
HERMIONE 'Tis Grace indeed.
Why, lo you now! I have spoke to th' purpose twice:
The one for ever earn'd a royal husband;
Th'other for some while a friend.
[*Gives her hand to Polixenes.*]
LEONTES [*Aside.*] Too hot, too hot!
To mingle friendship far is mingling bloods.
...
But to be paddling palms and pinching fingers,
As now they are, and making practic'd smiles,
As in a looking-glass; and then to sigh, as 'twere
The mort o' th' deer – O, that is entertainment
My bosom likes not, nor my brows! ... (1.2.101–21)

In Shakespeare's source for this play, Robert Greene's prose romance *Pandosto* (1588), the tragedy of jealousy is also effected through body language that is incorrectly decoded: 'While thus he noted their looks and gestures and suspected their thoughts and meanings, they two silly souls, who doubted nothing of this his treacherous intent, frequented daily each other's company' (158). Unlike Shakespeare, however, Greene only mentions the non-verbal behaviour in passing; its precise manner is not specified, and the important fact that the husband misunderstands the body language is only implied. In contrast, the body language in *The Winter's Tale* is presented in a manner that corresponds with its significance in the development of the plot and, most importantly, underscores the fact that it is misinterpreted.

A wider use of the expressive potential of body language can be observed only rarely in early English fiction. Significantly, most examples stem from the 'realistic' line of fiction, such as the works of Thomas Deloney or George Gascoigne.[3] Here, the body language often seems more 'authentic' than in the contemporary romance. In Deloney's narratives of bourgeois life, even the look of love is more rooted in reality than in the romantic tradition, as, for example, in *The Gentle Craft*:

On the Sundayes when he came into the Church, the Maides eyes were so firmely fixed on him that hee could neither looke forward, backeward, nor on any side, but that he should be sure to haue a winke of one, a smile of another, the third would giue a nod: and to be briefe, they would all cast on him such gracious lookes, that it was easie to guesse by their outward countenance, their inward good will. (141)

In the same text, a woman, when warning her husband, raises her finger in order to emphasize her words; this illustrator helps to make the episode appear vivid and visual: 'at what time his wife called after him, saying: and holding vp her finger. Husband, remember, you know what I haue said: take heed you dissemble not with God and the world, look to it Husband' (123).

George Gascoigne's *The Adventures of Master F.J.* (1573) is an early epistolary novel that was forgotten for a long time; it is recognized today as a rare beast in the tradition of Elizabethan courtly fiction.[4] In contrast to the romance, Gascoigne portrays aristocratic society critically and realistically, and in this context subtleties of non-verbal behaviour become important. During a game, for example, the Lady Elinor asks her admirer F.J. three questions. He thinks about his answers carefully, and in order not to be distracted, turns his eyes away. He is awakened from his reflection through a regulator with which another lady tries to gain his attention: 'F.J., abasing his eyes towards the ground, took good advisement in his answer, when a fair gentlewoman of the company clapped him on the shoulder, saying "How now, sir, is your hand on your halfpenny?"' (16). In this example, too, NVC helps to authenticate and dramatize the action.

However, even in the 'realistic' vein of fiction, such a use of NVC before Richardson must be seen as an exception. Even Daniel Defoe, whose novels are otherwise characterized by a particular attention to circumstance, used body language very sporadically. Not until the mid-eighteenth century is body language in prose fiction employed extensively, regularly, and in its full modal and functional spectrum.

5.2 Body Language in the Novel since Richardson

The extent to which novelists' awareness of body language and its expressive quality has increased since the mid-eighteenth century is obvious when we look at the two following examples. As was shown above, Thomas Lodge made the mistake of mentioning an instance of NVC twice within one brief passage of his *Rosalind*. Three centuries later, in George Eliot's *Middlemarch*, a character's body language is remembered even after a considerable lapse of narrative time; it seems to have a secure place in the writer's imagination and is subject to her artistic control:

> 'Good God!' Will burst out passionately, rising, with his hat still in his hand, and walking away to a marble table, where he suddenly turned and **leaned his back against it** ...
>
> Will was startled. Whatever the words might be, the tone seemed like a dismissal; and **quitting his leaning posture**, he walked a little way towards her. (3:13–15)

Increased attention to body language in the nineteenth century also becomes obvious in that it is often strongly emphasized – through detailed description, a glossing or comment, or a conspicuously poetic presentation, as in the similes and metaphors in the following quotations:

> 'Good heavens!' exclaimed the archdeacon, as he placed his foot on the gravel walk of the close, and raising his hat with one hand, passed the other somewhat violently over his now grizzled locks; smoke issued forth from the uplifted beaver as it were a cloud of wrath, and the safety-valve of his anger opened, and emitted a visible steam, preventing positive explosion and probable apoplexy. (Trollope, *Barchester Towers*, 1:41)

> His finely chiselled nostrils quivered, and some hidden nerve shook the scarlet of his lips and left them trembling ... His cool, white, flower-like hands, even, had a curious charm. They moved, as he spoke, like music, and seemed to have a language of their own. (Wilde, *The Picture of Dorian Gray*, 29–30)

Furthermore, the semiotic importance that body language is given in many novels since the last century is evident in the fact that it is often found prominently in the beginning or ending – important cornerstones – of a novel. Thomas Hardy's *Far from the Madding Crowd*, for example, begins with the description of a smile that introduces and characterizes one of the main characters; the body language thus carries a significant part of the expository information: 'When Farmer Oak smiled, the corners of his mouth spread till they were within an unimportant distance of his ears, his eyes were reduced to mere chinks, and diverging wrinkles appeared round them, extending upon his countenance like the rays in a rudimentary sketch of the rising sun' (1).[5] In George Meredith's *The Ordeal of Richard Feverel*, one of the central messages of the ending is conveyed by the eye behaviour of the protagonist (which is described by another character): '"Have you noticed the expression in the eyes of blind men? That is just how Richard looks, as he lies there silent in his bed – striving to image her on his brain"' (542). After his wife's death, Richard Feverel has ultimately become the victim of his father's fatal educational principles, and his deadly gaze is the expression of the death of his will to live. At the end of Graham Greene's *The Power and the Glory*, after the persecuted priest has been shot, a new clergyman is greeted with great respect:

> 'If you would let me come in,' the man said with an odd frightened smile, and suddenly lowering his voice he said to the boy, 'I am a priest.'
>
> 'You?' the boy exclaimed.
>
> 'Yes,' he said gently. 'My name is Father –' But the boy had already swung the door open and put his lips to his hand before the other could give himself a name. (221–2)

This final emblem of greeting and reverence, the kiss on the hand, indicates that the influence of the church cannot be defeated by the communist regime, and the end of the novel is thus given an unexpected, optimistic twist.

The change in status of body language indicated in the examples above can be said to begin with the 'sentimental' novel of Samuel Richardson and his contemporaries. Richardson's work is generally regarded as a turning point in the history of the novel, and this is also evident in his use of NVC. It is with Richardson that a novel tradition begins to emerge in which the expressive potential of body language can be exploited to the full. The new type of bourgeois novel presents nuances of psychological states and interpersonal relationships, both public and private. Everyday life gains significance as material for the novel; the concreteness and credibility of the world portrayed become important principles. Within the framework of this aesthetic, the frequency of body language increases noticeably, and the modal-functional grid in Table 5.2 is filled more regularly than it was in earlier centuries. Externalizers and illustrators are represented with much greater frequency, and functional classes also manifest themselves in a greater number of modes. The average frequency of NVC is increased again in the nineteenth century: novels in which there is no presence of body language whatsoever are now the exception rather than the rule. The full use of the expressive potential of NVC is accompanied by a tendency for

Prose fiction, 1740 to 1830		Functional classification			
Modal classification		emotional display	externalizer	illustrator	emblem
I. Kinesics	gesture				
	practical action				
	facial expression				
	eye behaviour				
	automatic reaction				
	posture				
II. Haptics					
III. Proxemics					

Table 5.2 Period Profile: Body Language in the Eighteenth-Century Novel since Richardson

an even modal-functional distribution, as documented in Table 5.3; increases in externalizers and illustrators are particularly evident in the period profile.

The twentieth-century novel differs only slightly from the preceding period in its use of the modal-functional spectrum of body language. In the sample investigated, a further rise in gestural illustrators points to the fact that body language accompanying speech is even more frequently described than it was in the Victorian novel. As far as decreases are concerned, only two seem to be significant: a decrease in gestural externalizers might be explained by the fact that conspicuous gestures are no longer used as frequently to characterize or identify characters as they were in the Victorian period; a decrease in automatic reactions to express emotional states could have to do with the fact that conventional repertoires of emotional displays, which contain a high level of automatic reactions, are used less and less. All in all, however, the twentieth-century novel appears to rely extensively on a 'grammar' of body language which was established in the second half of the eighteenth century and consolidated in the nineteenth century. The sections

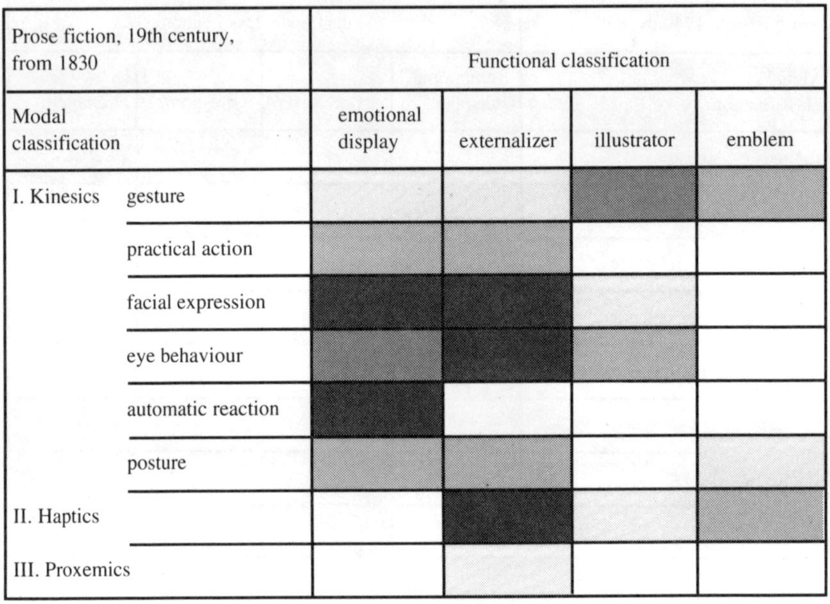

Table 5.3 Period Profile: Body Language in the Victorian Novel

that follow investigate a number of 'new' aesthetic principles that have encouraged the use of body language in the novel since Richardson.

5.3 The Attention to Detail

The modern novel, with its interest in the trivia of the fictional reality, gives body language careful attention. In the following passage from Graham Swift's *The Sweet Shop Owner* (1980), several characters meet in a pub; every minor change in the posture of one of the characters is recorded:

'Hello Frank.'

'Hello, helloh. Wangled some leave too?'

He rocked to and fro. Only his feet seemed to hold him to the ground, as if they were clamped with weights. One hand held his beer and the other was extended, palm forward, behind Irene's back.

'Fancy – ' He stood, open-mouthed, for a moment, as though embarrassed for something to say. 'Well – there goes the war.' He looked at the fire. He raised his beaker and **brought his mouth to it by leaning his whole body**.

'Look –' Irene said. She shifted forward.

'Soon be out of this, eh Willy?' Hancock tugged at his uniform 'Back to the shop?' He winked, **bobbed his head sideways, then stood, swaying**, looking at the fire. (86)

In examples like this, a development culminates that begins in the eighteenth century: in the context of a new need for illusion, the world of the novel becomes 'particular,' it pays attention to detail. In the case of the sentimental novel, this need for illusion is linked with a desired effect upon the reader: the action is to be presented in so vivid a manner that it will have an emotional and moral effect. The second letter of Richardson's *Clarissa* contains a passage in which the new attention to detail is programmatically expressed:

Excuse me, my dear, I never was thus particular before; ... you will always have me give you minute descriptions, nor suffer me to pass by the air and manner in which things are spoken that are to be taken notice of; rightly observing, that air and manner often express more than the accompanying words. (1:7–8)

It is also emphasized in Diderot's *Eloge de Richardson* (1761):

Sachez que c'est à cette multitude de petites choses que tient l'illusion: il y a bien de la difficulté à les imaginer: Il y en a bien encore à les rendre. Le geste est quelquefois aussi sublime que le mot; et puis ce sont toutes ces vérités de détail qui préparent l'âme aux impressions fortes des grands événements. (Diderot 1951, 1094)

Given such an agenda, body language is represented in fine nuances and precise descriptions. A passage from Laurence Sterne's *A Sentimental Journey*, for example, describes a facial expression with minute attention to physiological detail: 'but upon turning her face towards me, the spirit which had animated the reply was fled – **the muscles relaxed**, and I saw the same unprotected look of distress which first won me to her interest – melancholy! to see such sprightliness the prey of sorrow' (30). Similarly, the first-person narrator in Tobias Smollett's *Roderick Random* does not simply state that a character is crying, but describes how one single tear trickles down his cheek; this attention to detail is in keeping with the sensitivity with which the 'I' reacts to this tear: 'With these words I could perceive **a tear trickle down** his furrowed cheeks, which affected me so much, that I wept bitterly' (233).

As early as the end of the eighteenth century, Robert Bage's *Hermsprong* comments ironically on the detail with which emotional displays are commonly described in the novel of his time:

> Unless physiologists would do us the favour to explain what motions, solid or fluid, are going on within our microcosms, when, from a state of placidity, we grow in an instant raving mad, I know not why we novel writers should be at the trouble of noting the outward marks with precision, such as redness of face, or lividity, with swearing, or gnashing of teeth. (120)

If parody indicates how well established a device has become, the following quotation from Thomas Love Peacock's *Nightmare Abbey* (1818) can be considered a fitting proof of the novel's love of detail in describing body language:

> The whole party followed, with the exception of Scythrop, who threw himself into his arm-chair, crossed his left foot over his right knee, placed the hollow of his left hand on the interior ancle [*sic*] of his left leg, rested his right elbow on the elbow of the chair, placed the ball of his right thumb against his right temple, curved the forefinger along the upper part of his forehead, rested the point of the middle finger on the bridge of his nose, and the points of the two others on the lower part of the palm, fixed his eyes intently on the veins in the back of his left hand, and sat in this position like the immoveable Theseus, who, as is well known to many who have not been at college, and to some few who have, *sedet, aeternumque sedebit*. We hope the admirers of the *minutiae* in poetry and romance will appreciate this accurate description of a pensive attitude. (133–4)

In this lengthy description, the character freezes in a posture of reflection; the rigidity of his pose is emphasized through the allusion to the eternally immovable Theseus. However, the minuteness of description actually makes this body language unreadable – its signifier is split into so many individual components that it becomes impossible for the reader to put them together again into one expressive posture. A gloss is necessary to reveal the signified: 'a *pensive* attitude.' This gloss achieves the anticlimax intended by the parody, for it makes the preceding descriptive effort seem completely superfluous.

Peacock's detailed description of body language has a strongly visual character. In general, the new 'illusionist' novel since the mid-eighteenth century is marked by a conspicuous visual quality. Henry Home writes in *The Elements of Criticism* (1762): 'In narration as well as in description, facts and objects ought to be painted so accurately as to form in the mind of the reader distinct and lively images ... the narrative in an epic poem ought to rival a picture in the liveliness and accuracy of its representations: no circumstance must be omitted that tends to make a complete image ... (3:174–5). In the course of the nineteenth century, this visuality is even increased: 'Nineteenth-century fiction is full of attempts to make the reader *see* what is taking place ... Dickens and Trollope are two of many novelists to claim that the scenes and characters which they invent are directly perceived by them' (Irwin 1979, 2).[6] The genre-painting of the Dutch school became a model for the realistic novel of the nineteenth century. 'It is for this rare, precious quality of truthfulness that I delight in many Dutch paintings, which lofty-minded people despise,' George Eliot wrote in a frequently quoted passage from *Adam Bede* (1:246).[7] Apart from the old genre-paintings, the works of contemporary genre-painters like David Wilkie (at the beginning of the century) or William Powell Frith (in the 1850s and 1860s) enjoyed great popularity in the nineteenth century. These paintings depict scenes of everyday life with almost photographic precision and capture the body language of their subjects in minute detail.[8] The realistic novel of the time conveys non-verbal behaviour with equal precision:

'Ah!' said Mr. Blathers: not holding his wine-glass by the stem, but grasping the bottom **between the thumb and forefinger of his left hand** ... (Dickens, *Oliver Twist*, 188)

'That's the past tense, Tom,' returned Mr. James Harthouse, striking the ash from his cigar **with his little finger**. (Dickens, *Hard Times*, 102)

Other descriptions are careful to render body language in its temporal dimension:

her cheek, at first so deadly pale, **began gradually to be overspread with a faint blush** ... (Scott, *The Heart of Midlothian*, 230)

and the tears welled forth, and **hung glittering for an instant** on the shadowing eye-lashes **before rolling slowly down her cheeks**, and dropping, unheeded, on her dress. (Gaskell, *North and South*, 56)

Not only are the details of body language observed, but the description of this body language, too, becomes more and more detailed. The following quotation from George Eliot's *Middlemarch* is quite representative, despite the narrator's apology:

Accordingly, he took the paper and lowered his spectacles, measured the space at his command, reached his pen and examined it, dipped it in the ink and examined it again, then pushed the paper a little way from him, lifted up his spectacles again, showed a deepened depression in the outer angle of his bushy eyebrows, which gave his face a peculiar mildness (pardon these details for once, – you would have learned to love them if you had known Caleb Garth) ... (1:318–19)

The new attention to detail and the new visual quality of the novel, then, form an important basis for the use of body language since the end of the eighteenth century. Not only do novelists give this semiotic area greater attention, they also break new ground in its presentation. Two other literary functions of body language go hand in hand with the new attention to detail: dramatization and authentication.

5.4 Dramatization

The greater use of non-verbal detail alone contributes to an effect of full scenic representation of the fictional world, but body language accompanying the characters' speech especially makes for a dramatic effect. As we have seen above, the use of illustrators increases significantly since the middle of the eighteenth century; other classes of NVC are also encountered more frequently in the context of the characters' speech. By the nineteenth century, such non-verbal accompaniment to speech is an established fictional device, of which Charles Dickens has been deemed the master.[9] Walter Scott, too, showed his ability to render speech not only in his ear for dialect and prosodic detail,[10] but also in his eye for the body language that usually goes with every speech act:

'Who is she?' said the magistrate, looking round to some of his people.

'Other than a gude ane, sir,' said one of the city-officers, shrugging his shoulders, and smiling.

'Will ye say sae?' said the termagant, her eye gleaming with impotent fury ... (*The Heart of Midlothian*, 195–6)

Since the nineteenth century, we also increasingly find non-verbal behaviour that can be said to be semantically 'empty' but which helps to make a scene vivid and visually concrete:

'Well, Thquire,' he returned, taking off his hat, and **rubbing the lining with his pocket-handkerchief, which he kept inside for the purpose**. 'Ith it your intenthion to do anything for the poor girl, Thquire?' (Dickens, *Hard Times*, 29)

'I have thought over what you say,' she remarked to him, **moving her forefinger over the tablecloth**, her other hand, which bore the ring that mocked them both, supporting her forehead. 'It is quite true all of it; it must be. You must go away from me.' (Hardy, *Tess of the d'Urbervilles*, 287)

Many examples of this kind of body language can be found in the modern period:

'Oh well, be a nice surprise for Caro. You have a very admiring daughter. You know that?' **He squeezed his nose**. 'Actually, Dan, before I forget, she asked me to give you a ring.' (Fowles, *Daniel Martin*, 115)

'We don't want our girl upset,' he said judiciously, **removing a fleck of something from his tongue**. 'We don't want her under a strain.' (Brookner, *Lewis Percy*, 106)

In none of these quotations does the characters' non-verbal behaviour convey information about their personality traits or their momentary inner state. But, by suggesting pauses, it helps to create the impression of rhythmical speech and also gives this speech a dramatic quality; on the stage, too, pauses in the characters' speech would be bridged visually with body language. The examples considered show how closely authentication and dramatization are often linked, for the non-verbal behaviour used as a 'filler' for the pauses in the characters' speech also makes this speech seem more authentic.

5.5 Authentication

Clara Reeve was one of many writers in the eighteenth century who expounded the view that the novel should reflect reality as closely as possible. As she wrote in *The Progress of Romance* (1785): 'The Novel gives a familiar relation of such things as pass every day before our eyes, such as may happen to our friend or to ourselves; and the perfection of it is to represent every scene in so easy and natural a manner, and to make them appear so probable, as to deceive us into a persuasion (at least while we are reading) that all is real, until we are affected by the joys or distresses of the persons in the story as if they were our own.'[11] This shift to the 'familiar' is also reflected in the body language described in the novel. Thus the conviction that *all* non-verbal behaviour can be significant – not only the grand gestures – now becomes especially obvious. The following passage from *Tristram Shandy* (book 6, chapter 5) is even quoted in Freud's *The Psychopathology of Everyday Life* (1901) as an authentic example for symptomatic acts (see Freud 1966, 213); it would have been almost impossible to find such an example of body language represented in the majority of earlier novels:

– There is, continued my father, a certain mien and motion of the body and all its parts, both in acting and speaking, which argues a man *well within* ... There are a thousand unnoticed openings ... which let a penetrating eye at once into a man's soul; and I maintain it, added he, that a man of sense does not lay down his hat in coming into a room, – or take it up in going out of it, but something escapes, which discovers him.

It is for these reasons, continued my father, that the governor I make choice of shall neither lisp, or squint, or wink, or talk loud, or look fierce, or foolish; – or bite his lips, or grind his teeth, or speak through his nose, or pick it, or blow it with his fingers. –

He shall neither walk fast, – or slow, or fold his arms, – for that is laziness; – or hang them down, – for that is folly; or hide them in his pocket, for that is nonsense. –

He shall neither strike, or pinch, or tickle, – or bite, or cut his nails, or hawk, or spit, or snift, or drum with his feet or fingers in company ... (497–8)

The entire chapter 'The Translation' in *A Sentimental Journey* also reflects this insight into the significance of all non-verbal behaviour. The simple practical action of an officer is the starting point: he folds up his glasses and puts them into their case when Yorick enters his box in the Paris opera house. Yorick considers this behaviour as significant and 'translates' its meaning in a detailed gloss. He follows this gloss with a hymn of praise to the expressive power of everyday non-verbal behaviour:

There is not a secret so aiding to the progress of sociality, as to get master of this *short hand*, and to be quick in rendering the several turns of looks and limbs, with all their inflections and delineations, into plain words. For my own part, by long habitude, I do it so mechanically, that when I walk the streets of London, I go translating all the way; and have more than once stood behind the circle, where not three words have been said, and have brought off twenty different dialogues with me, which I could have fairly wrote down and sworn to. (105–6)

Sterne's novels can be seen as exceptional as far as the extent and manner of their description of body language is concerned – not only among the novels of the eighteenth century. But what appears to be excessive in Sterne's novels is also apparent, in a more moderate fashion, in works by other writers of this time. A marked increase in expressive practical actions is evident everywhere in the eighteenth century novel, as in the following examples of 'ordinary' emotional displays:

My Sister rose, with a face all over scarlet; and stepping to the table, **where lay a fan, she took it up, and ... fanned herself very violently**. (Richardson, *Clarissa*, 1:155)

Jones ... had been ready to sink with Fear. He sat **kicking his Heels, playing with his Fingers**, and looking more like a Fool, if it be possible, than a young booby Squire, when he is first introduced into a polite Assembly. (Fielding, *Tom Jones*, 734)

And then, staring full in his face, he **struck his cane on the ground**, with a violence that made him start. He did not, however, chuse [*sic*] to take any notice of this; but, **having bit his nails some time**, in manifest confusion, he turned very quick to me ... (Burney, *Evelina*, 81)

He **walked some turns backwards and forwards** in his room; he recalled the languid form of the fainting wretch to his mind; he wept at the recollection of her tears ... **He took a larger stride** – (Mackenzie, *The Man of Feeling*, 53)

Men and women no longer use canes or fans to express their inner anxiety, but the handling of objects is still an important modern behaviour pattern, as are chewing one's nails or rapping one's fingers. The character in a novel who displays his or her psychological state in such a way is much closer to the experience of modern (Western) readers than are the characters in earlier novels who were prone to fainting fits and other dramatic displays of emotion.

In the course of the nineteenth century, when human behaviour was first studied scientifically,[12] people became more and more convinced that all non-verbal behaviour is significant. 'Wise men read very sharply all your private history in your look and gait and behavior,' wrote Ralph Waldo Emerson in *The Conduct of Life* (1903 [1860], 170).[13] This conviction was also expressed in the novel of the time:

I watched every gesture, as if they must have some deep significance; **the very way in which they drank their coffee was a matter of interest to me**. I was almost disappointed to see them eat and chat like common men. (Kingsley, *Alton Locke*, 237)

Most of us have more or less frequently derived a similar impression, **from a man's manner of doing some very little thing**: plucking a flower, clearing away an obstacle, or even destroying an insentient object. (Dickens, *Little Dorrit*, 173)

Numerous examples in which the characters' ordinary non-verbal behaviour contributes to the overall effect of authenticity can be found in the novels of the nineteenth and the twentieth centuries.[14]

In the nineteenth-century novel in particular, body language is also used specifically for sociological and anthropological authentication. Just as the genre-painting of this time captures minute nuances of different social milieus, so the novel depicts a wide social spectrum, and the characters are given attributes, including body language, that correspond with their social status and the various social roles they play. In the grain auction episode of Thomas Hardy's *Far from the Madding Crowd*, for example, the farmers' non-verbal behaviour blends into the other details of the rural milieu:

The low though extensive hall ... was thronged with hot men who talked among each other in twos and threes, the speaker of the minute looking sideways into his auditor's face and concentrating his argument by a contraction of one eyelid during delivery. The greater number carried in their hands ground-ash saplings, using them partly as walking-sticks and partly for poking up pigs, sheep, neighbours with their backs turned, and restful things in general, which seemed to require such treatment in the course of their peregrinations. During conversations each subjected his saplings to great varieties of usage – bending it round his back, forming an arch of it between his two hands, overweighting it on the ground till it reached nearly a semicircle; or perhaps it was hastily tucked under the arm whilst the sample-bag was pulled forth and a handful of corn poured into the palm, which, after criticism, was flung upon the floor, an issue of events perfectly well known to half-a-dozen acute town-bred fowls which had as usual crept into the building unobserved, and waited the fulfilment of their anticipations with a high-stretched neck and oblique eye. (101–2)[15]

In other novels of the nineteenth century, one finds externalizers indicating a profession:

'Shure then, and yer a tailor, my young man?'
'Yes,' I said, nettled a little that my late loathed profession still betrayed itself in my gait. (Kingsley, *Alton Locke*, 199)[16]

or of belonging to a certain age-group:

'Wilt go to Cousin Hetty, my dilling, while mother gets ready to go to bed? Then Totty shall go into mother's bed, and sleep there all night.'
Before her mother had done speaking Totty had given her answer in an unmistakable manner, by knitting her brow, setting her tiny teeth against her under-lip, and leaning forward to slap Hetty on the arm with her utmost force. Then, without speaking, she nestled to her mother again. (George Eliot, *Adam Bede*, 1:204)

Although body language of this special kind of social realism appears to slightly decrease in the twentieth-century novel (according to the sample investigated), the role of NVC in authenticating the fictional world continues to be one of the main functions of literary body language.

5.6 Indication of Mental States

As we have seen, body language is, in all literary periods, encountered as an important means to indicate a character's feelings. The range of feelings suggested with body language, however, widens considerably in the course of time, increasingly including subtle psychological states. This refined psychology, in turn, requires more psychologically authentic forms of body language. In the nineteenth century, the description of practical actions to express a character's inner life is thus just as popular as it was in the preceding century. In the following quotations, body language conveys the embarrassment and anxiety of a character:

'Sarvant, sir!' said he, **slicking his hair down when he came into the room**: 'If hoo'l excuse me (looking at Margaret) for being i' my stockings; I'se been tramping a'day, and streets is none o' th' cleanest.' (Gaskell, *North and South*, 304)

'What do I think, Mrs. Bold?' and then **he rumbled his money with his hands in his trowsers** [*sic*] **pockets**, and looked and spoke very little like a thriving lover ... There was then a pause for a while, **during which Mr. Arabin continued to turn over his shillings and half-crowns.** (Trollope, *Barchester Towers*, 2:232)

These emotional displays do not differ greatly from the following, more recent example:

Hoylake **stopped doodling on his blotter** and looked through the window ... He **shuffled the papers on his desk** in an undecided yet intent kind of way, as if there were some way of arranging them which would say all he had to say for him. (Braine, *Room at the Top*, 141)

In a context of complex psychology, other mental states and processes than feelings are also increasingly portrayed and require greater attention to body language. In the following quotations, for example, one finds externalizers of the pensiveness and concentration of a character:

Mr. Losberne **thrust his hands into his pockets, and took several turns up and down the room; often stopping, and balancing himself on his toes**, and frowning frightfully. After various exclamations of 'I've got it now' and 'no, I haven't,' and as many renewals of the walking and frowning, he at length made a dead halt, and spoke as follows ... (Dickens, *Oliver Twist*, 180–1)

She bent low to the task, **holding her head slightly askew, putting the tip of her tongue between her lips**, and expending all the energy of her soul and body in an intense effort to do what she was doing as well as it could be done. (Bennett, *The Old Wives' Tale*, 78)

In the portrayal of mental states, the potential of an 'old' literary function of body language was continuously refined and enhanced over the centuries. In other areas, the expressive potential of NVC was hardly exploited until the eighteenth century. This has already been observed for the body language used to define character (see chapter 4, pages 134–5). It is even more evident in the portrayal of interpersonal relationships.

5.7 Indication of Interpersonal Relationships

One of the characteristics of NVC in the twentieth-century novel is the special attention given to the body language of interaction. Of the great number of externalizers represented in the twentieth-century novel, the majority are interpersonal, rather than subject-related. Again, this use of body language appears to begin in the eighteenth century. Until Richardson, externalizers of relationships were mainly used to express a love relationship. Externalizers of love remain an important group, but after the mid-eighteenth century the novel portrays a much wider spectrum of interpersonal relationships and forms of human interaction.

The eighteenth century in western Europe was an age of tremendous shifts in social structures; in particular, it was characterized by the emergence of a bourgeois society with complex social roles. It thus developed a heightened sensitivity towards the position of the individual in this society, and towards the various forms of human interaction. As a result of this new social experience, the human body gained a particular significance as a means through which a person presents him- or herself, but which also allows for a 'reading' of the other. One indication of this phenomenon was the enormous popularity which Lavater's writings on physiognomy enjoyed, despite the fact that they were also severely criticized. But the language of the body in motion also received special attention. In the novel of the period, it occurs with particular frequency in interactive situations.

Letter 11 of Fanny Burney's *Evelina*, for example, describes the nonverbal behaviour of participants at a ball. Here the men as well as the women are expected to play strictly defined roles and behave correspondingly: 'The gentlemen, as they passed and repassed, looked as if they thought we were quite at their disposal, and only waiting for the honour of their commands; and they sauntered about, in a careless indolent manner, as if with a view to keep us in suspense' (28). When Evelina, a newcomer to London society, comes in contact with a group of these gentlemen, she commits a *faux pas*. The gentlemen are taken aback, and Evelina's incorrect behaviour is immediately 'punished' through the men's body language:

> I interrupted him – I blush for my folly, – with laughing; yet I could not help it, for, added to the man's stately foppishness, (and he actually took snuff between every three words) when I looked round at Lord Orville, **I saw such extreme surprise in his face**, – the cause of which appeared so absurd, that I could not for my life preserve my gravity.
>
> I had not laughed before from the time I had left Miss Mirvan, and I had

much better have cried then; **Lord Orville actually stared at me**; the beau, I know not his name, **looked quite enraged**. 'Refrain – Madam,' (said he, with an important air,) 'a few moments refrain!' (33)

In this novel, social interaction, which has special rules for each situation, seems much more complex than, for example, in the world of the Elizabethan romance, in which a clearly defined courtly code ensures that there will be no misunderstandings in both the public and private realm of human interaction.

In a socially complex society, then, body language is of particular significance, and it is important to understand this body language in all its ramifications. In the novel, this consciousness is reflected in the fact that new modes of NVC are used and the significance of 'old' modes is broadened. As we have seen, distance behaviour of characters is very rarely depicted in the novel before the eighteenth century, and only since this century is touch behaviour increasingly used to indicate interpersonal relationships outside romantic love.[17] Eye behaviour in particular now comes to enjoy increased attention. Mechthild Albert concludes the following on the sociological significance of eye behaviour since the eighteenth century:

The isolation of the modern individual results in an almost pathological reference to the 'other' ... With growing functional differentiation, with the democratization of social structures and with the isolation of the subject, this reciprocal dependence increases ... The reference to the 'other' occurs in the form of visual processes, such as gaze and observation ... – we may thus conclude that there is an increasing visualization of social interaction. (Albert 1987, 161, my translation)[18]

Richardson's *Clarissa* contains numerous examples in which eye behaviour functions as a carrier of interpersonal messages, even outside the love relationship. Letter 8 of the novel describes how Clarissa is shunned by her family because she refuses to marry a man whom she does not love:

Such a Solemnity in every-body's countenance! – **My Mother's eyes were fixed upon the tea-cups; and when she looked up, it was heavily, as if her eyelids had weights upon them; and then not to me**. My Father sat half-aside in his elbow-chair, that his head might be turned from me; his hands clasped, and waving, as it were, up and down; his fingers, poor dear gentleman! in motion, as if angry to the very ends of them. My Sister sat swelling. **My Brother looked at me with scorn, having measured me, as I may say, with his eyes as I entered, from head to foot**. My Aunt was there, and **looked upon me as if with kindness restrained**, bending coldly to my compliment to her as she sat; and then **cast an eye first on my Brother, then on my Sister, as if to give the reason** (So I am willing to construe it) **of her unusual stiffness**. (1:51)

The passages in bold show that Clarissa receives a series of messages from the members of her family, especially through their eye behaviour, which clarify their different attitudes towards her: her mother cannot look her in the eye because of her sorrow; her brother punishes her with open contempt; her aunt shows her restrained friendliness, indicating, at the same time, why she has to be restrained.

The social significance of eye behaviour is also evident in the following passage from Henry Mackenzie's *The Man of Feeling*. A group of travellers from various social backgrounds are forced to interact with each other in the enclosed space of a stagecoach. Looks are an important means to show their relationships and attitudes to one another, ranging from avoidance of eye contact (the gentleman's averted gaze), to arrogance (the young officer), to outrage (the merchant), and secret pride (the merchant's wife):

The gentleman on the opposite side of the coach now **first turned his eye from the side-direction in which it had been fixed**, and begged Harley to exchange places with him, expressing his regret that he had not made the proposal before. Harley thanked him; and, upon being assured that both seats were alike to him, was about to accept of his offer, when the young gentleman of the sword, **putting on an arch look**, laid hold of the other's arm, 'So, my old boy,' said he, 'I find you have still some youthful blood about you; but, with your leave, I will do myself the honour of sitting by this lady;' and took his place accordingly. **The grocer stared him as full in the face** as his own short neck would allow; and his wife, who was a little round-fac'd woman, with a great deal of colour in her cheeks, drew up at the compliment that was paid her, **looking first at the officer, and then at the housekeeper**. (77)

In the novels of Jane Austen, looks also play a significant social role. Within the social confines of the characters, most of whom belong to the gentry, the behaviour of every individual is carefully registered and analysed by the others, as in the following passage from *Pride and Prejudice*:

Mrs. Gardiner and Elizabeth talked of all that had occurred ... The looks and behaviour of every body they had seen were discussed, except of the person who had mostly engaged their attention. (271–2)

Numerous glances not only suggest that everyone is constantly observing the others, but also carry diverse messages, as, for example, at the ball during which the affection between Jane and Bingley first becomes apparent to society:

'... Allow me to say, however, that your fair partner does not disgrace you, and that I must hope to have this pleasure often repeated, especially when a certain desirable event, my dear Miss Eliza, (**glancing at her sister and Bingley**,) shall take place. What congratulations will then flow in! I appeal to Mr. Darcy: ...'

The latter part of this address was scarcely heard by Darcy; but Sir William's allusion to his friend seemed to strike him forcibly, and **his eyes were directed with a very serious expression** towards Bingley and Jane, who were dancing together. (92–3)

Sir William's glance towards Jane and Bingley functions as a discreet illustrator replacing speech. Darcy's eye behaviour, however, is an unconscious externalizer of his reservations about a potential match between his friend Bingley and Miss Bennet. Glances can also convey judgments on a person that cannot be expressed in words, such as, for example, the look with which Miss Bingley communicates her contempt for Elizabeth's family to Darcy: 'Nothing but concern for Elizabeth could enable Bingley to keep his countenance. His sister was less delicate, and **directed her eye towards Mr. Darcy with a very expressive smile**' (43).

Summary

To fully develop its expressive potential, body language requires the kind of novel that first emerged in English literature with the novels of Samuel Richardson and his contemporaries. The aesthetic of this novel emphasizes the importance of detail, dramatic presentation, and authenticity. It finds its subject matter in the psychology of the characters and the diversity of human interaction. The nineteenth-century novel continues this agenda and brings it to its peak. The increasing importance of body language in the novel since the eighteenth century is also apparent in the role it plays within the structure of narrative transmission.

5.8 Body Language in the Structure of Narrative Transmission

Heterodiegetic narrators in the eighteenth-century novel have a tendency to gloss or comment on the characters' body language. But the eighteenth century, with its increased attention to individualism, is also a period in which homodiegetic forms of narration, with strongly subjective perspectives, reach a first climax. Again, the credit goes to Richardson, who used the subjectivity of his narrator-focalizers as a central artistic effect in his novels. As far as body language is concerned, one might criticize Richardson for including too many details for his epistolary novels to appear credible: as narrators, his letter writers seem to have an unusual capacity for memory and, as focalizers, they manifest an unusual awareness of the nuances of their own body language (see Och 1985, 79). For the first time, however, in Richardson's novels the NVC makes an essential contribution to perspectivization: in perceiving and decoding the body language of other characters, Richardson's letter writers reveal their sensitivity as well as their subjective way of seeing. In *Clarissa,* for example, the protagonist's perception is often influenced by her feelings. Her extreme dislike of Mr Solmes distorts her perception of his body language:

> I arose; the man hemming up for a speech, rising, and beginning to set his splay-feet (Indeed, my dear, the man in all his ways is hateful to me!) in an approaching posture. (1:101)

> The man stalked in. His usual walk is by pauses, as if (from the same vacuity of thought which made Dryden's Clown whistle) he was telling his steps ... (1:153)

As is evident in Clarissa's description of Solmes's postures and body techniques, the hated man becomes a caricature in her eyes – a view which does not correspond with the picture that is conveyed of him through the perception of other characters in the novel, at least not to this extreme degree.

Body language linked with specific perspectives also contributes to central messages and effects in a range of nineteenth-century novels. In Emily Brontë's *Wuthering Heights,* for example, the action regarding Heathcliff and Catherine Earnshaw is mainly conveyed through the view of marginal characters: the servant Nellie Dean and the tenant Lockwood. Direct access to the protagonists' thoughts and feelings is thus not possible; the novel's emotional drama is observed from the distanced perspective of less passionate characters, who describe Heathcliff and Catherine's excessive emotional displays, but do not really understand them. When Lockwood first meets Heathcliff, he is profoundly confused by the latter's emotional outburst in Cathy's old room:

> He got on to the bed, and wrenched open the lattice, bursting, as he pulled at it, into an uncontrollable passion of tears ...
>
> There was such anguish in the gush of grief that accompanied this raving, that my compassion made me overlook its folly, and I drew off, half angry to have listened at all, and vexed at having related my ridiculous nightmare, since it produced that agony; though *why*, was **beyond my comprehension**. (40)

In the episode when Catherine is dying, Nellie finds the emotional displays of Catherine and Heathcliff positively uncanny:

> His eyes, wide and wet, at last flashed fiercely on her; his breast heaved convulsively. An instant they held asunder, and then how they met I hardly saw, but Catherine made a spring, and he caught her, and they were locked in an embrace from which I thought my mistress would never be released alive: in fact, to my eyes, she seemed directly insensible. He flung himself into the nearest seat, and on my approaching hurriedly to ascertain if she had fainted he gnashed at me, and foamed like a mad dog, and gathered her to him with greedy jealousy. I did not feel as if I were in the company of a creature of my own species: it appeared that he would not understand, though I spoke to him; so, I stood off and held my tongue, **in great perplexity**. (239)

In the Victorian world, passionate and 'romantic' personalities such as Heathcliff and Catherine are outsiders; their emotions are not accessible to the 'normal' interpreter. In the narrative transmission of *Wuthering Heights*, this impression is strengthened, since the reader is not allowed direct access to the inner life of these highly emotional characters; their passion is conveyed through signs that can be perceived by the senses but are not understood by those who see and narrate them.

Charlotte Brontë's *Jane Eyre* is extremely conscious in its handling of perspective. The first-person narrator describes her own body language directly only when she is conscious of it within the narrated situation; the perception of her unconscious body language is consistently attributed to other characters; it is only through their reactions that Jane concludes anything at all about her own non-verbal behaviour: '"And so may you," I thought. My eye met his as the idea crossed my mind: **he**

seemed to read the glance, answering as if its import had been spoken as well as imagined ...' (1:225). Of special importance, however, is the body language of others perceived by Jane. The action is almost exclusively focalized through Jane as a character within the fictional situation. This limited view of the events serves to withhold information and thus to create and maintain suspense in the reader. Along with Jane, the reader perceives that there is a mystery around Rochester, but cannot solve it anymore than the protagonist herself.

The body language perceived by Jane serves to point towards Rochester's secret and the threat it poses for her happiness, even though Jane herself does not suspect his first wife's existence. When Rochester proposes marriage to Jane, she does not know that he will have to commit bigamy. Thus, she cannot correctly interpret the signs of his relief when she tells him the reason of her initial reservations:

> 'This is what I have to ask – Why did you take such pains to make me believe you wished to marry Miss Ingram?'
>
> 'Is that all? Thank God it is no worse!' And now he unknit his black brows; looked down, smiling at me, and stroked my hair, as if well pleased at seeing a danger averted. (2:39)

Similarly, she cannot understand why the housekeeper, who is fond of her (but knows Rochester's secret), is so sad about her upcoming marriage:

> Seeing me, she roused herself; she made a sort of effort to smile, and framed a few words of congratulation; but the smile expired, and the sentence was abandoned unfinished. She put up her spectacles, shut the Bible, and pushed her chair back from the table ...
>
> She surveyed my whole person: in her eyes I read that they there found no charm powerful enough to solve the enigma ...
>
> I was so hurt by her coldness and scepticism, that the tears rose to my eyes. (2:41–3)

The revelation at the wedding ceremony finally releases the tension which has been created, among other things, through the body language focalized by Jane.

With the steady increase in internal focalization in nineteenth-century novels, NVC achieves growing significance as an object of focalization: from the point of view of a character, information about the inner states of other characters can be gathered credibly only through explicit verbal information or through their body language. Thus there are more and more passages in which characters seek access to the thoughts, feelings, or attitudes of other characters through an observation of their body language. Elizabeth Gaskell's *North and South*, for example, describes repeatedly how a character consciously reads another's body language as an indication of his or her inner state. In chapter 16, Margaret, the main character, is told by a physician that her mother has very little time left to live; Margaret's reaction to this news is described from the doctor's perspective: 'He spoke two short sentences in a low voice, watching her all the time; for the pupils of her eyes dilated into a black horror, and the whiteness of her complexion became livid. He ceased speaking. He waited for that look to go off, – for her gasping breath to come' (126). In another passage, Margaret is observed by a police inspector, to whom she lies in order to protect her brother from arrest:

> The large dark eyes, gazing straight into the inspector's face, dilated a little. Otherwise there was no motion perceptible to his experienced observation. Her lips swelled out into a richer curve than ordinary, owing to the enforced tension of the muscles, but he did not know what was their usual appearance, so as to recognise the unwonted sullen defiance of the firm sweeping lines. She never blenched or trembled. She fixed him with her eye. (273)

Of special thematic relevance in this novel is the incorrect decoding of body language from a character's limited perspective. The novel explores the theme of the misunderstanding between the industrial north and the south of England. On a personal level, these regions are represented by Thornton, a factory owner, and the minister's daughter Margaret, who has moved into the community from the south. Before these two become a couple, they experience considerable difficulties in finding their way to each other, since they continually misunderstand each other. This is aptly conveyed through their touching behaviour. Misunderstandings even appear in haptic emblems, which carry different social meanings for Margaret and Thornton because of their different social backgrounds:

> When Mr. Thornton rose up to go away, after shaking hands with Mr. and Mrs. Hale, he made an advance to Margaret to wish her good-bye in a similar manner. It was the frank familiar custom of the place; but Margaret was not prepared for it. She simply bowed her farewell; although the instant she saw the

hand, half put out, quickly drawn back, she was sorry she had not been aware of the intention. Mr. Thornton, however, knew nothing of her sorrow, and, drawing himself up to his full height, walked off, muttering as he left the house –

'A more proud, disagreeable girl I never saw. Even her great beauty is blotted out of one's memory by her scornful ways.' (85)

A misunderstanding with most serious consequences occurs when Margaret embraces Thornton in order to protect him from an attack by workers who are on strike. Thornton concludes mistakenly that she loves him, and proposes marriage to her, which she rejects brusquely. In spite of this, Thornton is deeply affected when he sees Margaret at the train station, standing very close to a stranger; it is really her brother, but Thornton believes him to be Margaret's lover. Once again body language is misunderstood from this subjective point of view:

He could not forget the fond and earnest look that had passed between her and some other man – the attitude of familiar confidence, if not of positive endearment. The thought of this perpetually stung him; it was a picture before his eyes, wherever he went and whatever he was doing ... He thought of that look, that attitude! – how he would have laid his life at her feet for such tender glances, such fond detention! (309–10)

Only at the end of the novel do the characters clarify their misunderstandings, so that the central opposing factors of the novel may be reconciled.

Summary

We have seen how body language is used with increasing artistic care and fulfils a growing number of literary functions in the novel after the mid-eighteenth century. Thus, not only are the modal and functional classes of NVC employed in a much wider range than they were until this point, but also the frame conditions of NVC (see page 27) become more relevant for the analysis of these novels: body language appears much more frequently in interactive situations, and in these situations often accompanies speech. The question of the decoding of NVC within the fictional situation becomes important in the same proportion as a subjective point of view determines the structure of narrative transmission. Chapter 6 will demonstrate that such features as the consciousness and intentionality of non-verbal behaviour also start to gain significance in the course of the eighteenth century. At this point, however, the question remains to be asked whether and to what extent new trends in the development of literary body language are evident in the twentieth century.

5.9 Body Language in the Twentieth-Century Novel

5.9.1 Body Language and the Crisis of Language

A few differences in the presentation of body language with respect to the nineteenth-century novel can be linked to the decrease in overt narrators. On average, comments on body language become more 'discreet' and, along with a general reduction of extensive descriptions, the thoroughness with which body language is described also tends to decline. Body language in the twentieth-century novel is related in the narrative mode of report rather than that of description, and thus has a less static effect than is frequently the case in the eighteenth and nineteenth centuries. These broad developments are a result of general shifts in the techniques of novel writing.

Another question deals with the status of NVC in literature of the twentieth century. According to some historians of culture, the increased body awareness in the modern period can be considered a reaction to the over-emphasis on reason and *logos* in the Western 'civilizing process' (Elias 1994).[19] The move towards non-verbal means of presentation in twentieth-century drama and theatre as a result of modern scepticism about language has been frequently observed. In expressionist, surrealist, or absurd drama, non-verbal expression gains a particularly high degree of independence from the word and is often used to communicate messages discordant with the characters' speech.[20] In his study on the 'communication pathos' in modern literature, Winston Weathers (1981) discusses the importance of the non-verbal in the modern novel:

> Parallel with this movement toward seeing literature as 'thing,' 'artifact,' and 'object,' was the movement toward de-emphasizing language's role in human affairs even while keeping it around, in its most ordinary clothes, to do some of the pedestrian tasks of communication. This de-emphasis is easily seen in a growing celebration (ironically expressed *in* language) of nonverbal forms of 'communication.'
>
> D.H. Lawrence, perhaps more than any other author of our time, celebrated and insisted upon non-verbalization as a prime communication medium. (54)

In Lawrence's novels, the interaction between characters is frequently purely non-verbal, or occurs with a strong emphasis on non-verbal components, as in the following example from *Women in Love* (1921):

> He saw her bowed head, her rapt face, the face of an almost demoniacal ecstatic. Feeling him looking, she lifted her face and sought his eyes, her own beautiful grey eyes flaring him a great signal. But he avoided her look, she sank her head in torment and shame, the gnawing at her heart going on. And he too was tortured with shame, and ultimate dislike, and with acute pity for her, because he did not want to meet her eyes, he did not want to receive her flare of recognition. (23–4)

In this case, body language is the sole carrier of an emotional and sensual message that is exchanged between the characters Hermione and Birkin. This message never takes an explicit verbal form. When, towards the end of the novel, Gudrun embarrasses Gerald Crich in the presence of the painter Loerke and thus ends their relationship, NVC conveys the inner thoughts of the characters much more clearly than their clumsy words – Loerke's satisfaction, Gerald's dismay, and Gudrun's nervousness and confusion in the light of her spontaneous outburst:

> '*Bitte sagen Sie nicht immer, gnädige Frau,*' cried Gudrun, her eyes flashing, her cheeks burning. She looked like a vivid Medusa. Her voice was loud and clamorous, the other people in the room were startled.
>
> 'Please don't call me Mrs Crich,' she cried aloud ...
>
> The two men looked at her in amazement. Gerald went white at the cheek-bones.
>
> 'What shall I say, then?' asked Loerke, with soft, mocking insinuation.
>
> '*Sagen Sie nur nicht das,*' she muttered, her cheeks flushed crimson. 'Not that, at least.'
>
> She saw, by the dawning look on Loerke's face, that he had understood ...
>
> 'I am not married,' she said, with some hauteur ...
>
> Gerald sat erect, perfectly still, his face pale and calm, like the face of a statue ... He sat perfectly still in an unalterable calm. Loerke, meanwhile, was crouching and glancing up from under his ducked head.
>
> Gudrun was tortured for something to say, to relieve the suspense. She twisted her face in a smile and glanced knowingly, almost sneering, at Gerald.
>
> 'Truth is best,' she said to him, with a grimace. (505–6)

In some novels of our century, the correlation between mistrust of language and the high value given to NVC is made very obvious. As was shown, the NVC of the Neanderthals in William Golding's *The Inheritors* is given a positive moral value as opposed to the verbal communication of the *homo sapiens sapiens* (see pages 143–4). Another example is the split between language/logic and NVC/feeling in Margaret Atwood's *Surfacing* (see pages 153–5).[21] On the other hand, however, there seems to be no *general* increase in independent NVC or NVC that is discordant to the characters' speech in the twentieth-century novel. Rather, increased attention to NVC can also be observed in earlier periods whenever the value of speech as a means of communication is questioned, as will be shown in greater detail with regard to the eighteenth century (see page 216). Arguably, the fact that the modern novel appears to be not as extreme in its turn towards the non-verbal as some forms of theatre/drama can be attributed to the fact that the non-verbal must always be verbalized in the narrative text. Body language is thus never completely separated from the medium of language, and a contrast between the non-verbal and the verbal has less blatant results in a narrative text than it does in staged drama.

5.9.2 *A Modern Style of Body Language?*

It is always problematic to establish a style or styles specific to a period. Accordingly, when Wylie Sypher defines period style in his seminal study *Rococo to Cubism in Art and Literature* (1960), his definition is fairly open and vague: 'an expression of a prevailing, dominant, or authentically contemporary view of the world by those artists who have most successfully intuited the quality of human experience peculiar to their day and who are able to phrase this experience in forms deeply congenial to the thought, science, and technology which are part of that experience' (xix). Period styles of body language are more easily apparent in the visual arts than in literature, but in literature, too, one can occasionally observe styles that seem to be particularly related to a specific period. For example, the highly expressive emotional displays and emblems in medieval literature (see page 89) resemble the 'pictographic' style which Ernst Gombrich (1972, 381) has observed in early art of the Christian period: 'we can observe the re-emergence of frankly conceptual methods and a new standardization of symbolic or conceptual gestures ... These gestures of prayer, instruction, teaching or mourning, help rapidly to set up the context and to make the scene legible.'

We have seen above that the twentieth-century novel, on average, continues to employ the non-verbal 'grammar' consolidated in the nineteenth century. Although body language in the nineteenth-century novel can be stylized and exaggerated in melodramatic moments (see page 90), it is normally characterized by a style which allows it to contribute to the effect of reality in a text. Non-verbal styles in the twentieth-century novel are also fundamentally naturalistic rather than anti-naturalistic.

As far as body language in the visual arts of the twentieth century is concerned, however, it is often marked by an effect of estrangement. Expressionism freed itself from the principles of a realistic portrayal in order to give psychological facts the most intense expression possible. Edvard Munch's famous painting *The Scream* (1895) perfectly exemplifies the principles of expressionistic body language.[22] The face with its wide-open eyes and mouth and the raised hands are stylized and abstracted, so that no details distract the viewer from the essential features of the expression itself. The expressionist silent film of the first quarter of the twentieth century took on the stylized acting style of expressionistic theatre. Lotte Eisner (1969) describes the body language of the actors in *The Cabinet of Dr. Caligari* (1919):

> The stylization of the acting is dictated by the sets. Yet Werner Krauss in the part of the satanic Dr Caligari and Conrad Veidt in that of the sinister somnambulist are the only actors who really adapt themselves to it, and – in [Rudolf] Kurtz's words – achieve a 'dynamic synthesis of their being,' by concentrating their movements and facial expressions. Through a reduction of gesture they attain movements which are almost linear and which – despite a few curves that slip in – remain brusque, like the broken angles of the sets; and their movements from point to point never go beyond the limits of a given geometrical plane. (25)

The actors' faces in *Caligari* and other expressionist films are often frozen into grimaces; the actors' movements have an abrupt, tense, and mechanical quality. Modern theatre relies on a stylized and 'theatrical' body language, not only in its expressionistic but also in its absurd form.

In the modern novel, one occasionally encounters a body language that appears stylized for the sake of expressivity. The characteristic non-verbal style in Beckett's *Murphy* consists in the unnatural, puppet-like movements of Murphy and the other characters (see chapter 4, pages 91–2). A similar puppet-like behaviour is also apparent in passages of Conrad's *The Secret Agent* in which the main characters find themselves in an existential crisis and in which the world seems to spin out of their control. After the death of his brother-in-law in which he is implicated, Verloc seems to have become alienated from his own body; he moves like an automaton without a soul: 'Mr. Verloc obeyed woodenly, stony-eyed, and like an automaton whose face had been painted red. And this resemblance to a mechanical figure went so far that he had an automaton's absurd air of being aware of the machinery inside of him' (197). When she hears of her brother's death, Mrs Verloc freezes into a picture of grief, which, in its emphasis on the mask-like face and hands pressed to the face, resembles Munch's *The Scream*:

> She sat rigidly erect in the chair with two dirty pink pieces of paper lying spread out at her feet. The palms of her hands were pressed convulsively to her face, with the tips of the fingers contracted against the forehead, as though the skin had been a mask which she was ready to tear off violently. The perfect immobility of her pose expressed the agitation of rage and despair, all the potential violence of tragic passions, better than any shallow display of shrieks, with the beating of a distracted head against the walls, could have done. (212)

Conrad's novel unmistakably conveys an expressionist trait in the body language of its characters and thus manifests a non-verbal style of its period. On average, however, such antirealistic traits of body language are relatively rare in the modern novel, and the naturalistic style of body language continues to prevail.

We have seen in this chapter that historical trends in the use of body language in the novel are strongly influenced by overall developments in the genre. As the next chapter will show, however, they are also affected by changes of body language in real life, by the contemporary discussion of body language, and by the ways in which body language is employed in other forms of art.

6

Literary Body Language in Context

6.1 Changes of Body Language in Real Life

It is difficult to judge how 'accurately' literature reflects the non-verbal behaviour of a specific time or culture. However, the non-verbal competence of a writer's time and culture will, to a certain degree, always find its way into his or her work, and the body language of fictional characters is thus affected by the changes that occur in body language in real life. There are many examples to be found in which the body language of a literary character is quite obviously 'dated.' In William Congreve's play *The Way of the World* (1700), a historical shift in male touching behaviour is explicitly mentioned in the text, when Witwould, the fop, explains the following to his brother who lives in the country: 'But I tell you, 'tis not modish to know relations in town. You think you're in the country, where great lubberly brothers slabber and kiss one another when they meet, like a call of serjeants. 'Tis not the fashion here; 'tis not indeed, dear brother' (3. ll 470–4). In L.P. Hartley's novel *The Go-Between* (1953), an example of 'old-fashioned' touching behaviour serves to enhance the impression of the end of an era. In the following quotation, the narrator, an old man, describes a photograph taken in his childhood: 'I have my hand on Marcus's shoulder ... in the attitude of affection which, in those days, was permitted to the male sex when they were photographed together (undergraduates and even soldiers draped themselves about each other) ... '(40).

In these two instances, attention is drawn to a change in body language within the text itself, and the historical change in non-verbal behaviour is explicitly used to make a statement. More usually, however, non-verbal behaviour simply ages with the text in which it is described and may then seem strange to readers of a later date:

George Sampson, the friend of the Wilfer family, is by no means the only character in Dickens who thrusts the head of his stick into his mouth ... Contemporary sketches and paintings suggest that this practice was not uncommon ... It is obviously likely to appear grotesque to the modern reader because walking-sticks and canes are in such short supply. A wide range of Victorian gestures involved accoutrements that have now disappeared or become very scarce: hats, gloves, fans, monocles, parasols, snuff-boxes, pocket-watches, beards. Within the very recent past the handkerchief that could be drawn forth with a flourish to mop the brow has become an endangered species ... Men no longer shed tears or link arms. In terms of class and social convention Dickens's novels are so remote from our experience that we are liable to misread his finer detail, to overlook or misconstrue carefully recorded snubs, blunders, unorthodoxies. (Irwin 1979, 56–7)

In novels of the nineteenth and early twentieth centuries, male characters are often presented in what might be called a 'fireplace pose':

Mr. Darcy, who was leaning against the mantle-piece with his eyes fixed on her face, seemed to catch her words with no less resentment than surprise. (Austen, *Pride and Prejudice*, 190)

How he was preparing his thunder for successful rivals, standing like a British peer with his back to the sea-coal fire, and his hands in his breeches pockets ... (Trollope, *Barchester Towers*, 1:8)[1]

In nineteenth-century genre-painting, too, this pose frequently occurs, suggesting that it actually was a common pose for men during this time. The fact that it is almost exclusive to men[2] can be attributed in part to the different clothing worn by women and men: women, in their wide, floor-length skirts, would not have enjoyed standing close to even a cold fireplace. On the other hand, the privilege of an upright posture in the most prominent area of a room could also be linked to gender roles; propriety in the nineteenth century demanded that women were to appear in a sitting position, not in display poses, as in the examples above. In the early twentieth century, when gender roles (and women's fashion) were beginning to change, female characters are also increasingly found in the 'fireplace pose':

Isabel got up and walked over to the chimney-piece ... She stood with one elbow on the mantel-shelf in a graceful attitude which it was one of her most charming gifts to be able to assume without any appearance of intention. (Maugham, *The Razor's Edge*, 301)

But Anna, propping her elbow on the mantelpiece, looked at him with implacable melancholy. (Bowen, *The Death of the Heart*, 26)

Such observations are more interesting from the point of view of cultural studies than literary studies in a narrower sense. However, the poses described above could have created an effect of authenticity for contemporary readers, and aspects of period-specific body language may also be responsible for a reader's problems in fully understanding a text.

Socially coded emblems, in particular, are subject to the whims of fashion. For example, the novel reflects the change in greeting behaviour in Western civilization: while curtsies and bows dominated in the eighteenth century, hand shaking as a form of greeting increased in the following century (see Wildeblood 1973, 163). The form of greeting which one character offers another can – as is the case in *The Way of the World* – imply the social status of the character or the interpersonal relationship between the characters. To readers of a later date, such subtleties of forms of greeting may no longer be significant.

Body techniques are another area in which non-verbal behaviour changes. In nineteenth-century England, a woman's sitting posture might characterize her as unconventional and emancipated, as in the following example from Ellen Wood's *East Lynne*, in which the lawyer Carlyle's sister is described: 'In reply to this plain hint, Miss Carlyle deliberately seated herself in the client's chair, and crossed her legs, her shoes and her white stockings in full view' (31). To an English reader of today, this way of sitting seems perfectly 'normal,' and if he or she is not familiar with historical norms of etiquette, the significance of this behaviour is lost.

A loss in meaning may also be a result of the reader's unfamiliarity with historical theories of body language. As we shall see in the next section, literary preferences for certain kinds of NVC are often related to the general knowledge of the time about body language.

6.2 Body Language Theories

Academic reflection on the semiotics of the human body is to be found in almost all periods.[3] It can be assumed that this discussion, at least in its popularized forms, had an influence on the non-verbal competence of writers and readers and their alertness to non-verbal behaviour. For example, nineteenth-century British and American novelists could assume that their readers were familiar with the many allusions to physiognomy and phrenology in their works,[4] whereas these pose problems in interpretation to readers of today. Traces of the theoretical reflection on body language are not as clearly evident, but can certainly be found as well.

Thus the longevity of repertoires of emotional displays in literature (see chapter 4, page 89) could be linked with the fact that such repertoires were also circulated outside of literature. The main academic disciplines in which reflections on body language took place until the nineteenth century were rhetoric[5] and, from the Renaissance onwards, psychology. In the sixteenth and seventeenth centuries, both disciplines devoted special attention to the expression of affect and drew up inventories in which all feelings were associated with certain non-verbal displays. The following quotation from Sidney's *Arcadia* exemplifies this clear relation between non-verbal signifier and signified emotion:

> *Zelmanes* la[n]guishing cou[n]tena[n]ce with crost armes, and sometimes cast-up eyes, she thought to have an excellent grace: and therefore she also willingly put on the same countena[n]ce: til at the last ... she accepted not onely the band, but the service; **not only the signe, but the passion signified**. (170)

By imitating a certain emotional display, the character automatically also assumes the feeling that 'belongs' to it.

In academic writing, the notion that emotions and their forms of expression can be catalogued is to be found, for example, in the work of John Bulwer. With two influential volumes, Bulwer contributed to the disciplines of both psychology and rhetoric: *Pathomyotomia, or a Dissection of the Significative Muscles of the Affections of the Minde* (1649) and *Chirologia: Or the Naturall Language of the Hand ... Whereunto Is Added Chironomia: Or, the Art of Manual Rhetoricke* (1644). In the course of fifty-one chapters, the *Pathomyotomia* lists the expressive potential of individual body parts, such as, for example, head gestures:

> When we lightly *dislike, refuse, denie*, or *resent* a thing, we use a cast-up Nod of our Head, a motion diametrically opposite to the forward motion of assent ... (54)

In *Supplication, tendernesse of love* and *humility; servile respect, flattery, reverence*, and obsequious regard, &c. a *moderate bowing the head to one side* is often used, the better to move others to compassion, by that languishing posture of the Head. (74)

In Bulwer's *Chironomia*, the inventory of hand signifiers and their signifieds is even presented graphically, in the form of 'chirogrammatical' diagrams.[6]

Even if there are obvious points of contact between literary body language and the academic reflection on body language, however, the prose fiction of the sixteenth and seventeenth centuries hardly ever describes non-verbal behaviour in as great detail as do the psychological and rhetorical writings of the time. For example, the preening behaviour of a lover is described in many nuances in Robert Burton's *The Anatomy of Melancholy* (1621): 'No sooner doth a young man see his Sweetheart coming, but he smugs up himself, pulls up his cloak now fallen about his shoulders, ties his garters, points, sets his band, cuffs, slicks his hair, twirls his beard, &c.' (754). As we have seen (see pages 89, 129), much prose fiction of the sixteenth and seventeenth centuries does not make use of the detailed descriptions of emotional displays provided by contemporary psychology, but rather relies on literary tradition for the presentation of the mental states, especially stereotypical emotional displays.

The burgeoning use of body language in the eighteenth-century novel is, to a large extent, determined by overall changes occurring within the genre itself, such as those discussed in chapter 5. On the other hand, its greater use also occurs at a time when the language of the body received increased attention in philosophy, in particular, the philosophy of language as exemplified in Condillac's *Essai sur l'origine des connaissances humaines* (1746), Diderot's *Lettre sur les sourds et muets* (1751), Maupertuis's 'Dissertation sur les différens moyens dont les hommes se sont servis pour exprimer leurs idées' (1756), Herder's *Essay on the Origin of Language* (*Über den Ursprung der Sprache*, 1772), or Rousseau's *Essai sur l'origine des langues* (1781). These reflections may well have influenced the novelists' sensitivity to body language. In any case, the novel writers of the eighteenth century tend to pay special attention to exactly those aspects of NVC that are also prevalent in the philosophical discussion.

Philosophical reflection on language in the eighteenth century was particularly concerned with the relation between language and feeling, and it anticipated a central result of modern NVC research: intrinsically coded NVC is less subject to rational control than is the extrinsically coded word (see page 40). For the language philosophers, body language was thus a natural[7] – and the only reliable – expression of feeling. This conviction was soon echoed in contemporary writings on aesthetics. Henry Home, Lord Kames, for example, wrote in *The Elements of Criticism* (1762) that '[t]he natural signs of emotions ... form an universal language, which no distance of place, no difference of tribe, no diversity of tongue, can darken or render doubtful' (2:127).

Body language plays a central role in the expression of feeling in the literature of all periods. But it is only in the second half of the eighteenth century that a programmatic juxtaposition of language and body language is evident for the first time. As a means for the expression of feeling, language is regarded with growing scepticism; deep emotion is considered to be inexpressible in words, but it can be effectively expressed through the eloquence of the human body. Characters in the novel of the late eighteenth century typically become speechless in the presence of strong emotion.[8] Where, during the Renaissance, a character overwhelmed with emotions burst into monologues, in the eighteenth century the character exhibits a pantomime of affect. The mute scene thus becomes a new narrative device in the 18th century,[9] as in the following death scene in Robert Bage's *Hermsprong*:

> Mrs. Garnet entered. Lord Grondale put out towards her the only hand which now obeyed his will. His look asked forgiveness; hers granted it. He cast his eyes on his nephew, to whom he now held out his hand. Sir Charles took it with respect. He pressed it gently. Lord Grondale, with that strength he had, returned the pressure. Sir Charles understood this as an expression of contrition, and marked his sentiment of it by raising his uncle's hand to his lips. It seemed to animate his lordship; he beckoned Miss Campinet to approch [*sic*]; he took her hand, and motioned it towards his nephew. Sir Charles caught it, and imprinted upon it a respectful kiss. His uncle's last look seemed to express a faint degree of pleasure. But not longer able to support the effort of keeping awake, his head sunk upon the pillow, oppressed with his last sleep. He awoke, and died. (246)

In such mute scenes, body language serves as an independent carrier of meaning. When it accompanies speech, the relation between this speech and the body language of feeling is often discordant. In these cases, body language is usually given the greater credence:

> Notwithstanding the nicest Guard which *Sophia* endeavoured to set on her

Behaviour, she could not avoid letting some Appearances now and then slip forth: For love may again be likened to a Disease in this, that when it is denied a Vent in one Part, it will certainly break out in another. **What her Lips therefore concealed, her Eyes, her Blushes, and many little involuntary Actions, betrayed.** (Fielding, *Tom Jones*, 218–19)

'I cannot be detained Signor,' interrupted Ellena, still more embarrassed, 'or forgive myself for having permitted such a conversation;' **but as she spoke the last words, an involuntary smile seemed to contradict their meaning. Vivaldi believed the smile in spite of the words**; but, before he could express the lightning joy of conviction, she had left the pavilion; he followed through the garden – but she was gone. (Radcliffe, *The Italian*, 27)

The emphasis on the involuntariness of the body language in both quotations shows how two frame conditions of non-verbal behaviour gained a particular significance in the late eighteenth century: the unconsciousness and intentionality of non-verbal behaviour. In *The Elements of Criticism*, Henry Home expressly differentiated between 'voluntary and involuntary' external signs of the passions (2:199).

Consciousness and intentionality became important not only with respect to the expression of feelings, but also in the context of the new attention given to interpersonal relationships. While unconscious, natural body language has great credibility in the realm of interpersonal communication, intentional body language is suspect, because it can be used in order to deceive others. This deceptiveness was pointed out by Henry Fielding in his 'Essay on the Knowledge of the Characters of Men' (1743): 'Nature doth really imprint sufficient marks in the countenance to inform an accurate and discerning eye; but ... the generality of mankind mistake the affectation for the reality' (Fielding 1899, 187). William Hogarth, in *The Analysis of Beauty* (1753), also emphasized how unreliable a facial expression can be: 'the bad man, if he be an hypocrite, may so manage his muscles, by teaching them to contradict his heart, that little of his mind can be gather'd from his countenance' (Hogarth 1955, 137).

In many novels of the eighteenth century, the conscious control of body language was valued in a similarly negative way. A fundamental moral theme of Fielding's *Tom Jones* is the disillusionment of a naturally good person in the face of the deceptiveness of his fellow human beings. For example, controlled body language repeatedly characterizes Blifil, Tom's half-brother, as a sly opportunist:

Here *Allworthy* concluded his Sermon, to which *Blifil* had listened with the profoundest Attention, tho' it cost him some Pains to prevent now and then a small Discomposure of his Muscles. He now praised every Period of what he had heard, with the Warmth of a young Divine who hath the Honour to dine with a Bishop the same Day in which his Lordship hath mounted the Pulpit. (72)[10]

In Ann Radcliffe's *The Italian*, Schedoni's villainy is also reflected in his ability to control his body language: 'Yet, notwithstanding all this gloom and austerity, some rare occasions of interest had called forth a character upon his countenance entirely different; and he could adapt himself to the tempers and passions of persons, whom he wished to conciliate, with astonishing facility, and generally with complete triumph' (35). In Fanny Burney's *Evelina*, Evelina's spontaneous, natural body language is contrasted with the artificial body language of the genteel Londoners:

Not long after, a young man ... advanced, on tiptoe, towards me; he had a set smile on his face, and his dress was so foppish, that I really believe he even wished to be stared at; and yet he was very ugly.

Bowing almost to the ground, with a sort of swing, and waving his hand with the greatest conceit, after a short and silly pause, he said, 'Madam – may I presume?' – and stopt, offering to take my hand. I drew it back, but could scarce forbear laughing. (29)[11]

Henry Mackenzie's *The Man of Feeling* portrays a man who fails in a corrupt world because of his moral integrity. In his misguided belief in human benevolence, he regards body language as a universally honest reflection of the characteristics and feelings of his fellow men. This attitude makes him an object of ridicule:

Harley answered, 'That he could not but fancy the gentleman was mistaken, as he never saw a face promise more honesty than that of the old man he had met with.' – 'His face!' said a grave-looking man, who sat opposite to him, squirting the juice of his tobacco obliquely into the grate. There was something very emphatical in the action; for it was followed by a burst of laughter round the table. (52)[12]

Laclos's *Les Liaisons Dangereuses* (1782), finally, represents a peak of the social novel of the eighteenth century in which NVC is a central carrier of meaning. In accordance with the novel's main theme, love and its perversion in aristocratic circles, eye behaviour in particular is given special attention. In their letters, the Marquise de Merteuil and the Vicomte de Valmont report on their victims' eye behaviour as an indication for their success in playing with the feelings of others. They reveal their own perfidy in the way they consciously use the look of love for their own purposes. The manipulation of body language thus becomes an indicator for moral corruption:

De mon côté, je devins rêveuse, à tel point qu'on fut forcé de s'en apercevoir, et quand on m'en fit le reproche, j'eus l'adresse de m'en défendre maladroitement et de jeter sur Prévan un coup d'oeil prompt, mais timide et déconcerté, et propre à lui faire croire que toute ma crainte était qu'il ne devinât la cause de mon trouble ... Vous jugez bien que mes timides regards n'osaient chercher les yeux de mon vainqueur: mais dirigés vers lui d'une manière plus humble, ils m'apprirent bientôt que j'obtenais l'effet que je voulais produire. (187–8)

When body language is controlled, its unreliability increases, and the question whether it is interpreted correctly or incorrectly becomes particularly important.[13] In Sterne's *Tristram Shandy*, the fact that body language can be misunderstood is emphasized even for situations in which no deception is intended. In chapter 12 of book 4, Tristram's father and uncle are discussing the horrors of Mrs Shandy's imminent confinement, having, however, very different horrors in mind. When both of them shake their head, this thus means two totally divergent things. While Uncle Toby is showing the mother his sympathy, the future father is thinking about his own sex, which will suffer under the disturbance in the rhythm of the household:

'Tis a piteous burden upon 'em, continued he, shaking his head. – Yes, yes, 'tis a painful thing – said my father, shaking his head too – but certainly since shaking of heads came into fashion, never did two heads shake together, in concert, from two such different springs.

God bless } 'em all – said my uncle *Toby* and
Duce take } my father, each to himself. (340)

While the characters think they are both thinking the same thing, the narrator's gloss, in the form of a direct report of their thoughts, accentuates the contradictory signifieds of the body-language signifier.

The philosophy of language of the eighteenth century led to a heightened awareness not only of the characteristics of verbal language, but also of the expressive qualities of non-verbal communication. It thus formed a context which, besides the developments inherent to the genre itself, provided body language in the novel with new impulses.[14]

In the nineteenth century, due to an increased interest in psychology and sociology, human (expression) behaviour was explored with new, scientific methods. Many of the writings in this area were read by a wider public; in England, for example, the works of the anatomist Sir Charles Bell[15] and Charles Darwin's *The Expression of the Emotions in Man and Animals* (1872) were fairly popular.[16] This intensified interest may have sharpened the writers' sensitivity to the details of body language, which are increasingly evident in the nineteenth-century novel (see pages 188–90). At any rate, the characters and narrators in the novels themselves appear to be increasingly aware of body language and the messages it can convey; they think about and discuss body language within the fictional context. In American literature, Mark Twain's novels are a prominent example. In *A Connecticut Yankee in King Arthur's Court* (1889), the American democrat who finds himself transported to the Middle Ages gives the king a lesson about the behaviour proper to his role in society:

> 'Your soldierly stride, your lordly port – these will not do. You stand too straight, your looks are too high, too confident. The cares of a kingdom do not stoop the shoulders, they do not droop the chin, they do not depress the high level of the eye-glance, they do not put doubt and fear in the heart and hang out the signs of them in slouching body and unsure step. It is the sordid cares of the lowly born that do these things.' (274)[17]

For the twentieth-century novel, this kind of awareness of narrators and characters can be supported by many more examples:

> 'Oh, mother!' Constance protested. 'I think he's just lovely.'
>
> 'He never looks you straight in the face,' said Mrs. Baines. (Bennett, *The Old Wives' Tale*, 91)

> He looked, Mrs Viveash thought, peculiarly ugly when he laughed. His face seemed to go all to pieces; not a corner of it but was wrinkled and distorted by the violent grimace of mirth. Even the forehead was ruined when he laughed. Foreheads are generally the human part of people's faces. Let the nose twitch and the mouth grin and the eyes twinkle as monkeyishly as you like; the fore-

head can still be calm and serene, the forehead still knows how to be human. But when Casimir laughed, his forehead joined in the general disintegrating grimace. (Huxley, *Antic Hay*, 75)

Though I was watching his eyes pretty closely while we were exchanging these remarks I could discern only a natural surprise and pleasure, but no feeling more complicated. (Maugham, *The Razor's Edge*, 147)

The more recent the examples, the more frequently a specialized jargon is used in the description of non-verbal behaviour:

Portia, her hat pushed back from her forehead, stood askance under the light; she and Matchett blinked; there followed one of those pauses in which animals, face to face, appear to communicate. (Bowen, *The Death of the Heart*, 23)

He often thought what a good thing it would be if the wearing of masks or animals' heads could become customary for persons over a certain age. How restful social intercourse would be if the face did not have to assume any expression – the strained look of interest, the simulated delight or surprise, the anxious concern one didn't really feel. (Pym, *Less than Angels*, 54)

In particular, NVC research since the 1970s has provoked a more 'scientific' – and jargon-ridden – presentation of body language in the novel:

'He did seem a bit shifty,' said Robyn. 'All that fiddling with his pipe is an excuse to avoid eye contact.' (Lodge, *Nice Work*, 196)

'Do you know, when you talk sometimes, you tug your ear?'

'It's a defence reflex, Sophie. According to the books, tugging your ear, scratching the back of your head, is a disguised defence reflex. You lift your arm to strike your enemy. What do you say?' (Swift, *Out of This World*, 42)

In the last two quotations, the new jargon is used to address body language of interpersonal relationships. Apart from emotional displays, this is an area of NVC particularly emphasized in modern research and the popular handbooks derived from it. Since the popularization of NVC research, several aspects of interactive non-verbal behaviour appear in the novel which were never or only rarely mentioned before: for example, the angle at which one person faces another, or the way people build protective barricades between themselves and others. Both are aspects whose communicative relevance did not become public knowledge until Hall's ideas on proxemics had been widely circulated:

'I didn't say awful. Unpurged.' He goes and sits on the couch, at right angles to her chair. (Fowles, *Daniel Martin*, 57–8)

'Now, how can I be of help to you?' she said, taking her own seat behind the barrier of the desk. Roland meditated strategies of evasion of his own. (Byatt, *Possession*, 40)

A final question to be asked in this section concerns the extent to which the general body image of a period affects literary body language. The attention given to body language today is clearly embedded in a general awareness of the body – or even a cult of the body – in many areas of Western culture. To a considerable degree, however, literary body language seems to be quite independent of the general body image. For example, the conventional emotional displays that can be found in Western classical literature continue on into the nineteenth century quite regardless of considerable changes in general attitudes towards the body. Only on rare occasions can a direct correlation between the quantity or quality of body language and a specific body image be established.

In the work of D.H. Lawrence, a connection between preferred modes of NVC and the author's cult of the body can hardly be overlooked. In particular, the characters' touching behaviour – that is, the most sensuous mode of NVC – is described in great detail throughout Lawrence's novels. In *Women in Love*, for example, touch plays an important role in the relationship between the Brangwen sisters and Birkin and Gerald, as well as in the relationship between the two men. This is especially apparent in the chapter entitled 'Gladiatorial,' in which the men act out the erotic undertones of their friendship in a wrestling match. At the end of this match, the men confirm their friendship in a prolonged instance of touch:

He put out his hand to steady himself. It touched the hand of Gerald, that was lying out on the floor. And Gerald's hand closed warm and sudden over Birkin's, they remained exhausted and breathless, the one hand clasped closely over the other. It was Birkin whose hand, in swift response, had closed in a strong, warm clasp over the hand of the other. Gerald's clasp had been sudden and momentaneous. (307)

Lawrence was not alone in his attitude towards the body at a time when a general renaissance of the body was taking place in reaction against a culture increasingly perceived as logocentric. This renaissance is apparent, for example, in the areas of sports and dance, as well as nudism. In *Women in Love,* the swimming scenes, the Afro-rhythmic dances in which even Birkin can express his feelings, and especially the eurhythmic dances performed by Ursula and Gudrun demonstrate Lawrence's participation in this general movement of his time. But although some aspects of Lawrence's body language can certainly be connected to a specific body image, others, for example the NVC used to accompany dialogues, are quite untouched by it. Further research into the connections between body images and body language in literature is only possible when the history of the human body has been explored in more detail than it has up to now.

6.3 The Context of Other Literary Genres and Art Forms

Because of the close links between the genres of literature and their 'sister arts,' it is often impossible to determine in which direction an influence is taking place. Many affinities between the arts or between literary genres can be accounted for by the fact that they react to the same phenomena of their time. Occasionally, however, body language in the novel appears to be affected quite clearly by another literary genre or another art form.

6.3.1 Drama

We have seen how body language can help to dramatize the action of a novel (see pages 190–1). In fulfilling this function, it achieves an important status in the aesthetic of the novel since the late eighteenth century. As early as the seventeenth century, however, an awareness of the value of dramatic presentation began to emerge in both the theory and practice of novel writing. This awareness developed in close connection with drama, which occupied a higher rank in the contemporary hierarchy of genres.

During the Restoration, French *nouvelles* such as those by Madame de Lafayette were often translated and proved an important influence on the early English novel. These *nouvelles* were characterized by a greater concern with verisimilitude than was evident in the old romance (although the themes of the romance were often continued), and, in particular, they were concerned with a vivid, dramatic presentation of the action, for which body language became increasingly important.[18] They thus introduced a new direction for the novel that the eighteenth century could continue. It is certainly no coincidence that two novelists of the English Restoration period, Aphra Behn and William Congreve, were primarily active as dramatists. In his foreword to *Incognita* (1692), Congreve explicitly proclaimed that the novel needs 'to imitate *Dramatick* Writing.'

In the context of these early attempts at dramatic presentation in fiction, it is especially the characters' speech that experiences a decided change. In the Renaissance romance, the long monologue block is the dominant form for speech, and body language accompanying this speech is generally only mentioned in an initial position (see page 100). This type of body language is hardly capable of dramatizing the characters' speech. In the course of the seventeenth century, an important development of dialogue in the novel occurred when the speakers' utterances became shorter and the speakers changed more rapidly and frequently.[19] Such a kind of dialogue lends itself better to being supported by body language than the monologue blocks of the Renaissance. The following passage is taken from Aphra Behn's *The History of the Nun* (1689):

> At this Word, she grew pale, and started, as at some dreadful Sound, and cry'd, 'Hah! what is't you say? ... I will sooner dye, than yield to what ... Alas! I but too well approve!' These last words she spoke with a fainting Tone, and the Tears fell anew from her fair soft Eyes. 'If it be so,' said he, (with a Voice so languishing, it could scarce be heard) 'If it be so, and that you are resolv'd to try, if my Love be eternal without Hope, without expectation of any other Joy ...' (119)

Most striking in this passage is the attempt to create a sense of simultaneous speech and NVC. It is achieved by syntactic subordination (in the presentation of the man's paralanguage) as well as by clear indications where the character's speech is modified through NVC: 'at this word,' 'these last words.' The characters' speech is dramatized by being *interwoven* with NVC. A similar attempt to interweave the two is also evident in the dialogues of Congreve's *Incognita*:

> 'I believe you (says the Lady) and hope you are convinced of your error, since you must allow it impossible to tell who of all this Assembly did or did not make choice of their own Apparel. Not all (said *Aurelian*) there is an ungainness in some which betrays them. **Look ye there (says he) pointing to a Lady** who

stood playing with the Tassels of her Girdle, I dare answer for that Lady, though she be very well dress'd, 'tis more than she knows.' (18–19)

Here the resemblance of the characters' speech to natural speech is also heightened by a deictic illustrator, which allows an exophoric reference ('there') to occur within the speech (see page 140).

Among the writers who continued the tradition of the *nouvelle* in the beginning of the eighteenth century, Eliza Haywood is the best known today. She was also a playwright, and her effort to dramatize the novel was an important contribution to the further development of the genre. In *The Rash Resolve* (1724), for example, Haywood uses various devices to indicate the simultaneity of body language and speech, such as the parentheses in the following quotation:

GOOD Heaven! ... But you mistake her sure, and what is Over-Tenderness misconstrue Hate – You'll soon be able to judge whether I do not, (*resum'd* Berillia, *affecting an Air of Indignation*) – But I shall give my self no further trouble, but leave you to the Proof ... Forbid it Heaven (*resum'd she, softning her Voice and sitting down again*) that Love should have such Power over a Heart like yours ... (61)

The high regard which dramatic presentation enjoyed in the later eighteenth century is illustrated in a quotation from Henry Home's *The Elements of Criticism*. Drama is still considered to be a model for the novel: 'Writers of genius, sensible that the eye is the best avenue to the heart, represent every thing as passing in our sight; and from readers to hearers, transform us, as it were, into spectators. A skilful writer conceals himself, and presents his personages. In a word, every thing becomes dramatic as much as possible' (3:197). The development of dialogue under the influence of drama is considered one of the most important areas of progress in novel writing in the eighteenth century.[20] It coincides with the unprecedented role which body language now plays in the characters' interaction – in all modes of novel writing. There is even clearer evidence now of efforts to blend the characters' speech and body language. A conspicuous example, in which syntactical subordination and participle constructions are used for this purpose, is the episode in Sterne's *Tristram Shandy* in which Eugenius takes his final leave of the dying Yorick (book 1, chapter 12). Not only is the speaker's nonverbal behaviour inserted into his speech, but several reactions of the listener, Yorick, are also recorded:

He told him, he was within a few hours of giving his enemies the slip for ever. – I hope not, **answered *Eugenius*, with tears trickling down his cheeks,** and with the tenderest tone that ever man spoke, – I hope not, *Yorick*, said he ... – Come, – come, *Yorick*, **quoth *Eugenius*, wiping his eyes**, and summoning up the man within him, – my dear lad, be comforted, – let not all thy spirits and fortitude forsake thee at this crisis when thou most wants [*sic*] them; – who knows what resources are in store, and what the power of God may yet do for thee? – ***Yorick* laid his hand upon his heart, and gently shook his head**; – for my part, **continued *Eugenius*, crying bitterly as he uttered the words**, – I declare I know not, *Yorick*, how to part with thee ... – I beseech thee, *Eugenius*, **quoth *Yorick*, taking off his night-cap as well as he could with his left hand, – his right being still grasped close in that of *Eugenius***, – I beseech thee to take a view of my head ... *Yorick*'s last breath was hanging upon his trembling lips ready to depart as he uttered this; – yet still it was utter'd with something of a *cervantick* tone; – **and as he spoke it, *Eugenius* could perceive a stream of lambent fire lighted up for a moment in his eyes**; – faint picture of those flashes of his spirit, which (as *Shakespear* said of his ancestor) were wont to set the table in a roar! (33–4)

The non-verbal inserts in this passage not only give the episode a particular immediacy, but they also contribute to a sense of rhythm in the characters' speech in the way they create the impression of pauses and accentuate individual words or phrases. In the latter part of the eighteenth century, such inserts still frequently occur in the form of parentheses:

'I could not bear to see these poor Wretches naked and starving, and at the same Time know myself to have been the Occasion of all their Sufferings. – I could not bear it, Sir, upon my Soul, I could not.' (Here the Tears run down his Cheeks, and he thus proceeded) 'It was to save them from absolute Destruction, I parted with your dear Present ...' (Fielding, *Tom Jones*, 143)

'Oh, murder! (says I, clapping my hands) this is too bad, Jason.' – 'Why so? (said Jason) when it's all, and a great deal more to the back of it, lawfully mine was I to push for it.' 'Look at him (says I, pointing to Sir Condy, who was just leaning back in his arm chair, with his arms falling beside him like one stupefied) is it you, Jason, that can stand in his presence and recollect all he has been to us ...?' (Edgeworth, *Castle Rackrent*, 76–7)

In the nineteenth-century novel, however, the use of parentheses as a method to integrate body language and speech is conspicuously reduced. Instead, body language accompanying speech is generally inserted into the characters' speech with 'normal' punctuation marks, such as commas or full stops. Arguably, this may be an indication that body language accompanying speech is no longer regarded as a foreign element imported from drama, but as a regular, constitutive element of the novel.

Drama particularly affected the use and presentation of body language accompanying speech in the novel of the seventeenth and eighteenth centuries. Besides drama, the visual arts, especially theatre and painting, provide an important context for body language in the novel. Since the eighteenth century, there are numerous cross-references among the performing arts, painting, and literature.[21]

6.3.2 *Theatre and Painting*

Towards the end of the eighteenth century, the body language in the novel reflects a growing need for verisimilitude (see pages 191–3). At the same time, however, in the context of the contemporary interest in the passions, conventional emotional displays continue to be used for the portrayal of strong emotions (see page 90). This continuation of a conventional body language may have been encouraged by theatre and painting, art forms which still relied heavily on traditional repertoires of non-verbal expression and which also transformed the non-verbal inventories of seventeenth-century rhetoric and psychology into an aesthetic 'grammar' for the expression of feeling.

Reflections on the art of acting in the eighteenth century were particularly concerned with the body language of emotion, not least because of the attention given to it in the contemporary philosophy of language.[22] The basic tenor of these reflections was to encourage the move towards a more 'natural' body language of the actor, which was believed to imbue his expression of passion with great intensity. Denis Diderot was one of the main proponents of this idea in France; in England, Aaron Hill wrote the following in his 'Essay on the Art of Acting' (1746): 'To act a passion well, the actor never must attempt its imitation, until his fancy has conceived so strong an image, or idea, of it, as to move the same impressive springs within his mind, which form that passion, when it is undesigned, and natural' (Cole and Chinoy, eds 1970 [1949], 117). However, it was assumed that this intensive 'natural' expression could be achieved by following prescribed rules for the codification of emotion — a notion which seems somewhat paradoxical

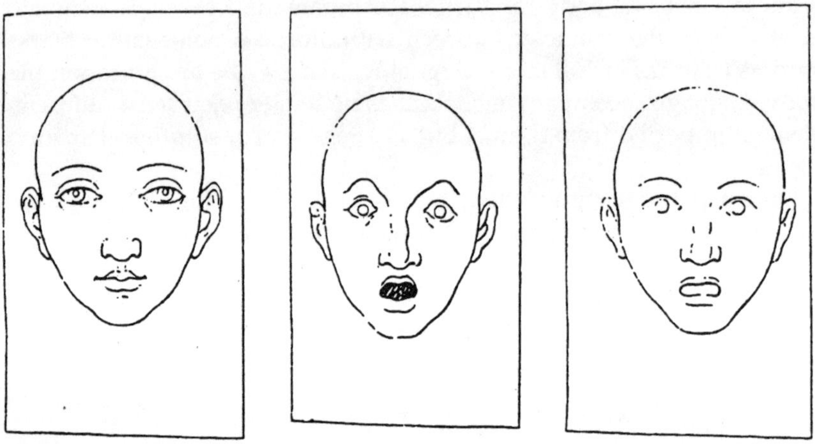

Figure 6.1 Charles Le Brun: Tranquillity – Astonishment – Admiration

from today's perspective. Johann Jakob Engel's *Ideen zu einer Mimik* (1786), a work that was influential in all of Europe, described such rules for a true 'expression of the inner operations and feelings of the soul' ('Ausdruck der innern Operationen und Empfindungen der Seele' [Engel, 1884:36]).[23] These rules were supposed to ensure that the non-verbal expression of an emotion would have a high degree of semantic clarity.

Engel's rules were, in many respects, anticipated in a work of the late seventeenth century which gained central importance in all visual arts of the eighteenth century: the *Conférences sur l'expression des différents caractères des passions* (1668), by the painter Charles Le Brun, compiled the 'grammar' of the passions which the French Academy painters had developed under the influence of Descartes's *Les passions de l'âme*. 'The codification of this expressiveness in the hands of the French Academy put the passions at the disposal of a public so wide that their signifyings could be taken for granted by painters, actors, and writers alike' (McKenzie 1990, 6).[24] In Le Brun's *Conférences*, every emotion is associated with a corresponding non-verbal expression and illustrated with a drawing. The illustrations in Figure 6.1. show, from left to right, Tranquillity, Astonishment, and Admiration.

The most impressive example of such a codification of expression in eighteenth-century theatre is a bravura performance for which David Garrick, who made his London debut as Richard III in 1741, was famous in all of Europe; Diderot describes Garrick's 'round of passions' in his *Paradoxe sur le comédien* (1777–8):

Garrick passe sa tête entre les deux battants d'une porte, et, dans l'intervalle de quatre à cinq secondes, son visage passe successivement de la joie folle à la joie modérée, de cette joie à la tranquillité, de la tranquillité à la surprise, de la surprise à l'étonnement, de l'étonnement à la tristesse, de la tristesse à l'abattement, de l'abattement à l'effroi, de l'effroie à l'horreur, de l'horreur au désespoir, et remonte de ce dernier degré à celui d'où il était descendu. (Diderot 1951, 1052)

In some novels of the eighteenth century, passages can be found that are strongly reminiscent of Garrick's round of passions, even when they are not exclusively concerned with facial expression:

Sir Philip grew every moment more affected by the recital; sometimes he clasped his hands together, he lifted them up to heaven, he smote his breast, he sighed, he exclaimed aloud; when Edmund related his dream, he breathed short, and seemed to devour him with attention; when he described the fatal closet, he trembled, sighed, sobbed, and was almost suffocated with his agitations ... (Reeve, *The Old English Baron*, 86)

During the recital, my friend [Strap] was strongly affected, according to the various situations described: He started with surprize, glowed with indignation, gaped with curiosity, smiled with pleasure, trembled with fear, and wept with sorrow, as the vicissitudes of my life inspired these different passions; and when my story was ended, signified his amazement on the whole, by lifting up his eyes and hands, and protesting, that tho' I was a young man, I had suffered more than all the blessed martyrs. (Smollett, *Roderick Random*, 253)

Outside his famous round of passions, too, Garrick relied heavily on formulas of emotional expression. Georg Christoph Lichtenberg gives a detailed account of Garrick's acting style in his *Visits to England* (*Briefe aus England*, 1776–8). In his description of a performance of *Hamlet*, for example, he praises Garrick's body language in the scene in which Hamlet, in shock, meets his father's ghost:

At these words Garrick turns sharply and at the same moment staggers back two or three paces with his knees giving way under him; his hat falls to the

Figure 6.2 William Hogarth: 'Mr. Garrick in the Character of Richard the 3rd' (Copyright © British Museum)

ground and both his arms, especially the left, are stretched out nearly to their full length, with the hands as high as his head, the right arm more bent and the hand lower, and the fingers apart; his mouth is open; thus he stands rooted to the spot, with legs apart, but no loss of dignity, supported by his friends, who are better acquainted with the apparition and fear lest he should collapse. (Lichtenberg 1938, 10)

A famous engraving by William Hogarth (Figure 6.2) depicts Garrick as Richard III, awakening from his nightmares before the Battle of Bosworth. This engraving supports the impression that Garrick's emotional displays were often formulaic. His portrayal of terror in this scene very closely resembles the description given by Lichtenberg.

The description of terror in many novels of the eighteenth century seems to suggest that the novelists were influenced by the formulas prevalent on the contemporary stage:

some of the vulgar spectators had run to the great church ... and came back **open-mouthed** ... (Walpole, *The Castle of Otranto*, 26)

She shuddered, and **recoiled a few paces**. (ibid., 35)

Bianca burst into the room, **with a wildness in her look and gestures that spoke the utmost terror**. (ibid., 131)

They stood **like statues petrified by fear** ... They **staggered to a seat, and sunk down upon it, ready to faint** ... (Reeve, *The Old English Baron*, 78)

In other cases, too, the body language in the eighteenth-century novel appears to be theatrical: for example, when characters express their overwhelming feelings in an exaggerated non-verbal style – large gestures and poses:

I threw my Apron over my Face, and laid my Head on a Chair, and cry'd as if my Heart would break, having no Power to stir. (Richardson, *Pamela*, 1:30)

Theodore! said Manfred, mournfully, and **striking his forehead** ... (Walpole, *The Castle of Otranto*, 107)

He **put his hands on his heart**, as if he really felt there the incurable wound he described bleed afresh. (Mackenzie, *The Man of Feeling*, 322)

'Wonderful!' cried he, **with uplifted hands and eyes**, 'most wonderful!' (Burney, *Evelina*, 183)

Like the body language on the contemporary stage, this body language distinguishes itself by its high level of clarity: not only is it impossible to misunderstand the signified, but it is virtually impossible to overlook its signifier.

The same clarity is evident in the formulaic body language of nineteenth-century melodrama. As was shown above (page 151), the novel of this period often relies on stereotypical emotional displays in its melodramatic moments. These emotional displays demonstrate considerable similarities to the repertoire of expression in the stage melodrama of the time: tearing one's hair in desperation, stamping one's feet in anger, grinding one's teeth, making a fist, rolling one's eyes, trembling and turning pale in fear, beating one's breast in guilt, holding one's forehead in pain, reaching out one's arms to the heavens in prayer, clasping one's hands above one's head in shock, etc.[25] The highly expressive style of this display of emotion can also be seen in the illustration in Figure 6.3; here a scene is captured from one of the numerous stage adaptations of Ellen Wood's popular novel *East Lynne*.

Similar gestures and postures can be found in melodramatic moments of numerous nineteenth-century novels. These have an especially theatrical effect when the emotional displays are exhibited with arms outstretched:

Deans raised the Bible with his left hand, so as partly to screen his face, and putting back his right as far as he could, held it towards Butler in that position, at the same time turning his body from him, as if to prevent his seeing the working of his countenance. (Scott, *The Heart of Midlothian*, 122)

She suddenly let go of me – she threw up her hands, and wrung them frantically in the air. (Wilkie Collins, *The Moonstone*, 393)

Up rose Lady Isabel, and flung her arms aloft in a storm of sobs. (Wood, *East Lynne*, 441)

A distinctly 'pictorial' method of portrayal in the theatre of the eighteenth and, in particular, the nineteenth century was the so-called 'tableau': at an emotional peak, an action-filled scene suddenly freezes into a motionless and mute picture.[26] Tableaus are also encountered in greater numbers in the novel of the time. One important precedent for the adoption of this 'visual' device was the fact that the novel in general became more pictorial than it was in earlier periods.[27] In a tableau in prose fiction, the narrative mode shifts from report to detailed description, and the action thus comes to a stop. A perfect example of a nonverbal tableau in the novel is the sentimental 'picture' that introduces the death scene in Richardson's *Clarissa*:

The Colonel was the first that took my attention, kneeling on the side of the bed, the Lady's right-hand in both his, which his face covered, bathing it with his tears; altho' she had been comforting him, as the women since told me, in elevated strains, but broken accents.

On the other side of the bed sat the good Widow; her face overwhelmed with tears, leaning her head against the bed's head in a most disconsolate manner; and turning her face to me, as soon as she saw me, O Mr. Belford, cried

Figure 6.3 *East Lynne* (V&A Picture Library)

she, with folded hands – The dear Lady – A heavy sob permitted her not to say more.

Mrs. Smith, with clasped fingers, and uplifted eyes, as if imploring help from the Only Power which could give it, was kneeling down at the bed's feet, tears in large drops trickling down her cheeks.

Her Nurse was kneeling between the Widow and Mrs. Smith, her arms extended. In one hand she held an ineffectual cordial, which she had just been offering to her dying mistress; her face was swoln with weeping (tho' used to such scenes as this); and she turned her eyes towards me, as if she called upon me by them to join in the helpless sorrow; a fresh stream bursting from them as I approached the bed.

The Maid of the house, with her face upon her folded arms, as she stood leaning against the wainscoat, more audibly expressed her grief than any of the others. (8:1–2)

In the centre of this carefully composed picture is Clarissa's deathbed. The other characters are all described, one after another, in relation to this centre, each one in a different pose.[28]

The melodrama of the nineteenth century still liked to use such emotional tableaus, on stage as well as in the novel. In Benjamin Disraeli's *Sybil*, for example, Sybil faints when she wants to warn her father, who is attending a secret workers' meeting, of the arrival of the police. At the dramatic climax of the episode, her father's arrest, the action freezes into a static picture: 'The light fell upon a group that did not move; the father holding the hand of his insensible child, while he extended his other arm as if to preserve her from the profanation of the touch of the invaders' (2:53). The phrase 'a group that did not move' strengthens the pictorial quality of the description; the effect of a concentrated ray of light further contributes to this pictorialism. The freezing of time, in addition, accentuates the figurative significance of the action: the father protects his daughter from the attack of the police as though to protect her from desecration – Sybil, the angelic woman, is guarded from the profane.

The non-verbal tableau is primarily found in eighteenth-century novels and in melodramatic passages in the nineteenth-century novel. It coincides with a fashion of the tableau on the contemporary stage, although it would be difficult to state a direction of influence in this particular case. Quite obviously, however, the non-verbal tableau was a device which resulted from a strong contemporary taste for the pictorial even in the temporal forms of art.

6.3.3 Photography and the Art of Motion Pictures

As Marshall McLuhan and others have pointed out, the media influence human behaviour and result in new patterns of perception and thought: 'All media work us over completely. They are so pervasive in their personal, political, economic, aesthetic, psychological, moral, ethical, and social consequences that they leave no part of us untouched, unaffected, unaltered. Any understanding of social and cultural change is impossible without a knowledge of the way media work as environments' (McLuhan 1967, 26).[29] In regarding a visible phenomenon such as body language, the question arises to what extent its presentation in literature has been affected by the visual media. The pictorialism observed above clearly relates to a historical facet of this aspect. This section is devoted to the question how body language has been affected by the more recent visual media of the nineteenth and twentieth centuries: photography and film.

As early as the beginning of our century, photography was observed to have left its mark on the body language in painting: 'Les gestes nous sont devenus familiers, non seulement dans leur aboutissement statique, qui est l'attitude, mais dans toute la variété de leurs progrès, où ils échappaient à la prise de la vision. Le plus grand dessinateur moderne, Degas, le premier qui ait représenté par centaines des gestes et des attitudes encore inconnus de l'art, est inexplicable, dans sa maturité si féconde, sans la photographie instantanée' (Reinach 1924, 78). It seems plausible – if difficult to prove – that the minute attention to subtleties of body language in the nineteenth-century novel (see pages 189–90) was given additional impetus through photography, a medium which could capture the human body and its movements in ways unknown until then. Facial expressions could be enlarged; photo series, such as those taken by Edweard Muybridge in the last quarter of the nineteenth century, made it possible to study the various stages of a particular movement.

The importance of body language in film was noted in the very early stages of this art form. In his enthusiasm for the new medium, Béla Balász (1970 [1926]), for example, saw the possibility that the (silent) film would restore the 'visibility' of human beings in a culture largely focused on the word: 'Man has again become visible' (41).[30] It is quite probable that after photography, film further heightened the general alertness to NVC. The text sample investigated for the present study does not suggest that body language in the novel increased in frequency due to the influence of film. In some instances, however, the kind of body language portrayed appears to show traces of the cinema. In a number of novels, the conviction that film enhances people's awareness of body language or may affect a person's non-verbal behaviour, is even explicitly expressed:

I took a gulp of the whisky and put on my belt, endeavouring to wear the expression of one who, contrary to appearances, is master of the situation. **The films provide one with useful conventions of this kind**. I looked Sammy up and down with deliberation. (Murdoch, *Under the Net*, 70)

and I saw his pose, standing with his back to the window **in a way that was like a caricature of that young American we see in the films** – sexy he-man, all balls and strenuous erection. He stood lounging, his thumbs hitched through his belt, fingers loose, but pointing as it were to his genitals – the pose that always amuses me when I see it on the films, because it goes with the young, unused, boyish American face – the boyish, disarming face, and the he-man's pose. (Lessing, *The Golden Notebook*, 535)

You emerge from the cinema ... Just for a while you possess an aura, a power, a stature. Your feet lift a little from the ground. It is a place for erotic training: the darkness, the clinches on the screen – what more instruction do you need? And how did you learn to walk, to stare, to stroke your jaw, to light your cigarette or toss it aside, in just that way? **You learnt it from the movies**. (Swift, *Out of This World*, 188)

Outside such reflections, too, the body language of characters in the novel occasionally has a distinctly cinematic effect. For example, characters exhibit non-verbal behaviour that seems more familiar from film than from real life:

Isabel gave me a long look as though she were trying to read my thoughts. She took a cigarette from the table beside her and, lighting it, leant back in her chair. She watched the smoke curl up into the air. (Maugham, *The Razor's Edge*, 163)

Madge came up to me. Her eyes were as hard as agate. 'This is real life, Jake,' she said. 'You'd better wake up.' And she struck me hard across the mouth. I recoiled slightly with the sudden pain of the blow. We stood so for a moment, and she sustained my gaze while the tears gathered slowly in her eyes. Then I received her into my arms. (Murdoch, *Under the Net*, 178)

The following passage from Graham Greene's *The Power and the Glory* reminds one of a cinematographic technique in which a character closes his eyes prior to a memory flashback:

> He leant his head back against the wall and half closed his eyes – he remembered Holy Week in the old days when a stuffed Judas was hanged from the belfry and boys made a clatter with tins and rattles as he swung out over the door ... (91)

In particular, film appears to have had an influence on the function with which eye behaviour is frequently observed in the contemporary novel. As Reinhold Rauh (1984) observes on the relation between words and looks in film: 'In real life, words and looks are always linked to each other. There is no speech that is not accompanied by ... looks ... In film, this link between language and looking is used quite consciously, sometimes even artistically, when both serve either as the basis of or as independently meaningful elements in the dramatic situation, in the succession of shots, or in the entire filmic narration' (30, my translation). As we have seen, in novels of all periods eye behaviour represents an important mode of NVC. Until the twentieth century, looks almost always have an emotional and/or interpersonal significance. In the twentieth century, however, eye behaviour often occurs in dialogue passages, and, to a great extent, functions primarily as a device to establish contact; in other words, it has a phatic rather than an expressive function. In this way the modern novel approaches real face-to-face interaction, in which phatic eye contact is generally very frequent, if completely unconscious. Film, which brought this type of eye contact to the screen, may have contributed to the fact that it is also found increasingly in narrative literature, as in the following interaction in John Fowles's *Daniel Martin*:

> He **stares at the glass** when she silently brings it, **then up into her eyes** with a wry smile.
>
> 'And fuck your great-grandmother.'
>
> **She holds his eyes, probing**. 'What's happened?'
>
> 'My erstwhile brother-in-law wants to see me.'
>
> 'But I thought ... the one with cancer?'
>
> He swallows half the whisky. **He stares down at the glass. He looks up at her, then down again**. 'We were very close once, Jenny. I've never really talked to you about all that.'

'You told me they'd excommunicated you.'

He turns away from her eyes, looks out again over the endless city. 'He was my best friend at Oxford. We were a ... sort of quartet. The two sisters. He and I.' He gives her a diffident grimace, **searching her reaction**. 'Ghosts.'

'But ...' she lets expostulation trail away. 'You're going?'

'It seems there's not much time left.' **She stares at him, and her eyes show two kinds of hurt honesty**, both a childlike and an adult. (55)

The glances described here serve as emotional displays and externalizers, but their phatic function is also important. If the episode were filmed, the characters' glances would probably indicate the points where a film editor would make his cuts from one speaker to another.

Photography and film may have affected not just the kind of body language portrayed in modern fiction. Even more importantly, they may have had an effect on how body language is presented in the novel. Of course, a strongly visual presentation in fiction does not first arise with photography and film. Indeed, 'photographic' or 'filmic' effects have been observed in texts written long before the invention of these media – not least since optical instruments invented before photography were also able to enhance or manipulate visual perception.[31] In novels written as early as the eighteenth century, for example, one finds 'close-ups' of body language. In Sterne's *Tristram Shandy*, Mr Shandy's emotional displays when he learns about his son's deformed nose are emphasized through an extremely close view of individual body parts:

The palm of his right hand, as he fell upon the bed, receiving his forehead, and covering the greatest part of both of his eyes, gently sunk down with his head (his elbow giving way backwards) till his nose touch'd the quilt; – his left arm hung insensible over the side of the bed, his knuckles reclining upon the handle of the chamber pot, which peep'd out beyond the valance, – his right leg (his left being drawn up towards his body) hung half over the side of the bed, the edge of it pressing upon his shin-bone – He felt it not. (255)

However, visual manipulations of body language are more frequently encountered in novels after the appearance of optical lenses[32] and the photographic arts they made possible. In the nineteenth-century novel, this is especially obvious in the work of Thomas Hardy.[33] A conspicuous close-up effect, for example, is found in the following quotation from *Tess of the d'Urbervilles*: 'She hardly observed that a tear descended slowly upon his cheek, a tear so large that it magnified the pores of the skin over which it rolled, like the object lens of a microscope' (273). The tear rolling down Angel Clare's face can be seen only at close proximity. Furthermore, the tear effects another close-up: it magnifies the pores of Angel's skin. In a relatively short passage, there is thus a double visual foregrounding of the body-language signifier.

A detail of Tess's face is 'enlarged' repeatedly: her mouth, which functions as a symbol of her sensuality throughout the novel.[34] When descriptions focus on details of Tess's mouth, this suggests a very close view of this part of her face and thus places it in the centre of attention:

her lower lip had a way of thrusting the middle of her top one upward, when they closed together after a word. (42–3)

the corners of her mouth trembling in her attempts not to cry. 'And I wouldn't ha' come if I had known!' (85)

Her lip lifted slightly, though there was little scorn, as a rule, in her large and impulsive nature. (112)

and in making the accusation symptoms of a smile gently lifted her upper lip in spite of her, so as to show the tips of her teeth, the lower lip remaining severely still. (161)

the sunk corners of her mouth betraying how purely mechanical were the means by which she retained that expression of chastened calm upon her face. (286)

At the end of *Tess of the d'Urbervilles*, another instance of visual foregrounding is reminiscent of a 'framed' photograph. Tess's intensive emotional displays just before she murders d'Urberville are conveyed from the point of view of the landlady looking through the keyhole:

The landlady looked through the keyhole ... Over the seat of the chair Tess's face was bowed, her posture being a kneeling one in front of it; her hands were clasped over her head, the skirts of her dressing-gown and the embroidery of her night-gown flowed upon the floor behind her, and her stockingless feet, from which the slippers had fallen, protruded upon the carpet ... In writhing, with her head on the chair, she turned her face towards the door, and Mrs Brooks could see the pain upon it; and that her lips were bleeding from the clench of her teeth upon them, and that the long lashes of her closed eyes stuck in wet tags to her cheeks. (432)

The visual frame provided by the keyhole focuses the reader's attention on Tess's body language and thus helps to direct the reader's sympathy in this passage. Her body language makes it obvious that Tess is in profound despair when she kills d'Urberville.

An example of the twentieth century which seems to have been inspired by film is found in Elizabeth Bowen's *The Death of the Heart*. In an episode at the cinema, the girl Portia notices that Eddie, whom she loves so much, is holding hands with another young woman, whom he has known for only a day. The emphasis which this gesture receives through its 'cinematic' presentation corresponds with Portia's intense shock: 'The light, with malicious accuracy, ran round a rim of cuff, a steel bangle, and made a thumb-nail flash. Not deep enough in the cleft between their *fauteuils* Eddie and Daphne were, with emphasis, holding hands. Eddie's fingers kept up a kneading movement: her thumb alertly twitched at the joint' (195). In the darkened cinema, the light of a match spotlights the object of Portia's attention, and again there is the effect of an extreme close-up in which even the twitching of a finger joint is captured.

Summary

Although this chapter had to be limited to a rather cursory sketch, it has suggested that some historical developments in the use of body language in the novel take place in the context of factors that are extrinsic to literature but that shape the non-verbal competence of writers and readers: changes that occur in the body language of real life and in the academic reflection on body language in various disciplines, from rhetoric to the philosophy of language to NVC research.

Of the parallel literary genres, drama in particular seems to have affected the presentation of NVC in the narrative text. When the novel started to become 'dramatic' at the end of the seventeenth century, it not only changed the presentation of the characters' speech, but also began to pay much greater attention to their non-verbal behaviour, in particular, body language that accompanies speech.

Since body language represents a visible element of fictional reality, the question finally arose whether and to what extent NVC in the narrative text was and is influenced by forms of visual art: theatre, painting, photography, and film. It is often difficult and almost impossible to discern a one-directional influence of one art form on other forms of art. However, several points could be observed in the history of the novel in which the presentation and/or the kind of NVC portrayed in a text show a special affinity to a sister art.

Conclusion

This study has shown that body language is an important signifying system in literature which can contribute in many ways to the meaning and effects of the literary text. Efforts to describe this area of literary semiotics made to date have tended to focus on individual writers, periods, or (sub)genres; they are frequently limited in their concept of body language, and they sometimes disregard the specifically *literary* presentation of this body language. The critical framework established in part II of the present study is based on NVC research *and* literary theory; it recognizes the broad expressive potential of literary body language by recording its many forms and functions with a much finer network of categories than was the case in earlier studies of this subject. Furthermore, these categories are presented in a two-part model which allows their systematic application as a heuristic tool in the analysis of a wide range of texts.

On the premise that body language in a fictional situation is first understood on the basis of a reader's knowledge about non-verbal behaviour in real life, the first component of the framework of categories is indebted to the results of recent scholarship on NVC. This interdisciplinary research (conducted in the areas of psychology, social psychology, sociology, anthropology, and linguistics) has supplied more precise categories for analysing natural body language than its predecessors such as rhetoric or expression psychology. It should have become obvious in the course of chapter 3 that in order fully to appreciate and understand body language in literature, it is necessary to bridge various disciplines. On the other hand, the concepts of NVC research have to be modified and complemented to accommodate the specific needs in literary analysis. The modal and functional classes discussed in chapter 3 thus do not present a comprehensive inventory of forms of body language, but are limited to categories especially relevant in an analysis of the literary text.

The second component of the framework of categories in chapter 4 is focused even more closely on the literariness of body language in literature: it comprises aspects of the presentation and the literary functions of body language in prose fiction, particularly the novel. Selected examples from other genres serve primarily to highlight the specifics of a narrative use of body language. The questions developed in chapter 4 can, however, easily be modified and complemented to serve the analysis of drama and poetry.

Finally, the system of categories developed in part II was applied in the area of historical analysis. As a universal aspect of human behaviour, body language appears in the literature of all periods, albeit in varying degrees and with different emphases. In the English novel, body language is used with great frequency and with its full expressive potential only since the mid-eighteenth century. Chapter 5 shows how this finding corresponds with the general development of the genre itself. On the other hand, as is demonstrated in chapter 6, body language in the novel is also part of a cultural network that comprises the history of body language in real life, academic reflection about it, and also the body semiotics of other literary genres and of the sister arts. With respect to the historical aspects of literary body language, this study could offer only a few points of departure for further study, which will also have to be interdisciplinary, making its observations in connection with findings in philosophy, psychology, anthropology, art history, and other areas.

The prime value of the critical framework developed in this study should consist in its effectiveness in text analysis: having a detailed network of categories for the analysis of body language in literature means that this body language will become more conspicuous to the reader and can thus be used in his or her construction of meaning from the text. Our framework thus aids in opening up and describing a semiotic area of the literary text which might otherwise be overlooked. As we have seen, for example, in the interpretation of Dickens's 'The Signalman' (pages 53–5), familiar texts may even appear in a new light if their use of body language is taken into account. In this and a number of other texts, such as the novels of Margaret Atwood, NVC emerges as a distinct level of significance additional – and sometimes contradictory – to the meanings conveyed in words or other semiotic systems within the text.

Paying attention to body language can thus sharpen awareness of the dynamics between various semiotic dimensions within the literary text, a semantic dynamics that is explored, for example, in the research conducted on irony.

Besides the areas investigated, there are many other possibilities for applying the approach of this study: body language in the novel has developed most fully in texts committed to an aesthetic of verisimilitude, and 'realistic' novels have therefore been given special emphasis in the present study. Although some other types of novels have also been considered, such as Beckett's novel of the 'absurd' or the metafictional novel, their special use of NVC could be more fully explored. Other subjects for further research could include scrutiny of the specifics of body language in the dramatic and poetic text, and a more thorough comparative look at how body language in literature interacts with body language in the other forms of art.

Beyond such specialized projects, a discussion of body language can be integrated in a number of discourses in literary studies. We have seen its relevance in relation to gender studies; its importance in other contexts of literary anthropology is also obvious. For example, characters' culture-specific body language can be an important factor in establishing the 'otherness' of a fictional world. On the other hand, as a universal medium of communication, body language may also be a means through which cultural difference can be bridged. In a specifically intercultural analysis, one might also investigate how the literatures of different cultures employ body language: is it used differently, for instance, in oral and written literature? In this respect, an investigation of body language is also relevant in medieval studies, where the relation between the oral and the written text is a key issue. In all 'cultural' approaches to body language in literature, it must be remembered that this body language is never simply a reflection of real life. The opposite, however, also holds true: in the final analysis, literary body language can only be studied within cultural contexts and demands an interdisciplinary approach.

APPENDIX

Notes on the Text Sample

Based on a selective sample of only eighty novels of the British Isles, the historical observations made in part III of the present study can make no claim to statistical reliability (see also page 16 in the introduction). On the other hand, being restricted to the novel of the British Isles, the sample ensures some measure of uniformity; furthermore, the texts chosen form a cross-section of representative varieties of novel writing, ranging from familiar canonical texts to popular bestsellers, which often reflect developmental tendencies particularly clearly. For each of the following 'periods,' twenty novels were examined. (Titles are given in their common, shortened forms.)

I Prose Fiction from the Sixteenth to the Early Eighteenth Century

'The Love of Alerane and Adelasia' from Painter, *The Palace of Pleasure* (1566); Gascoigne, *Adventures of Master F.J.* (1573); Lyly, *Euphues* (1578); Lodge, *Rosalind* (1590); Sidney, *The New Arcadia* (1590); Greene, *Pandosto* (1588); Nashe, *The Unfortunate Traveller* (1594); Deloney, *Jack of Newbury* (*c.* 1597) and *The Gentle Craft, Parts I* and *II* (*c.* 1597/*c.* 1600); Forde, *The Famous History of Montelion Knight of the Oracle* (*c.* 1600); Head, *The English Rogue* (1665); Bunyan, *The Pilgrim's Progress* (1678); Behn, *Oroonoko or The Royal Slave* (1688) and *The History of the Nun* (1689); Congreve, *Incognita* (1692); Defoe, *Robinson Crusoe* (1719) and *Moll Flanders* (1722); Aubin, *The Strange Adventures of the Count de Vinevil and His Family* (1721); Haywood, *The Rash Resolve* (1724); Swift, *Gulliver's Travels* (1726).

II The Novel between 1740 and 1830

Richardson, *Pamela* (1740–1) and *Clarissa* (1747–9); Smollett, *Roderick*

Random (1748); Fielding, *Tom Jones* (1749); Johnson, *Rasselas* (1759); Walpole, *The Castle of Otranto* (1764); Goldsmith, *The Vicar of Wakefield* (1766); Sterne, *Tristram Shandy* (1759–67) and *A Sentimental Journey* (1768); Mackenzie, *The Man of Feeling* (1771); Reeve, *The Old English Baron* (*The Champion of Virtue*) (1777); Burney, *Evelina* (1778); Radcliffe, *The Italian* (1797); Smith, *The Old Manor House* (1793); Bage, *Hermsprong* (1796); Edgeworth, *Castle Rackrent* (1800); Austen, *Pride and Prejudice* (1813); Shelley, *Frankenstein* (1818); Scott, *The Heart of Midlothian* (1818); Galt, *The Provost* (1822).

III The Victorian Novel

Dickens, *Oliver Twist* (1837–8); Disraeli, *Sybil* (1845); Charlotte Brontë, *Jane Eyre* (1847); Emily Brontë, *Wuthering Heights* (1847); Thackeray, *Vanity Fair* (1848); Kingsley, *Alton Locke* (1850); Dickens, *Hard Times* (1854); Gaskell, *North and South* (1854–5); Trollope, *Barchester Towers* (1857); Meredith, *The Ordeal of Richard Feverel* (1859); George Eliot, *Adam Bede* (1859) and *Middlemarch* (1871–2); Wood, *East Lynne* (1861); Collins, *The Moonstone* (1868); Hardy, *Far from the Madding Crowd* (1874) and *Tess of the d'Urbervilles* (1891); Haggard, *King Solomon's Mines* (1885); Gissing, *New Grub Street* (1891); Wilde, *The Picture of Dorian Gray* (1891); George Moore, *Esther Waters* (1894).

IV The Twentieth-Century Novel

Conrad, *The Secret Agent* (1907); Bennett, *The Old Wives' Tale* (1908); Forster, *Howards End* (1910); Joyce, *A Portrait of the Artist as a Young Man* (1916); Lawrence, *Women in Love* (1921); Huxley, *Antic Hay* (1923); Woolf, *Mrs Dalloway* (1925); Bowen, *The Death of the Heart* (1938); Greene, *The Power and the Glory* (1940); Maugham, *The Razor's Edge* (1944); Hartley, *The Go-Between* (1953); Murdoch, *Under the Net* (1954); Pym, *Less than Angels* (1955); Golding, *Pincher Martin* (1956); Braine, *Room at the Top* (1957); Lessing, *The Golden Notebook* (1962); Fowles, *Daniel Martin* (1977); McEwan, *The Comfort of Strangers* (1981); Brookner, *Lewis Percy* (1989); Byatt, *Possession* (1990).

The division of such a comprehensive genre as the (English) novel into periods requires at the very least a brief explanation. The date when the English novel began has been debated at length and, in light of the wide range of forms, is almost impossible to determine. It seems appropriate, as Paul Salzman (1985, 1) suggests, to end the search for the 'first'

English novel and instead concentrate on the connections between older and newer forms of prose fiction. According to Salzman (ibid., 2), 'a new interest in the possibilities of prose style can be seen in the work of Lyly, Sidney, and Nashe; vernacular prose was developed and explored with an increasing sense of its possibilities.' During the sixteenth century, however, the boundaries between shorter and longer forms of prose fiction were still indistinct, and, as the translations of novellas by Painter, Fenton, and Pettie represent an important step in the development of English prose fiction, an example from Painter's *The Palace of Pleasure* was included in the sample.

Spanning 150 years, the first 'period' considered seems rather long. However, between 1600 and 1660, very few innovative trends are evident in English prose fiction. Puritanism provided no fertile ground for the further development of a genre considered 'entertaining,' while the prose fiction of the preceding century still enjoyed great popularity (see Salzman 1985, 110). Novelists of the Restoration period, and even Defoe and Swift, are thus indebted to the older narrative tradition in many respects.

It is around 1740 that the English novel begins to be taken seriously as a 'literary' genre. This 'coming of age' of the novel is reflected in the way the production of novels grew steadily, as well as in the novelists' own reflections on this genre (see G.L. Barnett, ed. 1968). The novels of Richardson, Fielding, and their contemporaries not only deal with new material, they also establish new narrative techniques. The second 'period' considered includes the early nineteenth century. Even Jane Austen, despite her 'modern' narrative technique, is in other respects closer to the novels of the eighteenth century than to the Victorian novel.

The Victorian age is the period in which the 'realistic' novel flourished. Many literary histories treat the novel of the 1880s and 1890s as a transition into the modern period. However, in their use and presentation of body language, these novels do not differ significantly from earlier Victorian novels and are thus included in the third-period section of the sample.

No subdivisions were made for the twentieth century. The modern and contemporary novel develops in a variety of forms, from the stream-of-consciousness novel to the postmodern experiment; however, it is difficult to assign these various directions to subperiods, since many of them continue throughout the decades.

Notes

Chapter 1 Rationale and Purpose

1 The first instance of the use of 'body language' given in the *Oxford English Dictionary* (1989) is dated 1966.

2 For a more detailed discussion of the terms 'body language' and 'non-verbal communication,' see chapter 3, pages 25–8. Since this study uses NVC with a restricted meaning, the two terms can be understood as being synonymous.

3 Since the late 1960s, there has been a virtual explosion of NVC research in every discipline dealing with this field of study: anthropology (Birdwhistell, Hall) and behavioural science (Eibl-Eibesfeldt), sociology (Goffman) and social psychology (Argyle, Kendon, Ekman, and Friesen), psychology (K.R. Scherer and Wallbott), as well as linguistics and semiotics (Greimas, Sebeok, et al.). For selective bibliographies and reports of research see, for example, Hayes (1957), M. Davis (1972; 1979), Hewes (1975), Key (1975, 177–236, and 1977, 140–428), Davis and Skupien (1982), and Ellgring (1984). Fast (1970) and Morris (1977; 1985) are well-known contributors to the popular-science literature on body language.

4 See, among others, Fowler (1986, 169–70): 'Reading is a very active and constructive process, much dependent on what one brings to the text; it is not wholly fanciful to think of the reader actively *producing* a discourse from a text.'

5 See Magli (1989) for a historical overview of physiognomy. Tytler (1982) provides an excellent account of the influence of physiognomy on the European novel.

6 Accordingly, body language has been given very little attention in the study of poetry. One of the few exceptions is Fussell (1955) regarding T.S. Eliot.

7 See, for example, Rimmon-Kenan (1983, 86–105).

8 In oral story telling, on the other hand, a narrator's body language may contribute greatly to the effect of his or her narrative. See, among others, Haiding (1955), Sándor (1967), Calame-Griaule (1977), Sorin-Barreteau (1982), Wolfson (1982, 25), Bošković-Stulli (1985), and particularly Büchsenmann (1986).

9 For studies that look at author-specific use of body language see, for example, Smith (1976) on Kleist and Kafka, or Portch (1985) on the short stories of Hawthorne, Hemingway, and Flannery O'Connor.

10 See in particular the work of Rosenthal and Zuckerman listed in bibliography 3. M.L. Knapp (1980, 231–40) provides a summary of important results of these and other studies.

11 See chapter 3, pages 65–77 on haptics and proxemics.

12 See Halász (1987, 7).

13 For comparative and culture-specific studies of NVC see, among others, the work of Birdwhistell, E.T. Hall, Efron, La Barre, Hewes, and Mauss listed in bibliography 3.

14 See, among others, Culler (1975, 113–30), and Fowler (1986, 170).

15 See the following example from the Old Testament: 'He who winks his eyes plans perverse things, he who compresses his lips brings evil to pass' (Proverbs 16:30) (RSV).

16 Quintilian's discussion of 'actio' in his *Institutio Oratoria* (book XI) has been especially influential.

Chapter 2 Body Language in Literature and the Arts: Past and Present Research

1 This survey is restricted to work that may be considered most characteristic of the respective line of research. Further titles are included in bibliography 2.

2 See, for example, Bredtmann (1889), Lommatzsch (1910), Bolhöfer (1912), Zons (1933), and Frenzen (1936) on the French and German epic and romance.

3 See, for example, Schulz (1903), Hansen (1908), and W. Scherer (1908) on medieval literature, and Fischer (1908–9), Bathe (1917), Vlašimský (1910–11), Körver (1911), Hellermann (1912), Kostowa (1916), or Aulhorn (1924) on literature of the nineteenth and early twentieth centuries.

4 See, among others, Röhrich (1967). A survey of folkloric gesture research is provided by Kriss-Rettenbeck (1965) and Wehse (1987).

5 See, for example, Josephs (1969) on Diderot, and Och (1985) on Jean Paul.

6 See especially Johnson (1981) on Bellow; Portch (1985) on Hawthorne, Hem-

ingway, and Flannery O'Connor; K.R. Fell (1986) on Maugham; Raim (1986) on Maupassant; and Albert (1987) on Stendhal.

7 Most of these studies are devoted to German drama; see, for example, Lex (1901), Scheel (1923), Osterburg (1922), Lörges (1929), Engert (1934), and Ruppert (1941).

8 The catalogue of the Vienna exhibition on the 'Eloquence of the Body' (Barta Fliedl and Geissmar, eds 1992) includes Warburg's introduction to the atlas. The catalogue also provides an impression of the current state of the discussion of body language in art history.

9 See Gombrich (1959; 1966; 1972). See also the more recent overview by Cupchik (1988).

10 See also, among others, Elam (1980) and Pavis (1981; 1982).

11 For studies on special aspects of NVC in film see, for example, Garroni (1978) and Hairston (1989).

Chapter 3 Categories of Body Language

1 The discussion of the term is summarized in all relevant monographs and anthologies on NVC marked with an * in bibliography 3. Also see Kristeva (1968), Wiener et al. (1972), Scheflen (1979), Ekman and Friesen (1981 [1969]), Newman (1984), or Skupien (1984).

2 On paralanguage in narrative literature see Poyatos (1983, 281–6, and 1992), as well as Oldfield (1967), Schrero (1974), Johnson (1981), Hewitt (1984), Portch (1985), Purdy (1985), or Raim (1986, 131–60). The psychological study by Mahl (1987, 286–309) contains a chapter on 'Everyday Speech Disturbances in *Tom Sawyer*.'

3 In his *Confessions* (*c.* 400), for example, Augustine refers to bodily movement as the natural language of all people: 'hoc autem eos velle, ex motu corporis aperiebatur, tamquam verbis naturalibus omnium gentium' – 'And that they meant this or that thing, was discovered to me by the motion of their bodies, even by that natural language, as it were, of all nations' (Augustine, 1912, 24–5).

4 Intentional non-verbal behaviour and conscious non-verbal behaviour are not synonymous. It is possible, for example, to be conscious of unintentional body language, or to become conscious of it in retrospect. 'Awareness ... refers to whether the person knows he is engaging in a particular nonverbal act at the moment he does it, or whether he can recall with any ease what he has done. A person can be aware of his nonverbal behavior whether or not he engages in the act as an intentional attempt to communicate a specific message' (Ekman and Friesen 1981 [1969], 61).

5 The generally high amount of NVC in both novels corresponds with a principle which Ruesch and Kees (1956, 5) have observed in totalitarian systems: 'It has been widely noted how, under authoritarian regimes, human beings turn more and more toward the perception of the nonverbal, the evaluation of nonverbally codified things, and expression through gesture and action.'

6 See also Portch (1985, 122–43) for a more detailed discussion of the body language in this story.

7 'Noninteraction ... is a situation in which, despite the lack of another interactant and of any external eliciting factors, bodily behaviors ... are developed which reflect the effect of one's own mental and/or physical activities' (Poyatos 1983, 84).

8 'Psychonarration' is one of the terms coined by Dorrit Cohn (1978) to refer to techniques of presenting consciousness in fiction. In psychonarration, there is clear evidence of the narrator's mediation of a character's thoughts.

9 See especially Ekman and Friesen (1969 and 1974), as well as Ekman (1981); on deception and non-verbal leakage see also Cody and O'Hair (1983) and Zuckerman and Driver (1985).

10 For the modes and functions considered in the following discussion, only selected titles can be cited from the vast number of publications on NVC research. Relevant monographs and anthologies are listed in the bibliography but are generally not cited separately.

11 See titles listed in the bibliography.

12 See, in particular, the work of Adam Kendon (titles listed in the bibliography).

13 See especially the seminal studies on touching behaviour by Morris (1971), Montagu (1971), and Henley (1977, 141–82). On individual aspects of haptics, see also Frank (1957), Fisher, Rytting, and Heslin (1976), Heslin and Alper (1983), Jourard (1966), Andersen and Sull (1985), and Jones and Yarbrough (1985).

14 On proxemics, see especially the titles listed in the bibliography by Hall, Sommer, and Watson as well as Ashcraft and Scheflen (1976), Hayduk (1978), and Patterson and Edinger (1987), who include further references. On territorial behaviour see also the publications on behaviour research by Eibl-Eibesfeldt, as well as Esser, ed. (1971).

15 See especially Ekman and Friesen (1981 [1969]), whose categories were developed on the basis of the work by Efron (1941). For alternative classification systems see, among others, Guilhot (1962), Cosnier (1982), Patterson (1983), H.S. Scherer (1984), and, especially, K.R. Scherer (1977; 1980), who distinguishes between parasemantic, parasyntactic, parapragmatic, and dialogical functions.

16 See, for example, the detailed description of body language expressing anger in Seneca's *De ira*: 'flagrant ac micant oculi, multus ore toto rubor exaestuante ab imis praecordiis sanguine, labra quatiuntur, dentes comprimuntur, horrent ac surriguntur capilli' – 'his eyes blaze and sparkle, his whole face is crimson with the blood that surges from the lowest depths of the heart, his lips quiver, his teeth are clenched, his hair bristles and stands on end' (Seneca 1928, 108–9). See also Evans (1969, 8).

17 In Poyatos (1983) this term replaces the term 'affect display' used by Ekman and Friesen.

18 On the different expressive qualities of verbal and non-verbal communication see also Rastier (1968), Greimas (1968), Sanders (1985), and Dittmann (1987, 50, 60).

19 See Watzlawick (Watzlawick, Beavin, and Jackson 1968, 60–7) and Wilden (1972) on the dichotomy of analogic and digital coding.

20 This principle was already expressed in Quintilian's *Institutio Oratoria*: 'Contra si gestus ac vultus ab oratione dissentiat, tristia dicamus hilares, adfirmemus aliqua renuentes non auctoritas modo verbis, sed etiam fides desit' – 'On the other hand, if gesture and the expression of the face are out of harmony with the speech, if we look cheerful when our words are sad, or shake our heads when making a positive assertion, our words will not only lack weight, but will fail to carry conviction' (Quintilian 1958, 11.3.67).

21 'Greater liking is conveyed by standing close instead of far, leaning forward instead of back while seated, facing directly instead of turning to one side, touching, having mutual gaze or eye contact, extending bodily contact as during a handshake, prolonging goodbyes, or using gestures during a greeting which imply a reaching out toward the other person who is at a distance' (Mehrabian 1971, 22).

22 For recent contributions on this aspect see Ellyson and Dovidio, eds (1985).

23 See especially Henley (1977), Mayo and Henley, eds (1981), and Goffman (1979). Henley and LaFrance (1984) and Vrugt and Kerkstra (1984) as well as chapter 12 of Richmond, McCroskey, and Payne (1987) provide overviews of the most important results of this research. For individual aspects see also Frances (1979), Henley (1975), LaFrance and Mayo (1979), and J. Hall (1985).

24 'She walks demurely, head down, red-gloved hands clasped in front, with short little steps' (29); 'Usually we walked with heads bent down, our eyes on our hands or the ground' (142), and many other passages in the novel.

25 On cultural differences in gesticulation, see Efron's seminal study *Gesture and Environment* (1941).

26 These phenomena were first studied systematically by Condon and Ogston (1967; 1971) who used the terms 'self-synchrony' and 'interactional syn-

chrony' in their analyses. For more recent research in this area, see especially the work of McNeill; Beattie; Butterworth and Beattie; Ellis and Beattie; and Oliva listed in the bibliography. On the related issue of a link between gesticulation and thought processes see Freedman (1977), Grand (1977), and several contributions in Nespoulous, Perron, and Lecours, eds (1986).

27 See Scheflen (1974 [1973], 19–34).

28 Eye contact is a very strong social stimulus. Speakers who are engaged in a face-to-face conversation normally do not look directly into the eyes of an addressee until after the end of a phrase or a sentence, in order to avoid distractions (see Rutter 1984; Beattie 1983, 57; Ellis and Beattie 1986, 143; Ellgring 1989, 86). If a speaker makes direct eye contact outside of this normal strategy, it has the function of emphasis, and often also includes emotional components. 'Glances made by a speaker can act to emphasize particular words or phrases, just as increased loudness of voice or certain gestures can. A person trying to be persuasive looks more, and is seen as persuasive' (Argyle and Cook 1976, 120).

29 See especially the work by Duncan, Jr, listed in the bibliography, as well as Cappella (1985), and Rosenfeld (1987).

30 See also Morris et al. (1979) on gestural emblems.

31 See also Schmitt (1989) and, in particular, his comprehensive study *La raison des gestes dans l'occident médiéval* (1990); see also Vigarello (1989) and Schmidt-Wiegand (1982).

32 See Schiffrin (1974) and P. Hall and D.A.S. Hall (1983).

33 See L. Schmidt (1953, 248–9), Röhrich (1967, 18–19), and Burgoon, Buller, and Woodall (1989, 37) on this tradition.

34 See especially the work by Ekman and Friesen, as well as Izard, listed in the bibliography. Fridlund, Ekman, and Oster (1987) provide a report of important research.

35 Among the most important works on the portrayal of the face in literature are those by Charles Grivel (1981) and by Peter von Matt (1983), who lists the principles governing literary description of the face from the eighteenth century to the modern period.

36 See Goffman (1969, 3–103) on this term.

37 On the language of the eye in literature see, in particular, Starobinski (1961) and Weisrock (1990). Also see Gargano (1979), Johnson (1981), and Rogers (1980) on individual writers.

38 According to recent research, positive stimulants (sympathy, love, sexual attraction) cause pupils to dilate, whereas negative stimulants cause them to contract. Persons with dilated pupils appear to be friendlier and more attractive, and that is why women in earlier times used belladonna. See especially

Hess (1975), and also, for more recent observations, Hess and Petrovich (1987). In literary texts, however, pupil size is only rarely mentioned, as in Joseph Conrad's *The Secret Agent* (1907): 'With eyes whose pupils were extremely dilated she stared at the vision of her husband and poor Stevie walking up Brett Street side by side away from the shop' (243–4). In this instance, the character's pupils are dilated because of a positive feeling evoked through fantasy.

39 For a comprehensive report on modern research on eye behaviour, see Fehr and Exline (1987). Also see the work by Argyle, Exline, and Ellsworth listed in the bibliography, as well as Ehlich and Rehbein (1982), and Rutter (1984).

40 For earlier examples of the look of love in classical literature and in courtly poetry of the Middle Ages, see Peil (1975, 160–5).

41 See also the parody of the look of love in Sterne's *Tristram Shandy* in chapter 25 of book 8. Here Mrs Wadman shoots Uncle Toby a look that hits him like a cannon-ball.

42 There is also an element of power play when a woman is stared at by a man. In this case, the aura of dominance which the 'stronger' gender projects, seriously injures the woman's privacy. See Mulvey (1975) and Silverman (1984) for a study of this kind of male eye behaviour evident in literature and film.

43 On posture, see especially the work by Mehrabian listed in the bibliography, as well as Scheflen (1964).

44 On the openness of arms and legs as a signal of accessibility see Mehrabian (1969, 367ff).

45 Crying is also, in part, an automatic reaction. But since crying usually is accompanied by a characteristic facial expression, it is considered to be a form of facial expression in this study.

46 On the differences in touching behaviour between the genders, see, in particular, Vrugt and Kerkstra (1984, 14–15) and Patterson (1983, 99–100), as well as the chapter on touch in Henley (1977). In today's northern Western cultures, the fear that one will be suspected of homophilia is a much stronger factor in men who touch each other than is the case for women touching other women.

47 This list could be augmented with many other novels by contemporary female writers. For example, the novel *The Bone People* (1985) by New Zealand writer Keri Hulme also communicates its basic message with the use of haptics. Kerewin, a painter, suffers from a profound fear of entering relationships, which is expressed in her reluctance to have physical contact with others. Step by step she is freed from her isolation by the love of a Maori man and his adopted son. Instances of touch which indicate Kerewin's emotional recovery dominate the final episodes: 'There's herself, content in the

long wordless embrace given by her mother. Herself pushed and pummelled and hugged as though she were a child by all her tall brothers ... Herself, propped against her fat and comfortable moon-eyed sister, arms round each other's necks all good cheers and covered tears and matey friendship' (443).

48 One might arrive at a different conclusion for medieval epic literature, where the public and social use of space (characters making a ceremonial entrance or the placing of characters in a room according to their social rank) is very important.

49 Extroverted persons need less distance between themselves and other people than introverted persons do; psychological conditions such as schizophrenia often carry with them a need for greater personal space. See Cook (1970) and Bouvron (1985) on this phenomenon.

50 See the summary in Henley (1977).

Chapter 4 Body Language in the Narrative Text: A Literary-Critical Perspective

1 In this context, see also Stanzel (1984, 115–22) on the semiotic importance of fictional space.

2 Cook and Lalljee (1972, 218), observing telephone conversations, conclude that the lack of body-language signals in this form of non-visual interaction has hardly any effect on the exchange of information.

3 This term is also used by Zons (1933, 8–9) in his study of medieval German epics.

4 On this term see Bonheim (1982): 'In *virtual speech* what a character says is only imagined by another character, or by the narrator' (34).

5 See relevant chapters in Critchley (1971 [1939] and 1975) on conventionalized body language in Oriental arts; see also Fischer-Lichte (1992, 55) on gesture codes of the Peking Opera.

6 See Boggs (1934–40) on the fairy tale, as well as Habicht (1959) and Peil (1975) on the medieval epic.

7 In contrast, psychologists have identified pathological patterns of movement. Schizophrenics, for example, 'display angular, jerky, and uncoordinated movements which are carried out with uneven acceleration or deceleration at either too slow or too fast a tempo' (Ruesch 1972, 637).

8 See, among others, Fischer-Lichte (1992, part II) and Elam (1980, 76–7) on theatre; J.F. Scott (1975, chapter 6) on film, and Weisbach (1948, 30) on Carolingian art.

9 Various disciplines thus revert to graphic representations or special notation systems in order to avoid the limitations of language. Since the Renaissance,

choreography, for example, has attempted to create a notation system for movement. See, among others, Birdwhistell (1973 [1970]); Ekman, Friesen, and Tomkins (1971); Ekman (1980a); E.T. Hall (1974); Hess-Lüttich (1979b); and Kowal et al., eds (1995).

10 'Foregrounding' is a concept of Prague structuralism. Chapman (1973, 48) explains it as a textual device through which an element is given artistic emphasis in its context: '[Foregrounding] is helpfully described by M.A.K. Halliday as "prominence that is motivated."' See also Leech (1985, 47) and Fowler (1986, 71).

11 See also Leech and Short (1981, 176) on fictional sequencing in the narrative text.

12 See Genette (1972, 77–121). An 'analepsis' is a narration of a story-event at a point in the text after later events have been told. Its opposite, the foreshadowing of an event, is referred to as a 'prolepsis.'

13 See also Butterworth and Beattie (1978, 355–8) and Ehlich and Rehbein (1982, 13). Perhaps this preference for the initial position has also motivated the recommendation to actors that gestures should be made before the verbal utterance they belong to. Louis de Cahusac, for example, wrote in the *Encyclopédie* (1777 [1754]): 'Le *geste* au théatre [*sic*] doit toujours précéder la parole: on sent bien plutôt que la parole ne peut le dire; & le *geste* est beaucoup plus preste qu'elle; il faut des momens [*sic*] à la parole pour se former et pour frapper l'oreille; le *geste* que la sensibilité rend agile, part toujours au moment même où l'ame [*sic*] éprouve le sentiment' (112–13).

14 In dramatic texts of the seventeenth and eighteenth centuries, speech-synchronic body language is also found in the final position, as, for example, in the plays of William Wycherley, whose stage directions are exceptionally detailed for plays of his period. Here, the directions for non-verbal communication between the characters almost always follow their speech; for the reader of today, this makes it difficult to establish whether the body language is synchronic to the verbal utterance, or is to follow it.

15 The lack of apostrophes in the edition used follows Shaw's simplification of English orthography.

16 It might also be possible that James is influenced by the dramatic convention of placing the body language before speech. On James's interest in drama see, among others, Pelzer (1984, 10–11). In the novel *The Picture of Dorian Gray*, by the dramatist Oscar Wilde, the initial position of body language accompanying speech also occurs with remarkable frequency.

17 Smith (1976, 97) comes to a similar conclusion in his comparison of gestures in the work of Kleist and Kafka. Kafka's preference for independent clauses, as opposed to Kleist's syntactical subordinations, correlates with Smith's

observation that Kafka, to a much greater extent than Kleist, treats NVC as an independent means of expression.

18 Also see R.G. Benson (1980, 34) on the 'natural limitation on the gestures of the first-person narrator.' Michie (1987, 118) sees a general strategy to hide the body in first-person narration. Poyatos (1983, 288) completely ignores narrative technique when he concludes the following about the first-person narrator in Salinger's *The Catcher in the Rye*: 'But one cannot hastily decide what prevents Salinger from showing the personality-revealing gestures and manners that the reader tends to attach to Holden Cauldfield's [*sic*] most realistic language'; a brief look at the novel reveals that Holden certainly registers the non-verbal behaviour of other characters; his tendency to withhold descriptions of his own body language is motivated by the fact that the novel is told in the first person.

19 'Cooper regarded Indian civilization as vastly inferior to Christianity, and when he undertook in his later novels a realistic rendering of Indian character his subjects were "bad" Indians ... who could become noble only by becoming Christians' (Grossman 1950, 46).

20 It is interesting in this context to note that the body language of the elderly Hagar is presented with much greater frequency than that of the young Hagar in the parts of the novel which tell of her past. Her body language is of much less existential relevance to the young Hagar than it is to the old woman.

21 See Spiegel (1976) for a comprehensive discussion on 'seeing' in literary texts.

22 The term 'indexical' is adopted from Roland Barthes (1966).

23 See also Todorov (1968, 98–9) on this problem in differentiation.

24 See, for example, Cunningham (1951) on affect in Elizabethan tragedy.

25 Also see Brooks (1973–4, 559) on the primacy of the non-verbal in nineteenth-century stage melodrama.

26 See also Scholes and Kellogg (1966, 171–96) and Bleikasten (1985 [1975], 17–18) on the correlation between an external point of view and the proportion of NVC in narrative literature.

27 See, for example, the passages cited in chapter 4 from *Mrs Dalloway* (pages 112–13), *Moon Tiger* (pages 116–17), and *An Artist of the Floating World* (pages 120–2).

28 See also the passage from Graham Swift's *Waterland* discussed in connection with eye behaviour in chapter 3 (pages 59–60).

29 See also Chatman (1978, 119–38) and Margolin (1986).

30 This does not mean that characterization through stable body features was necessarily influenced by physiognomy. Even George Eliot, who expresses great doubts about physiognomy in chapter 15 of *Adam Bede*, uses permanent body features quite extensively in her characterizations.

31 In fact, Lavater's concept of physiognomy was wide enough to include 'alle passive und active Bewegungen, alle Lagen und Stellungen des menschlichen Körpers' (Lavater 1984, 21–2), that is, all active or passive movements, all positions and postures of the human body.

32 Hair preening – that is, touching and smoothing one's own hair – is an indication of vanity and, especially in women, is considered to be a form of flirtation or courting behaviour; see Poyatos (1983, 143), and Vrugt and Kerkstra (1984, 17).

33 See also Irwin (1979, 15, 42–7, 59).

34 See Wylie (1977) on the gesticulation of the French in comparison with the Americans. Although Wylie deals with body language of the French of today, many of his observations also hold true for *The American*: for example, the fact that the French upper class gesticulates less than the lower classes (viii–ix). In James's novel, the upwardly mobile Nioches differ from the aristocratic Bellegardes in their more lively gesticulation. Only Valentin de Bellegarde, the black sheep of the family, who also initiates a love relationship with Mademoiselle Nioche, sometimes exhibits the same theatrical body language as the Nioches do: 'He renewed his mysterious physiognomical play, making at the same time a rapid tremulous movement in the air with his fingers' (197); 'The two men looked at each other, and Valentin indulged in another flash of physiognomical eloquence' (198).

35 See Grace (1980, 93), Hill Rigney (1987, 29–31), or Carrington (1982). The novel itself gives clear support for this kind of interpretation through Duncan's comments: '"but really I'm not human at all, I come from the underground"' (132); '"Hey," he said finally in a different voice, "you look sort of like me in that"' (136).

36 See Smith (1976, 10), R.G. Benson (1980, 9), or Pelzer (1984, 3–4).

37 See Barthes (1982 [1968]).

38 Henry James in 'The Art of Fiction' (1957 [1884], 33).

39 Watt (1972 [1957], 34–5).

40 On the basic artificiality of literary dialogues, see also Leech and Short (1981, 160–6 and 289 *passim*), and especially Page (1988). On the contribution NVC makes in the creation of more 'natural' dialogues in fiction, see also Danow (1980), K.R. Fell (1982, 95), and Øyslebø (1987).

41 This is especially the case in the statement 'I stare at her,' since a speaker normally looks at the person being addressed only at the end of an utterance and thus when a pause is made (see chapter 3, n28).

42 See Anne Chisholm, 'Lost Worlds of Pleasure,' *Times Literary Supplement*, 14 Feb. 1986, 162.

43 See Poyatos (1983, 143), and Ramsey (1984, 152–3). On specific elements of

Japanese body language see also Ekman (1971, 239 *passim*), Barnlund (1975), Kunihiro (1980), and Morsbach (1988).

44 See Kirstein (1990; 1991). A French film of this genre, *La Guerre du feu*, portrays a 'primitive' body language specially developed by Desmond Morris; see P.L.W. Koch (1990).

45 While younger women usually sit with their legs together, older women develop a more masculine sitting position with their legs apart; see Klein (1984, 123).

46 The same is true of Richardson's Pamela, who suffers most from Mr B.'s obtrusive touch; see especially Letter 15 in *Pamela* (1740–1).

47 Smith (1976) uses the term 'scenic-dramatic representation.' A strong tendency of some writers to use NVC in narrative literature may perhaps be attributed to the fact that they are also dramatists, or at least have a special interest in the dramatic arts. See, for example, Kuepper (1970, 144) and Smith (1976, 11) on Kafka; Pelzer (1984, 10–11) on Henry James, or K.R. Fell (1982, 94) on Maugham.

48 In this context, also see studies on the 'grotesque' image of the body in comic and satiric literature, especially Bakhtin's seminal study on Rabelais (1968 [1965]).

49 On the comic-parodic potential of imitation see Bergson in *Le Rire*: 'Voilà aussi pourquoi des gestes, dont nous ne songions pas à rire, deviennent risibles quand une nouvelle personne les imite ... Nous ne commençons donc à devenir imitables que là où nous cessons d'être nous-mêmes. Je veux dire qu'on ne peut imiter de nos gestes que ce qu'ils ont de mécaniquement uniforme et, par là même, d'étranger à notre personnalité vivante. Imiter quelqu'un, c'est dégager la part d'automatisme qu'il a laissée s'introduire dans sa personne. C'est donc, par définition même, le rendre comique, et il n'est pas étonnant que l'imitation fasse rire' (Bergson 1975 [1900], 25).

50 See also *Hard Times* for a similar case of the worship of female angel figures. In this novel, Sissy Jupe, formerly a circus girl, and Rachael, a factory worker, function as 'angels in the house.' Both women are adored by other characters: 'Louisa raised the hand that it might clasp her neck and join its fellow there. She fell upon her knees, and clinging to this stroller's child looked up at her almost with veneration' (171); 'As she looked at him, saying, "Stephen?" he went down on his knee before her, on the poor mean stairs, and put an end of her shawl to his lips ... She raised her eyes for a moment as she said the words; and then they fell again, in all their gentleness and mildness, on his face' (68).

51 See Ruesch (1972, 637–41). On other symptoms of schizophrenia in *Surfacing*, also see Grace (1980, 109), Hill Rigney (1987, 47), and McLay (1975).

52 See also Bjerring (1976, 597) and Ewell (1981) on this subject.
53 According to Ruesch (1972, 638), a person suffering from schizophrenia is 'on the whole more versed in the use of numbers and words than in the use of objects and movements ... his understanding is logical, his approach speculative.'
54 See also Ruesch (1972, 638) on regression in schizophrenic patients: 'When a patient becomes psychotic, he relinquishes a way of communication [= verbal communication] that did not work in the first place ... It is as if such a patient knew that the basis for human relations is established in the non-verbal mode and that successful communication cannot be achieved until this step is mastered.'
55 See also Carrington (1983, 52–4).
56 See also Hill Rigney (1987, 106) on the negativity of seeing in *Bodily Harm.*
57 See, for example, Worthen (1983).
58 This is addressed, in particular, in chapter 6, which describes Murphy's consciousness: 'Thus Murphy felt himself split in two, a body and a mind. They had intercourse apparently, otherwise he could not have known that they had anything in common. But he felt his mind to be bodytight and did not understand through what channel the intercourse was effected nor how the two experiences came to overlap. He was satisfied that neither followed from the other. He neither thought a kick because he felt one nor felt a kick because he thought one' (64).
59 'Characters and action are subordinate to or expressive of an ontological dualism ... Thus, the opposition of mind and body establishes a polarity of characters. At one extreme there is the somatic Miss Counihan ... At the other extreme there is Mr. Endon, "a schizophrenic of the most amiable variety." He has withdrawn almost completely from the world of things into the world of his own mind' (Hesla 1971, 31).
60 On the puppet-like bodily movements in Beckett's novels, see also M. Benson (1984, 236–7), as well as Gidal (1986, 61, 187–8).
61 See also Portch (1985, 31).
62 The poem is also reprinted in Atwood (1976, 37).
63 R.G. Benson (1980) dedicates chapter 3 of his study on Chaucer to this question.
64 Hayes (1957, 236) cites the following result from an unpublished thesis by Paula Cohn, 'Gesture Found in Grimm's Household Tales': 'The variety of gestures found is small. Of 300 tales, 33 contain one or more gestures.'
65 On flirting and courting behaviour, see Scheflen and Scheflen (1972), A.E. Scheflen 1974 [1973], 71–9), Givens (1978), and Richmond, McCroskey, and Payne (1987, 216–17).

66 Cited in Haight, ed. (1954, 111); see also Stang (1959, 40–1).
67 'Major Brutt had met her eyes kindly, without a qualm' (49).

Chapter 5 Body Language and the Aesthetic of the Novel

1 The history of the human body and of body images has been extensively researched in various disciplines over the last few decades. For an overview see, for example, the essays in Feher et al., eds (1989). Gender studies in particular have made significant contributions; see Shorter's cultural history of the female body (1982) or the essays collected by Suleiman, ed. (1985) and Gallagher and Laqueur, eds (1987); Michie (1987) provides an overview of the reawakened interest in the female body both in theoretical and literary writing. In comparison, there are only a few studies devoted to the historicity of body *language*. Bremmer and Roodenburg, eds (1991) provide the first social history of gestures. Also see: Key (1975, 138–9 and 1977, 40–5) as well as Cresswell (1968, 122) on the decline in gesticulation accompanying speech in England since the eighteenth century; Lamb and Watson (1979, 31–7) on 'posture requirements' of various historical periods; Vigarello (1989) on body posture control from the Middle Ages to the seventeenth century; Schmitt (1989; 1990) on the disciplining of non-verbal behaviour in medieval education, philosophy, and theology. Wildeblood (1973) provides an overview of changes in etiquette in the British Isles.
2 Sidney's *Arcadia* (1590) is an exception, however. Although in this romance, too, the emotional displays are conventional (tears, blushing, self-injury as an expression of pain), this body language stands out through its unusual concreteness and abundance of detail. The detailed analyses of and comments on many emotional displays also foreground the body language in a way which is unusual in the prose fiction of this time.
3 This 'realistic' use of body language is not entirely unprecedented in the Middle Ages. R.G. Benson (1980, 11–12) makes the following observation regarding Chaucer's *fabliaux*: 'there are very few stylized gestures. In these comic tales, Chaucer exercised great freedom in selecting and rendering gestures. Indeed, spontaneous and frequently startling gestures are essential ingredients of Chaucer's comic art.'
4 See, for example, Davies (1969, 97).
5 Hardy generally tends to use characterizing body language at the beginning of his novels; see, in particular, *Under the Greenwood Tree*.
6 See also Witemeyer (1979): 'the Victorian audience liked to "see" its fiction, and novelists catered to the same taste by providing abundant visual description. Conrad was only reiterating a commonplace of Victorian aes-

thetics when he said that the "task which I am trying to achieve is, by the power of the written word, to make you hear, to make you feel – it is, before all, to make you see"' (1–2).

7 A few years before this, Charles Kingsley wrote in *Alton Locke*: 'By-the-bye, I have as yet given no description of the old eccentric's abode – an unpardonable omission, I suppose, in these days of Dutch painting and Boz' (62). The subtitle of Thomas Hardy's *Under the Greenwood Tree* is: 'A Rural Painting of the Dutch School.' See also Witemeyer (1979, 105) on the relations between the novel and genre-painting in the nineteenth century.

8 See Meisel (1983) for reproductions of these paintings.

9 See especially Page (1988, chapter 6).

10 The following passage is symptomatic of this prosodic precision, in which an emphasis in the direct speech is signalled both in the print itself and in an explanatory comment by the narrator: '"An *honest* woman's bairn, Maggie?" answered the peace-officer, smiling and shaking his head with an ironical emphasis on the adjective' (196).

11 Cited from G.L. Barnett, ed. (1968, 135); this volume also contains similar reflections by many other eighteenth-century novelists.

12 See, for instance, book VI of John Stuart Mill's *A System of Logic* (1843) on the need for a scientific ethology, sociology, and psychology.

13 See also Balzac's *Comédie humaine*, which contains a 'Théorie de la démarche' (1833).

14 In this respect, the novel precedes the theatre. In the art of acting, a shift towards natural, psychologically authentic body language is not observed until towards the end of the century – in England, in the theatrical style of Henry Irving (see Booth et al., eds 1975, 139–41); on the European continent, especially in Stanislawki (see R. Williams, 1968, 107–33).

15 Also see a similar market scene in *The Mayor of Casterbridge*: 'Here the face, the arms, the hat, the stick, the body throughout spoke equally with the tongue. To express satisfaction the Casterbridge market-man added to his utterance a broadening of the cheeks, a crevicing of the eyes, a throwing back of the shoulders, which was intelligible from the other end of the street. If he wondered ... you knew it from perceiving the inside of his crimson mouth, and a target-like circling of his eyes. Deliberation caused sundry attacks on the moss of adjoining walls with the end of his stick, a change of his hat from the horizontal to the less so; a sense of tediousness announced itself in a lowering of the person by spreading the knees to a lozenge-shaped aperture and contorting the arms' (72–3).

16 See also the butler Giles in Dickens's *Oliver Twist*: 'with his body drawn up to its full height, his head thrown back, and inclined the merest trifle on one

side, his left leg advanced, and his right hand thrust into his waistcoat, while his left hung down by his side, grasping a waiter, looked like one who laboured under a very agreeable sense of his own merits and importance' (176).

17 See chapter 3, page 69, on haptics, and page 73 on proxemics, as well as chapter 4, pages 144–5, on proxemics in *Clarissa*.

18 Also see Brooks (1969) on the French 'novel of worldliness' in the eighteenth century: 'The glance, the look of the eyes, is in fact the central physical and metaphorical expression of the closure and lack of privacy that are the primary conditions of life in society' (18). Eye behaviour in the novel is also discussed by Stewart (1973, 107), Robinson (1970), and Kleinspehn (1989).

19 See, for example, various contributions in in Benthall and Polhemus, eds (1975).

20 On the emancipation of body language from the word in modern drama and theatre see, among others, Kostelanetz (1968, 33), Brown (1972, 55–73), Kennedy (1975, 8 and 11–12), Goetsch (1977), Krysinski (1981), or Kane (1984). Antonin Artaud's 'Theatre of Cruelty' entails a programmatic turn towards non-verbal means of expression; see his *Théâtre et son double* (1938). On the significance of non-verbal expression in connection with the experience of the crisis of language also see Gerhard Austin (1981) on Hofmannsthal and, with regard to Pinter and Beckett, Santucci (1981), Murphy (1972), and Murch (1983).

21 Love (1968) makes a similar observation for Sherwood Anderson's *Winesburg, Ohio*, and Paden (1982–3) for Carson McCullers's *The Heart Is a Lonely Hunter*.

22 Reproduced, for example, in Gombrich (1989, 449).

Chapter 6 Literary Body Language in Context

1 Also see the following examples: 'After tea Mr. Hale got up, and stood with his elbow on the chimney-piece, leaning his head on his hand' (Gaskell, *North and South*, 32); 'Richard did not approach him. He leaned against the chimney-piece, glancing at the floor' (Meredith, *The Ordeal of Richard Feverel*, 526); 'Then he straightened himself up, and walked over to the fireplace, and stood there, looking at the burning logs' (Wilde, *The Picture of Dorian Gray*, 223); 'Mr Dedalus looked at himself in the pierglass above the mantelpiece, waxed out his moustache-ends and then, parting his coattails, stood with his back to the glowing fire' (Joyce, *A Portrait of the Artist as a Young Man*, 27); 'There he found Gerald standing with his back to the fire, in the library' (Lawrence, *Women in Love*, 300).

2 One exception in the novel is Becky Sharp in Thackeray's *Vanity Fair*, who leans against the mantle-piece in a dramatic, desperate pose: 'She held out one hand. She cried fit to break her heart; her ringlets fell over her face, and over the marble mantel-piece where she laid it' (1:177). However, her posture has a different quality from the men's, for this is a posture of helplessness, not a casual one.

3 On the antecedents of modern NVC research see Ancelin Schutzenberger (1978), M. Davis (1979), Asendorpf and Wallbott (1981–2), Kendon (1982; 1983c), and Winkin (1984).

4 Phrenology was concerned with the interpretation of personality traits on the basis of cranial contours. It caused quite a stir, especially in English-speaking countries in the nineteenth century. The most important publication of these teachings was undertaken by Johann Joseph Gall and Johann Kaspar Spurzheim in their *Anatomie et physiologie du systeme nerveux en général et du cerveau en particulier, avec des observations sur la possibilité de reconnaître plusieurs dispositions intellectuelles et morales de l'homme et des animaux par la configuration de leurs têtes* (1810–19). On the influence of phrenology on English and American writers see, among others, Hungerford (1930–1a; 1930–1b), Lokensgard (1940), Hillway (1949), and Pickrel (1986).

5 For a very clear trace of rhetoric in the eighteenth-century novel, see the orator's pose of Corporal Trim in Sterne's *Tristram Shandy* (book 2, chapter 17): 'He stood before them with his body swayed, and bent forwards just so far, as to make an angle of 85 degrees and a half upon the plain of the horizon; – which sound orators, to whom I address this, know very well, to be the true persuasive angle of incidence; – in any other angle you may talk and preach; – 'tis certain; – and it is done every day, – but with what effect, – I leave the world to judge!' (140).

6 For similar examples in the area of psychology, see Thomas Wright's *The Passions of the Minde in Generall* (1604), in particular book IV, and, of course, Descartes's *Les passions de l'âme*, which appeared in the same year as Bulwer's work; here, the 'signes extérieurs' of the various passions are carefully listed in articles 112 to 135. For inventories of rhetorical body language, see also, for example, Thomas Wilson's *Arte of Rhetorique* (1553), and the *Vacationes Autumnales* (1620) of Ludovicus Cresollius [Louis de Cressolles], whose second book deals with the orator's body language over the course of 300 pages, covering everything from head to foot.

7 In his article 'Geste' in the *Encyclopédie* (1777 [1754]), Louis de Cahusac, for example, described body and facial movements as 'une des premieres [*sic*] expressions du sentiment données à l'homme par la nature' (111).

8 See the following examples: 'Every one, all the time, remaining silent; their

countenances shewing a grief in their hearts too big for expression' (*Clarissa*, 8:74); 'She did not speak; she was not able: but the tears which had till then trembled in her eyes now stole down her cheeks' (Smith, *The Old Manor House*, 41); 'They supported him to a seat, where he recovered by degrees, but had no power to speak his feelings; he looked up to his Benefactors in the most affecting manner, he laid his hand upon his bosom, but was still silent' (Reeve, *The Old English Baron*, 141); 'He beckoned with his hand: he would have stopped the mention of his favours; but he could not speak, had it been to beg a diadem' (Mackenzie, *The Man of Feeling*, 66).

9 This development is also evident in the drama of this period: 'The mute scene and gesture are clearly linked for Diderot to moments of acute passion' (Brooks 1973–4, 554); also see Madland (1984) on the German Storm and Stress movement.

10 See also McKenzie (1990, chapter 6) for a detailed discussion of false expressions of feeling in Fielding's works.

11 In the eighteenth-century novel, fops are generally characterized negatively through their affected body language; see also Bage's *Hermsprong*: 'Mr. Fillygrove, at this instant, came dancing forward in the familiar style' (59).

12 The same is true for Harley's belief in physiognomy; see especially chapter 27 of the novel.

13 Ketcham (1981) comes to a similar conclusion when analysing the discussion on body language in Addison and Steele's *Spectator*: 'the *Spectator's* sense of gesture acknowledges that gestures constitute a socially learned language, with a possibility of disguise or imposture ... The *Spectator's* interpretation of gestures thus moves away from a correspondence theory of meaning (one sign equals one meaning) toward a theory of interpretation which is based on the double nature of the sign: the implicit physiognomy of conduct books or character sketches, where the meaning of a sign may be found in some kind of external catalogue of meanings, is replaced by a more novelistic "reading" of social performances, where the meaning of a sign must be read according to its context' (150–1).

14 The impact of language philosophy on body language in literature is also apparent in the fact that illustrators replacing speech are rather frequent in novels of the early eighteenth century which describe encounters between their protagonists and members of other cultures; see, for example, Defoe's *Robinson Crusoe* (1719) or Swift's *Gulliver's Travels* (1726). This exceptional attention to body language as a replacement for speech is found in the context of a time particularly interested in the question of a universal language. See also Knowlson (1965) and Seigel (1969) on the discussion of gesture as a universal language in the seventeenth and eighteenth centuries.

15 Bell's best-known work, *Essays on the Anatomy and Philosophy of Expression*, was first published in 1806 and posthumously republished in 1844 as *The Anatomy and Philosophy of Expression as Connected with the Fine Arts.* See Codell (1986) on Bell's influence on the Pre-Raphaelites.

16 Darwin's study became a bestseller in several simplified versions (see Ekman 1973a, 1). Other important contributions to expression psychology, which were read in all of Europe and in the United States, were the works of Guillaume Duchenne de Boulogne, Pierre Gratiolet, Paolo Mantegazza, and Theodor Piderit (see bibliography). For a survey of German expression psychology, which flourished in the 1920s and 1930s, see Asendorpf and Walbott (1981–2); among the most important representatives of this approach were Strehle, Lersch, Klages, and Leonhard. Expression psychology in the English-speaking countries during the first half of this century (represented by scholars such as Allport and Vernon, Frois-Wittmann, Krout, or Charlotte Wolff) is discussed in Allport (1961, 451–86).

17 See also the passage from *Huckleberry Finn* discussed in chapter 3, page 37.

18 Incidentally, this new need for the 'dramatic' is also evident in Dryden's adaptation of Chaucer's *Knight's Tale*, as Rogerson (1953, 90) observes: 'When Dryden refurbished Chaucer's *Knight's Tale*, he added line after line in which he spoke of the sighs, stampings, and silences of Palamon and Arcite, recording them as though he were seeing them displayed on a stage, or mounted in a historical painting.'

19 Before this time dialogue of this type is the exception – for example, in the prose fiction of Thomas Deloney.

20 See G. Watson (1979, 48). Richardson's connections with drama and theatre have been widely documented; see Konigsberg (1968, chapter 1) and Kinkead-Weekes (1973). For other discussions on the connection between drama and the novel in eighteenth-century England see also Loftis et al. (1976, 70–3).

21 On the interconnections among the arts in the eighteenth and nineteenth centuries, see the excellent and richly illustrated study by Meisel (1983). One should also bear in mind the many scenes in eighteenth-century novels in which a visit to the theatre is described – for example, in *Tom Jones* (book 16, chapter 5), *A Sentimental Journey* ('The Translation'), and *Evelina* (Letter 10). As far as the nineteenth century is concerned, Dickens's obsession with the theatre has been amply documented, but other novels, such as *Vanity Fair* and *The Picture of Dorian Gray*, also have numerous references to the theatre.

22 For a discussion of the connections between the philosophy of language and developments in the dramatic arts in the eighteenth century, see Fischer-Lichte (1989); a heavily abridged English version of this study is part II of

Fischer-Lichte (1992). D. Barnett (1987) provides an overview of body language on the European stages of the time, on the basis of extensive source material and numerous illustrations.

23 Engel's *Ideen* represents the first attempt at a systematic record of the semiotics of the body in motion. On Engel, see also Magli (1979), Veltrusky (1980), and Fischer-Lichte (1989, 156–77).

24 Also see Rogerson (1953) and Proust (1961) on Le Brun's influence on eighteenth-century acting. Hogarth's *The Analysis of Beauty* refers to Le Brun as an authority on the representation of the passions (1:138). Le Brun was, however, not the first painter to compile such a catalogue; ever since the Renaissance, treatises on painting have discussed the body language of affect (Gombrich 1972, 379).

25 See J.N. Schmidt (1986, 323–4). Stage melodrama flourished between 1790 and 1900. On this stage genre see also M.R. Booth (1965; 1975). On the affinities between melodrama on stage and melodrama in the novel see Brooks (1976), Worth (1978), and Easson (1988).

26 On the tableau in eighteenth-century theatre see also Preston (1974, 105).

27 Among the abundance of publications on literary pictorialism and the connections between literature and painting, see Praz (1970), Hunt, ed. (1971), Hunt (1976), Wendorf, ed. (1983), Torgovnick (1985), and D. Scott (1988). In a seminal study, Jean Hagstrum (1958) defined 'pictorialism' as follows: 'In order to be called "pictorial" a description or an image must be, in its essentials, capable of translation into painting or some other visual art' (xxi–xxii).

28 There is indeed an almost exact parallel in a death tableau by the French genre-painter Jean-Baptiste Greuze, *Le fils puni* (1778). Today this painting can be found in the collection of the Louvre; it is reproduced in Meisel (1983, 85). See also a similar tableau in *Clarissa*, when her corpse is brought to her parental home (8:71). Another family 'portrait' is given in Bage's *Hermsprong*, when a father is to be arrested for his debts at the beginning of chapter 62.

29 See also, among others, John Berger (1972).

30 See also Arnheim (1969 [1958], 114–19) on the importance of body language in the silent film.

31 Sergei Eisenstein writes in a famous essay (1964 [1944]) that the use of montage in Griffith's pioneering films was inspired by Dickens's novels. Sypher (1960, 186–7) shows that 'photographic' and 'cinematic' effects can be observed in painting long before the advent of the modern media.

32 Lenses that made fine magnifying or distorting effects possible were not developed until the nineteenth century. See J.L. Fell (1986 [1974]).

33 See, in particular, A.M. Jackson (1984) and Lodge (1977, 78).

34 This is particularly obvious in the episode in which Tess's defloration by

d'Urberville is anticipated when he feeds her strawberries: '"No – no!" she said quickly, putting her fingers between his hand and her lips. "I would rather take it in my own hand." "Nonsense!" he insisted; and in a slight distress she parted her lips and took it in' (70). Tess's futile gesture of negation draws attention to her mouth as representing d'Urberville's actual object of desire.

References

Bibliography 1 Primary Sources
Bibliography 2 Body Language in Literature, Theatre, Film, and Art: Secondary Sources
Bibliography 3 NVC Research and Other Secondary Sources

Note: There are a number of cross-references between bibliographies 2 and 3.

Bibliography 1 Primary Sources

Years given in brackets refer to the first edition of the text in question.

Ackroyd, Peter. 1984 [1982]. *The Great Fire of London*. London: Sphere.

Anderson, Sherwood. 1960 [1919]. *Winesburg, Ohio*. New York: Viking.

[Anon.] 1967. *Sir Gawain and the Green Knight*. Edited by J.R.R. Tolkien, E.V. Gordon, and Norman Davis. 2nd ed. Oxford: Clarendon Press.

Atwood, Margaret. 1976. *Selected Poems*. Toronto: Oxford University Press.

– 1982 [1979]. *Life before Man*. London: Virago.

– 1982 [1981]. *Bodily Harm*. Toronto: Seal.

– 1987. *The Edible Woman – Surfacing – Lady Oracle*. London: Treasure.

– 1987 [1985]. *The Handmaid's Tale*. London: Virago.

Aubin, Penelope. 1973 [1721]. *The Strange Adventures of the Count de Vinevil and His Family*. Foundations of the Novel. New York and London: Garland.

Austen, Jane. 1932 [1813]. *Pride and Prejudice*. The Novels of Jane Austen in Five Volumes. 3rd ed. London: Oxford University Press.

Bage, Robert. 1985 [1796]. *Hermsprong: Or Man as He Is Not*. Oxford: Oxford University Press.

Balzac, Honoré de. 1981 [1833]. 'Théorie de la démarche.' *La Comédie humaine*, 12:259–302. Paris: Gallimard.

Beckett, Samuel. 1965 [1956]. *Waiting for Godot*. London: Faber.

– 1973 [1938]. *Murphy*. London: Picador.

Behn, Aphra. 1930 [1688]. *Oroonoko: or, The Royal Slave: A True History*. In Philip Henderson, ed., *Shorter Novels: Seventeenth Century*, 145–224. London: Dent; New York: Dutton.

– 1970 [1689]. *The History of the Nun: or, The Fair Vow-Breaker*. In Charles C. Mish, ed., *Restoration Prose Fiction 1660–1700: An Anthology of Representative Pieces*, 93–142. Lincoln: University of Nebraska Press.

Bellow, Saul. 1989. *A Theft*. Harmondsworth: Penguin.

Bennett, Arnold. 1948 [1908]. *The Old Wives' Tale*. London: Hodder and Stoughton.

Bowen, Elizabeth. 1962 [1938]. *The Death of the Heart*. Harmondsworth: Penguin.

Braine, John. 1959 [1957]. *Room at the Top*. Harmondsworth: Penguin.

Brontë, Charlotte. 1924 [1847]. *Jane Eyre*. Thornton Edition of the Sisters Brontë. 2 vols. Edinburgh: Grant.

Brontë, Emily. 1924 [1847]. *Wuthering Heights*. Thornton Edition of the Sisters Brontë. Edinburgh: Grant.

Brookner, Anita. 1988 [1987]. *A Friend from England*. London: Grafton.

– 1990 [1989]. *Lewis Percy*. Harmondsworth: Penguin.

Bunyan, John. 1960 [1678]. *The Pilgrim's Progress: From This World to That Which Is to Come*. Edited by James Blanton Wharey and Roger Sharrock. 2nd ed. Oxford: Clarendon Press.

Burney, Fanny. 1982 [1778]. *Evelina: Or the History of a Young Lady's Entrance into the World*. Oxford: Oxford University Press.

Butler, Samuel. 1966 [1903]. *The Way of All Flesh*. Harmondsworth: Penguin.

Byatt, A.S. 1991 [1990]. *Possession: A Romance*. London: Vintage.

Calvino, Italo. 1977. *The Castle of Crossed Destinies*. London: Secker and Warburg. [Translation of *Il castello dei destini incrociati*, 1973.]

Carey, Peter. 1989 [1988]. *Oscar and Lucinda*. London: Faber and Faber.

Cather, Willa. 1989 [1905]. 'Paul's Case: A Study in Temperament.' In Hermione Lee, ed., *The Short Stories of Willa Cather*, 89–111. London: Virago.

Chaucer, Geoffrey. 1957. *The Works of Geoffrey Chaucer*. Edited by F.N. Robinson. 2nd ed. London: Oxford University Press.

Clemens, Samuel Langhorne [Mark Twain]. 1923 [1884]. *The Adventures of Huckleberry Finn*. The Writings of Mark Twain. Definitive Edition. New York: Wells.

– 1923 [1889]. *A Connecticut Yankee in King Arthur's Court*. The Writings of Mark Twain. Definitive Edition. New York: Wells.

Collins, William Wilkie. 1982 [1868]. *The Moonstone*. Oxford: Oxford University Press.

Congreve, William. 1971 [1692]. *Incognita: or, Love and Duty Reconcil'd*. Facsimile of first edition. Menston, Yorkshire: Scolar Press.

– 1975 [1700]. *The Way of the World*. Edited by Kathleen M. Lynch. Regents Restoration Drama Series. London: Arnold.

Conrad, Joseph. 1947 [1907]. *The Secret Agent: A Simple Tale*. Collected Edition of the Works of Joseph Conrad. London: Dent.

Cooper, James Fenimore. 1901 [1826]. *The Last of the Mohicans: A Narrative of 1757*. The Works of J. Fenimore Cooper. New York: Appleton.

Defoe, Daniel. 1927 [1719]. *The Life and Strange Surprising Adventures of Robinson Crusoe*. The Shakespeare Head Edition of the Novels and Selected Writings of Daniel Defoe. 3 vols. Oxford: Blackwell.

– 1927 [1722]. *The Fortunes and Misfortunes of the Famous Moll Flanders*. The Shakespeare Head Edition. 2 vols. Oxford: Blackwell.

Deloney, Thomas. 1912 [*c*. 1597]. *Iacke of Newberie*. In Francis Oscar Mann, ed., *The Works of Thomas Deloney*, 1–66. Oxford: Clarendon Press.

– 1912 [*c*. 1597–1600]. *The Gentle Craft, Parts I and II*. In Francis Oscar Mann, ed., *The Works of Thomas Deloney*, 67–210. Oxford: Clarendon Press.

Dickens, Charles. 1901 [1837–8]. *Oliver Twist*. The Authentic Edition: The Works of Charles Dickens in Twenty-one Volumes. London: Chapman and Hall; New York: Scribner's.

– 1901 [1849–50]. *The Personal History of David Copperfield*. The Authentic Edition. London: Chapman and Hall; New York: Scribner's.

– 1901 [1854]. *Hard Times*. The Authentic Edition. London: Chapman and Hall; New York: Scribner's.

– 1901 [1855–7]. *Little Dorrit*. The Authentic Edition. London: Chapman and Hall; New York: Scribner's.

– 1967 [1866]. 'The Signalman.' In Christopher Dolley, ed., *The Penguin Book of English Short Stories*, 11–24. Harmondsworth: Penguin.

Disraeli, Benjamin. 1904 [1845]. *Sybil or The Two Nations*. The Works of Benjamin Disraeli, Earl of Beaconsfield. 2 vols. New York and London: Dunne.

Dos Passos, John. 1930. *The 42nd Parallel*. New York: Harper.

Drabble, Margaret. 1988 [1987]. *The Radiant Way*. Harmondsworth: Penguin.

Edgeworth, Maria. 1964 [1800]. *Castle Rackrent*. Oxford: Oxford University Press.

Eliot, George. 1898 [1859]. *Adam Bede*. Holly Lodge Edition. 2 vols. Boston: Estes.

– 1898 [1871–2]. *Middlemarch: A Study of Provincial Life*. Holly Lodge Edition. 3 vols. Boston: Estes.

Ellis, Bret Easton. 1986 [1985]. *Less than Zero*. London: Picador.
Fielding, Henry. 1974 [1749]. *The History of Tom Jones a Foundling*. The Wesleyan Edition of the Works of Henry Fielding. 2 vols. Oxford: Clarendon Press.
Forde, Emanuel. 1680 [*c.* 1600]. *The Famous History of Montelion Knight of the Oracle*. London: Printed by T. Haly for W. Thackeray and T. Passinger.
Forster, E.M. 1947 [1910]. *Howards End*. London: Arnold.
– 1961 [1924]. *A Passage to India*. Harmondsworth: Penguin.
– 1978 [1908]. *A Room with a View*. Harmondsworth: Penguin.
Fowles, John. 1977. *Daniel Martin*. London: Cape.
Galt, John. 1982 [1822]. *The Provost*. Oxford: Oxford University Press.
Gascoigne, George. 1987 [1573]. *The Adventures of Master F.J.* In Salzman ed., *An Anthology of Elizabethan Prose Fiction*, 1–81.
Gaskell, Elizabeth. 1977 [1854–5]. *North and South*. Oxford: Oxford University Press.
Gissing, George. 1904 [1891]. *New Grub Street*. London: Smith, Elder.
Golding, William. 1955. *The Inheritors*. London: Faber.
– 1956. *Pincher Martin*. London: Faber.
Goldsmith, Oliver. 1901 [1766]. *The Vicar of Wakefield*. London: Oxford University Press.
Greene, Graham. 1971 [1940]. *The Power and the Glory*. Harmondsworth: Penguin.
Greene, Robert. 1987 [1588]. *Pandosto: The Triumph of Time*. In Salzman ed., *An Anthology of Elizabethan Prose Fiction*, 151–204.
Haggard, Henry Rider. 1989 [1885]. *King Solomon's Mines*. Oxford: Oxford University Press.
Hardy, Thomas. 1926 [1886]. *The Life and Death of the Mayor of Casterbridge*. The Wessex Edition of the Works of Thomas Hardy in Prose and Verse. London: Macmillan.
– 1923 [1871]. *Desperate Remedies*. The Wessex Edition. London: Macmillan.
– 1924 [1874]. *Far from the Madding Crowd*. The Wessex Edition. London: Macmillan.
– 1974 [1872]. *Under the Greenwood Tree or The Mellstock Quire: A Rural Painting of the Dutch School*. The New Wessex Edition. London: Macmillan.
– 1974 [1891]. *Tess of the d'Urbervilles: A Pure Woman*. The New Wessex Edition. London: Macmillan.
Hartley, L.P. 1958 [1953]. *The Go-Between*. Harmondsworth: Penguin.
Haywood, Eliza. 1973 [1724]. *The Rash Resolve: Or, The Untimely Discovery*. Foundations of the Novel. New York and London: Garland.
Head, Richard, and Francis Kirkman. 1928 [1665]. *The English Rogue Described in the Life of Meriton Latroon, a Witty Extravagant*. New York: Dodd, Mead.

Heller, Joseph. 1962 [1961]. *Catch-22*. London: Cape.
Hulme, Keri. 1986 [1985]. *The Bone People*. London: Picador.
Huxley, Aldous. 1947 [1928]. *Point Counter Point*. London: Chatto and Windus.
– 1949 [1923]. *Antic Hay*. London: Chatto and Windus.
Irving, Washington. 1851 [1819]. 'Rip van Winkle.' In *The Sketch-Book of Geoffrey Crayon, Gent., Vol I*, 42–74. The Writings of Washington Irving. New Sunnyside Edition. New York and London: G.P. Putnam's Sons.
Ishiguro, Kazuo. 1983 [1982]. *A Pale View of Hills*. Harmondsworth: Penguin.
– 1987 [1986]. *An Artist of the Floating World*. London: Faber.
James, Henry. 1921 [1881]. *The Portrait of a Lady*. 2 vols. London: Macmillan.
– 1981 [1876–7]. *The American*. Harmondsworth: Penguin.
James, P.D. 1985 [1963]. *A Mind to Murder*. London: Sphere.
Johnson, Samuel. 1887 [1759]. *History of Rasselas Prince of Abyssinia*. Oxford: Clarendon Press.
Joyce, James. 1966 [1916]. *A Portrait of the Artist as a Young Man*. New York: Viking.
– 1986 [1922]. *Ulysses*. A Critical and Synoptic Edition, edited by Hans Walter Gabler, Wolfhard Steppe, and Claus Melchior. 3 vols. New York and London: Garland.
Kafka, Franz. 1976. *The Trial*. In *Selected Works*, 11–128. London: Secker and Warburg/Octopus Press. [Translation of *Der Prozess*, 1925]
Kingsley, Charles. 1983 [1850]. *Alton Locke: Tailor and Poet*. Oxford: Oxford University Press.
Kleist, Heinrich von. 1964. *Erzählungen*. dtv-Gesamtausgabe. Munich: dtv.
Laclos, Pierre Choderlos de. 1964 [1782]. *Les Liaisons Dangereuses*. Paris: Garnier-Flammarion.
Laurence, Margaret. 1987 [1964]. *The Stone Angel*. London: Virago.
Lawrence, D.H. 1950 [1922]. *A Modern Lover and Other Stories*. New York: Avon.
– 1960 [1921]. *Women in Love*. Harmondsworth: Penguin.
Lessing, Doris. 1973 [1962]. *The Golden Notebook*. London: Granada.
Lively, Penelope. 1988 [1987]. *Moon Tiger*. Harmondsworth: Penguin.
Lodge, David. 1989 [1988]. *Nice Work*. Harmondsworth: Penguin.
Lodge, Thomas. 1967 [1590]. *Rosalind: Euphues' Golden Legacy Found after His Death in His Cell at Silexedra*. In Merritt Lawliss, ed., *Elizabethan Prose Fiction*, 278–394. Indianapolis and New York: Odyssey Press.
Lurie, Alison. 1986 [1974]. *The War between the Tates*. London: Sphere.
Lyly, John. 1987 [1578]. *Euphues: The Anatomy of Wit*. In Salzman, ed., *An Anthology of Elizabethan Prose Fiction*, 83–150.
McEwan, Ian. 1982 [1981]. *The Comfort of Strangers*. London: Picador.

Mackenzie, Henry. 1967 [1771]. *The Man of Feeling*. London: Oxford University Press.

Malamud, Bernard. 1968 [1966]. *The Fixer*. Harmondsworth: Penguin.

Maugham, W. Somerset. 1963 [1944]. *The Razor's Edge*. Harmondsworth: Penguin.

Melville, Herman. 1952 [1851]. *Moby-Dick or The Whale*. London: Oxford University Press.

Meredith, George. 1984 [1859]. *The Ordeal of Richard Feverel: A History of a Father and Son*. Oxford: Oxford University Press.

Moore, George. 1983 [1894]. *Esther Waters*. Oxford: Oxford University Press.

Murdoch, Iris. 1960 [1954]. *Under the Net*. Harmondsworth: Penguin.

Nashe, Thomas. 1987 [1594]. *The Unfortunate Traveller*. In Salzman, ed., *An Anthology of Elizabetan Prose Fiction*, 205–309.

O'Connor, Flannery. 1955. 'Good Country People.' *A Good Man Is Hard to Find and Other Stories*, 168–96. New York: Harcourt, Brace and World.

Orwell, George. 1954 [1949]. *Nineteen Eighty-Four*. Harmondsworth: Penguin.

Painter, William. 1966 [1566]. 'The Forty-Fourth Nouell: The Love of Alerane of Saxone, and of Adelasia the Doughter of the Emperour Otho the Thirde of That Name.' In his *The Palace of Pleasure*, edited by Joseph Jacobs, 1:249–84. 3 vols. New York: Dover.

Peacock, Thomas Love. 1924 [1818]. *Nightmare Abbey*. The Halliford Edition of the Works of Thomas Love Peacock. London: Constable; New York: Wells.

Piercy, Marge. 1987 [1972]. *Small Changes*. Harmondsworth: Penguin.

– 1987 [1976]. *Woman on the Edge of Time*. London: The Women's Press.

Pym, Barbara. 1980 [1955]. *Less than Angels*. London: Panther.

Pynchon, Thomas. 1979 [1966]. *The Crying of Lot 49*. London: Picador.

Rabelais, François. 1955. *Oeuvres Complètes*. Edited by Jacques Boulenger and Lucien Scheler. Bibliothèque de la Pléiade. Paris: Gallimard.

Radcliffe, Ann. 1981 [1797]. *The Italian: Or the Confessional of the Black Penitents*. Oxford: Oxford University Press.

Reeve, Clara. 1967 [1777]. *The Old English Baron: A Gothic Story*. London: Oxford University Press.

Richardson, Samuel. 1929 [1740–1]. *Pamela or, Virtue Rewarded*. The Shakespeare Head Edition of the Novels of Samuel Richardson. 4 vols. Oxford: Blackwell.

– 1930 [1747–9]. *Clarissa or, The History of a Young Lady*. The Shakespeare Head Edition. 8 vols. Oxford: Blackwell.

Rushdie, Salman. 1988. *The Satanic Verses*. London: Viking.

Salinger, J.D. 1964 [1950]. 'For Esmé – with Love and Squalor.' In his *Nine Stories*, 87–114. New York: Bantam.

– 1964 [1951]. 'Pretty Mouth and Green My Eyes.' In his *Nine Stories*, 115–29. New York: Bantam.

Salzman, Paul, ed. 1987. *An Anthology of Elizabethan Prose Fiction*. Oxford: Oxford University Press.

Scott, Walter. 1830 [1818]. *The Heart of Midlothian*. Waverley Novels. The Edinburgh Edition. Edinburgh: Paterson.

Shakespeare, William. 1974. *The Riverside Shakespeare*. Edited by G. Blakemore Evans. Boston: Houghton Mifflin.

Shaw, Bernard. 1941 [1914]. *Pygmalion: A Romance in Five Acts*. Harmondsworth: Penguin.

Shelley, Mary W. 1969 [1818]. *Frankenstein or The Modern Prometheus*. London: Oxford University Press.

Sidney, Philip. 1922 [1590]. *The Countesse of Pembrokes Arcadia*. Edited by Albert Feuillerat. Cambridge: Cambridge University Press.

Smith, Charlotte. 1969 [1793]. *The Old Manor House*. London: Oxford University Press.

Smollett, Tobias. 1981 [1748]. *The Adventures of Roderick Random*. Oxford: Oxford University Press.

Sterne, Laurence. 1928 [1768]. *A Sentimental Journey through France and Italy*. London: Oxford University Press.

– 1978 [1759–67]. *The Life and Opinions of Tristram Shandy, Gentleman*. The Florida Edition of the Works of Laurence Sterne. 2 vols. Gainesville: University Presses of Florida.

Swift, Graham. 1983 [1980]. *The Sweet Shop Owner*. Harmondsworth: Penguin.

– 1984 [1983]. *Waterland*. London: Picador.

– 1988. *Out of This World*. Harmondsworth: Penguin.

Swift, Jonathan. 1959 [1726]. *Gulliver's Travels*. Oxford: Blackwell.

Thackeray, William Makepeace. 1910 [1848]. *Vanity Fair: A Novel without a Hero*. The Centenary Biographical Edition of the Works of William Makepeace Thackeray. New York and London: Harper and Brothers.

Trollope, Anthony. 1980 [1857]. *Barchester Towers*. Oxford: Oxford University Press.

Twain, Mark. *See* Clemens, Samuel Langhorne.

Updike, John. 1987 [1986]. *Roger's Version*. Harmondsworth: Penguin.

van Herk, Aritha. 1989 [1981]. *The Tent Peg*. London: Virago.

Vonnegut, Kurt, Jr. 1973. *Breakfast of Champions: Or Goodbye Blue Monday*. New York: Delacorte.

Walpole, Horace. 1924 [1765]. *The Castle of Otranto* and *The Mysterious Mother*. London: Constable.

Weldon, Fay. 1989. *The Cloning of Joanna May*. Glasgow: Fontana.

Wilde, Oscar. 1905 [1891]. *The Picture of Dorian Gray*. Paris: Carrington.
Wolfe, Tom. 1987. *The Bonfire of the Vanities*. New York: Farrar, Straus, Giroux.
Wood, Mrs Henry [Ellen]. 1907 [1861]. *East Lynne*. London: Macmillan.
Woolf, Virginia. 1964 [1925]. *Mrs Dalloway*. Harmondsworth: Penguin.
Wycherley, William. 1979. *The Plays of William Wycherley*. Edited by Arthur Friedman. Oxford: Clarendon Press.

Bibliography 2 Body Language in Literature, Theatre, Film, and Art: Secondary Sources

Years given in brackets refer to first editions when later editions were used.

Aikins, Janet E. 1989. 'Richardson's "Speaking Pictures."' In M.A. Doody and P. Sabor, eds, *Samuel Richardson: Tercentenary Essays*, 146–66. Cambridge: Cambridge University Press.
Albert, Mechthild. 1987. *Unausgesprochene Botschaften: Zur nonverbalen Kommunikation in den Romanen Stendhals*. Romanica et Comparatistica, 7. Tübingen: Stauffenburg.
Alfieri, Gabriella. 1983. 'Processi sociocomunicativi e testo narrante: Codice gestuale in contesti "culturali" verghiani.' *Linguistica e anthropologia: Atti del XIV congresso internazionale di studi, 23–25 Lecce maggio 1980, a cura del Gruppo di Lecce*, 423–49. Rome: Bulzoni.
Altman, Leslie Joan Wolbarst. 1973. 'Gesture and Posture in the *Merchant's Tale*: A Study of Chaucer's Narrative Technique.' *Dissertation Abstracts International* 34: 1232A. [Ph.D. diss., Boston College 1973]
Amira, Karl von. 1905. 'Die Handgebärden in den Bilderhandschriften des Sachsenspiegels.' *Abhandlungen der Philosophisch-Philologischen Klasse der bayerischen Akademie der Wissenschaften*, 163–263. I. Klasse, Bd 23, II. Abt. Munich.
Amprimoz, Alexandre L. 1982. 'Fonction gestuelle: *Bonheur d'occasion* de Gabrielle Roy.' *Présence Francophone: Revue Littéraire* 24: 123–37.
Argelander, Ronald. 1973. 'Scott Burton's Behavior Tableaux (1970–72).' *Drama Review* 17, no. 3: 109–13.
Arnheim, Rudolf. 1969 [1958]. *Film as Art*. London: Faber and Faber. [Translation of *Film als Kunst*, 1932]
Artaud, Antonin. 1970 [1938]. *Le Théâtre et son double*. Paris: Gallimard.
'Die Aufklärung und ihr Körper: Beiträge zur Leibesgeschichte im 18. Jahrhundert.' 1990. *Das Achtzehnte Jahrhundert* 14, no. 2.
Aulhorn, Edith. 1924. 'Zur Gestaltung seelischer Vorgänge in neurer Erzählung.' In Julius Wahle and Victor Klemperer, eds, *Vom Geiste neuer Literaturforschung: Festschrift für O. Walzel*, 70–9. Wildpark-Potsdam: Athenaion.

Austin, Gerhard. 1981. *Phänomenologie der Gebärde bei Hugo von Hofmannsthal.* Frankfurter Beiträge zur Germanistik, 18. Heidelberg: Winter.

Austin, Gilbert. 1969 [1818]. *Die Kunst der rednerischen und theatralischen Declamation.* Faksimile der Originalausgabe 1818. Leipzig: Edition Leipzig. [Translation of *Chironomia*, 1806]

Baamonde Traveso, Gloria. 1986. 'Approximación semiológica a la expresión gestual en Valle-Inclán.' In Garrido Gallardo and Miguel Angel, eds, *Crítica semiológica de textos literarios hispánicos*, 835–41. Madrid: Consejo Superior de Investigaciones Científicas.

Bakhtin, Mikhail. 1968 [1965]. 'The Grotesque Image of the Body and Its Sources.' In his *Rabelais and His World*, 303–67. Cambridge, Mass. and London: MIT Press. [Translation of *Tvorchestvo Frasua Rable*, 1965]

Bal, Mieke. 1983. 'The Narrating and the Focalizing: A Theory of the Agents in Narrative.' *Style*. 17: 234–69.

Balász, Béla. 1970 [1926]. *Theory of the Film: Character and Growth of a New Art.* New York: Dover Publications.

Ballhausen, Günter. 1955. 'Der Wandel der Gebärde auf dem deutschen Theater im 18. Jahrhundert dargestellt an den Gebärdenbüchern.' Diss., Göttingen.

Barasch, Moshe. 1976. *Gestures of Despair in Medieval and Early Renaissance Art.* New York: New York University Press.

Barkan, Leonard. 1975. *Nature's Work of Art: The Human Body as Image of the World.* New Haven and London: Yale University Press.

Barker, Francis. 1984. *The Tremulous Private Body: Essays on Subjection.* London and New York: Methuen.

Barnett, Dene. 1987. *The Art of Gesture: The Practices and Principles of 18th Century Acting.* Heidelberg: Winter.

Barnett, George L., ed. 1968. *Eighteenth-Century British Novelists on the Novel.* New York: Appleton-Century-Crofts.

Barta, Ilsebill. 1986. 'Der disziplinierte Körper: Bürgerliche Körpersprache und ihre geschlechtsspezifische Differenzierung.' In I. Barta and Zita Breu et al., eds, *Frauen, Bilder, Männer, Mythen: Kunsthistorische Beiträge*, 84–106. Berlin: Reimer.

Barta Fliedl, Ilsebill, and Christoph Geissmar, eds. 1992. *Die Beredsamkeit des Leibes: Zur Körpersprache in der Kunst.* Veröffentlichung der Albertina, 31. Salzburg and Vienna: Residenz.

Barthes, Roland. 1966. 'Introduction à l'analyse structurale des récits.' *Communications* 8: 1–27.

– 1982 [1968]. 'The Reality Effect.' In Tzvetan Todorov, ed., *French Literary Theory Today: A Reader*, 11–17. Cambridge: Cambridge University Press, Paris:

Editions de la Maison des Sciences de L'Homme. [Translation of 'L'effet du réel,' 1968]

Bathe, Johannes. 1917. 'Die Bewegungen und Haltungen des menschlichen Körpers in Heinrich von Kleists Erzählungen.' Diss., Tübingen.

Baumeister, August. 1884–5. 'Geberdensprache in der Kunst.' In *Denkmäler des klassischen Altertums: Zur Erläuterung des Lebens der Griechen und Römer in Religion, Kunst und Sitte, Bd. I,* 586–92. Munich and Leipzig: Oldenbourg.

Bayne, Sheila Page. 1981. *Tears and Weeping: An Aspect of Emotional Climate Reflected in Seventeenth-Century French Literature.* Etudes littéraires françaises, 16. Tübingen: Narr; Paris: Place.

Beatty, Patricia V. 1981–2. 'Body Language in Harry Crews's *The Gypsy's Curse.*' *Critique* 23: 61–6.

Benson, Michael. 1984. 'Moving Bodies in Hardy and Beckett.' *Essays in Criticism* 34: 229–43.

Benson, Robert G. 1980. *Medieval Body Language: A Study of the Use of Gesture in Chaucer's Poetry.* Anglistica, 21. Kopenhagen: Rosenkilde and Bagger.

Berger, John. 1972. *Ways of Seeing.* Harmondsworth: Penguin.

Bergson, Henri. 1975 [1900]. *Le Rire: Essai sur la signification du comique.* Paris: Presses Universitaires de France.

Bestul, Thomas H. 1983. 'True and False *Cheere* in Chaucer's *Clerk's Tale.*' *Journal of English and Germanic Philology* 82: 500–14.

Beszard, L. 1903. 'Les larmes dans l'épopée, particulièrement dans l'épopée française jusqu'à la fin du XIIe siècle.' *Zeitschrift für romanische Philologie* 27: 385–413; 513–49; 641–74.

Bevington, David. 1984. *Action Is Eloquence: Shakespeare's Language of Gesture.* Cambridge, Mass., and London: Harvard University Press.

Bienheim, Erich. 1924. 'Die Gebärden im Alten Testament.' Diss., Würzburg.

Binder, Hartmut. 1976. *Kafka in neuer Sicht: Mimik, Gestik und Personengefüge als Darstellungsform des Autobiographischen.* Stuttgart: Metzler.

Bjerring, Nancy E. 1976. 'The Problem of Language in Margaret Atwood's *Surfacing.*' *Queen's Quarterly* 83: 597–612.

Blackmur, R.P. 1952 [1942]. 'Language as Gesture.' In his *Language as Gesture: Essays in Poetry,* 3–24. New York: Harcourt, Brace and Court.

Blaicher, Günther. 1966. 'Das Weinen in mittelenglischer Zeit: Studien zur Gebärde des Weinens in historischen Quellen und literarischen Texten.' Diss., Saarbrücken.

– 1970. 'Über das Lachen im englischen Mittelalter.' *Deutsche Vierteljahrsschrift für Literaturwissenschaft und Geistesgeschichte* 44: 508–29.

Bleikasten, André. 1985 [1975]. 'Terror and Nausea: Bodies in *Sanctuary.*' *The*

Faulkner Journal 1, no. 1: 17–29. [Translation of 'La terreur et la nausée, ou le langage des corps dans *Sanctuaire*,' 1975]

Bluestone, Max. 1974. *From Story to Stage: The Dramatic Adaptation of Prose Fiction in the Period of Shakespeare and His Contemporaries*. The Hague and Paris: Mouton.

Boggs, Ralph Steele. 1934–40. 'Gebärde.' In Lutz Mackensen, ed., *Handwörterbuch des deutschen Märchens*, 2:318–22. Berlin: de Gruyter.

Bohn, Ursula. 1938. *Bild und Gebärde in Adalbert Stifters 'Studien,' mit besonderer Berücksichtigung der Lesarten*. Germanistische Studien, 203. Berlin: Ebering.

Bolhöfer, Walther. 1912. 'Gruss und Abschied in Ahd. und Mhd. Zeit.' Diss., Göttingen.

Bonheim, Helmut. 1982. *The Narrative Modes: Techniques of the Short Story*. Cambridge: Brewer.

Booth, Michael R. 1965. *English Melodrama*. London: Herbert Jenkins.

Booth, Michael R., et al., eds. 1975. *The Revels History of Drama in English. Vol. VI: 1750–1880*. London: Methuen.

Bošković-Stulli, Maja. 1985. 'Darstellerische Aspekte des Erzählens.' *Fabula* 26: 58–71.

Bowers, Robert H. 1948. 'Gesticulation in Elizabethan Acting.' *Southern Folklore Quarterly* 12: 267–77.

Braeder, Anna. 1931. *Zur Rolle des Körperlichen in der altfranzösischen Literatur mit besonderer Berücksichtigung der Chansons de Geste*. Giessener Beiträge zur Romanischen Philologie, 24. Giessen: Romanisches Seminar.

Brecht, Bertolt. 1967 [1938]. 'Über gestische Musik.' In *Gesammelte Werke*, 15: 482–5. Frankfurt: Suhrkamp.

Bredtmann, Hermann. 1889. 'Der sprachliche Ausdruck einiger der geläufigsten Gesten im altfranzösischen Karlsepos.' Diss., Marburg.

Brilliant, Richard. 1963. *Gesture and Rank in Roman Art: The Use of Gestures to Denote Status in Roman Sculpture and Coinage*. Memoirs of the Connecticut Academy of Art and Sciences, 14. New Haven, Conn.: Academy of Art and Sciences.

Brooks, Peter. 1969. *The Novel of Worldliness: Crébillon, Marivaux, Laclos, Stendhal*. Princeton: Princeton University Press.

– 1973–4. 'The Text of Muteness.' *New Literary History*, 5: 549–64.

– 1976. *The Melodramatic Imagination: Balzac, Henry James, Melodrama, and the Mode of Excess*. New Haven and London: Yale University Press.

Brown, John Russell. 1972. *Theatre Language: A Study of Arden, Osborne, Pinter and Wesker*. London: Allen Lane and Penguin.

Bruyne, Luc de. 1943. 'L'imposition des mains dans l'art chrétien ancien: Contribution iconologique à l'histoire du geste.' *Rivista di Archeologia Cristiana* 20: 113–278.

Buchloh, Paul Gerhard. 1975. 'Die Bedeutung aussersprachlicher Mittel im modernen amerikanischen Theater.' In Siegfried Neuweiler and Alfred Weber, eds, *Amerikanisches Drama und Theater im zwanzigsten Jahrhundert: American Drama and Theater in the 20th Century*, 36–59. Göttingen: Vandenhoeck and Ruprecht.

Büchsenmann, Jens. 1986. *Nonverbale Ikonizität in narrativen Gesprächsbeiträgen: Beispiele anschaulichen Erzählens von Geschichten in Südfrankreich*. Frankfurt am Main: Lang.

Bullen, J.B. 1986. *The Expressive Eye: Fiction and Perception in the Work of Thomas Hardy*. Oxford: Clarendon Press.

Burke, Kenneth. 1963. 'The Thinking of the Body: Comments on the Imagery of Catharsis in Literature.' *Psychoanalytical Review* 50, no. 3: 25–68.

– 1966. 'Definition of Man.' In his *Language as Symbolic Action: Essays on Life, Literature, and Method*, 3–24. Berkeley and Los Angeles: University of California Press. [First published in *Hudson Review* 16, no. 4 (1963–4): 491–514]

Cahusac, Louis de. 1777 [1754]. 'Geste.' In Denis Diderot and Jean Le Rond d'Alembert, eds, *Encyclopédie, ou Dictionnaire Raisonné des Sciences, des Arts et des Métiers*. Nouvelle Edition. Geneva: Pellet.

Calame-Griaule, Geneviève. 1977. 'Pour une étude des gestes narratifs.' In her *Langages et cultures africaines: Essais d'ethno-linguistique*, 303–59. Paris: Maspero.

Cameron, Sharon. 1981. *The Corporeal Self: Allegories of the Body in Melville and Hawthorne*. Baltimore, Md.: Johns Hopkins University Press.

Carducci, Jane S. 1987. 'Shakespeare's *Titus Andronicus*: An Experiment in Expression.' *Cahiers Elisabéthains* 31: 1–9.

Carrington, Ildikó de Papp. 1982. '"I'm Stuck": The Secret Sharers in *The Edible Woman*.' *Essays on Canadian Writing* 23: 68–87.

– 1983. 'Another Symbolic Descent.' *Essays on Canadian Writing* 26: 45–63.

Chabert, Pierre. 1982. 'The Body in Beckett's Theatre.' *Journal of Beckett Studies* 8: 23–8.

Chapman, Raymond. 1973. *Linguistics and Literature: An Introduction to Literary Stylistics*. London: Arnold.

Charney, Maurice. 1961. *Shakespeare's Roman Plays: The Function of Imagery in the Drama*. Cambridge, Mass.: Harvard University Press.

Chatman, Seymour. 1975. 'The Structure of Narrative Transmission.' In Roger Fowler, ed., *Style and Structure in Literature: Essays in the New Stylistics*, 213–257. Oxford: Blackwell.

– 1978. *Story and Discourse: Narrative Structure in Fiction and Film*. Ithaca, N.Y., and London: Cornell University Press.

Codell, Julie F. 1986. 'Expression over Beauty: Facial Expression, Body Language, and Circumstantiality in the Paintings of the Pre-Raphaelite Brotherhood.' *Victorian Studies* 29: 255–90.

Cohen, Keith. 1979. *Film and Fiction: The Dynamics of Exchange*. New Haven and London: Yale University Press.

Cohn, Dorrit. 1978. *Transparent Minds: Narrative Modes for Presenting Consciousness in Fiction*. Princeton: Princeton University Press.

Colas, Louise. 1982. 'Chrétien de Troyes: Le corps et le geste.' *Europe* 642: 105–13.

Cole, Toby, and Helen Krich Chinoy, eds. 1970 [1949]. *Actors on Acting: The Theories, Techniques, and Practices of the Great Actors of All Times as Told in Their Own Words*. New York: Crown.

Cowley, Malcolm, ed. 1958. *Writers at Work: The Paris Review Interviews*. With an introduction by Malcolm Cowley. London: Secker and Warburg.

Cowling, Mary C. 1983. 'The Artist as Anthropologist in Mid-Victorian England: Frith's *Derby Day*, the *Railway Station* and the New Science of Mankind.' *Art History* 6: 461–77.

– 1989. *The Artist as Anthropologist: The Representation of Type and Character in Victorian Art*. Cambridge: Cambridge University Press.

Crompton, John. 1988. 'Eurybessie: Non-Verbal Communication in Conrad.' *The Conradian* 13: 183–91.

Culler, Jonathan. 1975. *Structuralist Poetics: Structuralism, Linguistics and the Study of Literature*. London: Routledge and Kegan Paul.

Cunningham, J.V. 1951. *Woe or Wonder: The Emotional Effect of Shakespearean Tragedy*. Denver, Colo.: University of Denver Press.

Cupchik, Gerald C. 1988. 'Nonverbal Communication in Paintings.' In Poyatos, ed., 1988, *Literary Anthropology*, 227–43.

Danow, David K. 1980. 'Semiotics of Gesture in Dostoevskian Dialogue.' *Russian Literature* 8: 41–75.

Davidson, Margaret E. 1986. 'The Hand in the Works of Heinrich von Kleist.' *Colloquia Germanica* 19: 228–41.

Davies, Walter R. 1969. *Idea and Act in Elizabethan Fiction*. Princeton: Princeton University Press.

Deleuze, Gilles. 1979. 'Pierre Klossowski oder Die Sprache des Körpers.' In Pierre Klossowski et al., *Sprachen des Körpers: Marginalien zum Werk von Pierre Klossowski*, 39–66. Berlin: Merve.

Delling, Hildegard. 1925. 'Studien über die Gebärdensprache in Dichtkunst und Bildkunst des frühen und hohen Mittelalters.' Diss., Leipzig.

Demisch, Heinz. 1984. *Erhobene Hände: Geschichte einer Gebärde in der bildenden Kunst*. Stuttgart: Urachhaus.

Deonna, W. 1914. *L'expression des sentiments dans l'art grec: Les facteurs expressifs*. Paris: Renouard.

Diderot, Denis. 1951. *Oeuvres*. Edited by André Billy. Bibliothèque de la Pléiade. Paris: Gallimard.

Dietrich, Anne-Margret. 1944. 'Wandel der Gebärde auf dem deutschen Theater vom 15. zum 17. Jahrhundert.' Diss., Vienna.

Doswald, Herman K. 1969. 'Nonverbal Expression in Hofmannsthal's *Elektra*.' *Germanic Review* 44: 199–210.

Duggan, Margaret. 1989. 'Gesture and Physical Attitude in Two Novels by Samuel Richardson.' *Studies on Voltaire and the Eighteenth Century* 265: 1608–10.

Easson, Angus. 1988. 'Emotion and Gesture in *Nicholas Nickleby*.' *Dickens Quarterly* 5: 136–51.

Eisenstein, Sergei. 1964 [1944]. 'Dickens, Griffith, and the Film Today.' In his *Film Form: Essays in Film Theory and the Film Sense*, 195–255. Cleveland and New York: Meridian Books.

Eisner, Lotte H. 1969. *The Haunted Screen: Expressionism in the German Cinema and the Influence of Max Reinhardt*. London: Thames and Hudson. [Translation of *Dämonische Leinwand: Die Blütezeit des deutschen Films*, 1955]

Elam, Keir. 1980. *The Semiotics of Theatre and Drama*. New Accents. London and New York: Methuen.

Engel, Johann Jakob. 1884 [1786]. *Ideen zu einer Mimik*. J.J. Engels Schriften, VII and VIII. Berlin: Mylius.

Engert, Fritz. 1934. *Das stumme Spiel im deutschen Drama von Lessing bis Kleist*. Leipzig: Frommhold and Wendler. [Diss., Leipzig 1928]

Eschholz, Paul A. 1973. 'Mark Twain and the Language of Gesture.' *Mark Twain Journal* 17: 5–8.

Esslin, Martin. 1980. *The Theatre of the Absurd*. 3rd ed. Harmondsworth: Penguin.

Evans, Elizabeth C. 1969. 'Physiognomics in the Ancient World.' *Transactions of the American Philosophical Society* N.S. 59: Part 5.

Ewell, Barbara C. 1981. 'The Language of Alienation in Margaret Atwood's *Surfacing*.' *The Centennial Review* 25, no. 2: 185–202.

Ewert, Sabine. 1978. 'Die Gebärde im Melodrama *Lenardo und Blandine* von Joseph Franz von Goetz.' Diss., Munich.

Fabre, Michel. 1983. 'From *The Stone Angel* to *The Diviners*: An Interview with Margaret Laurence.' In George Woodcock, ed., *A Place to Stand On: Essays by and about Margaret Laurence*, 193–209. Edmonton: NeWest.

Fahnestock, Jeanne. 1981. 'The Heroine of Irregular Features: Physiognomy and Conventions of Heroine Description.' *Victorian Studies* 24: 325–50.

Fell, John L. 1986 [1974]. *Film and the Narrative Tradition*. Berkeley and Los Angeles: University of California Press.

Fell, Katherine Rowe. 1982. 'The Unspoken Language of Edward Driffield.' *Language and Literature* 7: 93–106.

– 1986. '"A Silent Way Unseen": Maugham's Use of Nonverbal Behavior in Three Novels.' Ph.D. diss., Texas A and M University.

Fischer, Ottokar. 1908–9. 'Mimische Studien zu Heinrich von Kleist.' *Euphorion* 15: 488–510, 716–25; 16: 62–92, 412–25, 747–72.

Fischer-Lichte, Erika. 1988a. *Semiotik des Theaters: Eine Einführung. Bd. I: Das System der theatralischen Zeichen*. 2nd ed. Tübingen: Narr.

– 1988b. *Semiotik des Theaters: Eine Einführung. Bd. III: Die Aufführung als Text*. 2nd ed. Tübingen: Narr.

– 1989. *Semiotik des Theaters: Eine Einführung. Bd. II: Vom 'künstlichen' zum 'natürlichen' Zeichen – Theater des Barock und der Aufklärung*. 2nd ed. Tübingen: Narr.

– 1992. *The Semiotics of Theatre*. Bloomington and Indianapolis: Indiana University Press. [Abridged translation of the three-volume German edition]

Flannigan, Arthur. 1982. '"The Eye of the Witch": Non-Verbal Communication and the Exercise of Power in *Une Vie de Boy*.' *French Review* 56: 51–63.

Flynn, Carol Houlihan. 1990. *The Body in Swift and Defoe*. Cambridge Studies in Eighteenth-Century English Literature and Thought, 5. Cambridge: Cambridge University Press.

Fowler, Roger. 1986. *Linguistic Criticism*. Oxford: Oxford University Press.

Franz, Arthur. 1927. 'Seelische und körperliche Bewegung in Dantes *Divina Commedia*.' In *Estudios eruditos in memoriam de Adolfo Bonilla y San Martin*, 415–30. Madrid: Jaime Ratés.

Frappier-Mazur, Lucienne. 1967. 'Espace et regard dans *La Comédie humaine*.' *L'Anneé balzacienne 1967*, 325–38.

Frenzen, Wilhelm. 1936. 'Klagebilder und Klagegebärden in der deutschen Dichtung des höfischen Mittelalters.' Diss., Bonn.

Friedman, John Block. 1981. 'Another Look at Chaucer and the Physiognomists.' *Studies in Philology*, 78: 138–52.

Friedman, Lionel J. 1957–8. 'Occulta Cordis.' *Romance Philology* 11: 103–19.

Fussell, Paul, Jr. 1955. 'The Gestic Symbolism of T.S. Eliot.' *English Literary History* 22: 194–211.

Gargano, James W. 1979. 'The "Look" as a Major Event in James's Short Fiction.' *Arizona Quarterly* 35: 303–20.

Garroni, Emilio. 1978. 'Langage verbal et éléments non-verbaux dans le message filmico-télévisuel.' In Dominique Noguez, ed., *Cinéma, théorie, lectures*, 111–27. 2nd ed. Paris: Klincksieck.

Geitner, Ursula. 1990. '"Die Beredsamkeit des Leibes": Zur Unterscheidung von Bewusstsein und Kommunikation im 18. Jahrhundert.' *Das Achtzehnte Jahrhundert* 14, no. 2: 181–95.

Genette, Gérard. 1969 [1966]. 'Frontières du récit.' In his *Figures II: Essais*, 49–69. Paris: Seuil. [First published in *Communications*, 8 (1966): 152–63]

– 1972. *Figures III*. Paris: Seuil.

Gentges, Ignaz. 1923. 'Tiecks Märchenbühne: Die Geste als Wort und Gebärde im Drama Ludwig Tiecks.' *Das deutsche Theater: Jahrbuch für Drama und Bühne (1922/23)*, 144–60. Berlin and Leipzig: Schröder.

Gerstner-Hirzel, Arthur. 1957. *The Economy of Action and Word in Shakespeare's Plays*. The Cooper Monographs, 2. Bern: Francke.

Gidal, Peter. 1986. *Understanding Beckett: A Study of Monologue and Gesture in the Works of Samuel Beckett*. Houndmills: Macmillan.

Glättli, Walter. 1949. 'Die Behandlung des Affekts der Furcht im englischen Roman des 18. Jahrhunderts.' Diss., Zurich.

Goetsch, Paul. 1977. 'Gebärde.' In his *Bauformen des modernen englischen und amerikanischen Dramas*, 53–84. Darmstadt: Wissenschaftliche Buchgesellschaft.

Gombrich, E.H. 1959. *Art and Illusion*. London: Phaidon.

– 1966. 'Ritualized Gesture and Expression in Art.' *Philosophical Transactions of the Royal Society of London*, B, 251, Biological Sciences: 393–401.

– 1972. 'Action and Expression in Western Art.' In Hinde, ed., 1972, *Non-Verbal Communication*, 373–93. *See* bibliography 3.

– 1989. *The Story of Art*. 15th ed. London: Phaidon.

Grabes, Herbert. 1990. 'Creating to Dissect: Strategies of Character Portrayal and Evaluation in Short Stories by Margaret Laurence, Alice Munro and Mavis Gallant.' In Nischik and Korte, eds, 1990, *Modes of Narrative*, 119–28.

Grace, Sherrill E. 1980. *Violent Duality: A Study of Margaret Atwood*. Montreal: Véhicule.

Graf, Heinz Joachim. 1938. 'Untersuchungen zur Gebärde in der Íslendingasaga.' Diss., Bonn.

Grajew, Felix. 1934. 'Untersuchungen über die Bedeutung der Gebärden in der griechischen Epik.' Diss., Freiburg.

Grivel, Charles. 1981. 'L'Histoire dans le visage.' In Jean Decottignies, ed., *Les sujets de l'écriture*, 175–227. Lille: Presses Universitaires de Lille.

Grossman, James. 1950. *James Fenimore Cooper*. The American Men of Letters Series. London: Methuen.

Gruen, Ruth. 1981–2. 'L'impuissance à parler: Aspects du discours et du comportement non verbal dans *Armance*.' *Stendhal Club* 96, 24: 411–23.

Haas, Rudolf. 1980. 'Handlung und Gebärde in *Hamlet*.' In Hans-Heinrich Freitag and Peter Hühn, eds, *Literarische Ansichten der Wirklichkeit: Studien zur Wirklichkeitskonstitution in englischsprachiger Literatur: To Honour Johannes Kleinstück*, 73–87. Frankfurt am Main: Lang.

Habicht, Werner. 1959. *Die Gebärde in englischen Dichtungen des Mittelalters*. Bayerische Akademie der Wissenschaften, Abhandlungen der Philosophisch-Historischen Klasse, N.F., H. 46. Munich: Verlag der Bayerischen Akademie der Wissenschaften.

Habicht, Werner, and Ina Schabert, eds. 1978. *Sympathielenkung in den Dramen Shakespeares*. Munich: Fink.

Hacks, Charles. 1892. *Le Geste*. Paris: Marpon et Flammarion.

Hagstrum, Jean H. 1958. *The Sister Arts: The Tradition of Literary Pictorialism and English Poetry from Dryden to Gray*. Chicago: University of Chicago Press.

Haiding, Karl. 1955. *Von der Gebärdensprache der Märchenerzähler*. FF Communications, 155. Helsinki: Academia Scientiarum Fennica.

Haight, Gordon S., ed. 1954. *The George Eliot Letters: Vol. III 1859–1861*. London: Oxford University Press; New Haven, Conn.: Yale University Press.

Hairston, Robert Burl. 1990. 'An Examination of the Nonverbal Communication in Three Noir Films: "The Postman Always Rings Twice," "The Big Sleep," and "Murder My Sweet" in the Original and Remake Versions.' *Dissertation Abstracts International* 50: 3770A. [Diss., Florida State University, 1989]

Halász, László. 1987. 'Cognitive and Social Psychological Approaches to Literary Discourse: An Overview.' In László Halász, ed., *Literary Discourse: Aspects of Cognitive and Social Psychological Approaches*, 1–37. Berlin: de Gruyter.

Halliday, M.A.K. 1971. 'Linguistic Function and Literary Style: An Inquiry into the Language of William Golding's *The Inheritors*.' In Seymour Chatman, ed., *Literary Style: A Symposium*, 330–65. London and New York: Oxford University Press.

Hamon, Philippe. 1981. 'Rhetorical Status of the Descriptive.' In Philippe Hamon, ed., *Towards a Theory of Description*, 1–26. *Yale French Studies*, 61.

Hansen, Leopold. 1908. 'Die Ausdrucksformen der Affekte im Tristan Gottfrieds von Strassburg.' Diss., Kiel.

Hanson, Thomas Bradley. 1970. 'Stylized Man: The Poetic Use of Physiognomy in Chaucer's *Canterbury Tales*.' Ph.D. diss., University of Wisconsin.

Hapgood, Robert. 1966–7. 'Speak Hands for Me: Gesture as Language in *Julius Caesar*.' *Drama Survey* 5: 162–70.

Harbage, Alfred. 1939. 'Elizabethan Acting.' *PMLA* 54: 685–708.

– 1972. 'Shakespeare without Words.' In his *Shakespeare without Words and Other Essays*, 3–23. Cambridge, Mass.: Harvard University Press.

Hardy, Barbara. 1969–70. 'Dickens and the Passions.' *Nineteenth-Century Fiction* 24: 449–66.

– 1985. *Forms of Feeling in Victorian Fiction*. London: Owen.

Hart Nibbrig, Christiaan L. 1985. *Die Auferstehung des Körpers im Text*. Frankfurt am Main: Suhrkamp.

Hartmann, Georg. 1923. 'Die Gesten bei Shakespeare als Ausdruck von Gemütsbewegungen (Ein Beitrag zur Geschichte der Schauspieltechnik im Elisabethanischen Zeitalter).' Diss., Leipzig.

– 1924. 'Die Bühnengesten in Shakespeares Dramen als Ausdruck von Gemütsbewegungen: Ein Beitrag zur Geschichte der Schauspieltechnik im Elisabethanischen Zeitalter.' *Jahrbuch der Deutschen Shakespeare-Gesellschaft*, N.F. 1: 41–61.

Hasler, Jörg. 1975. 'Gestische Leitmotive in Shakespeare's *Henry VI*.' *Deutsche Shakespeare-Gesellschaft West, Jahrbuch 1975*, 163–73.

– 1978. '*Richard II*: Gestische Ironie und das Problem Bolingbroke.' In Habicht and Schabert, eds, 1978, *Sympathielenkung in den Dramen Shakespeares*, 142–53.

Hausmann, Frank-Rutger. 1990. 'Soupirs, larmes et pâleur: Aspects non verbaux de la "langue de l'amour" dans la littérature française des XVIe et XVIIe siècles.' *Offerts en hommage à Noémie Hepp*, 407–16. Traveaux de Littérature, 3. Paris: Adirel.

Hayman, David. 1974. 'Language of/as Gesture in Joyce.' In Louis Bonnerot et al. eds, *'Ulysses' Cinquante Ans Après: Témoignages Franco-Anglais sur le Chef-d'Oeuvre de James Joyce*, 209–21. Paris: Didier.

Heine, Thomas. 1983. 'The Force of Gestures: A New Approach to the Problem of Communication in Hofmansthal's *Der Schwierige*.' *German Quarterly* 56: 408–18.

Helbo, André. 1985. 'El personaje Corneliano: El cuerpo, la voz, el gesto.' In Luciana García Lorenzo, ed., *El personaje dramático*, 135–47. Madrid: Taurus.

Hellermann, Fritz. 1912. 'Mienenspiel und Gebärdensprache in Conrad Ferdinand Meyers Novellen: Die Ausdrucksbewegungen mit besonderer Berücksichtigung des Auges.' Diss., Giessen.

Hermann, John P. 1985. 'Gesture and Seduction in *Troilus and Criseyde*.' *Studies in the Age of Chaucer* 7: 107–35.

Hermann, Max. 1914. *Forschungen zur deutschen Theatergeschichte des Mittelalters und der Renaissance*. Berlin: Weidmann.

Hesla, David H. 1971. *The Shape of Chaos: An Interpretation of the Art of Samuel Beckett*. Minneapolis: University of Minnesota Press.

Hess-Lüttich, Ernest W.B. 1979a. 'Drama, Silence and Semiotics.' *Kodikas/Code* 1: 105–20.

– 1979b. *See* bibliography 3.

Hess-Lüttich, Ernest W.B., ed. 1982. *Multimedial Communication. Vol. II: Theatre Semiotics*. Kodikas/Code, Supplement 8. Tübingen: Narr.

– 1987. *Text Transfers: Probleme intermedialer Übersetzung*. Münster: Nodus.

Hess-Lüttich, Ernest W.B., and Roland Posner, eds. 1990. *Code-Wechsel: Texte im Medienvergleich*. Opladen: Westdeutscher Verlag.

Hewitt, Elizabeth Kennedy. 1984. 'More Effective than Words: The Role of Non-Verbal Communication in *Billy Budd*.' In Borbé, ed. *Semiotics Unfolding*, 519–26. *See* bibliography 3.

Hill Rigney, Barbara. 1987. *Margaret Atwood*. Women Writers. London: Macmillan.

Hillway, Tyrus. 1949. 'Melville's Use of Two Pseudo-Sciences.' *Modern Language Notes* 64: 145–50.

Hoffmann, Gerhard. 1978. *Raum, Situation, erzählte Wirklichkeit: Poetologische und historische Studien zum englischen und amerikanischen Roman*. Stuttgart: Metzler.

Hogarth, William. 1955 [1753]. *The Analysis of Beauty*. Edited by Joseph Burke. Oxford: Clarendon Press.

Holub, James P. 1992. 'Nonverbal Communication in the Classics: Research Opportunities.' In Poyatos, ed., *Advances in Nonverbal Communication*, 237–54.

Homan, Sydney, ed. 1980. *Shakespeare's 'More than Words Can Witness': Essays on Visual and Nonverbal Enactment in the Plays*. London: Associated University Presses.

Home, Henry, Lord Kames. 1967 [1762]. *The Elements of Criticism*. 3 vols. New York and London: Johnson Reprint Co.

Hoppe, Ruth. 1937. *Die romanische Geste im Rolandslied*. Schriften der Albertus-Universität, Geisteswissenschaftliche Reihe, 10. Königsberg and Berlin: Ost-Europa-Verlag.

Hornback, Bert G. 1978. 'Dickens's Language of Gesture: Creating Character.' *Dickens Studies Newsletter* 9, no. 4: 100–6.

Hösle, Johannes. 1981. '"Lo duca mio allor mi diè di piglio": Zur nichtverbalen Kommunikation in der *Divina Commedia*.' In Hans Gerd Rötzer and Herbert Walz, eds, *Europäische Lehrdichtung: Festschrift für Walter Naumann*, 74–85. Darmstadt: Wissenschaftliche Buchgesellschaft.

Hungerford, Edward. 1930–1a. 'Poe and Phrenology.' *American Literature* 2: 209–31.

– 1930–1b. 'Walt Whitman and His Chart of Bumps.' *American Literature* 2: 350–84.

Hunt, John Dixon. 1976. *The Figure in the Landscape: Poetry, Painting, and Gardening during the Eighteenth Century*. Baltimore, Md, and London: Johns Hopkins University Press.

Hunt, John Dixon, ed. 1971. *Encounters: Essays on Literature and the Visual Arts*. London: Studio Vista.

Idol, John L. 1991. '"A Linked Circle of Three" Plus One: Nonverbal Communication in *The Marble Faun*.' *Studies in the Novel* 23: 139–51.

Ingarden, Roman. 1965 [1931]. *Das literarische Kunstwerk: Mit einem Anhang von den Funktionen der Sprache im Theaterschauspiel*. 3rd ed. Tübingen: Niemeyer. [English translation: *The Literary Work of Art: An Investigation on the Borderline of Ontology, Logic, and Theory of Literature*. Evanston, Ill: Northwestern University Press]

Ionescu-Muresanu, Marina. 1981. 'Pour une lecture pragmatique de la narration.' *Degrés* 9: k1–k5.

Irwin, Michael. 1979. *Picturing: Description and Illusion in the Nineteenth-Century Novel.* London: Allen and Unwin.

Jackson, Arlene M. 1981. *Illustration and the Novels of Thomas Hardy.* Totowa, N.J.: Rowman and Littlefield.

– 1984. 'Photography as Style and Metaphor in the Art of Thomas Hardy.' In Norman Page, ed., *Thomas Hardy Annual No. 2,* 91–109. London: Macmillan.

Jackson, G. Donald. 1984. 'Gestes, déplacements et texte dans trois pièces de Molière.' *Papers on French Seventeenth-Century Literature* 11, no. 20: 37–59.

Jakobson, Roman. 1960. 'Closing Statement: Linguistics and Poetics.' In Thomas A. Sebeok, ed., *Style in Language,* 350–77. Cambridge, Mass.: MIT Press.

James, Henry. 1957 [1884]. 'The Art of Fiction.' In his *The House of Fiction,* 23–45. London: Hart-Davis.

Janković, Milan. 1972. 'Perspectives of Semantic Gesture.' *Poetics* 4: 16–27.

Johnson, Gregory Allen. 1981. '"Creatures and More": Codes of Nonverbal Dialogue in the Canon of Bellow.' Ph.D. diss., University of Washington.

Jones, George Fenwick. 1966. 'The Kiss in Middle High German Literature.' *Studia Neophilologica* 38: 195–210.

Jordan, Leo. 1931. 'Zur französischen Geste: Vom Roland bis heute.' *Zeitschrift für romanische Philologie* 51: 119–24.

Jorio, Andrea de. 1832. *La mimica degli Antichi investigata nel gestire napoletano.* Naples: Fibreno.

Joseph, Bertram L. 1964. *Elizabethan Acting.* 2nd ed. London: Oxford University Press.

Josephs, Herbert. 1969. *Diderot's Dialogue of Language and Gesture: 'Le Neveu de Rameau.'* Columbus: Ohio State University Press.

Josipovici, Gabriel. 1982. *Writing and the Body.* Brighton: Harvester Press.

Jucker-Scherrer, Ines. 1956. 'Der Gestus des Aposkopein: Ein Beitrag zur Gebärdensprache in der antiken Kunst.' Diss., Zurich.

Kahrmann, Cordula, et al. 1977. *Erzähltextanalyse: Eine Einführung in Grundlagen und Verfahren,* I. Kronberg: Athenäum.

Kalverkämper, Hartwig. 1991. 'Literatur und Körpersprache.' *Poetica* 23: 328–73.

Kane, Leslie. 1984. *The Language of Silence: On the Unspoken and the Unspeakable in Modern Drama.* Rutherford: Fairleigh Dickinson University Press; London and Toronto: Associated University Presses.

Kapp, Volker. 1991. 'Langage verbal et langage non-verbal dans le Bourgeois gentilhomme.' In Volker Kapp, ed., *Le Bourgeois gentilhomme: Problèmes de la comédie-ballet,* 95–113. Paris: Papers of French Seventeenth-Century Literature.

Kemp, Wolfgang. 1975. 'Die Beredsamkeit des Leibes: Körpersprache als künstlerisches und gesellschaftliches Problem der bürgerlichen Emanzipation.' *Städel-Jahrbuch* NF 5: 111–34.

Kennedy, Andrew K. 1975. *Six Dramatists in Search of a Language: Studies in Dramatic Language.* Cambridge: Cambridge University Press.

Kenner, Hedwig. 1960. *Weinen und Lachen in der griechischen Kunst.* Österreichische Akademie der Wissenschaften, Philosophisch-Historische Klasse, Sitzungsberichte, 234, 2. Abhandlung. Vienna: Rohrer.

Kenner, Hugh. 1962. *Samuel Beckett: A Critical Study.* London: Calder.

Ketcham, Michael G. 1981. 'The Arts of Gesture: *The Spectator* and Its Relationship to Physiognomy, Painting and the Theater.' *Modern Language Quarterly* 42: 137–52.

Kindermann, Wolf. 1989. 'Visual Motion in Faulkner's Visual Art.' In *Faulkner's Discourse: An International Symposium,* 46–52. Tübingen: Niemeyer.

Kinkead-Weekes, Mark. 1973. *Samuel Richardson: Dramatic Novelist.* Ithaca, N.Y.: Cornell University Press.

Kirstein, Boni. 1990. '*Quest for Fire* and Some Functions of Paleofiction.' In W.A. Koch, ed., *Geneses of Language,* 413–16.

– 1991. 'Paleofiction and Language Origins.' In Walburga von Raffler-Engel, et al., eds, *Studies in Language Origins II,* 311–29. Amsterdam and Philadelphia: Benjamins.

Kleinspehn, Thomas. 1989. *Der flüchtige Blick: Sehen und Identität in der Kultur der Neuzeit.* Reinbek: Rowohlt.

Klineberg, Otto. 1938. 'Emotional Expression in Chinese Literature.' *Journal of Abnormal and Social Psychology* 33: 517–20.

Koch, Peter L.W. 1990. 'Some Remarks on the Film *La Guerre du feu.*' In Walter A. Koch, ed., *Geneses of Language,* 374–85.

Koch, Walter A., ed. 1990. *Geneses of Language / Genesen der Sprache.* Bochum Publications in Evolutionary Cultural Semiotics. Bochum: Brockmeyer.

Koelb, Clayton. 1984. 'The Language of Presence in Varley's "The Persistence of Vision."' *Science-Fiction Studies* 11: 154–65.

Konigsberg, Ira. 1968. *Samuel Richardson and the Dramatic Novel.* Lexington, Ky: University of Kentucky Press.

'Körper und Körpersprache bei Shakespeare.' 1989. *Deutsche Shakespeare-Gesellschaft West, Jahrbuch 1989,* 174–265.

Korte, Barbara. 1993. *Körpersprache in der Literatur: Theorie und Geschichte am Beispiel des englischsprachigen Romans.* Tübingen: Francke.

– 1996. 'Silent Eloquence: Notes on the Evolution of Body Language in the English Sentimental Novel.' In Gudrun M. Grabher and Ulrike Jessner, eds, *Semantics of Silences in Linguistics and Literature,* 113–26. Heidelberg: Winter.

– 1996. 'Berührung durch Text: Zur Semiotik der Berührung in der Literatur.' In Kunst- und Ausstellungshalle der Bundesrepublik Deutschland, ed., *Tasten,* 125–42. Schriftenreihe Forum, 7. Göttingen: Steidl Verlag.

Körver, Carl. 1911. *Stendhal und der Ausdruck der Gemütsbewegungen in seinen Werken.* Beihefte der Zeitschrift für Romanische Philologie, 35. Halle: Niemeyer.

Kostelanetz, Richard. 1968. *The Theater of Mixed Means: An Introduction to Happenings, Kinetic Environments, and Other Mixed-Means Performances.* New York: Dial Press.

Kostowa, Wera. 1916. 'Die Bewegungen und Haltungen des menschlichen Körpers in Conrad Ferdinand Meyers Erzählungen: Eine psychologisch-statistische Untersuchung.' *Zeitschrift für angewandte Psychologie* 11: 29–89.

Kracauer, Siegfried. 1965 [1960]. *Theory of Film: The Redemption of Physical Reality.* New York: Oxford University Press.

Kraemer, Christiane K. 1984. 'Die Gebärden in der mittelhochdeutschen Heldenepik.' Ph.D. diss., Ohio State University.

Kremer, Karl Richard. 1961. 'Das Lachen in der deutschen Sprache und Literatur des Mittelalters.' Diss., Bonn.

Kriss-Rettenbeck, Lenz. 1965. 'Probleme der volkskundlichen Gebärdenforschung.' *Bayerisches Jahrbuch für Volkskunde 1964–65,* 14–46. Volkach vor Würzburg: Hart.

Krysinski, Wladimir. 1981. 'Semiotic Modalities of the Body in Modern Theater.' *Poetics Today,* 2: 141–61.

Kuepper, Karl J. 1970. 'Gesture and Posture as Elemental Symbolism in Kafka's *The Trial.*' *Mosaic* 3, no. 4: 143–52.

Kultermann, Erika. 1957. 'Die Bedeutung der Pantomime in den Dramen Heinrich von Kleists.' *Maske und Kothurn* 3: 70–81.

Lateiner, Donald. 1992. 'Affect Displays in the Epic Poetry of Homer, Vergil, and Ovid.' In Poyatos, ed., *Advances in Nonverbal Communication,* 255–69.

Le Brun, Charles. 1982 [1668]. *Méthode pour apprendre à dessiner les passions proposée dans une conférence sur l'expression générale et particulière.* Reprint of the 1702 edition. Hildesheim, Zürich, and New York: Olms.

Lee, Virgil Jackson. 1969. 'The Face in Shakespeare: A Study of Facial Gesture and Attitude as Aspects of Dramatic *Energeia.*' *Dissertation Abstracts,* 30: 4416–A.

Leech, Geoffrey N. 1985. 'Stylistics.' In Teun A. van Dijk, ed., *Discourse and Literature,* 39–57. Critical Theory. Amsterdam: Benjamins.

Leech, Geoffrey N., and Michael H. Short. 1981. *Style in Fiction: A Linguistic Introduction to English Fictional Prose.* London and New York: Longman.

Leimberg, Inge. 1987. '"Give Me Thy Hand": Some Notes on the Phrase in Shakespeare's Comedies and Tragedies.' In Bernhard Fabian and Kurt Tetzeli von Rosador, eds, *Shakespeare: Text, Language, Criticism: Essays in Honour of Marvin Spevack,* 118–46. Hildesheim: Olms-Weidmann.

Lessing, Gotthold Ephraim. 1964 [1766]. *Laokoon oder Über die Grenzen der Malerei und Poesie*. Stuttgart: Reclam. [English translation: *Laocöon, Nathan the Wise, and Minna von Barnhelm*. London: Dent; New York: Dutton 1930]

Levitine, George. 1954. 'The Influence of Lavater and Girodet's *Expression des Sentiments de l'Ame*.' *Art Bulletin* 36: 33–44.

Lex, Michael. 1901. '"Körperliche Beredsamkeit" in den Dramen der (deutschen) Klassizisten.' Diss., Munich.

Lichtenberg, Georg Christoph. 1938. *Lichtenberg's Visits to England*. Edited by Margaret L. Mare and W.H. Quarrell. Oxford: Clarendon Press. [Translation of *Briefe aus England*, 1776–8]

Link, Hannelore. 1980. *Rezeptionsforschung: Eine Einführung in Methoden und Probleme*. 2nd ed. Stuttgart: Kohlhammer.

Lodge, David. 1977. 'Thomas Hardy as a Cinematic Novelist.' In Lance St John Butler, ed., *Thomas Hardy after Fifty Years*, 78–89. London: Macmillan.

Loeschke, Walter. 1965. 'Der Griff ans Handgelenk: Skizze einer motivgeschichtlichen Untersuchung.' In Ursula Schlegel and Claus Zoege von Manteufel, eds, *Festschrift für Peter Metz*, 46–73. Berlin: de Gruyter.

Loftis, John, et al. 1976. *The Revels History of Drama in English. Vol. V: 1660–1750*. London: Methuen.

Lohr, Günther. 1987. *Körpertext: Historische Semiotik und komische Praxis*. Opladen: Westdeutscher Verlag.

Lokensgard, Hjalmar O. 1940. 'Oliver Wendell Holmes's "Phrenological Character."' *New England Quarterly* 13: 711–18.

Lommatzsch, Erhard. 1910. 'System der Gebärden: Dargestellt auf Grund der mittelalterlichen Literatur Frankreichs.' Diss., Berlin.

– 1924. 'Darstellung von Trauer und Schmerz in der altfranzösischen Literatur.' *Zeitschrift für romanische Philologie* 43: 20–67.

Lörges, Karl Robert. 1929. *Mimische Studien zu Franz Grillparzers Dramen mit besonderer Berücksichtigung der Beziehungen zwischen Wort und Gebärde*. Die Schaubühne, 3. Bonn: Klopp.

Lotman, Jurij M. 1972 [1970]. *Die Struktur literarischer Texte*. Munich: Fink. [Translation of *Struktura khudozhestvennogo teksta*, 1970]

Love, Glen A. 1968. '*Winesburg, Ohio* and the Rhetoric of Silence.' *American Literature* 40: 38–57.

McAleer, Janice K. 1982. '*El campo*, de Griselda Gambaro: Una contradicción de mensajes.' *Revista Canadiense de Estudios Hispánicos* 7, no. 1: 159–71.

McKenzie, Alan T. 1990. *Certain, Lively Episodes: The Articulation of Passion in Eighteenth-Century Prose*. Athens, Ga, and London: University of Georgia Press.

McLay, Catherine. 1975. 'The Divided Self: Theme and Pattern in Margaret Atwood's *Surfacing*.' *Journal of Canadian Fiction* 4, no. 1: 82–95.

Madland, Helga Stipa. 1984. 'Gesture as Evidence of Language Skepticism in Lenz's *Der Hofmeister* and *Die Soldaten*.' *German Quarterly* 57: 546–57.

Magli, Patrizia. 1979. 'The System of the Passions in Eighteenth Century Dramatic Mime.' *Versus* 22: 32–47.

Mahr, August. 1911. *Formen und Formeln der Begrüssung in England von der normannischen Eroberung bis zur Mitte des 15. Jahrhunderts.* Frankfurt am Main: Knauer.

Maresca, Carol J. 1966. 'Gestures as Meaning in Sherwood Anderson's *Winesburg, Ohio*.' *College Language Association Journal* 9: 279–83.

Margolin, Uri. 1986. 'The Doer and the Deed: Action as a Basis for Characterization in Narrative.' *Poetics Today* 7: 205–25.

Marks, Sita Patricia. 1974. 'A Silent Morality: Nonverbal Expression in *The Ambassadors*.' *South Atlantic Bulletin* 39: 102–6.

Masé, Armin. 1953. *Die Darstellung des Affekts der Furcht im englischen Roman zu Anfang des 19. Jahrhunderts.* Zurich: Juris.

Matt, Peter von. 1983. *... fertig ist das Angesicht: Zur Literaturgeschichte des menschlichen Gesichts.* Munich and Vienna: Hanser.

Mattenklott, Gert. 1982. *Der übersinnliche Leib: Beiträge zur Metaphysik des Körpers.* Reinbek bei Hamburg: Rowohlt.

Mauser, Wolfram. 1961. *Bild und Gebärde in der Sprache Hofmannsthals.* Österreichische Akademie der Wissenschaften, Philosophisch-Historische Klasse, Sitzungsberichte, 238, 1. Abhandlung. Vienna: Böhlau.

Meidow, Erika. 1945. 'Das Motiv, den Kopf in die Hand zu stützen.' Diss., Greifswald.

Meisel, Martin. 1983. *Realizations: Narrative, Pictorial, and Theatrical Arts in Nineteenth-Century England.* Princeton: Princeton University Press.

Ménard, Philippe. 1969. *Le rire et le sourire dans le roman courtois en France au Moyen Age (1150–1250).* Publications Romances et Françaises, 105. Geneva: Droz.

– 1984. 'Les gestes et les expressions corporelles dans la *Chanson de Roland*: Les attitudes de commandement et de défi.' In Wolfgang van Emden et al., eds, *Guillaume d'Orange and the Chanson de Geste*, 85–92. Reading: Soc. Rencesvals.

Michie, Helena. 1987. *The Flesh Made Word: Female Figures and Women's Bodies.* New York and Oxford: Oxford University Press.

Miller, Jonathan. 1972. 'Plays and Players.' In Hinde, ed., *Non-Verbal Communication*, 359–72. *See* bibliography 3.

Mish, Charles C. 1970. 'Introduction.' In Charles C. Mish, ed., *Restoration Prose Fiction 1660–1700: An Anthology of Representative Pieces*, vii–xiv. Lincoln: University of Nebraska Press.

Möller, Karl Dietmar. 1985. 'Zum Verhältnis von Interaktion, nonverbaler Kommunikation und Dialog im Spielfilm.' In Bentele and Hess-Lüttich, eds, *Zeichengebrauch in Massenmedien*, 303–15. *See* bibliography 3.

Monti, Claudia, et al., eds. 1996. *Körpersprache und Sprachkörper / La parola del corpo – il corpo della parola: Semiotische Interferenzen in der deutschen Literatur / Tensioni semiotiche nella literatura tedesca*. Essay und Poesie, 3. Innsbruck: Studien Verlag.

Mowat, Barbara. 1970. 'The Beckoning Ghost: Stage-Gesture in Shakespeare.' *Renaissance Papers*; 41–54.

Mulvey, Laura. 1975. 'Visual Pleasure and Narrative Cinema.' *Screen* 16, no. 3: 6–18.

Murch, Anne C. 1983. 'Considérations sur la proxémique dans le théâtre de Samuel Beckett.' *Australian Journal of French Studies* 20: 307–39.

Murphy, Robert P. 1972. 'Non-Verbal Communication and the Overlooked Action in Pinter's *The Caretaker*.' *Quarterly Journal of Speech* 58: 41–7.

Mylne, Vivienne. 1965. *The Eighteenth-Century French Novel: Techniques of Illusion*. Manchester: Manchester University Press.

Nehring, Wolfgang. 1970. 'Die Gebärdensprache E.T.A. Hoffmanns.' *Zeitschrift für deutsche Philologie* 89: 207–21.

Neumann, Gerhard. 1965. *Gesten und Gebärden in der griechischen Kunst*. Berlin: de Gruyter.

Newbold, Ronald. 1992. 'Nonverbal Expressiveness in Late Greek Epic: Quintus of Smyrna, and Nonnus.' In Poyatos, ed., *Advances in Nonverbal Communication*, 271–83.

Ngenge, Tayoba Tata. 1987. 'Gesture in Modern African Narrative.' Ph.D. diss., University of Texas at Austin.

Nischik, Reingard M. 1991. 'Körpersprache im Drama: Ein Beitrag zur Semiotik des Dramas.' *Germanisch-Romanische Monatsschrift* NF, 41: 257–69.

Nischik, Reingard M., and Barbara Korte, eds. 1990. *Modes of Narrative: Approaches to American, Canadian and British Fiction*. Würzburg: Königshausen und Neumann.

Nissen, Theodor. 1924. 'Die Physiologie und Psychologie der Furcht in der Ilias.' *Archiv für die gesamte Psychologie* 46: 70–97.

– 1925. 'Die Physiologie und Psychologie der Furcht in der Odyssee.' *Archiv für die gesamte Psychologie* 52: 177–94.

Nuessel, Frank. 1985. 'Teaching Kinesics through Literature.' *Canadian Modern Language Review* 41, no. 6: 1014–19.

Och, Gunnar. 1985. *Der Körper als Zeichen: Zur Bedeutung des mimisch-gestischen und physiognomischen Ausdrucks im Werk Jean Pauls*. Erlanger Studien, 62. Erlangen: Palm und Enke.

Oldfield, Derek. 1967. 'The Language of the Novel: The Character of Dorothea.'

In Barbara Hardy, ed., *Middlemarch: Critical Approaches to the Novel*, 63–86. London: Athlone Press.

Onuska, John T., Jr. 1981. 'Bringing Shakespeare's Characters down to Earth: The Significance of Kneeling.' *Iowa State Journal of Research* 56, no. 1: 31–41.

Osterburg, Karl Hermann. 1922. 'Das stumme Spiel in Schillers Jugenddramen.' Diss., Munich.

Øyslebø, Olaf. 1987. 'Nonverbal Presentation of Narrative Characters: Two Aspects of the Visualizing Art of Jonas Lie in *The Family at Gilje*.' *Livstegn* 1: 181–92.

Paden, Frances Freeman. 1982–3. 'Autistic Gestures in *The Heart Is a Lonely Hunter*.' *Modern Fiction Studies* 28: 453–63.

Page, Norman. 1988. *Speech in the English Novel*. 2nd ed. Houndmills: Macmillan.

Pavis, Patrice. 1981. 'Problems of a Semiology of Theatrical Gesture.' *Poetics Today* 2: 65–93.

– 1982. *Languages of the Stage: Essays in the Semiology of Theatre*. New York: Performing Arts Journal Publications.

Peil, Dietmar. 1975. *Die Gebärde bei Chrétien, Hartmann und Wolfram: Erec – Iwein – Parzival*. Medium Aevum, Philologische Studien, 28. Munich: Fink.

Pelzer, Linda Claycomb. 1984. 'Henry James and the Rhetoric of Gesture.' Ph.D. diss., University of Notre Dame.

Petsch, Robert. 1930. 'Die dramatische Gebärde.' *Das Nationaltheater* 3: 41–6.

Pickrel, Paul. 1986. '*Jane Eyre*: The Apocalypse of the Body.' *ELH* 53: 165–82.

Pongs, Hermann. 1965. 'Die Gebärde als Sinnbildausdruck.' In his *Das Bild in der Dichtung*, 25–42. Marburg: Elwert.

Porena, Manfredi. 1902. *Delle manifestazioni plastiche del sentimento nei personaggi della Divina Commedia*. Milan: Hoepli.

Portch, Stephen R. 1985. *Literature's Silent Language: Nonverbal Communication*. American Universities Studies, Series IV: English Language and Literature, 19. New York: Lang. [Ph.D. diss., Pennsylvania State University 1982]

Powell, Jocelyn. 1987. 'Making Faces: Character and Physiognomy in *L'Ecole des Femmes* and *L'Avare*.' *Seventeenth-Century French Studies* 9: 94–112.

Poyatos, Fernando. 1981. 'Literary Anthropology: A New Interdisciplinary Perspective of Man through His Narrative Literature.' *Versus: Quaderni di studi semiotici* 28 (Gennaio/Aprile): 3–28.

– 1983. *See* bibliography 3.

– 1988. 'Introduction.' In Poyatos, ed., *Literary Anthropology*, xi–xxiii.

– 1992. 'Paralanguage and Quasiparalinguistic Sounds as a Concern of Literary Analysis.' In Poyatos, ed., *Advances in Nonverbal Communication*, 301–19.

Poyatos, Fernando, ed. 1988a. *Literary Anthropology: A New Interdisciplinary Approach to People, Signs and Literature*. Amsterdam: Benjamins.

– 1988b. *See* bibliography 3.
– 1992. *Advances in Nonverbal Communication: Sociocultural, Clinical, Esthetic and Literary Perspectives*. Amsterdam: Benjamins.
Praz, Mario. 1970. *Mnemosyne: The Parallel between Literature and the Visual Arts*. Bollingen Series, 35, 16. Princeton and London: Princeton University Press.
Preston, Thomas R. 1974. 'The "Stage Passions" and Smollett's Characterization.' *Studies in Philology* 71: 105–25.
Promies, Wolfgang. 1957. 'Mimik und Gebärde in Lope de Vegas "El Caballero del Milagro."' *Maske und Kothurn* 3: 116–27.
Proust, Jacques. 1961. 'Diderot et la Physiognomie.' *Cahiers de l'Association Internationale des Etudes Françaises* 13: 317–29.
Purdy, Anthony. 1985. 'Echanges non verbaux et communication paralinguistique dans les romans de Stendhal.' In V. Del Litto, ed., *La création romanesque chez Stendhal: Actes du XVIe Congrès International Stendhalien*, 267–87. Geneva: Droz.
Rabkin, Leslie Y., ed. 1966. *Psychopathology and Literature*. San Francisco: Chandler.
Radmehr, Ingeborg. 1980. *Typik der Gefühlsdarstellung in der frühneuhochdeutschen Erzählprosa*. GRATIA, Bamberger Schriften zur Renaissanceforschung, 8. Göttingen: Gratia-Verlag.
Raim, Anne Marmot. 1986. *La communication non-verbale chez Maupassant*. Paris: Nizet. [Ph.D. diss., University of California at Los Angeles, 1983]
Ramon Resina, Joan. 1988. 'Gesture: Kafka's Means to Silence.' *International Fiction Review* 15: 14–20.
Rauh, Reinhold. 1984. 'Worte und Blicke im Film.' *Sprache im technischen Zeitalter* 89: 30–53.
Rautenfeld, George von. 1981. 'Nonverbal Communication in the *Nibelungenlied* Compared with That in the *Chanson de Roland* and the *Poema Di Mio Cid*.' *Dissertation Abstracts International*, 42: 722A. [Ph.D. diss., University of Maryland, 1980]
Reinach, Salomon. 1924. 'L'Histoire des gestes.' *Revue archéologique* 5th series, 20: 64–79.
Rhodes, Neil. 1980. *Elizabethan Grotesque*. London: Routledge and Kegan Paul.
Richards, I.A. 1964 [1929]. *Practical Criticism: A Study of Literary Judgment*. London: Routledge and Kegan Paul.
Riehle, Wolfgang. 1978. '*Coriolanus*: Die Gebärde als sympathielenkendes Element.' In Habicht and Schabert, eds, *Sympathielenkung in den Dramen Shakespeares*, 132–41.
Riemschneider-Hoerner, Margarete. 1939. *Der Wandel der Gebärde in der Kunst*. Frankfurt am Main: Klostermann.

Rimmon-Kenan, Shlomith. 1983. *Narrative Fiction: Contemporary Poetics*. New Accents. London and New York: Routledge.

Roberts, Ruth E. 1982. 'Nonverbal Communication in *The Great Gatsby*.' *Language and Literature* 7: 107–29.

Robinson, Peter Holbrook. 1970. 'Convention and Originality in the Description of the Eye and the Glance in the French Realist Novel, 1800–1860.' Diss., University of Pennsylvania.

Roeder, Anke. 1974. *Die Gebärde im Drama des Mittelalters: Osterfeiern – Osterspiele*. Münchener Texte und Untersuchungen zur deutschen Literatur des Mittelalters, 49. Munich: Beck.

Rogers, Nancy E. 1980. 'The Use of Eye Language in Stendhal's *Le Rouge et le Noir*.' *Romance Notes* 20: 339–43.

Rogerson, Brewster. 1953. 'The Art of Painting the Passions.' *Journal of the History of Ideas* 14: 68–94.

Röhrich, Lutz. 1967. 'Gebärdensprache und Sprachgebärde.' In *Gebärde – Metapher – Parodie: Studien zur Sprache und Volksdichtung*, 7–36. Wirkendes Wort, Schriftenreihe, 4. Düsseldorf: Schwann. [First published in Wayland D. Hand and Gustav O. Arlt, eds, *Humaniora: Essays in Literature, Folklore and Bibliography*, 121–49. Locust Valley, N.Y.: Augustin 1960]

Roos, Renate. 1975. 'Begrüssung, Abschied, Mahlzeit: Studien zur Darstellung höfischer Lebensweise in Werken der Zeit von 1150–1320.' Diss., Bonn.

Rothschild, Judith Rice. 1985. 'Manipulative Gestures and Behaviors in the *Lais* of Marie de France.' In Glyn S. Burgess and Robert A. Taylor et al., eds, *The Spirit of the Court: Selected Proceedings of the Fourth Congress of the International Courtly Literature Society (Toronto 1983)*, 283–8. Dover, N.H.: Brewer.

Ruppert, Hans. 1941. 'Die Darstellung der Leidenschaften und Affekte im Drama des Sturmes und Dranges.' Diss., Bonn.

Rychner, Jean. 1990. *La narration des sentiments, des pensées et des discours dans quelques oeuvres des XIIe et XIIIe siècles*. Publications Romanes et Françaises, 192. Geneva: Droz.

Salzman, Paul. 1985. *English Prose Fiction 1558–1700: A Critical History*. Oxford: Clarendon Press.

Sándor, István. 1967. 'Dramaturgy of Tale-Telling.' *Acta Ethnographica* 16: 305–38.

Santucci, Lino Falzon. 1981. *Harold Pinter: Explorations in Verbal and Nonverbal Interaction*. Messina: Peloritana Editrice.

Saxl, F. 1979 [1932]. 'Die Ausdrucksgebärden der bildenden Kunst.' In Dieter Wuttke, ed., *Aby M. Warburg, Ausgewählte Schriften und Würdigungen*, 419–31. Saecula Spiritalia, 1. Baden-Baden: Koerner.

Scarry, Elaine, ed. 1988. *Literature and the Body: Essays on Populations and Persons.* Selected Papers from the English Institute, N.S. 12. Baltimore, Md, and London: Johns Hopkins University Press.

Schäfer, Martin. 1960. 'Die Kunst der aussersprachlichen, sogenannten "mimischen" Mittel im Spätwerk Hofmannsthals.' Diss., Saarbrücken.

Schechner, Richard, and Cynthia Mintz. 1973. 'Kinesics and Performance.' *The Drama Review* 17, no. 3: 102–8.

Scheel, Hans Ludwig. 1923. 'Der mimische Gehalt im Drama Lessings und seiner Zeitgenossen.' Diss., Munich.

Scheick, William J. 1977. '"An Intercourse Not Well Designed": Talk and Touch in the Plays of Tennessee Williams.' In Jac Tharpe, ed., *Tennessee Williams: A Tribute*, 763–73. Jackson: University Press of Mississippi.

Scherer, Wilhelm. 1908. 'Der Ausdruck des Schmerzes und der Freude in mittelhochdeutschen Dichtungen der Blütezeit.' Diss., Strassburg.

Schmid, Eduard E. 1960. 'Über die Gebärde in Ballade, Novelle und Drama.' *Wirkendes Wort* 10: 238–49.

Schmidt, Johann N. 1986. *Ästhetik des Melodramas: Studien zu einem Genre des populären Theaters im England des 19. Jahrhunderts.* Heidelberg: Winter.

Schmidt, Leopold. 1953. 'Die volkstümlichen Grundlagen der Gebärdensprache.' In Ingeborg Weber-Kellermann and Wolfgang Steinitz, eds, *Beiträge zur sprachlichen Volksüberlieferung: Festschrift für Adolf Spamer*, 233–49. Berlin: Akad. Verlag.

Scholes, Robert. 1982. *Semiotics and Interpretation.* New Haven and London: Yale University Press.

Scholes, Robert, and Robert Kellogg. 1966. *The Nature of Narrative.* New York: Oxford University Press.

Schrero, Elliot M. 1974. 'Intonation in Nineteenth-Century Fiction: The Voices of Paraphrase.' *Quarterly Journal of Speech* 60: 289–95.

Schulz, Otto. 1903. 'Die Darstellung psychologischer Vorgänge in den Romanen des Kristian von Troyes.' Diss., Breslau.

Schwalbe, Jürgen. 1970. 'Sprache und Gebärde im Werk Hugo von Hofmannsthals.' Diss., Freiburg.

Scott, David. 1988. *Pictorialist Poetics: Poetry and the Visual Arts in Nineteenth-Century France.* Cambridge: Cambridge University Press.

Scott, James F. 1975. *Film: The Medium and the Maker.* New York: Holt, Rinehart and Winston.

Seigel, Jules Paul. 1969. 'The Enlightenment and the Evolution of a Language of Signs in France and England.' *Journal of the History of Ideas* 30: 96–115.

Sena, John F. 1983. 'The Language of Gestures in *Gulliver's Travels*.' *Papers on Language and Literature* 19: 145–66.

Shorley, Christopher. 1981. '"Joindre le geste à la parole": Raymond Queneau and the Uses of Non-Verbal Communication.' *French Studies* 35: 408–20.

Silverman, Kaja. 1984. 'History, Figuration and Female Subjectivity in *Tess of the d'Urbervilles*.' *Novel* 18, no. 1: 5–28.

Simmel, Georg. 1957 [1901]. 'Die ästhetische Bedeutung des Gesichts.' In M. Landmann and M. Susman, eds, *Brücke und Tor: Essays des Philosophen zur Geschichte, Religion, Kunst und Gesellschaft*, 153–9. Stuttgart: Koehler.

Sittl, Carl. 1890. *Die Gebärden der Griechen und Römer*. Leipzig: Teubner.

Skilton, David. 1988. 'The Relation between Illustration and Text in the Victorian Novel: A New Perspective.' In Karl Joseph Höltgen, Peter M. Daly, and Wolfgang Lottes, eds, *Word and Visual Imagination: Studies in the Interaction of English Literature and the Visual Arts*, 303–25. Erlangen: Universitätsbund Erlangen/Nürnberg.

Skrotzki, Ditmar. 1971. *Die Gebärde des Errötens im Werk Heinrich von Kleists*. Marburger Beiträge zur Germanistik, 37. Marburg: Elwert.

Skwarczyńska, Stefania. 1974. 'Anmerkungen zur Semantik der theatralischen Gestik.' In Walter Kroll and Aleksandar Flaker, eds, *Literaturtheoretische Modelle und kommunikatives System: Zur aktuellen Diskussion in der polnischen Literaturwissenschaft*, 328–70. Skripten Literaturwissenschaft, 4. Kronberg/Ts: Scriptor.

Smith, David E. 1976. *Gesture as a Stylistic Device in Kleist's 'Michael Kohlhaas' and Kafka's 'Der Prozess.'* Stanford German Studies, 11. Frankfurt am Main: Lang.

Sorin-Barreteau, Liliane. 1982. 'Gestes narratifs et langage gestuel chez les Mofu (Nord-Cameroun).' *Cahiers de Littérature Orale* 11: 37–93.

Soupel, Serge. 1978. 'Le corps, le coeur, et l'oeil: Esquisse d'une physiologie de l'affectivité dans quelques romans secondaires 1740–1771.' *Bulletin de la Société d'Etudes Anglo-Américaines des XVIIe et XVIIIe Siècles* 6: 77–95.

Spiegel, Alan. 1976. *Fiction and the Camera Eye: Visual Consciousness in Film and the Modern Novel*. Charlottesville: University Press of Virginia.

Stang, Richard. 1959. *The Theory of the Novel in England 1850–1870*. New York: Columbia University Press; London: Routledge and Kegan Paul.

Stanzel, Franz K. 1984. *A Theory of Narrative*. Cambridge: Cambridge University Press.

Starobinski, Jean. 1961. *L'oeil vivant: Essai (Corneille, Racine, Rousseau, Stendhal)*. Paris: Gallimard.

– 1989. 'The Natural and Literary History of Bodily Sensation.' In Feher et al., eds, 1989, *Fragments for a History of the Human Body*, 350–405. *See* bibliography 3.

Steppacher, Ulrike. 1996. *Körpersprache in Jean Pauls 'Unsichtbare Loge.'* Würzburg: Königshausen und Neumann.

Sternberg, Ellen W. 1985–6. 'Verbal and Visual Seduction in "The Defence of Guenevere."' *The Journal of Pre-Raphaelite Studies* 6, no. 2: 45–53.

Stewart, Philip. 1973. *Le Masque et La Parole: Le langage de l'amour au XVIIIe siècle*. Paris: Corti.

Sullivan, Francis A. 1968. '*Tendere Manus*: Gestures in the *Aeneid*.' *Classical Journal* 63: 358–62.

Sulzer, Johann Georg. 1792. 'Gebehrden.' In his *Allgemeine Theorie der Schönen Künste*, Part II: 314–18. 2nd ed. Leipzig: Weidmann.

Suntrup, Rudolf. 1978. *Die Bedeutung der liturgischen Gebärden und Bewegungen in lateinischen und deutschen Auslegungen des 9. bis 13. Jahrhunderts*. Münstersche Mittelalter-Schriften, 37. Munich: Fink.

Sypher, Wylie. 1960. *Rococo to Cubism in Art and Literature*. New York: Vintage.

Teubner, Bernhard. 1989. *Sprache – Körper – Traum: Zur karnevalesken Tradition in der romanischen Literatur aus früher Neuzeit*. Mimesis, 4. Tübingen: Niemeyer.

Teuchert, Brigitte. 1988. *Kommunikative Elemente und ihre literarische Vermittlung: Zur Bedeutung nonverbaler Kommunikation und der verba dicendi in den Prosawerken Bölls, Dürrenmatts und Hesses*. Regensburger Beiträge zur deutschen Sprach- und Literaturwissenschaft, 37. Frankfurt am Main: Lang. [Diss., Regensburg 1987]

Tikkanen, J.J. 1912. *Die Beinstellungen in der Kunstgeschichte: Ein Beitrag zur Geschichte der künstlerischen Motive*. Acta Societatis Scientiarum Fennicae, 42, no. 1. Helsingfors: Finnische Literaturgesellschaft.

– 1913. *Zwei Gebärden mit dem Zeigefinger*. Acta Societatis Scientiarum Fennicae, 43, no. 2. Helsinki: Finnische Literaturgesellschaft.

Todorov, Tzvetan. 1968. 'La grammaire du récit.' *Langages* 12: 94–102.

– 1975. 'La lecture comme construction.' *Poétique* 6: 417–25.

Torgovnick, Marianna. 1980. 'Gestural Pattern and Meaning in *The Golden Bowl*.' *Twentieth Century Literature* 26: 445–57.

– 1985. *The Visual Arts, Pictorialism, and the Novel: James, Lawrence, and Woolf*. Princeton: Princeton University Press.

Tytler, Graeme. 1982. *Physiognomy in the European Novel: Faces and Fortunes*. Princeton: Princeton University Press.

Urbahn, Therese. 1936. 'Die Geste in Sternes *Tristram Shandy*.' In *Arbeiten aus dem Seminar für englische Sprache und Kultur an der Hansischen Universität gesammelt aus Anlass seines 25jährigen Bestehens*, 171–87. Britannica, 13. Hamburg: Friederichsen, de Gruyter and Co.

Uspensky, Boris. 1973 [1970]. *A Poetics of Composition: The Structure of the Artistic Text and Typology of a Compositional Form*. Berkeley: University of California Press. [Translation of *Poetica komposizii*, 1970]

Van Dyke, Joyce. 1977. 'Making a Scene: Language and Gesture in *Coriolanus*.' *Shakespeare Survey* 30: 135–46.

Veltrusky, Jarmila. 1980. 'Engel's *Ideas for a Theory of Acting.*' *Drama Review* 24, no. 4: 71–80.

Vincent-Buffault, Anne. 1991. *The History of Tears: Sensibility and Sentimentality in France 1700–1900*. London: Macmillan.

Vlašimský, J. 1910–11. 'Mimische Studien zu Th. Storm.' *Euphorion* 17: 636–50; 18: 150–7, 468–78.

Vorwahl, Heinrich. 1932. 'Die Gebärdensprache im Alten Testament.' Diss., Berlin.

Vosskamp, Wilhelm. 1973. *Romantheorie in Deutschland: Von Martin Opitz bis Friedrich von Blankenburg*. Stuttgart: Metzler.

Wahrig, Gerhard. 1955. 'Das Lachen im Altenglischen und Mittelenglischen.' *Zeitschrift für Anglistik und Amerikanistik* 3: 274–304, 389–418.

Walker, Albert L. 1938. 'Convention in Shakespeare's Description of Emotion.' *Philological Quarterly* 17: 26–66.

Wandruska, Mario. 1954. *Haltung und Gebärde der Romanen*. Beihefte zur Zeitschrift für Romanische Philologie, 96. Tübingen: Niemeyer.

Warner, Janet A. 1970. 'Blake's Use of Gesture.' In David Vorse Erdman and John Ernest Grant, eds, *Blake's Visionary Forms Dramatic*, 174–95. Princeton: Princeton University Press.

Watson, George. 1979. *The Story of the Novel*. London: Macmillan.

Watt, Ian. 1972 [1957]. *The Rise of the Novel: Studies in Defoe, Richardson and Fielding*. Harmondsworth: Penguin.

Weathers, Winston. 1981. *The Broken Word: The Communication Pathos in Modern Literature*. Communication and the Human Condition, 1. New York: Gordon and Breach.

Wehse, Rainer. 1987. 'Gebärde.' In Rainer Wilhelm Brednich, ed., *Enzyklopädie des Märchens*, 782–92. Berlin and New York: de Gruyter.

Weinand, Heinz-Gerd. 1958. *Tränen: Untersuchungen über das Weinen in der deutschen Sprache und Literatur des Mittelalters*. Bonn: Bouvier.

Weir, Lorraine. 1977. 'The Choreography of Gesture: Marcel Jousse and *Finnegans Wake*.' *James Joyce Quarterly* 14: 313–25.

Weisbach, Werner. 1948. *Ausdrucksgestaltung in mittelalterlicher Kunst*. Einsiedeln and Zurich: Benziger.

Weisrock, Katharina. 1990. *Götterblick und Zaubermacht: Auge, Blick und Wahrnehmung in Aufklärung und Romantik*. Opladen: Westdeutscher Verlag.

Weiss, Wolfgang. 1989. '"There Is Language in Her Eye, Her Cheek, Her Lip": Körper und Körpersprache in *Troilus and Cressida, All's Well That Ends Well* und *Measure for Measure*.' *Deutsche Shakespeare-Gesellschaft West, Jahrbuch 1989*, 196–208.

Weltzien, Erich. 1926. 'Die Gebärden der Furcht in Thomas Hardys Wessex-romanen.' Diss., Greifswald.

Wendorf, Richard, ed. 1983. *Articulate Images: The Sister Arts from Hogarth to Tennyson*. Minneapolis: University of Minnesota Press.

Wespi, Hans-Ulrich. 1949. *Die Geste als Ausdrucksform und ihre Beziehungen zur Rede: Darstellung anhand von Beispielen aus der französischen Literatur zwischen 1900 und 1945*. Romanica Helvetica, 33. Bern: Francke.

Wiegand, Julius. 1917. 'Die Gesten in der deutschen erzählenden Dichtung.' *Neue Jahrbücher für das klassische Altertum, Geschichte und deutsche Literatur und für Pädagogik* 40: 332–44.

Will, Gerd. 1934. *Die Darstellung der Gemütsbewegungen in den Liedern der Edda*. Nordische Brücke, 2. Hamburg: Friederichsen and de Gruyter.

Williams, Raymond. 1968. *Drama in Performance*. 2nd ed. London: Watts.

Windeatt, Barry. 1979. 'Gesture in Chaucer.' *Medievalia et Humanistica*, N.S. 9: 143–61.

Witemeyer, Hugh. 1979. *George Eliot and the Visual Arts*. New Haven and London: Yale University Press.

Wolfson, Nessa. 1982. *CHP: The Conversational Historical Present in American English Narrative*. Topics in Sociolinguistics, 1. Dordrecht and Cinnaminson: Foris.

Worth, George J. 1978. *Dickensian Melodrama: A Reading of the Novels*. University of Kansas Humanistic Studies, 50. Lawrence: University of Kansas.

Worthen, William B. 1983. 'Beckett's Actor.' *Modern Drama* 26: 415–24.

Wuttke, Bernard. 1973. 'Nichtsprachliche Darstellungsmittel des Theaters: Kommunikations- und zeichentheoretische Studien unter besonderer Berücksichtigung des satirischen Theaters.' Diss., Münster.

York, Lorraine M. 1984. '"Its Better Nature Lost": The Importance of the Word in Sinclair Ross's *As for Me and My House*.' *Canadian Literature* 102: 166–74.

Zappert, Georg. 1854. 'Über den Ausdruck des geistigen Schmerzes im Mittelalter.' In *Denkschriften der Kaiserlichen Akademie der Wissenschaften*, 73–136. Philosophisch-Historische Classe, 5. Vienna: Hof- und Staatsdruckerei.

Zons, Franz Bernard. 1933. 'Von der Auffassung der Gebärde in der mhd. Epik: Studie über drei Hauptarten mal. Gebärdendarstellung.' Diss., Münster.

Zschietzschmann, Willy. 1924. 'Untersuchungen zur Gebärdensprache in der älteren Griechischen Kunst.' Diss., Jena.

Bibliography 3 NVC Research and Other Secondary Sources

Basic articles, monographs, handbooks, and anthologies are preceded by an *.

Abercrombie, David. 1954–5. 'Gesture.' *English Language Teaching* 9: 3–12.

Addison, Joseph. 1898 [1711]. 'No. 86, Friday, June 8, 1711.' In George A. Aitken, ed., *The Spectator*, 8 vols, 2:24–9. London: Nimmo.

Albert, Mechthild. 1989. 'L'Eloquence du corps: Conversation et sémiotique corporelle au siècle classique.' *Germanisch-Romanische Monatsschrift* 39: 156–79.

Allport, Gordon W. 1961. *Pattern and Growth in Personality*. New York: Holt, Rinehart and Winston.

Allport, Gordon W., and Philip E. Vernon. 1933. *Studies in Expressive Movement*. New York: Macmillan.

* Ancelin Schutzenberger, Anne. 1978. *Contribution à l'étude de la communication non verbale*. 2 vols. Paris: Champion.

Andersen, Peter A., and Karen Kuish Sull. 1985. 'Out of Touch, Out of Reach: Tactile Predispositions as Predictors of Interpersonal Distance.' *Western Journal of Speech Communication* 49: 57–72.

Argyle, Michael. 1967. *The Psychology of Interpersonal Behaviour*. Harmondsworth: Penguin.

– 1969. *Social Interaction*. London: Methuen.

– 1972. 'Non-Verbal Communication in Human Social Interaction.' In Hinde, ed., *Non-Verbal Communication*, 243–69.

– 1973. 'The Syntaxes of Bodily Communication.' *International Journal of Psycholinguistics* 2: 71–89.

*– 1975. *Bodily Communication*. London: Methuen.

* Argyle, Michael, ed. 1973. *Social Encounters: Readings in Social Interaction*. Harmondsworth: Penguin.

Argyle, Michael, and Mark Cook. 1976. *Gaze and Mutual Gaze*. Cambridge: Cambridge University Press.

Argyle, Michael, and Janet Dean. 1965. 'Eye Contact, Distance and Affiliation.' *Sociometry* 28: 289–304. [Reprinted in Laver and Hutcheson, eds, 1972, *Communication in Face to Face Interaction*, 301–16, and in Argyle, ed., 1973, *Social Encounters*, 173–87]

Argyle, Michael, and Roger Ingham. 1972. 'Gaze, Mutual Gaze, and Proximity.' *Semiotica* 6: 32–49.

Argyle, Michael, and Adam Kendon. 1972. 'The Experimental Analysis of Social Performance.' In Laver and Hutcheson, eds, 1972, *Communication in Face to Face Interaction*, 19–63. [First published in Leonard Berkowitz, ed., *Advances in Experimental Social Psychology*, 55–98. New York: Academic Press 1967]

Argyle, Michael, Mansur Lalljee, and Mark Cook. 1968. 'The Effects of Visibility on Interaction in a Dyad.' *Human Relations* 21: 3–17.

Argyle, Michael, et al. 1981. 'The Different Functions of Gaze.' In Kendon, ed., *Nonverbal Communication*, 283–95.

Asendorpf, Jens, and Harald G. Wallbott. 1981–2. 'Contributions of the German

"Expression Psychology" to Nonverbal Communication Research, Parts I, II.' *Journal of Nonverbal Behavior* 6: 135–47, 199–219.

Ashcraft, Norman, and Albert E. Scheflen. 1976. *People Space: Making and Breaking of Human Boundaries*. Garden City, N.Y.: Anchor Books.

Augustine. 1912. *St. Augustine's Confessions in Two Volumes*. Translated by William Watts. The Loeb Classical Library. Cambridge, Mass.: Harvard University Press.

Bacon, Francis. 1861 [1604]. *Of the Proficience and Advancement of Learning*. London: Bell and Daldy.

Barnlund, Dean C. 1975. 'Communicative Styles in Two Cultures: Japan and the United States.' In Kendon, Harris, and Key, eds, *Organization of Behavior*, 427–56.

Barnlund, Dean C., ed. 1968. *Interpersonal Communication: Survey and Studies*. Boston: Houghton Mifflin.

Beattie, Geoffrey W. 1980. 'The Role of Language Production Processes in the Organization of Behaviour in Face-to-Face Interaction.' In Brian Butterworth, ed., *Language Production, Vol. I: Speech and Talk*, 69–107. London: Academic Press.

– 1981. 'Sequential Temporal Patterns of Speech and Gaze in Dialogue.' In Kendon, ed., *Nonverbal Communication*, 297–320.

– 1983. *Talk: An Analysis of Speech and Non-Verbal Behaviour in Conversation*. Milton Keynes: Open University Press.

Bell, Sir Charles. 1847 [1806]. *The Anatomy and Philosophy of Expression as Connected with the Fine Arts*. 4th ed. London: Murray.

* Benson, Thomas W., and Kenneth D. Frandsen. 1982. *Nonverbal Communication*. Modules in Speech Communication. 2nd ed. Chicago: Science Research Associates.

Bentele, Günter, and Ernest W.B. Hess-Lüttich, eds. 1985. *Zeichengebrauch in Massenmedien: Zum Verhältnis von sprachlicher und nichtsprachlicher Information in Hörfunk, Film und Fernsehen*. Medien in Forschung und Unterricht, Serie A, 17. Tübingen: Niemeyer.

Benthall, Jonathan. 1975. 'A Prospectus as Published in *Studio International*, July 1972.' In Benthall and Polhemus, eds, *The Body as a Medium of Expression*, 5–12.

Benthall, Jonathan, and Ted Polhemus, eds. 1975. *The Body as a Medium of Expression*. London: Allen Lane and Penguin.

Bernard, Michel. 1976. *L'expressivité du corps: Recherche sur les fondements de la théatralité*. Paris: Delarge.

Birdwhistell, Ray L. 1952. *Introduction to Kinesics*. Foreign Service Institute. Louisville: University of Louisville Press.

– 1971. 'Kinesics: Inter- and Intra-Channel Communication Research.' In Kristeva, Rey-De Bove, and Umiker, eds, 1971, *Essays in Semiotics*, 527–46.

– 1973 [1968]. 'Kinesics.' In Argyle, ed., *Social Encounters*, 93–102. [First published in *International Encyclopaedia of Social Sciences* 1968]

*– 1973 [1970]. *Kinesics and Context: Essays on Body-Motion Communication*. Harmondsworth: Penguin.

– 1975. 'Background Considerations to the Study of the Body as a Medium of "Expression."' In Benthall and Polhemus, eds, *The Body as a Medium of Expression*, 36–58.

– 1983. 'Background to Kinesics.' *Et cetera* 13, no. 1: 352–61.

Blake, William H. 1933. 'A Preliminary Study of the Interpretation of Bodily Expression.' Ph.D. diss., Columbia University, New York.

Borbé, Tasso, ed. 1984. *Semiotics Unfolding: Proceedings of the Second Congress of the International Association for Semiotic Studies, Vienna, July 1979, Vol. I*. Approaches to Semiotics, 68. Berlin: Mouton.

*Bosmajian, Haig A., ed. 1971. *The Rhetoric of Nonverbal Communication: Readings*. Glenview, Ill.; London: Scott, Foresman.

Bouissac, Paul. 1973. *La mesure des gestes: Prolégomènes à la sémiotique gestuelle*. Approaches to Semiotics, 3. The Hague and Paris: Mouton.

Bouvron, Anne-Marie. 1985. 'L'homme et "son" espace: Étude expérimentale des effets du narcissisme et de la "difference" sur l'espace personnel.' In Rodolfo Ghiglione, ed., *La communication, ses faires, ses dires, ses effets*, 25–39. Paris: Colin.

*Bremmer, Jan, and Herman Roodenburg, eds. 1991. *A Cultural History of Gestures: From Antiquity to the Present*. Cambridge: Polity Press.

Bühler, Karl. 1965 [1934]. *Sprachtheorie: Die Darstellungsfunktion der Sprache*. 2nd ed. Stuttgart: Fischer.

– 1968 [1933]. *Ausdruckstheorie: Das System an der Geschichte aufgezeigt*. 2nd ed. Stuttgart: Fischer.

*Bull, Peter. 1983. *Body Movement and Interpersonal Communication*. Chichester: Wiley.

Bulwer, John. 1649. *Pathomyotomia, or a Dissection of the Significative Muscles of the Affections of the Minde*. London: W.W. for Humphrey Moseley.

– 1648 [1644]. *Chirologia: Or the Naturall Language of the Hand ... Whereunto Is Added Chironomia: Or, the Art of Manual Rhetoricke*. London: Printed by T.H.

Burger, Harald. 1976. '"Die Achseln zucken": Zur sprachlichen Kodierung nicht-sprachlicher Kommunikation.' *Wirkendes Wort* 26: 311–34.

*Burgoon, Judee K., David B. Buller, and W. Gill Woodall. 1989. *Nonverbal Communication: The Unspoken Dialogue*. New York: Harper and Row.

*Burgoon, Judee K., and Thomas Saine. 1978. *The Unspoken Dialogue: An Introduction to Nonverbal Communication*. Boston: Houghton Mifflin.

Burton, Robert. 1948 [1621]. *The Anatomy of Melancholy*. Edited by Floyd Dell and Paul Jordan-Smith. New York: Tudor.

Buser, Remo. 1973. *Ausdruckspsychologie: Problemgeschichte, Methodik und Systematik der Ausdruckswissenschaft*. Munich and Basel: Reinhardt.

Butterworth, Brian, and Geoffrey Beattie. 1978. 'Gesture and Silence as Indicators of Planning in Speech.' In Robin N. Campbell and Philip T. Smith, eds, *Recent Advances in the Psychology of Language: Formal and Experimental Approaches*, 347–60. New York and London: Plenum Press.

Calbris, Geneviève. 1990. *The Semiotics of French Gestures*. Advances in Semiotics. Bloomington: Indiana University Press.

Cappella, Joseph N. 1985. 'Controlling the Floor in Conversation.' In Siegman and Feldstein, eds, *Multichannel Integration*, 69–103.

Castiglione, Baldassare. 1900 [1561]. *The Book of the Courtier from the Italian of Count Baldassare Castiglione*. Done into English by Sir Thomas Hoby Anno 1561. The Tudor Translations, 23. London: Nutt. [Translation of *Il Libro del Cortegiano*, 1528]

Cody, Michael J., and H. Dan O'Hair. 1983. 'Nonverbal Communication and Deception: Differences in Deception Cues Due to Gender and Communicator Dominance.' *Communication Monographs* 50: 175–92.

Condon, W.S., and W.D. Ogston. 1967. 'A Segmentation of Behavior.' *Journal of Psychiatric Research* 5: 221–35.

– 1971. 'Speech and Body Motion Synchrony of the Speaker-Hearer.' In David L. Horton and James J. Jenkins, eds, *Perception of Language*, 150–73. Columbus, Ohio: Merrill.

Cook, Mark. 1970. 'Experiments on Orientation and Proxemics.' *Human Relations* 23: 61–76.

Cook, Mark, and Mansur G. Lalljee. 1972. 'Verbal Substitutes for Visual Signals in Interaction.' *Semiotica* 6: 212–21.

*Corraze, Jacques. 1980. *Les communications non-verbales*. Le Psychologue, 78. Paris: Presses Universitaires de France.

Cosnier, Jacques. 1982. 'Communications et langages gestuels.' In Jacques Cosnier et al., eds, *Les voies du langage: Communications verbales gestuelles et animales*, 255–302. Paris: Dunod.

Cranach, Mario von, and Ian Vine, eds. 1973. *Social Communication and Movement: Studies of Interaction in Man and Chimpanzee*. European Monographs in Social Psychology, 4. London and New York: Academic Press.

Cresollius, Ludovicus [Louis de Cressolles]. 1620. *Vacationes Autumnales sive De Perfecta Oratoris, Actione et Pronuntiatione*. Libri III. Paris: Ex Officina Nivelliana, sumptibus Sebastiani Cramoisy.

Cresswell, Robert. 1968. 'Le geste manuel associé au langage.' In Greimas, ed., *Langages*, 119–27.

* Critchley, Macdonald. 1971 [1939]. *The Language of Gesture*. New York: Haskell House.
*– 1975. *Silent Language*. London: Butterworths.
Darwin, Charles. 1904 [1872]. *The Expression of the Emotions in Man and Animals*. Popular Edition. Edited by Francis Darwin. London: Murray.
* Davis, Flora. 1971. *Inside Intuition: What We Know about Non-Verbal Communication*. New York: McGraw-Hill.
Davis, Martha. 1972. *Understanding Body Movement: An Annotated Bibliography*. New York: Arno Press.
– 1979. 'The State of the Art: Past and Present Trends in Body Movement Research.' In Wolfgang, ed., *Nonverbal Behavior*, 51–66.
Davis, Martha, and Janet Skupien, eds. 1982. *Body Movement and Nonverbal Communication: An Annotated Bibliography, 1971–1981*. Bloomington: Indiana University Press.
Della Casa, Giovanni. 1942 [1558]. *Galateo Ovvero de' Costumi*. Edited by Pietro Pancrazi. Florence: Felice Le Monnier.
Delsarte System of Oratory. 1893 [1882]. 4th ed. New York: Werner.
Descartes, René. 1953 [1649]. *Les passions de l'âme*. In his *Oeuvres et Lettres*, edited by André Bridoux, 695–802. Bibliothèque de la Pléiade, 40. Paris: Gallimard.
* Dittmann, Allen T. 1972. *Interpersonal Messages of Emotion*. New York: Springer.
– 1987. 'The Role of Body Movement in Communication.' In Siegman and Feldstein, eds, *Nonverbal Behavior*, 37–64.
* Druckman, Daniel, Richard M. Rozelle, and James C. Baxter. 1982. *Nonverbal Communication: Survey, Theory, and Research*. Sage Library of Social Research, 139. Beverly Hills: Sage.
Duchenne de Boulogne, Guillaume. 1862. *Méchanisme de la physionomie humaine, ou analyse électro-physiologique de l'expression des passions, applicable à la pratique des arts plastiques*. Paris: Renouard.
Duncan, Starkey, Jr. 1972. 'Some Signals and Rules for Taking Speaking Turns in Conversations.' *Journal of Personality and Social Psychology* 23: 283–92. [Reprinted in Weitz, ed., *Nonverbal Communication*, 298–311]
– 1975. 'Interaction Units during Speaking Turns in Dyadic, Face-to-Face Conversations.' In Kendon, Harris, and Key, eds, *Organization of Behavior*, 199–213.
– 1981. 'Conversational Strategies.' In Sebeok and Rosenthal, eds, *The Clever Hans Phenomenon*, 144–51.
– 1983. 'Speaking Turns: Studies of Structure and Individual Differences.' In Wiemann and Harrison, eds, *Nonverbal Interaction*, 149–78.
Duncan, Starkey, Jr., and Donald W. Fiske. 1977. *Face-to-Face Interaction: Research, Methods, and Theory*. Hillsdale, N.J.: Erlbaum.
Duncan, Starkey, Jr., Lawrence J. Brunner, and Donald W. Fiske. 1979. 'Strategy

Signals in Face-to-Face Interaction.' *Journal of Personality and Social Psychology* 37: 301–13.

Eco, Umberto. 1977. *Zeichen: Einführung in einen Begriff und seine Geschichte.* Frankfurt am Main: Suhrkamp. [Translation of *Segno* 1973]

Efron, David. 1941. *Gesture and Environment.* Morningside Heights, N.Y.: King's Crown Press. [Published later as *Gesture, Race and Culture.* The Hague: Mouton 1972]

Ehlich, Konrad, and Jochen Rehbein. 1981. 'Zur Notierung nonverbaler Kommunikation für diskursanalytische Zwecke.' In Peter Winkler, ed., *Methoden der Analyse von Face-to-Face Situationen*, 302–329. Stuttgart: Metzler.

– 1982. *Augenkommunikation: Methodenreflexion und Beispielanalyse.* Linguistik Aktuell, 2. Amsterdam: Benjamins.

Eibl-Eibesfeldt, Irenäus. 1970. *Liebe und Hass: Zur Naturgeschichte elementarer Verhaltensweisen.* Munich: Piper.

– 1972. 'Similarities and Differences between Cultures in Expressive Movements.' In Hinde, ed., *Non-Verbal Communication*, 297–312. [Reprinted in Weitz, ed., 1974, *Nonverbal Communication*, 20–33]

– 1973. *Der vorprogrammierte Mensch: Das Ererbte als bestimmender Faktor im menschlichen Verhalten.* Vienna: Molden.

– 1975 [1970]. *Ethology: The Biology of Behavior.* 2nd ed. New York: Holt, Rinehart and Winston. [Translation of *Grundriss der vergleichenden Verhaltensforschung* 1970]

– 1979. 'Universals in Human Expressive Behavior.' In Wolfgang, ed., *Nonverbal Behavior*, 17–30.

* Eisenberg, Abne M., and Ralph V. Smith, Jr. 1971. *Nonverbal Communication.* Indianapolis and New York: Bobbs-Merrill.

Ekman, Paul. 1971. 'Universals and Cultural Differences in Facial Expressions of Emotions.' In James K. Cole, ed., *Nebraska Symposium on Motivation 1971*, 207–83. Lincoln: University of Nebraska Press.

– 1973a. 'Introduction.' In Ekman, ed., *Darwin and Facial Expression*, 1–10.

– 1973b. 'Cross-Cultural Studies of Facial Expression.' In Ekman, ed., *Darwin and Facial Expression*, 169–222.

– 1978. 'Facial Signs: Facts, Fantasies, and Possibilities.' In Sebeok, ed., *Sight, Sound, and Sense*, 124–56.

– 1980a. 'Facial Signals.' In Rauch and Carr, eds, *The Signifying Animal*, 227–39.

– 1980b. *The Face of Man: Expressions of Universal Emotions in a New Guinea Village.* New York and London: Garland.

– 1981. 'Mistakes When Deceiving.' In Sebeok and Rosenthal, eds, *The Clever Hans Phenomenon*, 269–78.

Ekman, Paul, ed. 1973. *Darwin and Facial Expression: A Century of Research in Review*. New York and London: Academic Press.

Ekman, Paul, and Wallace V. Friesen. 1968. 'Nonverbal Behavior in Psychotherapy Research.' In John M. Shlien, ed., *Research in Psychotherapy: Proceedings of the Third Conference, Chicago, Illinois, 1966, Vol. III*, 179–216. Washington, D.C.: American Psychological Association.

– 1969. 'Non-Verbal Leakage and Clues to Deception.' *Psychiatry* 32: 88–106. [Reprinted in Argyle, ed., 1973, *Social Encounters*, 132–48, and Weitz, ed., 1974, *Nonverbal Communication*, 269–90]

– 1971. 'Constants across Cultures in the Face and Emotion.' *Journal of Personality and Social Psychology* 17: 124–29.

– 1974. 'Detecting Deception from the Body or Face.' *Journal of Personality and Social Psychology* 29: 288–98.

– 1975. *Unmasking the Face: A Guide to Recognizing Emotions from Facial Cues*. Englewood Cliffs, N.J.: Prentice-Hall.

*– 1981 [1969]. 'The Repertoire of Nonverbal Behavior: Categories, Origins, Usage and Coding.' In Kendon, ed., *Nonverbal Communication*, 57–105. [First published as 'Origin, Usage and Coding: The Basis for Five Categories of Non-Verbal Behavior.' *Semiotica* 1 (1969): 49–98]

Ekman, Paul, Wallace V. Friesen, and Phoebe Ellsworth. 1972. *Emotion in the Human Face*. Elmsford, N.Y.: Pergamon.

Ekman, Paul, Wallace V. Friesen, and Silvan S. Tomkins. 1971. 'Facial Affect Scoring Technique (FAST): A First Validity Study.' *Semiotica* 3: 37–58. [Reprinted in Weitz, ed., 1974, *Nonverbal Communication*, 34–50]

Ekman, Paul, Wallace V. Friesen, et al. 1980. 'Relative Importance of Face, Body, and Speech in Judgments of Personality and Affect.' *Journal of Personality and Social Psychology* 38: 270–7.

– 1987. 'Universals and Cultural Differences in the Judgements of Facial Expressions of Emotion.' *Journal of Personality and Social Psychology* 53: 712–17.

Ekman, Paul, Richard Sorenson, and Wallace V. Friesen. 1969. 'Pan-Cultural Elements in Facial Displays of Emotion.' *Science* 164: 86–8.

Elias, Norbert. 1994. *The Civilizing Process: The History of Manners and State Formation and Civilization*. Oxford: Blackwell. [Translation of *Über den Prozess der Zivilisation: Soziogenetische und psychogenetische Untersuchungen* 1936]

Ellgring, Heiner. 1984. 'The Study of Nonverbal Behavior and Its Applications: State of the Art in Europe.' In Wolfgang, ed., *Nonverbal Behavior*, 115–38.

– 1989. *Nonverbal Communication in Depression*. European Monographs in Social Psychology. Cambridge: Cambridge University Press.

Ellis, Andrew, and Geoffrey Beattie. 1986. *The Psychology of Language and Communication*. London: Weidenfeld and Nicolson.

Ellsworth, Phoebe C. 1975. 'Direct Gaze as a Social Stimulus: The Example of Aggression.' In Pliner, Krames, and Alloway, eds, *Advances*, 53–75.

Ellsworth, Phoebe C., and Ellen J. Langer. 1983 [1976]. 'Staring and Approach: An Interpretation of the Stare as a Nonspecific Activator.' In Katz and Katz, eds, *Foundations of Nonverbal Communication*, 111–18. [First published in *Journal of Personality and Social Psychology* 33 (1976): 117–22]

Ellsworth, Phoebe C., and Linda M. Ludwig. 1972. 'Visual Behavior in Social Interaction.' In Harrison and Knapp, eds, *Journal of Communication* Special Issue, 375–403.

Ellyson, Steve L., and John F. Dovidio, eds., 1985. *Power, Dominance, and Nonverbal Behavior*. Springer Series in Social Psychology. New York: Springer.

Emerson, Ralph Waldo. 1903 [1860]. 'Behavior.' In *The Conduct of Life*, 163–89. Emerson's Complete Works, 6. London: Routledge.

Esser, Aristide H., ed. 1971. *Behavior and Environment: The Use of Space by Animals and Man*. New York and London: Plenum Press.

Exline, Ralph V. 1971. 'Visual Interaction: The Glances of Power and Preference.' In James K. Cole, ed., *Nebraska Symposium on Motivation 1971*, 163–206. Lincoln: University of Nebraska Press.

Exline, Ralph V., Steve L. Ellyson, and Barbara Long. 1975. 'Visual Behavior as an Aspect of Power Role Relationship.' In Pliner, Krames, and Alloway, eds, *Advances*, 21–52.

Fast, Julius. 1970. *Body Language*. New York: Evans.

Feher, Michel, et al., eds. 1989. *Fragments for a History of the Human Body*, Parts I, II. Zone 3, 4. New York: Zone.

Fehr, B.J., and Ralph V. Exline. 1987. 'Social Visual Interaction: A Conceptual and Literature Review.' In Siegman and Feldstein, eds, *Nonverbal Behavior*, 225–326.

Fielding, Henry. 1899. 'An Essay on the Knowledge of the Characters of Men.' In *The Works of Henry Fielding*, 11:175–212. Westminster: Constable; New York: Scribner's.

Fisher, Jeffrey, Marvin Rytting, and Richard Heslin. 1976. 'Hands Touching Hands: Affective and Evaluative Effects of an Interpersonal Touch.' *Sociometry* 39: 416–21.

Flachskampf, Ludwig. 1938. 'Spanische Gebärdensprache.' *Romanische Forschungen* 52: 205–58.

Florio, John, trans. 1904–6 [1603]. *The Essayes of Michael Lord of Montaigne*. 3 vols. London: Oxford University Press/Frowde.

Foucault, Michel. 1976–. *Histoire de la sexualité*. Paris: Gallimard.

Frances, Susan J. 1979. 'Sex Differences in Nonverbal Behavior.' *Sex Roles* 5: 519–35.

Frank, Lawrence K. 1957. 'Tactile Communication.' *Genetic Psychology Monographs* 56: 209–55. [Reprinted in Bosmajian, ed., 1971, *Rhetoric*, 34–57]

Freedman, Norbert. 1977. 'Hands, Words, and Mind: On the Structuralization of Body Movements during Discourse and the Capacity for Verbal Representation.' In Freedman and Grand, eds, *Communicative Structures*, 109–32.

Freedman, Norbert, and Stanley Grand, eds. 1977. *Communicative Structures and Psychic Structures: A Psychoanalytic Interpretation of Communication*. New York and London: Plenum Press.

Freud, Sigmund. 1966. *The Psychopathology of Everyday Life*. Edited by James Strachey. Translated by Allan Tyson. London: Ernest Benn.

Frey, Siegfried, Hans-Peter Hirsbrunner, and Ulrich Borns. 1982. 'Time-Series Notation: A Coding Principle for the Unified Assessment of Speech and Movement in Communication Research.' In Hess-Lüttich, ed., *Multimedial Communication*, 30–58.

Fridlund, Alan J., Paul Ekman, and Harriet Oster. 1987. 'Facial Expressions of Emotion: Review of Literature, 1970–1983.' In Siegman and Feldstein, eds, *Nonverbal Behavior*, 143–224.

Frijda, Nico H. 1953. 'The Understanding of Facial Expression of Emotion.' *Acta Psychologica* 9: 294–362.

– 1969. 'Recognition of Emotion.' In Leonard Berkowitz, ed., *Advances in Experimental Social Psychology*, 4:167–223. New York and London: Academic Press.

– 1973. 'The Relation between Emotion and Expression.' In Cranach and Vine, eds, *Social Communication*, 325–39.

– 1982. 'The Meanings of Emotional Expression.' In Key, ed., *Nonverbal Communication Today*, 103–19.

Frois-Wittmann, J. 1930. 'The Judgment of Facial Expression.' *Journal of Experimental Psychology* 13: 113–51.

Gallagher, Catherine, and Thomas Laqueur, eds. 1987. *The Making of the Modern Body: Sexuality and Society in the Nineteenth Century*. Berkeley, Los Angeles, and London: University of California Press.

Givens, David B. 1978. 'The Nonverbal Basis of Attraction: Flirtation, Courtship, and Seduction.' *Psychiatry* 41: 346–59.

Goffman, Erving. 1956. *The Presentation of Self in Everyday Life*. Edinburgh: Edinburgh University Press.

– 1963. *Behavior in Public Places: Notes on the Social Organization of Gatherings*. New York: Free Press.

– 1967. *Interaction Ritual*. Chicago: Aldine.

– 1969. *Strategic Interaction*. Philadelphia: Philadelphia University Press.

– 1971. *Relations in Public: Microstudies of the Public Order*. New York: Basic Books.

– 1974. *Frame Analysis*. New York: Harper and Row.

– 1979. *Gender Advertisements*. London: Macmillan.

Goldstein, Melvin A., M. Catherine Kilroy, and David Van de Voort. 1976. 'Gaze as a Function of Conversation and Degree of Love.' *Journal of Psychology* 92: 227–34.

Grand, Stanley. 1977. 'On Hand Movements during Speech: Studies of the Role of Self-Stimulation in Communication under Conditions of Psychopathology, Sensory Deficit, and Bilingualism.' In Freedman and Grand, eds, *Communicative Structures*, 199–211.

Grant, James. 1785. 'Origin of Language.' In his *Essays on the Origin of Society, Language, Property, Government, Jurisdiction, Contracts, and Marriage*, 27–61. London: Robinson; Edinburgh: Elliot.

Gratiolet, Pierre. 1865. *De la physionomie et des mouvements d'expression*. Paris: Hetzel.

Greimas, Algirdas Julien. 1968. 'Conditions d'une sémiotique du monde naturel.' In Greimas, ed., *Langages*, 3–35.

Greimas, Algirdas Julien, ed. 1968. *Langages*, No. 10: 'Pratiques et langages gestuels.'

Grice, H. Paul. 1975. 'Logic and Conversation.' In Peter Cole and Jerry L. Morgan, eds, *Speech Acts*, 41–58. Syntax and Semantics, 3. New York: Academic Press.

Guilhot, Jean. 1962. *La dynamique de l'expression et de la communication: La voix, la parole, les mimiques et les gestes auxiliaires*. Publications du Centre de Psychiatrie Sociale. Paris and the Hague: Mouton.

Habicht, Werner. 1967. 'Zur Bedeutungsgeschichte des englischen Wortes *countenance*.' *Archiv* 203: 32–51.

Hall, Edward T. 1959. *The Silent Language*. Garden City, N.Y.: Doubleday.

– 1963. 'A System for the Notation of Proxemic Behavior.' *American Anthropologist* 65: 1003–26. [Reprinted in Laver and Hutcheson, eds, 1972, *Communication*, 247–73]

– 1964. 'Silent Assumptions in Social Communication.' *Disorders of Communication* 42: 41–55. [Reprinted in Matson, et al., eds, 1967, *The Human Dialogue*, 491–505, and Laver and Hutcheson, eds, 1972, *Communication*, 274–87]

– 1966. *The Hidden Dimension*. Garden City, N.Y.: Doubleday.

– 1968. 'Proxemics.' *Current Anthropology* 9: 83–108. [Reprinted in Katz and Katz, eds, 1983, *Foundations of Nonverbal Communication*, 5–27, and Weitz, ed., 1974, *Nonverbal Communication*, 205–29]

– 1974. *Handbook for Proxemic Research*. Studies in the Anthropology of Visual Communication. Philadelphia: Society for the Anthropology of Visual Communication.

– 1977 [1976]. *Beyond Culture*. Garden City, N.Y.: Anchor Books.

Hall, Judith A. 1985. 'Male and Female Nonverbal Behavior.' In Siegman and Feldstein, eds, *Multichannel Integration*, 195–225.

Hall, Peter M., and Dee Ann Spencer Hall. 1983. 'The Handshake as Interaction.' *Semiotica* 45: 249–64.

Harper, Robert G. 1985. 'Power, Dominance, and Nonverbal Behavior: An Overview.' In Ellyson and Dovidio, eds, *Power*, 29–48.

* Harper, Robert G., Arthur N. Wiens, and Joseph D. Matarazzo. 1978. *Nonverbal Communication: The State of the Art*. New York: Wiley.

Harrison, Randall P. 1973. 'Nonverbal Communication.' In Ithiel de Sola Pool et al., eds, *Handbook of Communication*, 93–115. Chicago: Rand McNally.

* Harrison, Randall P., and Mark L. Knapp, eds. 1972. *The Journal of Communication* 22, no. 4: Special Issue on Nonverbal Communication.

Hayduk, Leslie Alec. 1978. 'Personal Space: An Evaluative and Orienting Overview.' *Psychological Bulletin* 85: 117–34.

Hayes, Francis C. 1957. 'Gestures: A Working Bibliography.' *Southern Folklore Quarterly* 21: 218–317.

Henley, Nancy M. 1975. 'Power, Sex, and Nonverbal Communication.' In Barrie Thorne and Nancy Henley, eds, *Language and Sex: Difference and Dominance*, 184–203. Rowley, Mass.: Newbury House.

– 1977. *Body Politics*. Englewood Cliffs, N.J.: Prentice-Hall.

Henley, Nancy M., and Marianne LaFrance. 1984. 'Gender as Culture: Difference and Dominance in Nonverbal Behavior.' In Wolfgang, ed., *Nonverbal Behavior*, 351–71.

Heslin, Richard, and Tari Alper. 1983. 'Touch: A Bonding Gesture.' In Wiemann and Harrison, eds, *Nonverbal Interaction*, 47–75.

* Heslin, Richard, and Miles L. Patterson. 1982. *Nonverbal Behavior and Social Psychology*. New York and London: Plenum Press.

Hess, Eckhard H. 1975. *The Tell-Tale Eye: How Your Eyes Reveal Hidden Thoughts and Emotions*. New York: Van Nostrand Reinhold.

Hess, Eckhard H., and Slobodan B. Petrovich. 1987. 'Pupillary Behavior in Communication.' In Siegman and Feldstein, eds, *Nonverbal Behavior*, 327–48.

Hess-Lüttich, Ernest W.B. 1979a. *See* bibliography 2.

– 1979b. 'Korpus, Kode und Kommunikation: Probleme der Verschriftlichung direkter Interaktion.' *Kodikas/Code* 1: 199–215.

– 1985. 'Komplementarität der Codes in öffentlicher Kommunikation: Zum Gebrauch sprachlicher und nicht-sprachlicher Zeichensysteme in den Massenmedien: Eine Einführung.' In Bentele and Hess-Lüttich, eds, *Zeichengebrauch*, 1–21.

Hess-Lüttich, Ernest W.B., ed. 1982. *Multimedial Communication Vol. I: Semiotic Problems of Its Notation*. Kodikas/Code Supplement 8. Tübingen: Narr.

Hewes, Gordon Winant. 1955. 'World Distribution of Certain Postural Habits.' *American Anthropologist* 57: 231–44.

– 1957. 'Anthropology of Posture.' *Scientific American* 196 (Feb. 1957): 123–32.

– 1975. *Language Origins: A Bibliography*. 2 vols. 2nd ed. The Hague: Mouton.

*Hinde, R.A., ed. 1972. *Non-Verbal Communication*. Cambridge: Cambridge University Press.

Hindmarch, Ian. 1973. 'Eyes, Eye-Spots and Pupil Dilation in Non-Verbal Communication.' In Cranach and Vine, eds, *Social Communication*, 299–321.

Hirsbrunner, Hans-Peter, A. Florin, and Siegfried Frey. 1981. 'Das Berner System zur Untersuchung nonverbaler Interaktion: II. Die Auswertung von Zeitreihen visuell-auditiver Information.' In Peter Winkler, ed., *Methoden der Analyse von Face-to-Face Situationen*, 237–68. Stuttgart: Metzler.

Hirsbrunner, Hans-Peter, Siegfried Frey, and Robert Crawford. 1987. 'Movement in Human Interaction: Description, Parameter Formation and Analysis.' In Siegman and Feldstein, eds, *Nonverbal Behavior*, 99–140.

Hjortsjö, Carl-Herman. 1969. *Man's Face and Mimic Language*. Lund: Studentlitteratur.

Hübler, Axel. 1984. 'Nonverbal Interaction.' LAUT-Paper, Series B, No. 100/21. Trier: Linguistic Agency University of Trier.

Izard, Carroll E. 1971. *The Face of Emotion*. New York: Meredith Corporation (Appleton-Century-Crofts).

– 1979. 'Facial Expression, Emotion, and Motivation.' In Wolfgang, ed., *Nonverbal Behavior*, 31–49.

Izard, Carroll E., and Barbara S. Izard. 1980. 'Expression of Emotions as a Transcultural Language in Social Interactions and Theatrical Performance.' In Raffler-Engel, ed., *Aspects of Nonverbal Communication*, 253–64.

Joly, André. 1985. 'Pour une analyse systématique des modalités non verbales de la communication.' In G. Debusscher and J.P. van Noppen, eds, *Communiquer et Traduire: Hommages à Jean Dierickx*, 131–41. Brussels: Editions de l'Université de Bruxelles.

Jones, Stanley E., and Elayne Yarbrough. 1985. 'A Naturalistic Study of the Meanings of Touch.' *Communication Monographs* 52: 19–56.

Jourard, Sidney M. 1966. 'An Exploratory Study of Body-Accessibility.' *British Journal of Social Clinical Psychology* 5: 221–31. [Reprinted in Katz and Katz, eds, 1983, *Foundations*, 148–57]

Katz, Albert M., and Virginia T. Katz. 1983. 'Introduction.' In Katz and Katz, eds, *Foundations*, xv–xvii.

*Katz, Albert M., and Virginia T. Katz, eds. 1983. *Foundations of Nonverbal Commu-*

nication: Readings, Exercises, and Commentary. Carbondale: Southern Illinois University Press.

Kendon, Adam. 1967. 'Some Functions of Gaze-Direction in Social Interaction.' *Acta Psychologica* 26: 22–63. [Reprinted in Kendon, 1977, *Studies*, 13–51]

– 1972. 'Some Relationships between Body Motion and Speech: An Analysis of an Example.' In Aron W. Siegman and Benjamin Pope, eds, *Studies in Dyadic Communication*, 177–210. New York: Pergamon.

– 1973. 'The Role of Visible Behaviour in the Organization of Social Interaction.' In Cranach and Vine, eds, *Social Communication*, 29–74.

*– 1977. *Studies in the Behavior of Social Interaction*. Studies in Semiotics, 6. Bloomington: Indiana University Press.

– 1980. 'Gesticulation and Speech: Two Aspects of the Process of Utterance.' In Key, ed., *Relationship of Verbal and Nonverbal Communication*, 207–27.

*– 1981. 'Introduction.' Kendon, ed., *Nonverbal Communication*, 1–53.

– 1982. 'The Study of Gesture: Some Observations on Its History.' *Recherches sémiotiques* 2, no. 1: 45–62.

– 1983a. 'Gesture.' *Journal of Visual Verbal Languaging* 3: 21–36.

– 1983b. 'Gesture and Speech: How They Interact.' In Wiemann and Harrison, eds, *Nonverbal Interaction*, 13–45.

– 1983c. 'The Study of Gesture: Some Remarks on Its History.' In John N. Deely and Margot D. Lenhart, eds, *Semiotics 1981*, 153–64. New York and London: Plenum Press.

– 1984. 'Did Gesture Have the Happiness to Escape the Curse at the Confusion of Babel?' In Wolfgang, ed., *Nonverbal Behavior*, 75–114.

– 1985. 'Some Uses of Gesture.' In Deborah Tannen and Muriel Saville-Troike, eds, *Perspectives on Silence*, 215–34. Norwood, N.J.: Ablex.

– 1987. 'On Gesture: Its Complementary Relationship with Speech.' In Siegman and Feldstein, eds, *Nonverbal Behavior*, 65–97.

– 1989. *Sign Languages of Aboriginal Australia: Cultural, Semiotic and Communicative Perspectives*. Cambridge: Cambridge University Press.

*Kendon, Adam, ed. 1981. *Nonverbal Communication, Interaction, and Gesture: Selections from 'Semiotica.'* The Hague: Mouton.

*Kendon, Adam, Richard M. Harris, and Mary Ritchie Key, eds. 1975. *Organization of Behavior in Face-to-Face Interaction*. The Hague: Mouton.

*Key, Mary Ritchie. 1975. *Paralanguage and Kinesics (Nonverbal Communication)*. Metuchen, N.J.: Scarecrow Press.

*– 1977. *Nonverbal Communication: A Research Guide and Bibliography*. Metuchen, N.J.: Scarecrow Press.

*Key, Mary Ritchie, ed. 1980. *The Relationship of Verbal and Nonverbal Communication*. The Hague: Mouton.

*– 1982. *Nonverbal Communication Today: Current Research.* Contributions to the Theory of Language, 33. Berlin: Mouton.

Kirchhoff, Robert, ed. 1965. *Handbuch der Psychologie. Bd. V: Ausdruckspsychologie.* Göttingen: Verlag für Psychologie.

Klages, Ludwig. 1964 [1950]. *Grundlegung der Wissenschaft vom Ausdruck.* 8th ed. Bonn: Bouvier.

Klein, Zdenek. 1984. 'Sitting Postures in Males and Females.' *Semiotica* 48: 119–31.

Kleinpaul, Rudolph. 1869. 'Zur Theorie der Geberdensprache.' *Zeitschrift für Völkerpsychologie und Sprachwissenschaft* 6: 353–75.

– 1893 [1888]. *Sprache ohne Worte: Idee einer allgemeinen Wissenschaft der Sprache.* Leipzig: Friedrich.

* Knapp, Mark L. 1972. *Nonverbal Communication in Human Interaction.* New York: Holt, Rinehart and Winston.

*– 1980. *Essentials of Nonverbal Communication.* New York: Holt, Rinehart and Winston.

Knapp, Peter H., ed. 1963. *Expression of the Emotions in Man.* New York: International Universities Press.

Knowlson, James R. 1965. 'The Idea of Gesture as a Universal Language in the XVIIth and XVIIIth Centuries.' *Journal of the History of Ideas* 26: 495–508.

Kowal, Sabine, Daniel C. O'Connell, and Roland Posner, eds. 1995. *Kodikas/Code,* 18, Nos. 1–3: *Signs for Time: Notation and Transscription of Movements.*

Kristeva, Julia. 1968. 'Le geste, pratique ou communication?' In Greimas, ed., *Langages,* 48–64.

Kristeva, Julia, Josette Rey-De Bove, and Donna Jean Umiker, eds. 1971. *Essays in Semiotics / Essais de Sémiotique.* Approaches to Semiotics, 4. The Hague and Paris: Mouton.

Krout, Maurice H. 1939. 'Understanding Human Gestures.' *Scientific Monthly* 49: 167–72.

Kunihiro, Tetsuya. 1980. 'Personality-Structure and Communicative Behavior: A Comparison of Japanese and Americans.' In Raffler-Engel, ed., *Aspects of Nonverbal Communication,* 329–33.

La Barre, Weston. 1947. 'The Cultural Basis of Emotions and Gestures.' *Journal of Personality* 16: 49–68. [Reprinted in Laver and Hutcheson, eds, 1972, *Communication,* 207–24]

– 1964. 'Paralinguistics, Kinesics, and Cultural Anthropology.' In Sebeok, et al., eds, *Approaches to Semiotics,* 191–220.

LaFrance, Marianne, and Clara Mayo. 1979. 'A Review of Nonverbal Behaviors of Women and Men.' *Western Journal of Speech Communication* 43: 96–107.

Lamb, Warren, and Elizabeth Watson. 1979. *Body Code: The Meaning in Movement.* London: Routledge and Kegan Paul.

Lavater, Johann Caspar. 1984. *Physiognomische Fragmente zur Beförderung der Menschenkenntnis und Menschenliebe: Eine Auswahl*. Edited by Christoph Siegrist. Stuttgart: Reclam. [English translation: *Essays on Physiognomy, Designated to Promote the Knowledge and the Love of Mankind*. London: Murray 1789–1798]

Laver, John, and Sandy Hutcheson. 1972. 'Introduction.' In Laver and Hutcheson, eds, *Communication*, 11–15.

* Laver, John, and Sandy Hutcheson, eds. 1972. *Communication in Face to Face Interaction: Selected Readings*. Harmondsworth: Penguin.

* Leathers, Dale G. 1976. *Nonverbal Communication Systems*. Boston: Allyn and Bacon.

Leonhard, Karl. 1949. *Ausdruckssprache der Seele: Darstellung der Mimik, Gestik und Phonik des Menschen*. Berlin: Haug.

Lersch, Phillip. 1932. *Gesicht und Seele: Grundlinien einer mimischen Diagnostik*. Munich: Reinhardt.

Lichtenberg, Georg Christoph. 1972 [1778]. 'Über Physiognomik; wider die Physiognomen.' In his *Schriften und Briefe, III: Aufsätze, Entwürfe, Gedichte, Erklärung der Hogarthischen Kupferstiche*, 256–95. Darmstadt: Wissenschaftliche Buchgesellschaft.

McLuhan, Marshall. 1967. *The Medium Is the Massage: An Inventory of Effects*. New York: Bantam.

McNeill, David. 1980. 'Iconic Relationships between Language and Motor Action.' In Rauch and Carr, eds, *The Signifying Animal*, 240–51.

– 1981. 'Action, Thought, and Language.' *Cognition* 10: 201–8.

– 1985. 'So You Think Gestures Are Nonverbal?' *Psychological Review* 92: 350–71.

Magli, Patrizia. 1989. 'The Face and the Soul.' Feher, et al., eds, *Fragments*, Part II, 87–127.

Mahl, George F. 1987. *Explorations in Nonverbal and Verbal Behavior*. Hillsdale, N.J., and London: Erlbaum.

Mallery, Garrick. 1972 [1881]. *Sign Language among North American Indians: Compared with That among Other Peoples and Deaf-Mutes*. Approaches to Semiotics, 14. The Hague and Paris: Mouton.

Mantegazza, Paolo. 1885 [1881]. *La physionomie et l'expression des sentiments*. Paris: Alcan. [Translation of *Fisionomia e mimica* 1881]

Matson, Floyd W., et al., eds. 1967. *The Human Dialogue: Perspectives on Communication*. New York: Free Press.

Maupertuis, Pierre-Louis Moreau de. 1965. 'Dissertation sur les différens moyens dont les hommes se sont servis pour exprimer leurs idées.' In his *Oeuvres*, III: 437–68. Hildesheim: Olms. [Reprint of the 1768 edition]

Mauss, Marcel. 1935. 'Les techniques du corps.' *Journal de psychologie normale et pathologique* 32: 271–93.

Mayo, Clara, and Nancy M. Henley, eds. 1981. *Gender and Nonverbal Behavior.* New York: Springer.

Mehrabian, Albert. 1969. 'Significance of Posture and Position in the Communication of Attitude and Status Relationships.' *Psychological Bulletin,* 71: 359–72.

– 1971. *Silent Messages.* Belmont, Calif: Wadsworth.

*– 1972. *Nonverbal Communication.* Chicago: Aldine.

– 1973 [1968]. 'Inference of Attitudes from the Posture, Orientation and Distance of a Communication.' In Argyle, ed., *Social Encounters,* 103–18. [First published in *Journal of Consulting and Clinical Psychology* 32 (1968): 296–308]

Mehrabian, Albert, and Susan R. Ferris. 1967. 'Inference of Attitudes from Nonverbal Communication in Two Channels.' *Journal of Consulting Psychology* 31: 248–52. [Reprinted in Weitz, ed., 1974, *Nonverbal Communication,* 291–7]

Mill, John Stuart. 1974 [1843]. *A System of Logic Rationative and Inductive: Being a Connected View of the Principles of Evidence and the Methods of Scientific Investigation.* Edited by J.M. Robson. 2 vols. Collected Works of John Stuart Mill, 7/8. Toronto: University of Toronto Press.

Montagu, Ashley. 1971. *Touching: The Human Significance of the Skin.* New York: Columbia University Press.

Morris, Desmond. 1971. *Intimate Behaviour.* London: Cape.

– 1977. *Manwatching: A Field Guide to Human Behavior.* New York: Abrams.

– 1985. *Bodywatching.* London: Cape.

Morris, Desmond, et al. 1979. *Gestures: Their Origins and Distribution.* London: Cape.

Morsbach, Helmut. 1988. 'Nonverbal Communication and Hierarchical Relationships: The Case of Bowing in Japan.' In Poyatos, ed., *Cross-Cultural Perspectives,* 189–99.

Müller, Jürgen E. 1982. 'Face-to-Face Interaction and Its Notation.' In Hess-Lüttich, ed., *Multimedial Communication,* 18–29.

Nespoulous, Jean-Luc, Paul Perron, and André Roch Lecours, eds. 1986. *The Biological Foundations of Gestures: Motor and Semiotic Aspects.* Hillsdale, N.J., and London: Erlbaum.

Newman, John B. 1984. 'On the Counterverbality of "Nonverbal" as a Verbal Term.' In Lawrence R. Raphael et al., eds, *Language and Cognition: Essays in Honor of Arthur J. Bronstein,* 203–39. New York and London: Plenum Press.

Noller, Patricia. 1984. *Nonverbal Communication and Marital Interaction.* International Series in Experimental Social Psychology, 9. Oxford: Pergamon.

* Nöth, Winfried. 1985. 'Nonverbale Kommunikation.' In his *Handbuch der Semiotik,* 321–80. Stuttgart: Metzler.

– 1990. 'Nonverbal Communication: Introduction.' In his *Handbook of Semiotics*. Bloomington and Indianapolis: Indiana University Press 1990. [Enlarged and completely revised translation of Nöth 1985]

Oliva, Joseph. 1981. 'Synchronic versus Rhythmic Sign Vehicles.' In Annemarie Lange-Seidl, ed., *Zeichenkonstitution: Akten des 2. Semiotischen Kolloquiums Regensburg 1978*, 2:224–8. 2 vols. Berlin and New York: De Gruyter.

– 1984. 'Rhythmicity and Iconicity in Signed Discourse.' In Borbé, ed., *Semiotics Unfolding*, 579–83.

* Patterson, Miles L. 1983. *Nonverbal Behavior: A Functional Perspective*. New York: Springer.

Patterson, Miles L., and Joyce A. Edinger. 1987. 'A Functional Analysis of Space in Social Interaction.' In Siegman and Feldstein, eds, *Nonverbal Behavior*, 523–62.

Piderit, Theodor. 1858. *Grundsätze der Mimik und Physiognomik*. Braunschweig: Vieweg.

– 1886. *Mimik und Physiognomik*. 2nd ed. Detmold: Meyer.

Pliner, Patricia, Lester Krames, and Thomas Alloway, eds. 1975. *Advances in the Study of Communication and Affect. Vol. II: Nonverbal Communication of Aggression*. New York and London: Plenum Press.

Polhemus, Ted. 1975. 'Social Bodies.' In Benthall and Polhemus, eds, *The Body as a Medium of Expression*, 13–35.

Posner, Roland. 1985. 'Nonverbale Zeichen in öffentlicher Kommunikation: Zu Geschichte und Gebrauch der Begriffe "verbal" und "nonverbal," "Interaktion" und "Kommunikation" ...' *Zeitschrift für Semiotik* 7: 235–71.

Potter, Charles Francis. 1972. 'Gestures.' In *Funk and Wagnall's Standard Dictionary of Folklore, Mythology and Legend*, 451–3. New York: New English Library.

Poyatos, Fernando. 1976. *Man beyond Words: Theory and Methodology of Nonverbal Communication*. Oswego: New York State English Council.

*– 1983. *New Perspectives in Nonverbal Communication: Studies in Cultural Anthropology, Social Psychology, Linguistics, Literature and Semiotics*. Oxford: Pergamon.

Poyatos, Fernando, ed. 1988a. *See* bibliography 2.

– 1988b. *Cross-Cultural Perspectives in Non-Verbal Communication*. Toronto: Hogrefe.

Quintilian, Marcus Fabius. 1958. *The Institutio Oratoria of Quintilian*. Translated by H.E. Butler. The Loeb Classical Library. London: Heinemann; Cambridge, Mass.: Harvard University Press.

* Raffler-Engel, Walburga von, ed. 1980. *Aspects of Nonverbal Communication*. Lisse: Swets and Zeitlinger.

Ramsey, Sheila. 1984. 'Double Vision: Nonverbal Behavior East and West.' In Wolfgang, ed., 1984, *Nonverbal Behavior*, 139–67.

Rastier, François. 1968. 'Comportement et Signification.' In Greimas, ed., *Langages*, 76–86.

Rauch, Irmengard, and Gerald F. Carr, eds. 1980. *The Signifying Animal: The Grammar of Language and Experience*. Advances in Semiotics. Bloomington: Indiana University Press.

* Richmond, Virginia P., James McCroskey, and Steven K. Payne. 1987. *Nonverbal Behavior in Interpersonal Relations*. Englewood Cliffs, N.J.: Prentice-Hall.

Rittner, Volker. 1976. 'Handlung, Lebenswelt und Subjektivierung.' In Dietmar Kamper and Volker Rittner, eds, *Zur Geschichte des Körpers*, 13–66. Munich and Vienna: Hanser.

Rosenfeld, Howard M. 1987. 'Conversational Control Functions of Nonverbal Behavior.' In Siegman and Feldstein, eds, *Nonverbal Behavior*, 563–601.

Rosenthal, Robert, et al. 1979. *Sensitivity to Nonverbal Communication: The PONS Test*. Baltimore and London: Johns Hopkins University Press.

Rosenthal, Robert, ed. 1979. *Skill in Nonverbal Communication: Individual Differences*. Cambridge, Mass.: Oelgeschlager, Gunn and Hain.

Ruesch, Jürgen. 1972. *Semiotic Approaches to Human Relations*. Approaches to Semiotics. 25. The Hague and Paris: Mouton.

* Ruesch, Jürgen, and Weldon Kees. 1956. *Nonverbal Communication: Notes on the Visual Perception of Human Relations*. Berkeley and Los Angeles: University of California Press.

Rutter, Derek R. 1984. *Looking and Seeing: The Role of Visual Communication in Social Interaction*. Chichester and New York: Wiley.

St.Clair, Robert N., and Howard Giles, eds. 1980. *The Social and Psychological Context of Language*. Hillsdale, N.J.: Erlbaum.

Sanders, Robert E. 1985. 'The Interpretation of Nonverbals.' *Semiotica* 55: 195–216.

Scheflen, Albert E. 1974 [1973]. *How Behavior Means: Exploring the Contexts of Speech and Meaning: Kinesics, Posture, Interaction, Setting, and Culture*. Garden City, N.Y.: Anchor Books.

– 1964. 'The Significance of Posture in Communication Systems.' *Psychiatry* 27: 316–31.

* Scheflen, Albert E., and A. Scheflen. 1972. *Body Language and the Social Order: Communication as Behavioral Control*. Englewood Cliffs, N.J.: Prentice-Hall.

– 1979. 'On Communicational Processes.' In Wolfgang, ed., *Nonverbal Behavior*, 1–16.

Scherer, Hans Siegfried. 1984. 'Nonverbale Kommunikation.' In his *Sprechen im situativen Kontext*, 108–46. Tübingen: Stauffenberg.

*Scherer, Klaus R. 1973 [1970]. *Non-verbale Kommunikation*. Forschungsberichte des Instituts für Kommunikationsforschung und Phonetik der Universität Bonn. 3rd ed. Hamburg: Buske.

– 1977. 'Die Funktionen des nonverbalen Verhaltens im Gespräch.' In Dirk Wegner, ed., *Gesprächsanalysen: Vorträge gehalten anlässlich des 5. Kolloquiums des Instituts für Kommunikationsforschung und Phonetik, Bonn, 14.–16. Okt. 1976*, 275–97. Hamburg: Buske. [Reprinted in Scherer and Wallbott, eds, 1984, *Nonverbale Kommunikation*, 25–32]

– 1980. 'The Functions of Nonverbal Signs in Conversation.' In St. Clair and Giles, eds, *Social and Psychological Context*, 225–44.

– 1984. 'The Nonverbal Dimension: A Fad, a Field, or a Behavioural Modality?' In Henry Tajfel, ed., *The Social Dimension: European Developments in Social Psychology, Vol. I*, 160–83. Cambridge: Cambridge University Press.

Scherer, Klaus R., and Paul Ekman, eds. 1982. *Handbook of Methods in Nonverbal Behavior Research*. Cambridge: Cambridge University Press; Paris: Editions de la Maison des Sciences de l'Homme.

Scherer, Klaus R., and Harald G. Wallbott. 1985. 'Analysis of Nonverbal Behavior.' In Teun A. van Dijk, ed., *Handbook of Discourse Analysis, Vol. II: Dimensions of Discourse*, 199–230. London: Academic Press.

Scherer, Klaus R., et al. 1979. 'Methoden zur Klassifikation von Bewegungsverhalten: Ein funktionaler Ansatz.' *Zeitschrift für Semiotik* 1: 177–92.

*Scherer, Klaus R., and Harald G. Wallbott, eds. 1984. *Nonverbale Kommunikation: Forschungsberichte zum Interaktionsverhalten*. 2nd ed. Weinheim and Basel: Beltz.

Schiffrin, Deborah. 1974. 'Handwork as Ceremony: The Case of the Handshake.' *Semiotica* 12: 189–202. [Reprinted in Kendon, ed., 1981, *Nonverbal Communication*, 237–50]

Schmidt-Wiegand, Ruth. 1982. 'Gebärdensprache im mittelalterlichen Recht.' *Frühmittelalterliche Studien* 16: 363–79.

Schmitt, Jean-Claude. 1989. 'The Ethics of Gesture.' In Feher et al., eds, *Fragments*, Part II, 129–47.

– 1990. *La raison des gestes dans l'occident médiéval*. Paris: Gallimard.

Sebeok, Thomas A. 1979. *The Sign and Its Masters*. Austin and London: University of Texas Press.

Sebeok, Thomas A., ed. 1978. *Sight, Sound, and Sense*. Advances in Semiotics. Bloomington and London: Indiana University Press.

Sebeok, Thomas A., and Robert Rosenthal, eds. 1981. *The Clever Hans Phenomenon: Communication with Horses, Whales, Apes and People*. Annals of the New York Academy of Sciences, 364. New York: New York Academy of Sciences.

Sebeok, Thomas A., et al., eds. 1964. *Approaches to Semiotics: Cultural Anthropol-*

ogy, Education, Linguistics, Psychiatry, Psychology: Transactions of the Indiana University Conference on Paralinguistics and Kinesics. The Hague and Paris: Mouton.

Seigel, Jules Paul. 1969. 'The Enlightenment and the Evolution of a Language of Signs in France and England.' *Journal of the History of Ideas* 30: 96–115.

Seneca, L. Annaeus. 1928. *De ira. Seneca in Ten Volumes*. Translated by John W. Basore. Vol. 1. The Loeb Classical Library. Cambridge, Mass.: Harvard University Press.

Shorter, Edward. 1982. *A History of Women's Bodies*. New York: Basic Books.

* Siegman, Aron W., and Stanley Feldstein, eds. 1985. *Multichannel Integration of Nonverbal Behavior*. Hillsdale, N.J., and London: Erlbaum.

*– 1987. *Nonverbal Behavior and Communication*. 2nd ed. Hillsdale, N.J., and London: Erlbaum.

Simmel, Georg. 1958 [1908]. 'Exkurs über die Soziologie der Sinne.' In his *Soziologie: Untersuchungen über die Formen der Vergesellschaftung*, 483–93. 4th ed. Berlin: Duncker und Humblot.

Skupien, Janet. 1984. 'Behavior as Sign.' *Semiotica* 50: 359–69.

Sommer, Robert. 1969. *Personal Space: The Behavioral Basis of Design*. Englewood Cliffs, N.J.: Prentice-Hall.

Strehle, Hermann. 1934. *Analyse des Gebarens: Erforschung des Ausdrucks der Körperbewegung*. Berlin: Bernard und Graefe. [Diss., Berlin 1934]

Suleiman, Susan Rubin, ed. 1985. *The Female Body in Western Culture: Contemporary Perspectives*. Cambridge, Mass., and London: Harvard University Press.

Vigarello, Georges. 1989. 'The Upward Training of the Body from the Age of Chivalry to Courtly Civility.' In Feher et al., eds, *Fragments*, Part II, 148–99.

Vine, Ian. 1970. 'Communication by Facial-Visual Signals.' In John Hurrell Crook, ed., *Social Behaviour in Birds and Mammals: Essays on the Social Ethology of Animals and Man*, 279–354. London and New York: Academic Press.

Vrugt, Anneke, and Ada Kerkstra. 1984. 'Sex Differences in Nonverbal Communication.' *Semiotica* 50: 1–41.

Wallbott, Harald G. 1980. 'The Measurement of Human Expression.' In Raffler-Engel, ed., *Aspects of Nonverbal Communication*, 203–28.

– 1982. *Bewegungsstil und Bewegungsqualität: Untersuchungen zum Ausdruck und Eindruck gestischen Verhaltens*. Weinheim and Basel: Beltz.

– 1984. 'Nonverbales Verhalten und Sprechausdruck.' In Lothar Berger, ed., *Sprechausdruck*, 57–67. Sprache und Sprechen, 13. Frankfurt am Main: Scriptor.

Watson, O. Michael. 1970. *Proxemic Behavior: A Cross-Cultural Study*. Approaches to Semiotics, 8. The Hague and Paris: Mouton.

– 1972. 'Proxemics as Non-Verbal Communication.' In Samir K. Ghosh, ed.,

Man, Language and Society: Contributions to the Sociology of Language, 224–31. Ianua Linguarum, Series Minor, 109. The Hague: Mouton.

Watzlawick, Paul, Janet Helmick Beavin, and Don D. Jackson. 1968 [1967]. *Pragmatics of Human Communication: A Study of Interactional Patterns, Pathologies, and Paradoxes*. London: Faber and Faber.

* Weitz, Shirley, ed. 1974. *Nonverbal Communication: Readings with Commentary*. New York: Oxford University Press.

* Wiemann, John M., and Randall P. Harrison, eds. 1983. *Nonverbal Interaction*. Sage Annual Reviews of Communication Research. Beverley Hills: Sage.

Wiener, Morton, et al. 1972. 'Nonverbal Behavior and Nonverbal Communication.' *Psychological Review* 79: 185–214.

Wildeblood, Joan. 1973. *The Polite World: A Guide to the Deportment of the English in Former Times*. London: Davis-Poynter.

Wilden, Anthony. 1972. 'Analog and Digital Communication: On the Relationship between Negotiation, Signification and the Emergence of the Discrete Element.' *Semiotica* 6: 50–82.

Wilson, Thomas. 1909. *Wilson's Arte of Rhetorique 1560*. Edited by G.H. Mair. Oxford: Clarendon Press.

Winkin, Yves. 1984. 'Esquisse d'une archéologie de la recherche en communication non-verbale.' In Borbé, ed., *Semiotics Unfolding*, 663–70.

Wolff, Charlotte. 1972 [1945]. *A Psychology of Gesture*. Body Movement: Perspectives in Research. New York: Arno Press.

* Wolfgang, Aaron, ed. 1979. *Nonverbal Behavior: Applications and Cultural Implications*. New York: Academic Press.

* – 1984. *Nonverbal Behavior: Perspectives, Applications, Intercultural Insights*. Lewiston, N.Y., and Toronto: Hogrefe.

Wright, Thomas. 1604. *The Passions of the Minde in Generall*. London: Valentine Simmes for Walter Burre.

Wundt, Wilhelm. 1900. *Völkerpsychologie: Eine Untersuchung der Entwicklungsgesetze von Sprache, Mythus und Sitte. Erster Band: Die Sprache. Erster Theil.* Leipzig: Engelmann [I. 'Ausdrucksbewegungen'; II. 'Geberdensprache']. [English translation: *Elements of Folk Psychology: Outlines of a Psychological History of the Development of Mankind*. London: George Allen and Unwin, 1916. Chapter 2 of Part I was retranslated as *The Language of Gestures*. The Hague: Mouton, 1973.]

– 1903 [1874]. *Grundzüge der Physiologischen Psychologie*, III. 5th ed. Leipzig: Engelmann.

Wylie, Laurence. 1977. *Beaux Gestes: A Guide to French Body Talk*. Cambridge, Mass.: Undergraduate Press; New York: Dutton.

Xenophon. 1923. *Memorabilia, Oeconomicus, Symposium, Apology*. Translated by

E.C. Marchant and O.J. Todd. The Loeb Classical Library. Cambridge, Mass., and London: Harvard University Press.

Zuckerman, Miron, and Robert E. Driver. 1985. 'Telling Lies: Verbal and Nonverbal Correlates of Deception.' In Siegman and Feldstein, eds, *Multichannel Integration*, 129–47.

Zuckerman, Miron, et al. 1975. 'Encoding and Decoding Nonverbal Cues of Emotion.' *Journal of Personality and Social Psychology* 32: 1068–76.

– 1976. 'Encoding and Decoding of Spontaneous and Posed Facial Expressions.' *Journal of Personality and Social Psychology* 34: 966–77.

– 1979. 'Posed and Spontaneous Communication of Emotion via Facial and Vocal Cues.' *Journal of Personality* 47: 712–33.

– 1981. 'Controlling Nonverbal Displays: Facial Expressions and Tone of Voice.' *Journal of Experimental Social Psychology* 17: 506–24.

Index